AF754450

Our Daily Breath
DEVOTIONAL

TYNDALE
MOMENTUM™

A Tyndale nonfiction imprint

365 Prayers & Practices
That Whisper Peace in a Shouting World

Our Daily Breath

DEVOTIONAL

KAYLA CRAIG

Visit Tyndale online at tyndale.com.

Visit the author online at kaylacraig.com.

Tyndale, Tyndale's quill logo, *Tyndale Momentum*, and the Tyndale Momentum logo are registered and/or common law trademarks of Tyndale House Ministries in the USA and various other jurisdictions around the world. All rights reserved. See tyndale.com for a full list of trademarks owned by Tyndale House Ministries. Tyndale Momentum is a nonfiction imprint of Tyndale House Publishers, Carol Stream, Illinois.

Our Daily Breath Devotional: 365 Prayers and Practices That Whisper Peace in a Shouting World

Copyright © 2026 by Kayla Craig. All rights reserved.

Cover and interior illustration of abstract field copyright © Zaien/Adobe Stock. All rights reserved. Interior illustration of torso and lungs designed by Freepik.

Author photo taken by Deven Holley Photography, copyright © 2026. All rights reserved.

Cover design by Eva M. Winters

Interior design by Eva M. Winters and Laura Cruise

Edited by Stephanie Rische

Published in association with the literary agency of Gardner Literary LLC. www.gardner-literary.com.

Scripture quotations marked AMP are taken from the Amplified® Bible (AMP), copyright © 2015 by The Lockman Foundation. Used by permission. www.lockman.org.

Scripture quotations marked CEB are taken from the Common English Bible, copyright 2011. Used by permission. All rights reserved.

Scripture quotations marked ESV are from The ESV® Bible (The Holy Bible, English Standard Version®), copyright © 2001 by Crossway, a publishing ministry of Good News Publishers. Used by permission. All rights reserved.

Scripture quotations marked FNV are reproduced from First Nations Version, copyright © 2021 by Rain Ministries Inc. Used by permission of InterVarsity Press, Downers Grove, IL. All rights reserved.

Scripture quotations marked GNT are taken from the Good News Translation in Today's English Version, Second Edition, copyright © 1992 by American Bible Society. Used by permission.

Scripture quotations marked ISV are taken from the Holy Bible: International Standard Version.® Copyright © 2003 by The ISV Foundation. Used by permission of Davidson Press, Inc. All rights reserved internationally.

Scripture quotations marked MSG are taken from *The Message*, copyright © 1993, 2002, 2018 by Eugene H. Peterson. Used by permission of NavPress. All rights reserved. Represented by Tyndale House Publishers.

Scripture quotations marked NET are taken from the New English Translation, NET Bible,® copyright ©1996–2006 by Biblical Studies Press, L.L.C. http://netbible.com. All rights reserved.

Scripture quotations marked NIV are taken from the Holy Bible, *New International Version*,® *NIV*.® Copyright © 1973, 1978, 1984, 2011 by Biblica, Inc.® Used by permission. All rights reserved worldwide.

Scripture quotations marked *NLT* are taken from the *Holy Bible*, New Living Translation, copyright © 1996, 2004, 2015 by Tyndale House Foundation. Used by permission of Tyndale House Publishers, Carol Stream, Illinois 60188. All rights reserved.

Scripture quotations marked NRSV are taken from the New Revised Standard Version Bible, copyright © 1989 National Council of the Churches of Christ in the United States of America. Used by permission. All rights reserved worldwide.

Scripture quotations marked The Voice are taken from The Voice,™ copyright © 2012 by Ecclesia Bible Society. Used by permission. All rights reserved.

The URLs in this book were verified prior to publication. The publisher is not responsible for content in the links, links that have expired, or websites that have changed ownership after that time.

For information about special discounts for bulk purchases, please contact Tyndale House Publishers at csresponse@tyndale.com, or call 1-855-277-9400.

ISBN 978-1-4964-7715-6

Printed in China

32 31 30 29 28 27 26
7 6 5 4 3 2 1

INTRODUCTION

Snowy days in the Midwest can be breathtaking—and bitterly cold. I know winter has arrived when I can see my breath forming small, wispy clouds against the dark cover of night. It's not a new phenomenon, yet I'm mesmerized by seeing what has been there all along—a vapor formed in my lungs and sent into the world, the invisible made visible.

I usually notice this as I'm letting my dogs outside before bed. I continue to exhale, now with intention, watching my warm breath float into the cold abyss of my backyard as I whisper-shout to my oversize goldendoodle to stop barking.

In the comings and goings of our days, it's easy to forget our breath. To take the many daily inhales and exhales (around twenty thousand) for granted. It's like that with our experiences of God too.

We want to connect with God, but we can barely catch our collective breath.

We're bombarded with digital noise, family needs, work demands, and heartbreaking headlines. Making time, summoning energy, and finding space for prayer can feel impossible. If you're tired, overstimulated, or stretched thin, you're not alone.

When the world swirls outside of us, our pulse quickens. Breathing becomes shallow. Our minds race. Our bodies ache. Our souls feel empty. We were never meant to live like this.

You've been holding your breath far too long.

What would it look like for you to exhale?

AS YOU LIVE AND BREATHE

This book is a collection of prayers and practices that whisper peace in a shouting world. Each day offers a simple way to pause, breathe, and awaken to the presence of God. It's for anyone who longs to breathe again—to pray in real life. It invites you into a rhythm of contemplation and action: inhale and exhale.

Breath prayers are simple phrases as you pray with your inhale and exhale. These short prayers match the rhythm of your breathing, helping you focus your body and mind on the One who gives each breath.

Do you have one minute to spare while commuting to work or standing in line at the grocery store? Then you have enough time to borrow a breath prayer.

For me, practicing simple breath prayers like "You are with me" on the inhale and "In every breath" on the exhale has been a powerful part of my spiritual journey.

By simply praying (silently or aloud) the *inhale* words as you breathe in and the *exhale* words as you let your breath go, you can find solid ground for your body and your soul. These simple prayers can return you to the Spirit of God, who is always with you (even when you forget that sacred truth).

SAMPLE BREATH PRAYER

Inhale through your nose for four seconds, hold, exhale for six seconds.

INHALE: You are with me
EXHALE: In every breath.

When you integrate breath prayer into your day, you don't need the perfect place or the perfect words to pray. Anyone with breath in their lungs and a heart that beats can pray alongside their breath.

In Isaiah 42:5, we read that our breath is a gift from the Creator, "who spreads out the earth with all that springs from it, who gives breath to its people, and life to those who walk on it."[*]

No matter who you are or where you are, whether you're aware of it or not, you have your breath. And that's all you need to awaken to the presence of God in you and around you. Breath prayers help us stay mindful of God's loving presence, which permeates every nook and cranny of our busy days. They are a grab-and-go practice, an offering to tuck into your heart and unfold throughout the day.

In 1 Thessalonians 5:17, Paul encourages the people of God to "pray without ceasing."[†] As we pray with our inhale and exhale, we become more awake to the presence of God in our messy, holy lives—our real lives, not the lives we wish we had, the ones we feel like we should have, or the ones we shine up for social media.

As we breathe deep the presence of Christ and then release our worries and fears with each exhale, we open ourselves to the transformative work of the Holy Spirit.

Prayerfully breathing into your day is one way to love the Lord your God with all your heart, soul, mind, and strength. And in God's generosity, it's a way to receive the grace of God too.

[*] NIV.
[†] NRSV.

GIVE US THIS DAY

The Lord's Prayer is perhaps the most well-known Christian prayer, spoken across languages, countries, and traditions every day. Jesus invites us to use it as scaffolding for our prayers—a structure to help us stay rooted and grow in faith.

Prayer is a way to enter the ongoing conversation our Creator has been having with us all along.

In Acts 17:24-25, we're reminded that God draws near to us: "He is the God who made the world and everything in it. Since he is Lord of heaven and earth, he doesn't live in man-made temples, and human hands can't serve his needs—for he has no needs. He himself gives life and breath to everything, and he satisfies every need."* The One who gives life and breath satisfies every need.

In the Lord's Prayer, Jesus prays, "Give us this day our daily bread." We can't hoard our daily bread (it would turn into croutons!), just as we can't hoard our breath (we'd die of carbon dioxide poisoning!).

We must rely, day by day, on God's provision to nourish both body and soul.

When my daughter was in the hospital with pneumonia, her pulmonologist got creative to help us understand what was happening. He grabbed a thick black marker and began sketching lungs on the glass wall of her room in the intensive care unit. "In your lungs, the main airways are called bronchi. They branch off into smaller and smaller passageways," he explained. "Your daughter is experiencing bronchospasms, which are making it hard for her to breathe."

I absorbed this information as I watched a machine breathe for my little girl, praying for her life. I stared at the drawing, struck by how much the lungs he drew resembled a root system—spreading, growing, sustaining life.

By the grace of God (and the help of modern medicine), my daughter began to breathe on her own again. Years have passed, but when I close my eyes, I can still see that hospital drawing. I can still hear that prayer I held on to when I didn't know what else to pray.

Give us this day our daily breath.

It's a prayer of the heart that asks God to give us roots, to help us grow, and to nourish us—mind, body, and soul.

What would it look like to trust God to care for you with every breath you take?

PRACTICING PEACE

The pages that await you offer daily words to borrow, prayers to exhale, and space to connect with God right where you are. This collection offers breathing room to rediscover spiritual practices through meaningful (but short) daily readings.

They take the same time to read as it would to watch a viral video of a cat riding a robot vacuum. (I can't promise I'll be as hilarious as a hairball on wheels, but I think the hope we unearth together will make up for it.)

---

* NLT.

In times that seem increasingly turbulent with each passing breath, my prayer is that these short readings will serve as compassionate companions on your journey of learning to know and love yourself, God, and your neighbor more fully.

There's no shame in missing a day (or week, or month), but if you can (and you can!), you'll find spiritual, mental, emotional, and physical benefits to intentionally getting into a daily rhythm of prayer.

Along the way, you'll find scientific discoveries, poems, art, and words of wisdom. Each entry follows the natural and liturgical rhythms of the year, day by day, season by season. You'll journey through Ordinary Time, Lent, and Advent, and you'll also find holy days that have been celebrated by the church over the centuries, which I've included because they remind us we belong to a wider story.

Each day, you'll find the following:

- **Scripture:** an anchor for your reflection
- **Breath prayer:** a short phrase to pray with your inhale and exhale
- **Reflection:** a brief devotion to help you awaken to God's presence in everyday life
- **Concluding thought:** simple tools and reflections, such as facts about breath, short takeaways, wisdom from others, invitations for self-reflection, prayerful practices and exercises, prayers to borrow and make your own, and prayerful poetry.

HERE'S HOW TO BEGIN

1. **Pause:** Rest your hand on your heart.
2. **Breathe:** Pray the inhale/exhale lines once or twice.
3. **Carry:** Borrow that prayer throughout your day.

You may pray alone, but you're never praying by yourself.

Across neighborhoods and nations, people are inhaling mercy and exhaling peace. This is our shared daily breath.

May each day be an invitation to a new rhythm—where contemplation meets compassion, where prayer becomes practice, where we inhale God's presence and exhale love. May each breath prayer help you listen for God's whisper and live it out in the noise of the world.

May the days to come offer an exhale for the breath you've been holding.

A PRAYER TO BEGIN

God who breathed life into being,
Creator of all,
Nourisher of souls,
Redeemer of life,
Who exists in and beyond all things,
We marvel at who You are
And pray that every breath we take
Would be an overflow of adoration,
Would honor and glorify You,
That every breath would whisper Your ways.
Holy God, bring the rhythms of Your grace
Into our daily comings and goings.
We belong to You;
No other comes close.
Reorder our realities
To reflect Your goodness and grace.
Creation groans, out of breath,
Gasping for air under the weight of us
Trying to do it our own way
Instead of shaping the way of our world
To bear Your glory.
O cosmic Christ, give us this day
Our daily breath.
Spirit, remind us that You
Dwell deep inside us,
That each inhale, each exhale,
Is a sacred gift from You alone.
Amen.

JANUARY 1

The Spirit of God made me what I am,
the breath of God Almighty gave me life!

JOB 33:4 (MSG)

INHALE: You were with me then;
EXHALE: You are with me now.

Excited. Overwhelmed. Unsure. As you look to this New Year, how are you feeling, *really*?

When we pray alongside our breath, we signal to our brains and bodies that, whatever the circumstances, at *this* moment, we are safe.

Inhale for four seconds. Hold for another four, and then slowly exhale for six to eight seconds.[1]

Rest, even for a moment, in the truth that God's grace holds you now and will hold you in the future. With each breath, remember that you aren't alone in this big, terrible, beautiful, complicated world. You don't have to know what the future holds to rest in the promise that the One who holds the future holds you.

Breath by breath, God is writing your story. You aren't alone. Take heart.

This is only the beginning.

SACRED ECHOES

The grace of God means something like: "Here is your life. You might never have been, but you *are*, because the party wouldn't have been complete without you. Here is the world. Beautiful and terrible things will happen. Don't be afraid. I am with you. Nothing can ever separate us. It's for you I created the universe. I love you."[2]

Frederick Buechner

JANUARY 2

SAINT BASIL THE GREAT

The best thing you can do right now is to finish what you started last year and not let those good intentions grow stale.

2 CORINTHIANS 8:10 (MSG)

INHALE: I trust your unfolding work;
EXHALE: You're not finished with me yet.

At the beginning of a New Year, enthusiasm comes easily. We jot down resolutions. We vow to do more, to work harder, to just *be better*. (Whatever that means.)

But as time passes, distractions creep in, real life hits hard, and the work we meant to continue—whether in our faith, in our relationships, or at the gym—begins to stall.

Thousands of years ago, the church in Corinth was going through a similar struggle. They'd started strong in their generosity, eager to give and support others, but their follow-through was crumbling. When Paul wrote to them, he didn't come at them with shame or guilt. He just pointed them back to the truth that they didn't need to prove anything to God. They just needed to keep moving forward.

Saint Basil the Great, who is remembered today, embodied the spirit of perseverance Paul wrote about. A thoughtful theologian and fierce advocate for the poor in the fourth century, Basil moved beyond good intentions. He faithfully followed through, founding hospitals, caring for the forgotten, and shaping Christian thought for future generations. His life was a testament to the belief that faith is what we profess *and* what we continue to live out, step by step, breath by breath.

God isn't measuring your progress with a checklist or tallying up your failures. What God began in you, God will be faithful to complete.*

What would it look like to stop chasing after some unattainable perfection? To release that breath you've been holding as you look ahead to the New Year?

LET IT LINGER

All you have to do is keep going—to let God's slow, steady work in you unfold as you continue showing up in love. The good work you bring into your home, your community, and your world isn't wasted.

As you live and breathe, God is moving in you, through you, and ahead of you.

Small steps still get you where you're going.

* See Philippians 1:6.

JANUARY 3

Create in me a clean heart, O God,
and put a new and right spirit within me.

PSALM 51:10 (NRSV)

INHALE: Create in me
EXHALE: A clean heart, O God.

RHYTHM OF BREATH

Every fresh heartbeat
Is an invitation to begin.
Each exhale holds promise
That new life is here.
As you wake,
You have breath—
A gift,
A reminder
That you are not alone.

Every breath proves that God is still at work in us. Each heartbeat is an invitation to begin again—not through our own effort, but by receiving the renewal offered by the One who gives each breath.

The self-improvement industry is projected to reach $86.54 billion by 2034.[3] But Psalm 51 offers a way to a deeper kind of peace—a way that *surrenders* instead of *strives*.

David doesn't declare, "I will fix my heart." Instead, he asks God to do what only God can do: "Create in me a clean heart."

The same Creator who formed the heavens and the earth is still shaping you.

You don't have to force transformation. Renewal unfolds in the quiet moments: a deep inhale before rushing ahead, a moment of pausing to truly listen, a release of what no longer serves you.

Richard Rohr says that at the dawn of a New Year "we celebrate the rebirth of time. We wait for our God to do new things. We wait for who we are. We wait for the coming of grace, for the revelation of God. We wait for the truth. We wait for the vision of the whole. But we cannot just wait. We must pray."[4]

Take a breath. Let your inhale become a prayer. And as you exhale, release the pressure to fix yourself and instead, like David, ask God to do what only God can do.

JANUARY 4

Trust God from the bottom of your heart; don't try to figure out everything on your own. Listen for God's voice in everything you do, everywhere you go; he's the one who will keep you on track.

PROVERBS 3:5-6 (MSG)

INHALE: I listen for Your voice

EXHALE: In every place, in everything.

As much as we crave clarity, some questions simply don't have answers. In a culture that constantly pushes for certainty and control, it can feel impossible to let go of the pressure to make everything *figureoutable*.

What if hearing God is simply listening with your heart in the everyday corners of life?

In everything you do, everywhere you go, God is already there. Not just in the obvious places. Not just in the quiet moments you manage to carve out. But in the *everything*—the exhaustion of work, the weight of the world, the breaking news, the unanswered prayers, the dinner dishes, the things you wish were different.

Take a deep breath.

As you exhale, listen to what God might be whispering to you.

SACRED ECHOES

Christian mindfulness is a practice of listening to God's voice as well as to the internal narrative that warps God's voice.[5]

Regina Chow Trammel and John Trent

JANUARY 5

When they saw the star, they were filled with joy!

MATTHEW 2:10 (NLT)

INHALE: Breath of life,
EXHALE: Light my way.

In times of division and upheaval, it can seem out of touch to hold on to hope. But the darkest times are when we desperately need glimmers of goodness.

Poet Jan Richardson writes,

Blessed are you
who bear the light
in unbearable times.[6]

Her words serve as a gentle reminder that we're not just searching for the Light of the World, but we are also called to carry this Light. In the shadows of our lives, the Light hasn't disappeared; it's simply waiting for us to notice it again.

The One who illuminated the sky thousands of years ago continues to guide us today. When darkness closes in, it's easy to lose sight of that truth.

What does holding on to stubborn hope look like right now? How might you open your heart a little wider to make space for Light to get in, even when everything seems dark? And how can you embrace joy in your life?

As you take a deep breath, picture the shimmering light of Christ meeting you in the shadows—a sanctuary shining upon you and reaching out to you, even here, even now.

RHYTHM OF BREATH

Darkness is near,
This is true.
But the candle you hold—
The tiniest flicker—
Can illuminate
More than what you can see.
The whole world
Held in the palm
Of the One who lights the way.
Don't you think
That God can hold you too?
Don't be afraid.
Watch for the Light.
Inhale, exhale
Divine love for humanity,
Breath of life,
Breath of Light.
Let your breath be more than a wish,
More than a prayer.
Hope hides in the shadows.

JANUARY 6

EPIPHANY

Arise, shine, for your light has come, and the glory of the LORD rises upon you.

ISAIAH 60:1 (NIV)

INHALE: Light of the World,
EXHALE: Lead me in Your love.

Epiphany honors the moment when the magi, following the brilliance of a star, arrived at the feet of Jesus. When the radiance of heaven broke through the darkness of the world and those who had been searching finally found what they were longing for.

It's easy to think of Epiphany as something that happened long ago, but the invitation still stands to set aside what we're told will fulfill us—popularity, prestige, power—and move toward the Light that gives us life.

Maybe you're still waiting for your own epiphany, for something to change everything. But here's the truth: The Light has already come.

Even when the night is long. Even when clarity feels out of reach. Even when you are still searching.

The same God who placed a star in the sky illuminates your path. The same God who guided the magi guides you today.

God is still revealing, still illuminating, still leading the weary traveler home. Take a breath.

The Light will meet you where you are.

To find out more about Epiphany, see the liturgical calendar in appendix A.

PAUSE AND PONDER

In what areas of your life are you carrying doubt or exhaustion into the New Year?

Where does the path ahead feel uncertain or unclear?

JANUARY 7

Let us consider how we may spur one another on toward love and good deeds.

HEBREWS 10:24 (NIV)

INHALE: You made us
EXHALE: To move toward love.

My son's kindergarten teacher gave out a cookie at the end of the day to anyone he noticed being a "smart cookie." I can still hear my son's excitement bubbling over as he climbed into the van, proudly proclaiming, "I got a 'smart cookie' cookie!"

We have to call out the good we see in others. Like a Christmas Eve candlelight service—one flame passed to another until the whole room glows—when we light a fire of encouragement, it spreads.

It's easy to fixate on what's wrong with the world, to spiral headfirst into cynicism and despair. Honestly, it takes very little effort to be a critic. The harder (and I'd say holier) work is to notice love alongside the hate.

If all we ever see is what's wrong, we'll never help create what's right.

The book of Hebrews reminds us, "Let us consider how we may spur one another on toward love and good deeds." The word *spur* isn't passive—it means "to stir up" or even "to provoke."

We're not called to slap a spiritual bandage over the world's wounds. We're called to actively disrupt the evil of the world and point one another toward love, to help one another keep the flame alive. And that takes knowing one another. It takes choosing community when isolation is easier.

After all, if no one tends the flame, even a candlelight service would go dark.

PAUSE AND PONDER

Like a teacher noticing the goodness of a child, where might you offer encouragement today? Whose flame might you help ignite?

JANUARY 8

Let us walk the path of peace in a manner that lifts up and strengthens the heart of each person.

ROMANS 14:19 (FNV)

INHALE: Lead me on
EXHALE: The path of peace.

I grew up on a steady diet of fairy tales and princess stories. I'd like to think of the path of peace as one filled with singing sparrows, dressmaking mice, and wide-eyed deer.

But choosing the path of peace isn't all rainbows and butterflies. We don't have to spend much time reading headlines to know that the peaceful way is not always a popular path. It's overgrown with brambles and branches, ice-slicked and thorny to navigate. It confounds the wise, frustrates the foolish, and slows even the strong. And still, we are called to seek and strive for peace together.

Paul's words remind us that the path of peace isn't just for our own souls' comfort. It's a way of living that lifts others up, strengthens the weary, and creates space for someone else to exhale. Mother Teresa is quoted as saying, "If we have no peace, it is because we have forgotten that we belong to each other."

Peace in Christ is more than the absence of conflict—it's "a state of wholeness and harmony. This peace is both internal and communal, reflecting the Hebrew concept of 'shalom.'"[7]

In Nordic countries (and Northern states), there's a saying: "There's no such thing as bad weather, only the wrong clothing." The path of peace is like that. Conditions might be harsh. The wind might sting. But with the right gear—truth, gentleness, patience, mutual care—we can keep going. And we can come alongside others on the journey too, cultivating a better world for all of us.

PRACTICING THE WAY

Bundle up. Layer your socks. Wrap your scarf. Step outside, if you're able—or simply turn your face toward the window and notice the world beyond the glass.

Let the cold remind you: Peace isn't always comfortable.

- Pray for the needs of your neighborhood: the family on the corner with a broken-down car, the elderly neighbor who lives alone, the kids walking to school. Say the names of those who come to mind—teachers, coworkers, caregivers.
- Open your news app to read the top three headlines. Offer each one to God with a breath prayer: "Lord, have mercy. Christ, bring peace."
- Picture someone you love—along with someone who's difficult for you to love. Imagine God's peace reaching them both, and ask God to help you be an active peacemaker.

(If it's not winter where you live, let whatever season you're in remind you that peace is still possible—right here, right now.)

JANUARY 9

Search me, O God, and know my heart; test me and know my anxious thoughts. Point out anything in me that offends you, and lead me along the path of everlasting life.

PSALM 139:23-24 (NLT)

INHALE: I give you
EXHALE: My anxious heart.

Anxiety often lives not just in our racing thoughts but in our bodies too. It shortens our breath, tightens our chests, and narrows our view of the world. But God invites us to open our hearts.

Therapist and author Aundi Kolber writes,

> *Each of our lives tells a story, and our bodies were created to give us valuable information as we experience those stories.*[8]

She explains that as a therapist, she specifically pays attention to her clients' autonomic nervous system—the part of the body that governs unconscious functions, such as breathing, heart rate, and how we react to threats.[9]

Our anxious thoughts are not moral failures. They are signals telling us something isn't safe, is too much, or needs care.

In my training to become a spiritual director (someone who listens, asks gentle questions, and accompanies others on their faith journey), one of my instructors offered this image: *God is like a divine therapist.*

God searches our hearts—not to shame us, but to *know* us. Our hearts are intricate maps our Creator intimately understands. God sees the anxious thoughts we hide, the fears we carry, and the stories we still don't know how to tell. And God does not leave us there.

Psalm 139 reminds us that God knows every corner of who we are. In Christ, God meets us where we are, going before us and alongside us in tenderness and patience, leading us along the path of everlasting life.

Where do you feel anxiety in your body today? What might it be trying to tell you? What stories have shaped your anxious thoughts? How might God meet you in those stories with gentleness?

RHYTHM OF BREATH

When you are not sure
What to do,
Where to go,
Why you're here,
Or who you are,
Remember:
Your heart is a map
With rivers of hope
And valleys of despair.
Open the map of your heart—
Unfurl it.
Let the One who *is*
Search it
And know it
And lead you home.

JANUARY 10

If you don't know what you're doing, pray to the Father. He loves to help.

JAMES 1:5 (MSG)

INHALE: God, I don't know;
EXHALE: Help me in the unknowing.

I'm no stranger to a good, old-fashioned pros and cons list. Throughout my life, I've found that listing my options has helped me figure out what to do. In high school, I used a wide-ruled notebook to choose between the tennis team and the spring play. Later, my lists guided choices on a college, a major, and—eventually—bigger life steps, like marriage and parenting.

For a long time, I kept my lists and my prayers separate. I wanted to follow God's will for my life, but it felt so mysterious and out of reach. I'd scribble the details and *then* ask God for guidance, as if God wasn't already in the details of my life. Over time, I've come to realize that God is big enough to be in every small detail of our lives.

Henri Nouwen writes, "The purpose of discernment is to know God's will, that is, to find, *accept*, and *affirm* the unique way in which God's love is manifest in our life."[10]

Contemplative discernment is a prayerful way of making decisions. When we enter into contemplative discernment, we lay down our desire to find the "perfect" answer and we invite the Holy Spirit to reveal hidden motives, free us from our fears or need for control, and guide us toward wise choices.[11]

We can turn to this process in any season of unknowns—whether we're seeking God's help about relationships, work, time, money, a move, or even our uneasiness about existing commitments.

When you feel stuck, unsettled, or faced with a big decision, try this:

- **Pray first.** Acknowledge God's goodness, and ask for wisdom and an open heart. Ask the Holy Spirit, "What is before me? What is God asking of me?"
- **Name your issue.** Fill in the blank: What are the advantages and disadvantages of ______________? Be specific, and include a time frame for when you'd like to take action.
- **Write the pros and cons.** As you sit with your lists, notice (and jot down) thoughts, emotions, or stories that surface.
- **Let go of your attachment** to either outcome.
- **Be open to God's presence** throughout the process.
- **Return to this exercise as needed** until a sense of clarity (not necessarily certainty) emerges.[12]

Discernment is slow, ongoing work, even after a decision is made. Trust that the One who gives each breath will meet you not just in an aha moment but in the steady rhythm of noticing, listening, and surrendering.

Even if you don't know what you're doing, you're not alone. God loves to help.

PAUSE AND PONDER

Contemplative discernment

What are the advantages of ____________?	What are the disadvantages of ____________?

JANUARY 11

Don't indulge your ego at the expense of your soul.

1 PETER 2:11 (MSG)

INHALE: I find my truest self

EXHALE: In You alone.

When I was in my twenties, I was a business reporter for a newspaper. In that role, I interviewed titans of industry, budding entrepreneurs, and everyone in between. I often found myself at after-work networking events, balancing a paper plate of mixed fruit and mini cupcakes, listening to the same first question ripple through the room: "What do you do?"

Our egos *love* that question (at least, if we have a title the world approves of). The ego thrives on job titles, polished résumés, and all the ways we prove our worth. That's the false self—the part of us shaped by what we produce, how we perform, or how we're perceived. Often, this false self is formed early in life by our longing for power and control, affection and esteem, or belonging to a group.[13]

I saw a glimpse of this at my son's soccer game when a parent introduced their children this way: "This is my athlete, and over there is my poet." There's nothing wrong with naming interests, but if we overidentify with roles or abilities, we risk creating a self-image rooted in achievement rather than in our belovedness.

Our *true self* is who we are in Christ. The truest part of each of us, Thomas Keating writes, is "the image and likeness of God in us . . . the uniqueness that God has called us to be."[14]

Jesus says, "Those who remain in me, and I in them, will bear much fruit."* The fruit comes not from striving but from living in the deep, abiding love of God.

My husband is a pastor who has walked with many who feel the tension between their false self and true self as they enter retirement. Without a title, they wonder, *Who am I now?* In our productivity-driven culture, it's easy to overidentify with what we *do*, rather than simply who we *are*.

The false self will never bear as much fruit as even the simplest acts done from the rootedness of who we are as God's beloved children.

Jesus frees us from the need to prove ourselves and calls us to live from the center of God's love.

Take a breath. Let the striving fall away.

You are so much more than what you do.

You are God's beloved.

* John 15:5, GNT.

LET IT LINGER

False Self (Who We Are on Our Own)	True Self (Who We Are in Christ)
Unsure of love	Resting in God's unshakable love and care
Rooted in performance, productivity, and how we're perceived	Anchored in Christ apart from achievement
Trying to prove, defend, and protect its image	Free to live from abundance—strivings cease
Fearful, fragile, and insecure	Secure in God's care
Holding tightly to control	Trusting God to carry and guide
Striving to earn love	Living from the truth that we're already beloved[15]

JANUARY 12

He does our praying in and for us, making prayer out of our wordless sighs, our aching groans.

ROMANS 8:26 (MSG)

INHALE: Not a single sigh
EXHALE: Goes unheard by You.

My daughter Eliza is nonspeaking. She has Down syndrome and, as a baby, developed a seizure disorder that forever changed the shape of her life. She lives with significant cognitive, developmental, and physical disabilities.

Eliza has broken open the neat boxes I once held about language, prayer, and even God. She often communicates in sounds—tones, hums, vocalizations—what some might call "wordless sighs." And every single sound is heard by the One who made her.

There's a psalm that says, "I call to God; God will help me. At dusk, dawn, and noon I sigh deep sighs—he hears, he rescues."* At every hour of the day, God bends close enough to hold even the faintest sigh or smallest breath.

Maybe you feel too overwhelmed to pray lately, unsure of what to say or exhausted by the thought of finding the "right" words. Take heart: God already knows what you need before you ask.† God will not forget your needs if you forget to pray them.

Prayer is not about informing God of a single thing but about drawing near and resting in the presence of the One who gives each breath. You don't have to ask for your next inhale. It's freely given. And so is God's nearness. The same God who knit your lungs together and who sustains each life-giving breath knows the heaviness you carry, the hope you hold, and the doubts you're afraid to speak aloud.

Sometimes prayer is nothing more (and nothing less) than turning toward God, like a child falling into the arms of a loving Parent. *All you have to do is breathe.*

BREATHE THIS IN

Even wordless sighs can be sacred resets for your body and soul. When you release a long, audible sigh, your body activates the parasympathetic nervous system, lowering stress, slowing heart rate, and reducing blood pressure. Try *cyclic sighing*, a breathing exercise researched by Dr. David Spiegel and his team at Stanford Medicine.

1. Breathe in through your nose until your lungs feel comfortably full.
2. Take a second, smaller sip of air to fill them completely.
3. Exhale slowly through your mouth until all the air is gone.[16]

* Psalm 55:16-17, MSG.
† See Matthew 6:8.

JANUARY 13

The old life is gone; a new life emerges! Look at it! All this comes from the God who settled the relationship between us and him, and then called us to settle our relationships with each other.

2 CORINTHIANS 5:17-18 (MSG)

INHALE: You make
EXHALE: All things new.

Across time, cultures, and faith traditions, prayer and breath have been intertwined.

Science is only now catching up to what people of faith have known for centuries: God has designed us for renewal. As James Nestor puts it, slow breathing "goes by another name: prayer."[17]

Just as each deep inhale and slow exhale nourishes us at a cellular level, God breathes new life into our weary souls, making us new. This renewal extends outward. The God who restores us also calls us to be restorers, to live in rhythms of grace with one another.

As you anticipate the year ahead, what would it look like to receive the renewal God freely gives?

BREATHE THIS IN

Reciting prayers naturally leads to a breathing pattern of 5.5 breaths per minute, shifting the body into a state where "the functions of heart, circulation, and nervous system are coordinated to peak efficiency."[18]

JANUARY 14

God keeps renewing the promise and setting the date as *today*.

HEBREWS 4:7 (MSG)

INHALE: Each breath is a chance
EXHALE: To begin again.

How do you approach rest?

We know that God, in the swirl of the cosmos, rested after breathing life into existence.

We know that Jesus, again and again, slipped away from crowds to pray, to breathe, to *be*.

But how do *we* rest, really?

Our culture insists that time is money. But our God is timeless. To live in Christ is to live beyond the ticking clock and into the fullness of time. Yes, there is an eternal rest we hold in hope, but there is also rest available here and now, available in this very breath.

The writer of Hebrews urges us not to miss this gift. The first generation of God's people in the wilderness missed it—not because the promise wasn't real but because they couldn't receive it with faith. This rest that we're invited into is, as Dr. Madison N. Pierce says, "a promise for every person to enter this space where God has been all along."[19]

You don't have to go anywhere or do anything to receive the promise that where you are, God already is. You just have to receive the promise with faith.

You're not running out of time. Breathe. Receive. And ask God to lead you to true rest.

BORROW THIS PRAYER

Keeper of time,
Giver of breath—
You renew
And keep renewing
Your promises,
Setting the date as today.
Not tomorrow
Or someday.
But now,
In this present moment.

Help us remember, O God:
In the glow of morning,
Each breath is a gift.
In the darkness of night,
Each breath is a gift.
In the promise of dawn,
Each breath is a gift.
In the stillness of dusk,
Each breath is a gift.
As time turns over,
You write a new story
With every sunrise
And every sunset,
With every inhale
And every exhale.

Help us remember
Each breath
Is a new beginning.
Help us remember
The story isn't over.

Help us believe
So that we might find
True rest.
Amen.

JANUARY 15

We know that we are held firm by God.

1 JOHN 5:19 (MSG)

INHALE: When I'm tired,
EXHALE: You hold me close.

Some days the path is clear. The sky is wide, the way is open, and all things seem to fall into place.

And then there are days when exhaustion settles in your bones. When the weight of the world presses down, weariness clings like fog, and all you want is to let go.

But even when you can't hold yourself together, you are held by the One who calls you by name.

When your spirit is weary, you don't have to push through. When you don't feel strong enough to keep going, you don't have to carry the burden alone.

That breath you're holding? You can let it out.

Because God is holding you.

The world is full of people barely keeping it together—the neighbor who carries quiet grief, the friend who won't ask for help, the stranger whose weariness mirrors your own.

Let the Love that holds you be the love that makes space for others.

LET IT LINGER

God is not watching from afar, waiting for you to regain your strength. God is as near as the breath in your lungs, catching you when you stumble, steadying you when you falter, wrapping you in a love that does not waver.

JANUARY 16

Everything that we have—right thinking and right living, a clean slate and a fresh start—comes from God by way of Jesus Christ.

1 CORINTHIANS 1:30 (MSG)

INHALE: It's not too late

EXHALE: To wipe the slate clean.

This time of year, we're drawn to fresh starts—shiny new calendars, planners brimming with promise, resolutions to finally get our lives in order. We want to shrug off the old and imagine what it would be like to "wipe the slate clean."

It's no wonder more than fifteen thousand self-help books are published *each year*.[20] We're all looking for a reset. There's something in us that aches for a new beginning, for a clean slate. We want wisdom to lean on, guidance for the future, words that will change us.

None of that is inherently bad—but it is *incomplete*.

The early church in Corinth longed for wisdom and guidance too. Most members weren't powerful or influential. In fact, many lived on the margins, overlooked by society. Through Christ, they were given a new identity—holy, free, and made right with God—no matter their status, education, or social standing.

Paul contrasted this divine wisdom with the human wisdom the community was tempted to value, like clever arguments, status, and reputation. The wisdom of God can't be captured in a splashy bestseller. It is embodied in Jesus Christ, who frees us from the ways of the world and invites us to extend this new beginning to others.

Where in your life are you aching for a fresh start? Christ meets you there. You don't have to move through this New Year alone. The One who is your wisdom will not leave you—and is in fact inviting you to share this new start with others.

Take a breath. The slate is clean. It's just the right time to begin again.

PAUSE AND PONDER

Where are you longing for a fresh start? In your relationships, routines, work, or attitude? What are you holding on to that you need to release?

____

____

____

What "marks" on your life's slate feel impossible to erase? How might Christ's mercy meet you there?

____

____

____

JANUARY 17

Let petitions and praises shape your worries into prayers, letting God know your concerns.

PHILIPPIANS 4:6 (MSG)

INHALE: I give You my worry;
EXHALE: You give me Your peace.

Sometimes we believe that saying something difficult aloud will make it real. But the truth is that only by *naming* our worries, emotions, fears, and anxieties can we begin to move *through* them.

What are you afraid to say out loud? To admit even to yourself, let alone to God?

Identifying what's going on inside us can feel vulnerable. But we can trust God—not just that God won't condemn us or cause more pain but that God will *protect* our hearts.

As Dr. Alison Cook writes,

> *Naming is a profound act of noticing, acknowledging, and validating the truth of what you're thinking and feeling at any given moment. You stop anxiously ruminating, impulsively reacting, or grasping for a solution and start paying attention to what's happening inside your own mind. What am I feeling right now? What's happening inside? Naming the truth of your inner experience is a powerful step toward clarity.*[21]

You might not always have the exact words for what you're feeling—especially in complicated situations that stir up a mix of emotions. That's okay.

Today, give yourself permission to name what's inside. Be brave enough to share those feelings. Let God shape your worries into prayers.

PRACTICING THE WAY

Let this guided prayer help you turn all you're holding into a conversation with God, allowing God to shape your worries into prayer and your breath into peace. You can whisper each step, write it down, or simply hold it quietly before God.

1. **Name your worry:** What's weighing on you today?
2. **Tell God what you need:** Just speak honestly. God already knows.
3. **Give thanks:** Even here, there is goodness. What is something you can thank God for right now?
4. **Receive peace:** Imagine Jesus placing peace over you like a blanket.
5. **Go forth, living in Christ:** Picture yourself stepping into the rest of this day with Jesus guiding you.
6. **Trust that Christ will protect your heart:** Release your heart into God's care, trusting you will be held in love.
7. **Trust that Christ will protect your mind:** Bring your racing thoughts to God. Ask God to be your shield against fear, confusion, and lies.

JANUARY 18

He will cover you with his feathers, and under his wings you will find refuge; his faithfulness will be your shield and rampart.

PSALM 91:4 (NIV)

INHALE: I find refuge

EXHALE: In the shelter of Your wings.

When a baby is swaddled in a parent's arms, the baby's heart rate slows and their breathing becomes steady. We're created to seek nurture, care, and protection.

When we feel unsafe or overwhelmed, our breathing becomes shallow and our blood pressure increases. Our bodies brace for what's next.

Picture being caught in a fierce blizzard, with cold winds hitting your face, frostbite threatening, and the windchill so intense that stepping outside takes your breath away. (I recall walking across campus in college during some of those freezing, harsh days. Let's just say I'm glad to not ever have to do *that* frigid trek again.)

But when you come inside, protected from the storm, your breath can calm and you can breathe more easily, finding comfort and safety. You can finally release a sigh of relief.

Perhaps you've never known God as a safe place—nurturing and protective, both gentle and strong. Maybe the church hasn't been a refuge for you. Maybe God's name was misused to harm rather than heal.

Life's storms may hurt you, but God never will.

When you are exhausted and worn out, God is always there to gently nurture and fiercely protect you, offering love and safety exactly when you need it most. When ice coats the branches, when your cheeks sting, when the chill in the air steals your breath—remember this: *God is your shelter.*

BREATHE THIS IN

Intentional, unhurried breathing (like the kind that happens when you feel truly safe) not only calms your mind but soothes your body too. Research from the American Heart Association shows that slow, steady breaths can ease your heart rate, lower blood pressure, and reduce stress hormones.[22] It's the body's way of responding to safety—like resting in the shelter of God's wings.

JANUARY 19

By coming up with a new plan, God put the old plan on the shelf. And there it stays, gathering dust.

HEBREWS 8:13 (MSG)

INHALE: The old ways are gone;
EXHALE: You are making me new.

When I worked at a national magazine, I watched from my cubicle as a trio of people in suits disappeared into a large office for their performance review, stacks of manila envelopes in hand. Those who went in came out with drawn faces, clutching papers that determined their worth (or lack thereof) to the company.

I sat at my desk, reordering sticky notes and mentally rehearsing accomplishments—ready to prove I deserved to stay.

God is not like that. In the Kingdom of God, there are no performance reviews. No quarterly reports. No "rightsizing" or "termination assistance." Because of Jesus, we aren't bound to a law-based relationship where our standing depends on meeting certain metrics. The old covenant—with all its rituals, sacrifices, and rules written on tablets—has been fulfilled.

Jesus ushered in something new: love written on our hearts, transformation through the Spirit, and a grace-based relationship with God that transcends everything we thought we knew. You don't have to do anything to earn God's love. Your name is not on the chopping block if you fail to measure up.

Grace radically reorients our lives. We don't have to perform our way into God's love.

But if we're honest, grace is easy to forget. We compare ourselves to others, competing as if there's only one job opening or one seat at the table—as the disciples once did, angling for the spot at Jesus' right hand.

Grace says the old ways are gone. We are free to rest from proving our worth. Forgiven for our shortcomings, we can, as poet Anis Mojgani says, "shake the dust" and live differently.[23] "If anyone is in Christ, the new creation has come: The old has gone, the new is here!"*

Grace is good news for you and for everyone else (including those you envy, misunderstand, or resist). God puts the old performance-driven ways on the shelf, where they gather dust, and invites us into a new reality of restoration and reconciliation.

What old ways of proving yourself do you need to leave behind? Where is God inviting you to stop striving and rest in grace?

Take a deep breath. Shake the dust. Rest in Christ's outstretched love. And become a harbinger of hope in a world still stuck in the old ways.

RHYTHM OF BREATH

In the dawn of a New Year,
I will place
My expectations on the shelf.
I will resolve to do less,
More often.

* 2 Corinthians 5:17, NIV.

JANUARY 20

Those who do not love a brother or sister whom they have seen, cannot love God whom they have not seen.

1 JOHN 4:20 (NRSV)

INHALE: Help me love others
EXHALE: The way You love me.

On the third Monday of January every year, we reflect on the life and legacy of Dr. Martin Luther King Jr., whose vision for a more just and loving world continues to challenge and inspire us.

Dr. King was shaped by the mentorship of Howard Thurman, a theologian and educator raised by his grandmother, who had lived through the horrors of enslavement. Thurman lived his life in Christ, holding together deep contemplation and courageous action for the flourishing of all people.

In his book *The Luminous Darkness*, Thurman describes the pain of seeing white Christians proclaim the gospel of Jesus while refusing to affirm the dignity of people of other races—fighting, sometimes violently, to *preserve* segregation.

"Because a man is a Christian," Thurman wrote, "is no indication to me what his attitude may be toward me in any given circumstance."[24] While legalized segregation may be over, adding "Christian" to our list of identifiers still means little if we refuse to love others in tangible ways. Injustice is still alive and well—an invisible thread sewn into the fabric of our society, showing up in personal attitudes and daily choices. It can be blatant, but it can also be passive.

Thurman warned, "Whether the acceptance is deliberate or indifferent, [a person] becomes the party to a monstrous evil executed in his name and maintained in his behalf."[25]

The words of this verse cut to the heart: If we can't love the people in front of us, we can't claim to love God. If we proclaim Christ, we must also embody Christ. We love because Jesus first loved us, and that love propels us to extend that mending type of love to others.

What would it look like for you to move toward others in love? What would it look like for you to love the people right in front of you? To honor the image of God in those you meet today?

BORROW THIS PRAYER

May we honor the work of Dr. King
And countless other women and men
Fighting for civil rights,
Yesterday and today,
By not shying away from the contact burns
It takes to keep the fires of freedom
Burning in our hearts.

When given the choice, may we
Know to choose community.
May we choose the love of neighbor
That flows out of the love of God—
A love that overcomes.
A love that, as Dr. King said,
Is the most durable power in the world.[26]

Adapted from "A Prayer for Martin Luther King Jr. Day" in To Light Their Way

JANUARY 21

He took a deep breath and breathed into them. "Receive the Holy Spirit."

JOHN 20:22 (MSG)

INHALE: Spirit, breathe
EXHALE: New life into me.

In the beginning, God breathed.

And God has been breathing new life into us ever since.

The breath of God is powerful enough to form life from dust and change the course of history *forever*.

God breathed life into Adam in the garden, and Jesus echoed that moment when he breathed onto the disciples, filling them with the Holy Spirit and sending them into a new way of living.

Like our lungs, the stories of Scripture are connected, expanding and contracting together. Just as we can't take a breath without both lungs working in harmony, we can't fully understand God's story without seeing how the Spirit moves through both the Old and New Testaments.

- In Hebrew, *ruach* means both "breath" and "spirit."
- In Greek, the same is true of *pneuma*.[27]
- In Ezekiel 37:9-10, the breath of God sweeps through a valley of dry bones, bringing life where there was only death.
- In Acts 2, the Spirit rushes in like a mighty wind, empowering ordinary people for an extraordinary mission.

When Jesus breathes on the disciples, something in the air changes—and their lives will never be the same.

That same Spirit-breath is offered to us today.

As you breathe, feel your lungs filling and emptying, your whole body participating in this holy rhythm. Let each inhale remind you that the Spirit of God dwells in you. Let each exhale make room for the new life only God can give.

BORROW THIS PRAYER

You are the breath
In my lungs.
You are the air
That I breathe.

Breathe new life
Into me.
Be the wind
That carries me
Across the water.

Beacon of hope,
Ever-present help,
Carry me on the
Whispering night sea.
Bring me to morning
In the shelter
Of Your wings.
Amen.

JANUARY 22

Ask for the ancient paths, where the good way lies; and walk in it.

JEREMIAH 6:16 (NRSV)

INHALE: Show me the way
EXHALE: To true peace, O God.

We understand which way leads to peace, but it can be tempting to overlook God's clear guidance that can truly restore and renew us.

This isn't a new thing. Throughout Scripture, God's people are shown the right path but choose not to follow it.

Part of being human is that we tend to steer away from paths of peace and onto the rocky terrain of self-interest. This leaves us unfulfilled and searching for more. It's easy to *know* what the Bible says but still fail to live by it. It's easy to prioritize love of self over love of neighbor, greed over generosity, and power over humility.

Recognizing the good way isn't enough—we're called to live it, empowered by the Spirit.

While following the good path often looks countercultural, we can trust God that doing so will bring deeper peace and rest for our souls. Our world can be a dark place, making it easy to lose our footing and take wrong turns. But it's never too late to find our course again.

When you grow weary and burdened, trying to check religious or cultural boxes, take a breath. Let go. Get back to where the good way lies.

In Christ, may you find true rest for today and hope for tomorrow, free from the burdens of past missteps.

RHYTHM OF BREATH

Ask—
And walk through the door.
Let the cold meet you.
Watch your exhale
Form clouds
That go before
In the now and not yet.

Step into the darkness
And let the breath of heaven
Guide you in the night.

When it seems as though
The light
Will never be again,
Breathe.
Trudge the ancient paths
Where the good way lies.

Go—
And let your lungs fill
With the newness of life.
Walk in it,
Travel its path,
And peace will find
Your tired soul.

JANUARY 23

This is what the Sovereign Lord says: "Look! I am going to put breath into you and make you live again!"

EZEKIEL 37:5 (NLT)

INHALE: I give you my burdens;
EXHALE: You give me my next breath.

God so seamlessly provides us with our next breath that we often forget it's happening.

Each inhale is a promise. Each exhale is a gift. The One who breathed life into dust still sustains us—so faithfully, so quietly, that we can overlook His generosity. And then, when hardship comes, we wonder if the Giver of life is truly trustworthy.

Spoiler alert: You can trust God.

Without effort, your lungs fill and empty, working in an unceasing rhythm God designed. And yet, as opposed to so many other automatic functions, you can also choose to slow your breath, deepen it, and be mindful of it.

The hope we have in Christ is that what is dead doesn't stay dead.

Every breath is an invitation to start fresh. The new life we receive offers hope for today and for the future—and it also calls us to act, to join in bringing God's Kingdom into a world still aching for healing.

How might being mindful that your breath is a gift change the way you go about your day today?

As you pray, try inhaling for a count of four seconds, holding that breath for a count of four, and then exhaling for a count of six.

SACRED ECHOES

We rally around your newness that is both our hope and our work.[28]

Walter Brueggemann

JANUARY 24

I pray to God—my life a prayer—and wait for what he'll say and do.

PSALM 130:5 (MSG)

INHALE: May all my life
EXHALE: Be a prayer.

May all of your life—your fantastic, dirty, messy, holy life—be a prayer. It's how I end so many of the blessings I write, because I need the reminder too.

Have you ever thought of prayer that way? Like your whole life—even the chaotic and complicated parts—could be a prayer of its own?

My husband and I adopted our daughter, Eliza, when she was three weeks old. She has Down syndrome and significant disabilities due to infantile seizures. She is now in upper elementary school but still needs constant care, including help with bathroom routines, since she wears Pull-Ups.

I don't often dwell on what-if worries about the future, but these messy moments sometimes trigger my worst anxieties. Changing a baby's diaper is one thing. But caring for a growing child in a very real mess—trying to honor her dignity and keep my sanity while scrubbing the bathroom floor—is its own kind of sacred labor.

This recurring need began to draw me into prayer. "God, be with Eliza," I'd whisper. "Help her." As I prayed, God began to shape not just my prayers but also *me*. I started seeing changing diapers as an invitation to let *my life* become a prayer. I prayed for Eliza and began to understand that God brought us together so I might extend Christ's compassion and care through my life.

Theologian Ronald Rolheiser explains that when we pray and say "through Jesus Christ our Lord" or "in Christ," we are praying through the *body* of Christ, which includes us as believers here on earth.[29] We are inviting our own bodies into the prayer.

We are part of how God is at work. We are part of how God heals. We are part of how God shows up.

Breath prayers are a way to pray throughout the day, reminding us that all aspects of our lives—including the mundane, ordinary, unseen moments—matter, and that all of our lives can be entered into and offered up as a prayer.

Breath prayers are a form of "active prayer," something we can revisit amid our daily routines to center us back to the truth that in Christ, we're not just praying—we *are* the prayer.

Where is God inviting you to let your life become a prayer? Return to today's breath prayer as you go about your day—and wait to see what God does.

SACRED ECHOES

To pray as a Christian demands concrete involvement in trying to bring about what is pleaded for in the prayer.[30]

Ronald Rolheiser

JANUARY 25

What you say about yourself means nothing in God's work.
It's what God says about you that makes the difference.

2 CORINTHIANS 10:18 (MSG)

INHALE: Help me receive
EXHALE: Your perfect love.

It's easy to get entangled in a world that measures worth by achievement, appearance, and accolades. We often define ourselves by our successes and failures, seeking approval from others and holding ourselves to unattainable standards. But our self-assessments (and the yardsticks of others) don't measure up to what God values.

Bombarding ourselves with negative self-talk is easy. And it's tempting to try to sanctify the mean things we say to ourselves, the *I should be better*s and the *I'm not good enough*s, to believe that's what God says about us.

But God isn't swayed by our accomplishments or our shortcomings. We're seen beyond our circumstances and in the depths of who we really are: *loved*. The love of God is unconditional. And that love is not something to be earned but received.

Before Jesus began ministry, before he performed miracles or preached to the masses, a voice from heaven declared, "This is my Son, whom I love; with him I am well pleased."* Jesus received the Father's affirmation not based on works but on identity as the beloved Son.

Our identity is rooted in being God's beloved children. In light of this, we can stop living *for* approval but instead live *from* a place of already being cherished by the Creator.

How might this perspective shift free you from a relentless pursuit of validation?

As you go throughout today, may this breath prayer anchor you in the truth of God's unwavering love. Breathe in the promise that it is Christ who defines your worth.

SACRED ECHOES

The world is loud, God.
Only you can convince me
Of how embarrassingly lovable I can be.[31]

Kate Bowler

* Matthew 3:17, NIV.

JANUARY 26

Be strong and courageous. Do not be afraid; do not be discouraged, for the LORD your God will be with you wherever you go.

JOSHUA 1:9 (NIV)

INHALE: God, You are with me;
EXHALE: I am safe with You.

Our bodies know we're scared before our minds do.

Pause for a moment to notice your breath. Is it slow and steady or shallow and staggered?

Dr. Michael Breus writes that rapid breathing is one of the body's early warning systems that triggers the stress response, sometimes before we even realize we're afraid.

"You don't even have to feel scared," he notes, "for the body to think it's under attack."[32]

When our breath quickens, our adrenal glands send the stress hormone cortisol into our system, redirecting blood to our muscles and heart so we can fight or flee.[33] But when we slow our breathing (like when we practice intentional, slow breaths with breath prayers), we give our bodies a different cue: *You are safe.*

And in the loving arms of our Creator, we truly are.

Our world may not always be a safe place. But God always is.

When God told Joshua not to be afraid, it wasn't because the road ahead would be smooth (or because Joshua needed to man up and be brave) but because God was promising to go with him as he led the Israelites into the Promised Land. The command to "be strong and courageous" was followed by a promise: "I will be with you wherever you go."

There was nowhere Joshua could go where God wouldn't be with him. There is no place beyond God's reach.

Let your breath become a prayer today. As you breathe slow, steady breaths, remember that you are safe in this moment because God is with you. You can be strong and courageous because you are not—and never have been—alone.

BREATHE THIS IN

- Sit up straight in a chair or lie on your back.
- Lay one hand on your stomach and the other hand on your chest.
- Inhale slowly through your nose, breathing deep into your belly so the hand on your stomach rises while the hand on your chest stays mostly still.
- Notice the natural pause before you exhale.
- Exhale slowly, feeling your belly fall.
- Continue this gentle rise-and-fall breathing for five minutes, pairing it with a simple breath prayer.[34]

JANUARY 27

God can do anything, you know—far more than you could ever imagine or guess or request in your wildest dreams! He does it not by pushing us around but by working within us, his Spirit deeply and gently within us.

EPHESIANS 3:20 (MSG)

INHALE: You are bigger
EXHALE: Than my wildest dreams.

I have an active imagination. My husband is used to me turning to him and starting a question with "What if . . . ?" before unleashing some big dream into the world. But even my boldest *what-ifs* bump into the edges of my mind.

God's power and creativity, though, are limitless—beyond our wildest dreams. Every spark of creativity or curiosity we carry is just a glimmer of the One who speaks galaxies into being in a single breath.

God's imagination for the world—and for *you*—is bigger and brighter than any of us can fathom. Paul says God works "deeply and gently within us." The same Spirit who scattered the stars and set planets into motion is imagining a life that would take your breath away.

What would it look like to trust the promise that God can do far more than you could ever dream up or ask for?

As kids, we're often told to step out of our daydreams and into the "real world." But what if the depth of our dreams and the heartbeat of our hopes are hints of the One who breathed the world into existence and who still breathes new life into us every moment?

We don't always notice the slow, steady work God is doing in our lives. But one day, I think we'll see that God's vision for us is far greater than anything we could paint in our minds.

Today, bring your too-big dreams and your barely whispered prayers to the One who imagined you before you were even born. And trust that God is still shaping you—beyond your understanding, unhindered by your limitations, and toward something better than you can imagine.

Open your heart. Have a willing spirit. And trust in the promise that, as Thomas Keating said, "transformation is completely God's work."[35]

PAUSE AND PONDER

When have you seen God's work turn out more beautiful than you expected? How might remembering that shape your hope today?

What would it look like to pray without editing or shrinking your requests this week?

JANUARY 28

May Jesus himself and God our Father, who reached out in love and surprised you with gifts of unending help and confidence, put a fresh heart in you, invigorate your work, enliven your speech.

2 THESSALONIANS 2:16-17 (MSG)

INHALE: I need Your help;
EXHALE: Put a fresh heart in me.

It's easy for me to think of prayer as something I do—a reaching out to God. But I wonder how my understanding of prayer might change if I thought of prayer as God reaching out to me. If only I'd take the call.

Our world is weary. In so many ways, we need help. The Psalms are jam-packed with prayers and poems that cry out to God, begging for help in a world bent on destruction and death. Over and over, Scripture tells us that God is our helper: "Surely God is my help; the Lord is the one who sustains me."*

And God doesn't help reluctantly—God *loves* to help.†

Boy, do we need that help. All around us, creation groans. Things aren't as they should be. Wars erupt. Injustices abound. We fall into cycles of cynicism or cruelty or corruption. We deal with the reverberations of sin and suffering all the time. That's what it is to be human. But the promise we have as believers is that God moves *toward* us—reaching out in love, offering endless help in a helpless world, giving us what we need to love others the same way, in our work and our words.

Because, yes, we need help in the big parts of our lives, but if I'm being honest, sometimes I need help just to be patient with my son when he can't find his left shoe and we're late for school drop-off.

Our help isn't found in some distant realm. God reaches out to us in love right here in our actual lives. Jesus broke into this messy, complicated reality of being human—and has never left us. In Psalm 124, we're told that the same God who made heaven and earth is our help in the here and now. This, says Eugene Peterson, pastor and translator of *The Message* Bible paraphrase, "takes the majesty of the One who pulled a universe into order and beauty, and finds this same God involved in the local troubles of a quite ordinary person."[36]

Holding hope doesn't mean that bad things won't happen. But when we hold hope, we make space for help to enter in.

Whatever you're holding today, remember that you're not alone. As you breathe, remember that God loves to help.

SACRED ECHOES

We are not scavenging in the dark alleys of the world, poking in its garbage cans for a bare subsistence. We are traveling in the light, toward God who is rich in mercy and strong to save. It is Christ, not culture, that defines our lives. It is the help we experience, not the hazards we risk, that shapes our days.[37]

Eugene Peterson

---

* Psalm 54:4, NIV.

† See James 1:5-8.

JANUARY 29

Keep your eyes open, hold tight to your convictions, give it all you've got, be resolute, and love without stopping.

1 CORINTHIANS 16:13-14 (MSG)

INHALE: Renew my tired spirit;
EXHALE: In You, I can carry on.

The way of Jesus is a rhythm we live, right here and right now, in the mess of our real lives.

But I'd be lying if I said there aren't days when the headlines keep coming, the weight of my own life presses in, and it feels easier to retreat. To turn away from the harsh realities of this weary world. To close my eyes or turn my back because showing up in this world in love feels like more than I can manage.

The church in Corinth understood this tension of being called to live in a new way while surrounded by old patterns. Paul's words cut through the noise then, and they still speak to us now:

- Keep your eyes open—even when the world feels overwhelming.
- Hold tight to your convictions—even when doubts creep in.
- Give it all you've got—even when you feel like you have little left.
- Be resolute—even in uncertainty.
- Love without stopping—even when it costs you something.

Every year, our city hosts a festival celebrating Irish and Scottish heritage. One of the most popular events is the caber toss—a competition where athletes lift and throw a full-length pine log, flipping it end over end, aiming for perfect alignment. It takes incredible physical strength.

When I think of strength, I often picture that kind of brute force that comes from lifting weights (or in this case, hoisting giant logs). But the strength that comes from God is something else entirely. It's the resilience of the single mother keeping everything together for her three kids. It's the teacher showing up for his students while he undergoes cancer treatments. It's the foster child who bravely enters a new home with their few belongings in a garbage bag.

When Paul wrote this letter to the Corinthians, he wasn't telling folks to push past their limits or ignore their exhaustion. He wasn't encouraging them to load up on protein powder and "get swole" for Jesus. He was reminding them that the way to stay awake, stand firm, and keep showing up in this weary world is to draw strength from the One who renews and restores.

Take a breath. Let your soul exhale. You are not alone in this. You don't have to carry the weight alone or rely on your own power. God is the One who will sustain you.

So keep going.

BREATHE THIS IN

Regular deep breathing—like what we experience in breath prayer—can reduce tension, boost blood flow and oxygenation, and help you increase strength and endurance.[38] In every breath, God meets you, strengthening you in both body and soul.

JANUARY 30

He himself gives life and breath to everything, and he satisfies every need.

ACTS 17:25 (NLT)

INHALE: Help me remember
EXHALE: Each breath is a gift.

Sometimes my husband forgets to breathe. If we're on the couch watching a particularly riveting movie, I'll notice stillness—and then hear a sudden, sharp inhale, as if his body has just remembered that breathing is not optional.

He's not alone. Former Apple and Microsoft employee Linda Stone coined the terms *email apnea* and *screen apnea* to describe the shallow or suspended breathing we often fall into while on a screen. In her observations of two hundred people using computers, a whopping 80 percent held their breath. The ones who didn't were trained in intentional breathwork—athletes, dancers, and musicians.[39]

We're living in a time like no other. From rolling over first thing in the morning to silence our alarms (and check the weather . . . and maybe an email or two) to doomscrolling in bed at night, we're saturated with screens from dawn to dusk. They connect us, inform us, entertain us, and, ironically, even track our health. We're convinced we have everything we need—and infinitely more—at our fingertips.

But sometimes I wonder if these glowing rectangles are curses disguised as blessings. They seem to give us everything, yet they're literally robbing us of our breath. Of life itself.

Breathing may seem like nothing more than a biological reflex, but Scripture reminds us it is a divine gift. Each rise and fall of our chest is sustained by the One who gave us breath in the beginning and is giving us breath still.

Our phones seem to be so good, making us feel prepared for or protected from the world. But as Frederick Buechner wrote, the same things that shield us from reality also steel us against "being opened and transformed by the holy power that life itself comes from."[40]

Even the ping of a new text or news alert can cause us to hold our breath, keeping our bodies in a low-grade state of stress—exhausted, inflamed, and headed toward burnout.[41]

Not only is God the One who *gave* us life—God is actively *giving* us every single breath we take. No matter how many notifications are vying for your attention, the rise and fall of your chest is sustained by the Giver of life.

Today, remember not just to breathe but also that the Giver of each breath is the One who meets your every need.

SACRED ECHOES

You can survive on your own. You can grow strong on your own. You can even prevail on your own. But you cannot become human on your own. . . . The rich man is so effective at getting for himself everything he needs that he does not see that what he needs more than anything else in the world can be had only as a gift.[42]

Frederick Buechner

JANUARY 31

You're well-known as good and forgiving,
bighearted to all who ask for help.

PSALM 86:5 (MSG)

INHALE: Help me remember
EXHALE: I can ask for help.

I can't stand asking for help. When I come home from grocery shopping, I lace my arms from wrist to shoulder with shopping bags as I trudge up the stairs, balancing keys in my mouth, more willing to let a dozen apples cascade down the stairs than to ask for help.

But asking for help isn't admitting defeat. Asking for help simply acknowledges what's already true: We're *human.*

None of us gets to where we are all alone. We've all had help and handholds along the way.

We can accept help because we have a God who has given us the Holy Spirit, called our Helper.* Some people claim that God is menacing or retributive. But the psalmist says God is good. Forgiving. Bighearted.

We have two takeaways here:

1. **It's good to ask for help.** Everyone needs help. It's not a sign of weakness or defeat; it's a sign of being human. And spoiler alert: You're human.
2. **God is our Helper.** God's goodness isn't reserved for a select few. God forgives. God listens. God comes to our aid.

We don't have to live as people who have to do it all by ourselves, as those who bear the burdens of our guilt and the brunt of our shame. We are free to breathe deep the love of God. And because of this goodness, we can exhale it into the world.

Because God is good, we can remember that goodness is a fruit of the Spirit.† We can forgive because we've been forgiven. We can be tender to those who ask for help because we know what it's like to be helped.

Maybe people turn coldhearted and cruel to those who are suffering because they view God as condemning themselves. But Scripture tells another truth: Our God is good and forgiving, bighearted to all who ask for help.

Take a breath. Ask for help from others. And from God. Then extend that help to others.

PAUSE AND PONDER

Where in your life do you resist asking for help? What might change if you saw asking for help as an act of trust rather than an act of weakness?

Who in your life might need a reminder of God's goodness and bighearted help? How could you tangibly extend that help?

* See John 14:26, ESV.

† See Galatians 5:22.

FEBRUARY 1

When you give them your breath, life is created,
and you renew the face of the earth.

PSALM 104:30 (NLT)

INHALE: You renew me
EXHALE: With every breath.

A shimmering world greets me as I step outside my front door. Powdered-sugar snow sparkles in the sun. Ice-coated branches scatter sunlight in a thousand directions. The sharp air steals my breath, and as I exhale, clouds of vapor dissolve like last summer's cotton candy.

I squint at the midday sun, the horizon a seamless blend of bright sky and snow-covered ground. The earth that was once brown and gray has been blanketed in new life. Everything feels fresh and full of promise.

The psalmist tells us that God's breath renews the face of the earth. This is not a one-time act of creation but an ongoing rhythm, steady as our own breathing. Just as each inhale brings oxygen to refresh our cells and each exhale makes room for new air to enter, the breath of God is forever and always inviting us into restoration and renewal.

Without breathing alongside God, we'll run out of steam, no matter how pure our intentions. "Our spirits are breathless until they breathe with God," Douglas Scott Dent writes. "The aim of Christian discipleship, indeed the whole of Christian life, is to discover how to breathe in harmony with God," Dent continues. "When we learn to breathe with God, we begin to breathe deeply with Jesus Christ, and to breathe in harmony with the Holy Spirit for the reclamation of the world."[43]

The same breath that gives you life also renews the earth. As you turn your breath into prayer, close your eyes and imagine the Spirit moving through you and into the far corners of the earth, breathing life into a world longing for restoration.

SACRED ECHOES

Just as God breathed the breath of life into the first living being, so our deep, instinctive taking of breath is receiving again the gift of life from God for each moment.[44]

Flora Slosson Wuellner

FEBRUARY 2

FEAST OF THE PRESENTATION

I have seen your salvation, which you have prepared for all people.

LUKE 2:30-31 (NLT)

INHALE: Light of the World,
EXHALE: You are with me in the wait.

Though February is the shortest month of the year, it sometimes feels like the *longest*. The excitement of resolutions and fresh starts fades, and the darkness of winter lingers. The days stretch on, gray and heavy, and we ache for light, both around us and within us.

Some Christian traditions mark today as the Feast of the Presentation, remembering when Mary and Joseph brought their newborn son to the Temple in Jerusalem. There, in the Temple courts, they met two faithful souls who had spent their whole lives waiting.

The aging Simeon had been told he would see the Messiah before he died. Anna, a widow for most of her life, was a prophet who spent her days in the Temple, fasting and praying. They waited through silence, through darkness, through the ache of expectation. And then, one day, a young mother walked in, cradling a newborn.

When he saw a small baby in Mary's arms, Simeon exhaled a lifetime of waiting.

If today feels dark, if you're grasping for the light but only finding shadows, if your prayers feel like whispers into the void, take heart. God hasn't forgotten you.

PRACTICING THE WAY

Some traditions observe Candlemas today by blessing the candles that will be used in worship throughout the year. In some churches, a candlelight procession winds through the aisles, a quiet defiance against winter's shadow.

Light a candle (any kind will do). As you watch the flame flicker and dance, let go of the breath you've been holding. Ask God to be with you in the wait. When you're ready, blow out the candle with a deep, slow exhale. As you smell the smoke and watch it linger, remember that no matter how dark things seem, the Light of the World cannot be extinguished.

FEBRUARY 3

This is the kind of fasting I want: Free those who are wrongly imprisoned; lighten the burden of those who work for you. Let the oppressed go free.

ISAIAH 58:6 (NLT)

INHALE: Help me care for others
EXHALE: The way You care for me.

God doesn't ask for much, really. Spiritual practices can be beautiful tools for formation, but we don't have to devote ourselves to dramatic fasting or specific religious rituals to earn God's favor.

We're just called to . . . love God and others. Easier said than done, right?

When God spoke through Isaiah, the message cut through the noise: *Worship that doesn't lead to loving others isn't worship at all.* True worship is marked not by how well we perform religion but by how fully we follow God's call to love.

That love looks like breaking chains and setting the oppressed free, echoing the mission of Jesus, who came to bring good news to the poor and set captives free.* In Christ, we are free from pious obligation so that we can actually *live* what we proclaim.

This call is not abstract work, and it's rarely convenient. Karl Barth, a theologian who refused to swear loyalty to Adolf Hitler, described our call as "a willing, working, and doing . . . according to the need, disposition, and direction of others."[45] Barth was deported from Germany for his commitment to the words of Isaiah. But that didn't stop him from holding firm in his conviction.

God doesn't just call us to *avoid* harm. God calls us to *undo* it.

Maybe you feel like you're one of the only ones still trying. Maybe you've been misunderstood or tempted toward cynicism. Take heart. Even when the loudest voices ring hollow, your quiet acts of love matter.

Compassion becomes action. Because here's the paradox of God's Kingdom: When we pour ourselves out in love, we don't end up empty. We find ourselves more alive, more free, more connected to the heart of the One who is—right now—breathing life into the world and asking us to join in.

PAUSE AND PONDER

Make this prayer your own by filling in the blanks. Let yourself be honest with God as you choose your words. Take all the time you need.

Generous and just God, I admit that it's difficult for me to ______________. Will You help me to follow Your rhythms of ______________ and ______________ today?

Breathe in me a spirit of ______________ so I might contribute to healing. Help me share my ______________ and help me live with open hands and an open heart.

Give me ______________ when I am weary and grant me ______________ when I don't know which way to turn. Remind me that You are ______________ when I am ______________.

---

* See Luke 4:18-19.

FEBRUARY 4

The LORD is my light and my salvation—so why should I be afraid?

PSALM 27:1 (NLT)

INHALE: Light of the World,
EXHALE: I release my fears.

As a mom to four kids, I'm no stranger to being called into a darkened bedroom after a bad dream wakes someone from their sleep. I've done my fair share of checking for monsters, shining a light under the bed to prove nothing is lurking in the shadows. But sometimes my kids cry out while they're still tangled in the nightmare. In those moments, all I can do is climb into bed beside them, wrap them in my arms, and remind them to breathe while I wait for them to wake up.

When fear grips us, our nervous systems kick into high gear. Hearts race. Palms sweat. Breath becomes fast and shallow. Our bodies instinctively move into fight, flight, or freeze, trying to protect us from danger.

A daily scan of the headlines reminds us there are plenty of reasons to be afraid in our grown-up world. The media knows how to keep us on edge. Politicians leverage fear to divide and conquer. If only the monsters that haunt us could be scared away with a quick flashlight sweep. But very real fear follows us into our days.

We are not made to live on constant high alert. But what can we do when it seems like we're living in a nightmarish world?

Prayerful breathing can calm our bodies and minds by lowering our heart rate, steadying our shaky hands, and helping us shift from panic to God's presence.

As you let your breath become prayer today, rest in the comfort that we have the One who doesn't just shine a light under the bed but *is* the Light of the World. A Light that the darkness can never extinguish. That holds us close and whispers again and again, *You are safe. You are safe. You are safe.*

PAUSE AND PONDER

What fears have been keeping you in survival mode this week? How can you let yourself be held by God?

Recall a time when you felt afraid. What was comforting to you? How can you extend that comfort to others?

FEBRUARY 5

We live by faith, not by sight.
2 CORINTHIANS 5:7 (NIV)

INHALE: Help me live by faith,
EXHALE: Not by sight.

As a child, I wore out our VHS recording of *The Wizard of Oz.* I was captivated by the yellow brick road and those glittering ruby slippers. But what fascinated me most was when Dorothy finally pulled back the curtain (spoiler alert) and discovered that the great and powerful wizard wasn't all-knowing after all—just a man fumbling with levers and smoke.

In our complicated world, we long for certainty. (I'm still waiting for someone to tell me everything will unfold exactly as I want and then invite me and my friends into a hot air balloon!) We like to believe we can predict what's ahead. We have algorithms at our fingertips to anticipate our every need. But no matter how advanced our technology gets, we'll never see tomorrow with clarity.

My mom used to sing "Que Sera, Sera" while she folded laundry: "Whatever will be, will be. The future's not ours to see." As a kid, I found that line frustrating. It sounded like the lyrical equivalent of shrugging your shoulders and giving in! But I hear it differently now, realizing it's not so much a resignation as it is an invitation to release my grip on what I cannot control.

Faith is not the same as sight. We go with God in mystery, trusting that even when the road twists and fog settles in, the Spirit is still there.

When we pray, we may not get the answers we want (or any answers at all), but we don't pray to a self-made wizard cloaked in smoke and mirrors. We pray to the One who will never leave or forsake us. We receive something better than certainty: the Advocate, the Holy Spirit, who is with us wherever the road takes us.

SACRED ECHOES

"Do you think things always have an explanation?"

"Yes. I believe that they do. But I think that with our human limitations we're not always able to understand the explanations. But you see, Meg, just because we don't understand doesn't mean that the explanation doesn't exist. . . ."

"We do not know what things *look* like. . . . We know what things *are* like. It must be a very limiting thing, this seeing."[46]

Madeleine L'Engle, A Wrinkle in Time

FEBRUARY 6

Long before he laid down earth's foundations, he had us in mind, had settled on us as the focus of his love, to be made whole and holy by his love.

EPHESIANS 1:4 (MSG)

INHALE: In You, I am made holy;
EXHALE: In You, I am made whole.

Long before the first sunrise, before soil was shaped or seas were stirred, God had us—had *you*—in mind.

From the very beginning, God's plan was to send the Son—not only to redeem us, but to walk among us, to be one of us. To know the texture of our skin, the salt of our tears, and the cadence of our laughter.

Before time itself, the Word was with God and the Word was God. And then the Word became flesh, choosing to live, breathe, and feel what it's like to be in our skin.* By choosing a body, God embraced the fullness of our humanity.

When we talk about the incarnation, we mean God coming close—Jesus living an entire human life. He didn't just arrive, skip to the cross, and rise again. He was a baby, a toddler, a boy with dusty feet. He was a teenager figuring things out, a man who laughed at weddings, felt hunger in the wilderness, and wept at a friend's tomb. Fully God and fully human, Jesus experienced it all. None of it was accidental.

We see faint glimpses of this kind of planning in human creativity, like the way Pixar slips hidden nods into its movies or how pop stars layer their work with clues for attentive fans to discover. But God's purposeful planning goes beyond what the most clever mastermind could plan—infinitely more complete, infinitely more loving.

God chose not just to create us and then be like us, but to love us and pursue us. Your emotions, your wonderings, your aches and pains are not distractions from faith but part of how you relate to and experience God, how God relates to and experiences you, and how you relate to and experience others.

From each breath to every heartbeat, you are loved in your entirety. And that love was planned from the very beginning. As you breathe, rest in the truth that God is making you *whole* and *holy*—and has been all along.

SACRED ECHOES

Because our faith is rooted in the incarnation of Jesus, any form of spirituality we claim must also be incarnational, which by definition includes the wholeness of the person. This will profoundly influence our relationship to our communities and our world.[47]

Flora Slosson Wuellner

---

* John 1:1, 14, NLT.

FEBRUARY 7

Depart from evil, and do good; seek peace, and pursue it.

PSALM 34:14 (NRSV)

INHALE: Help me do the good
EXHALE: That is mine to do.

We live in a culture where division is encouraged. We're told to huddle in our camps and draw lines in the sand, shutting out those who are different from us.

In the Disney animated classic *Beauty and the Beast*, Gaston—the hulking hunter who wants to kill the Beast—rallies the townspeople, shouting, "If you're not with us, you're against us!" That "us versus them" posture permeates our lives today, from political arguments to online outrage at anyone who looks, thinks, acts, or worships differently than we do.

So how do we "seek peace, and pursue it" when all around, people are gathering proverbial pitchforks? James Finley encourages us to "find your contemplative practice and practice it."[48]

Intentional prayer or stillness opens our hearts to Christ's transforming work. Without it, we risk adding to the noise. Drawing near to God for a peace that surpasses understanding steadies us in turbulent times. As the Spirit shapes us, we gain the inner strength needed to move forward in love. And we become people who not only *long for* peace but actively *make it*—retreating from our camps and cultivating peace in our homes, workplaces, and neighborhoods.

What practice might help you seek peace and pursue it? Begin with the breath prayer at the beginning of today's reading. As you breathe, linger over Psalm 34:14 in silence. Even something as seemingly small as praying with your breath can open your heart for the peace of Christ to change you—and, through you, to change the world.

Today, seek peace and keep pursuing it—trusting that Christ's peace is at work in you.

PAUSE AND PONDER

In what areas of your life are you most tempted to huddle in your camp to avoid, dismiss, or judge those who are different from you?

What small spiritual practice could you choose this week that moves you from longing for peace to actively pursuing it?

FEBRUARY 8

Just as the body is dead without breath,
so also faith is dead without good works.

JAMES 2:26 (NLT)

INHALE: With every breath,
EXHALE: Help me reflect You.

Here in the Midwest, wildfire smoke sometimes drifts in from hundreds of miles away, painting the sky in hazy orange hues. It's strangely beautiful. But the wonder of the warm glow comes at a cost. Hidden in the haze are fine particles that can irritate and inflame the lungs, making it harder to breathe.

Faith without works is like a body without breath—it cannot live.

We inhale the goodness of God so we can breathe out that goodness into the world: kindness in our words, compassion in our actions, hope in how we show up in this weary world. If faith isn't embodied, it isn't really faith at all. It is not living and breathing.

The Coca-Cola Company once trademarked the slogan "Put good in. Get good out." for its Minute Maid juices. The marketing line sticks with us because it reflects a deeper truth: What we take in influences what flows out.

When we inhale the love of God, our faith has fresh air to breathe. But when we breathe in what is polluted (maybe even things that look good from the outside but are actually harmful for us), our hearts grow clouded.

As long as you have breath, the Spirit will help you live out your faith. Breathe deep the love of God so you can carry it into a world running on fumes.

What will you inhale today? And what will you exhale into the lives of those around you?

BREATHE THIS IN

When we inhale, we draw oxygen and nitrogen from the atmosphere into the nose and mouth.

When we exhale, we send carbon dioxide and nitrogen out through the nose and mouth into the atmosphere.

That two-part process, the cycle of inhalation and exhalation, is what "taking a breath" means. You can't have inhalation without exhalation because both are essential to staying alive.[49]

Michael Breus

FEBRUARY 9

Rejoice in our confident hope. Be patient in trouble, and keep on praying.

ROMANS 12:12 (NLT)

INHALE: Breathe hope
EXHALE: Into my waiting heart.

I don't always feel confident in hope. My patience wears thin. My weariness grows. And in my exhaustion, I wonder if my prayers make any difference at all.

I know I'm not the only one. Sometimes it feels like the whole of humanity is waiting for the breath of heaven to make all things new.

When Paul wrote in his letter to the church in Rome to rejoice in "confident hope," he wasn't forcing positivity on them or telling them to live without doubt. He was encouraging them that even in the troubling times they faced, they could hold on to a hope beyond what they could see.

Waiting in hope isn't passive—it's actively choosing to believe there is more than what we can see. Hope is an act of humility, trusting that God is bigger than our circumstances, greater than any awful thing life can throw at us.

The hope Paul described wasn't wishful thinking but a confident expectation rooted in the promises of God.[50] Paul didn't promise that we won't have trouble. He said that *when* trouble comes, we can have joy in a hope that is bigger than ourselves. Confidence in hope means that despite all the heartache, evil won't have the final say. Our pain will not last forever. Every tear is held now and will someday be wiped away.

Paul encouraged the Romans that even in the midst of struggles, prayer still matters. Breath prayers remind us that the One who gives each breath is with us now. They remind us that the One who gives each breath is near, that unseen hope can still be trusted—just like the unseen breath we need to live.

Loosen your shoulders. As you inhale, name one thing you're waiting for. As you let your breath go, ask God to fill you with hope.

SACRED ECHOES

Hope springs from the continuing experience of God's compassion and help. Patience is hope in action. It waits for the saving help of God without giving up, giving in, or going away.[51]

Thomas Keating

FEBRUARY 10

Great is his faithfulness; his mercies begin afresh each morning.

LAMENTATIONS 3:23 (NLT)

INHALE: Your mercies are new
EXHALE: Each morning.

Mornings aren't my thing. It takes me a while (and at least two cups of coffee) before I'm ready to face the world. But even night owls like me have to admit that something shifts with the sunrise. In the light of day, the worries that kept me up at night don't seem so bleak.

Just like our breath, the rhythms of our days are beyond our control—day falls into night, night rises into a new day. As sure as the moon lights the night and the sun rises to meet the morning, we're given a chance to start anew.

The rhythm of inhale and exhale, night into morning and morning into night, whispers of God's mercy. Every new breath is an opportunity for renewal.

Jesus once told a story about a man who owed what would be billions of dollars today.* It's hard for most of us to grasp that kind of debt. Yet after the man pleaded his case, the king forgave it all. Jesus said that's what the Kingdom of God is like—endless mercy that surprises us. Mercy that doesn't add up, that feels absurd in a world obsessed with keeping score.

But here's the twist. The same man who'd just been forgiven his enormous debt encountered someone who owed him around a few thousand dollars in today's money—*pennies* compared to what he'd just been released from. But instead of passing on the mercy he'd received, he lashed out, violently demanding repayment.

Mercy is the air we breathe in and what we breathe out. We live in mercy so we can give mercy—not because it makes sense, but because this is the radical reordering of Jesus.

Mercy begets mercy. Breath by breath, morning after morning, mercy overflows. No matter how dark the night, we can carry a hope that fills our lungs, rising with the sun and lingering with each dusk.

You don't have to be a morning person for that to be true.

PRACTICING THE WAY

Plan a morning this week to reflect and reset. Choose one or two simple practices:

- **Disconnect:** Leave your phone outside your bedroom at night so it's not the first thing you see in the morning. (You might have to invest in an analog alarm clock!)
- **Pray:** Before getting out of bed, pray Psalm 118:24: "This is the day the LORD has made; we will rejoice and be glad in it."
- **Write:** Practice three "morning pages" (a practice popularized by Julia Cameron in *The Artist's Way*[52]) to clear your mind. Set a timer, grab a journal, and let yourself process what you're thinking and feeling by freewriting for a set time—no edits allowed.
- **Breathe:** As you brew coffee or make your toast, turn making breakfast into a time of breath prayer.
- **Walk:** Notice the light, the air, and the sounds around you.
- **Listen:** Tune in to the daily *Pray as You Go* podcast as you walk or get ready for the day.

* Matthew 18:21-35, NLT.

FEBRUARY 11

Let the light of this new day guide you onto a path of honor.

ROMANS 13:13 (FNV)

INHALE: Guide me

EXHALE: On the right path.

My husband and I recently purchased a new-to-us vehicle. I was floored the first night I drove it—the headlights were so bright I thought I had my high beams on. I had grown so used to our old minivan that I didn't realize how dull its lights had become.

It's easy to slip into autopilot without noticing how murky things get—how our connection with God, with ourselves, and with others slowly dims until something shakes us awake.

February is a tough month. Though it's the shortest, it often drags like the longest. We ache for spring's renewal, but life lacks a bit of its luster.

And yet the Light of the World we anticipated and celebrated just a few months ago is still here. Just as God gave the Israelites a cloud by day and fire by night to guide them,* the Spirit still guides us onto paths of honor, even on muddy, gray February days. Even when you feel overworked or underappreciated. Even when your own light seems faint and you feel like you're just going through the motions.

If you're feeling a little spiritually burned out today, you are not alone. God's love is forever lighting the way so you can keep walking the road of love. Take a breath.

As you breathe, remember that whatever today holds, the Light will guide your path.

* See Exodus 13:21.

RHYTHM OF BREATH

God of the night,
When words won't come
And sleep won't either,
Be near in the darkness.

God of the morning,
When dawn breaks
And so does my heart,
Be near in the morning light.

When time unfolds
And I can't catch my breath,
When my mind spins
And my bones ache,
Help me remember You—
You, the God of
Each sleepless night,
You, the God of
Every exhausted morning.

I bring my weary heart
To the altar of Your love.
There's no place
You've never been;
There's no place
You'll never go.
Whisper Your new mercy
Over me,
Over and over again.

FEBRUARY 12

Don't be afraid, I've redeemed you. I've called your name. You're mine. When you're in over your head, I'll be there with you.

ISAIAH 43:1 (MSG)

INHALE: You've called my name;
EXHALE: I am Yours.

When I'm overwhelmed—when my mind races and doubt floods in—it's easy to wonder if everything I've believed about God is . . . wrong.

Is it foolish to believe in something *more* when scarcity and suffering shout so loudly?

In those moments, I return to this: *Faith isn't the absence of doubt. Faith is the stubborn hope planted in the very soil of doubt.* Like a gardener, sometimes we need dirt under our nails for good things to grow.

Because I *remember*. I remember moments that can only be explained by something beyond me—bigger than me, bigger than life itself. Connections I never could have orchestrated, beauty I could not have created, mercy I could not have earned, glimpses of God's love breaking through, over and over again, in my seemingly ordinary life. Those memories play like an old film inside my mind, bringing me back to hope, however faint.

We all know disappointment. Plans unravel. People fail us. Following Christ doesn't spare us from devastation—but even when we don't feel it, God is still with us. God is not afraid of our doubts, our laments, our anger. We can bring them to God, and God still whispers, *I'm here. When you're in over your head, I'm with you.*

Through some cosmic truth that cuts across time and space, what Moses told Israel thousands of years ago still rings true today: God goes with you. God will never leave you nor forsake you.*

It's true—sometimes we don't *feel* God's presence. But that doesn't mean God isn't still there, with us in the muck and mire of real life.

From the Red Sea to the Jordan River, God's people have always come back to this same truth: The waters may rise, but God's presence does not fail. We may not tangibly see or hear God, but we experience the fullness of God in ways we can barely put to words. And these are the moments we go back to when we need help finding our way again.

When the world is loud and you feel yourself forgetting, reflect on where you've known God's faithfulness before, and let that memory anchor you again.

Today, take a breath. The world around might not feel safe, but God is. Let your nervous system settle down. God knows your name. And God calls it still.

As you breathe and pray, remember: You're not alone—you never have been.

SACRED ECHOES

Listen to "Always with Me" by Paul Zach and The Porter's Gate. As you do, listen for the words or phrases that stand out to you. How might it change your day if you trusted that God truly is near to you—even here, even now?

* Deuteronomy 31:6, NLT.

FEBRUARY 13

It's quite simple: Do what is fair and just to your neighbor, be compassionate and loyal in your love.

MICAH 6:8 (MSG)

INHALE: Help me love others
EXHALE: The way You love me.

Every February, pink and red displays try to sell us what love is. But in God's Kingdom, love is far more than what can fit on a valentine.

In eighth grade, my boyfriend gave me a fancy card where he'd traced, "After all this time, you're still the one." We'd been "going out" for *maybe* three weeks, and our relationship mostly consisted of waving in the hallway and chatting on instant messenger.

The love God invites us into is far more expansive than syrupy-sweet gestures or our culture's prepackaged definitions. Christ not only lavishes love upon us but *propels us* to extend that love to others too. (Even those who don't make it easy.)

Yet some who call themselves Christians treat love as a cheapened commodity, resisting compassion or justice. I wonder if that's because they've never truly experienced God's love for themselves. Because when we do, it overflows. We act justly, choose mercy, walk humbly, and love loyally. Without that? We're a clanging cymbal.*

Love is a central part of who we are. Christ is the center, and we are called to move out and move toward.

Love is the way we *live*. It's who we are. When we truly experience the vast love of Jesus, we can't help but share it with others. We won't always get it right—I know I don't. But living in Christ means asking for help, seeking forgiveness when we fail, and stepping back into the beautiful rhythm of receiving God's love and sharing it.

We live in this beautiful, never-ending circle: God breathes love into us, and we pass it on. It's a love that reshapes our hearts, our relationships, and our world—and it's far sweeter and more beautiful than any card or candy.

BORROW THIS PRAYER

When people are difficult to love—
And sometimes they are—
Grow in me compassion.
Nurture me in Your love.

Give me imagination
To understand that they, too,
Were made in Your image.
Grow in me Your loving-kindness
So that I might extend Your love,
Even when it's difficult,
Even when I don't want to.

Help me not to waver
But to stand firm
In what I know
To be true—
That You are good,
That I can trust You,
That I only love
Because You first loved me.

* See 1 Corinthians 13:1.

FEBRUARY 14

SAINT VALENTINE'S DAY

Love each other. Just as I have loved you, you should love each other.

JOHN 13:34 (NLT)

INHALE: You are love;
EXHALE: Show me the way.

All around us, our culture tells us who is worthy of love. It's easy to fall into that way of thinking, even unintentionally. But Jesus wasn't like that. He didn't carry around a scroll of who was in and who was out.

Jesus—Love incarnate—was present to the people right in front of Him.

Who is easy for you to love? Who is . . . more challenging? Sometimes what frustrates us in others points to something unhealed within ourselves. These questions invite us into deeper reflection about who we love—and how we show it.

We can *say* we love our neighbors—we can even say we love our enemies—but how do they know? What are we saying without saying a word?

I know that my nonspeaking daughter Eliza loves me. She tells me this not with words but by touching my face or nestling her cheek against mine. I see the same love in the way she gazes at my husband and grins when he walks into a room.

Think about where you're going today: the work you'll be doing, the people you'll cross paths with, the places you'll go. How will you show the kind of love that God shows?

We're not talking about *eros* (romantic love) but *agapē*, the kind of love that honors, forgives, and endures. In John 13:34, Jesus uses the word *agapate*—calling us to love one another with the same self-giving love He has shown us.[53]

When we see others as image bearers of God, we see God in a new light. And as we come to know God more deeply, we begin to see ourselves more clearly too. This is the sacred cycle of love.

As you breathe today, reflect on this truth: *Love never fails.**

BORROW THIS PRAYER

I want to see
Your face in the cashier,
To know the stories
Etched in the lines of her brow.
I want to see
Your face in the child,
To feel the unabashed joy
Of chocolate-covered cheeks.
I want to see
Your face in the man on the street,
Frostbite on his nose,
A thousand stories leading
To the cardboard sign in his hands.
I want to see
Your face in the neighbor
I do not know,
In the enemy
I do not understand.
Help us see each other
As You see us—
You, who makes friends out of strangers,
Family out of enemies.
You, who whispers peace
Into a world at war.
Help me know others,
So that I may know You.

* See 1 Corinthians 13:8.

FEBRUARY 15

God knew what he was doing from the very beginning. He decided from the outset to shape the lives of those who love him along the same lines as the life of his Son. The Son stands first in the line of humanity he restored. We see the original and intended shape of our lives there in him.

ROMANS 8:29 (MSG)

INHALE: You restore;
EXHALE: You shape my soul.

My friends tilt their heads back, lost in laughter. I laugh too, but inside, a deep sense of loneliness blooms. Feeling alone in a crowded room is its own kind of pain. Have you ever felt like people know you, but you aren't *known*?

When we think about the Creator of the universe, it's easy to marvel at God's bigness. At any given moment, someone is being born and someone else is taking their last breath. Somewhere, someone is living their best day, while another is living their worst.

Can God really be present in it *all*? And can we really be known by God?

We live in a world where telescopes peer into black holes and news feeds bring us global updates in real time. We're constantly reminded of how small we are. And yet Scripture insists: God's knowing is not distant foresight but intimate, relational love.[54] Like a parent who knows a baby's different cries and hears the truth behind a teenager's "I'm fine," God *knows* us.

Our restorative God has been shaping you since long before you took your first breath. God *knows* you. Remember that God is shaping you more and more into the image of Jesus.

As you breathe today, remember that this work is ongoing. With each inhale, God is shaping you, restoring you, and making you whole.

LET IT LINGER

Your soul bears the fingerprints of the One who gives each breath. Even now, God is shaping you. How is who you are going to be shaped by the One who is? Who are you becoming?

FEBRUARY 16

Everyone should be quick to listen,
slow to speak and slow to become angry.

JAMES 1:19 (NIV)

INHALE: Slow me down;
EXHALE: Help me listen.

I can't tell you how many times I've hammered out an . . . *unsanctified* response online, only to hold my finger on the delete key at the last minute and watch my snarky words disappear.

Because it doesn't matter if I'm *right.* It doesn't matter if I have the right to shout my opinions into the void if I'm not loving God or loving others as I love myself.

When I feel reactive—when I sense my nervous system shifting into fight-or-flight—I try to ask myself two questions:

- Is what I'm going to put out into the world helpful?
- Is what I'm about to say hopeful?

If neither of those things is true, I usually have my answer to whether I should post it. If I'm still feeling rattled and activated, I run my response through the fruits of the Spirit: *love, joy, peace, patience, kindness, goodness, faithfulness, gentleness, self-control.**

Of course, being slow to speak doesn't mean staying silent about injustice. In today's verse, James isn't calling us to passivity but inviting us into wisdom. The question is not just *what* we say but *how* we say it.

God formed our bodies with a built-in reset: our breath.

When we're triggered and our nervous system is activated, breath prayer offers a way to practice James's call to slow down, pause before speaking, and resist the pull of anger. Our biology may push us toward fight-or-flight (and sometimes that's needed), but breath prayer beckons us back to safety in God's presence.

Intentional breathing can interrupt our bodies' stress responses and restore connection with ourselves, God, and others.

With God's help, we can practice exhaling unhealthy anger before it takes root and causes harm. We read Scripture not for a list of dos and don'ts but as God-breathed wisdom that gives us embodied peace in a shouting world.

* See Galatians 5:22-23.

PRACTICING THE WAY

Use this guided breath practice to reconnect with your body and with God's presence:

- **Notice your breath.** Is it short and shallow, only reaching your collarbone? Is your chest tight, your jaw clenched, your forehead furrowed?
- **Slow your breathing.** Begin to deepen your inhales and lengthen your exhales. Let your body settle as you feel the rise and fall of your breath.
- **Engage your senses.** What do you see around you? What scents do you notice in the air? What surface is holding and supporting you right now? What do your ears hear, near and far?[55]

FEBRUARY 17

Love is patient, love is kind. It does not envy, it does not boast, it is not proud. It does not dishonor others, it is not self-seeking, it is not easily angered, it keeps no record of wrongs.

1 CORINTHIANS 13:4-5 (NIV)

INHALE: Help me, O God,
EXHALE: To live in love.

God is not just loving. God *is* love.*

The attributes Paul lists in today's passage are not distant ideals but a living portrait of our Creator. We can't even begin to fathom the depths of this love.† But in 1 Corinthians 13, we are given a blueprint of love so we might "know and rely on the love God has for us" because "God is love."‡

Make these verses personal, replacing the word *love* with *God*:

- God is patient with you.
- God is kind toward you.
- God doesn't boast or force His way.
- God is not hot-headed or full of anger toward you.
- God isn't tracking your wrongs.§

This is who God is. Not tallying up failures on a score sheet. Not puffed up or demanding. But meeting you with patience, kindness, and compassion.

Even if you've been told otherwise.

Even if the world feels harsh.

Even if you feel unworthy.

And if this is what we *know* about who God is, then this is also what we're called to become. As 1 John 4:8 says, "Anyone who does not love does not know God, for God is love." And we aren't left alone in this call to love. "Whoever lives in love lives in God, and God in them."¶

What would change if you truly believed God looks at you with compassion instead of criticism? And how might that reshape how you extend patience and kindness toward others? What would it look like—for you, today—to live in love?

* See 1 John 4:8.
† See Romans 11:34; Job 9:10.
‡ 1 John 4:16, NIV.
§ See 1 Corinthians 13:4-5.
¶ 1 John 4:16, NIV

PRACTICING THE WAY

When leaders set high expectations for others, those individuals often rise to meet them. Psychologists call it the "Pygmalion effect." The term comes from a Greek myth of a sculptor whose vision of beauty for his statue causes it to come alive.[56]

Imagine how God calls out belovedness in you by replacing *love* with your name:

- [Your Name] is patient.
- [Your Name] is kind.
- [Your Name] does not envy or boast.
- [Your Name] is not proud.
- [Your Name] does not keep a record of wrongs.

Notice what rises in you as you read it. What feels hard to believe? What might shift if you lived as though God's expectation of love is true of you?

FEBRUARY 18

Mostly what God does is love you.
Keep company with him and learn a life of love.

EPHESIANS 5:2 (MSG)

INHALE: Help me learn
EXHALE: A life of love.

When a toddler is learning to walk, they stumble and tumble—but we wouldn't shame them for falling. They're learning. They're training their brain and their muscles to work together. They're figuring it out as they go.

We're all still learning as we go. I used to think I'd reach an age when the way of love would feel effortless, but I'm beginning to realize that's not how it works. The problems set in when we start believing we *have* it figured out.

In Ephesians 5:2, we're reminded, "Mostly what God does is love you."

Not judge you.
Not test you.
Not ignore you.
Love.

And because of that, we're invited into rhythms with God where prayer is not bound to a place or a moment—it becomes the shape of our whole lives. We keep company with God, and in the process, we learn a life of love.

God is patient with us as we take our wobbly steps. We won't always get it right. God knows we're still learning. Life is complicated. Every day we hear voices telling us that we're not enough—or that we're too much. The messages swirl until we feel lost.

Pause. Take a breath.

All you need to do today is keep company with the One who delights to be with you—the One who cheers when you take even a small step in love. The One who opens arms wide and catches you like a loving parent.

In Jesus, we are taught the way of love. In the Spirit, we are guided and kept in it.

Life is confusing. This is true. But when in doubt—love. After all, that's mostly what God does.

BORROW THIS PRAYER

Help me, O God,
To love like You.
I want to learn Your ways.

You set a table
In a world that slams doors.
You bring hope to the weary,
Love to the hurting,
And power to the people
Who have been cast off,
Tossed aside,
And told they do not matter.
You see the unseen,
And You love those
Who have been sold the lie
That they are unlovable.

Help me, O God,
To love like You.
I want to learn Your ways.
Amen.

FEBRUARY 19

Don't push your way to the front; don't sweet-talk your way to the top. Put yourself aside, and help others get ahead.

PHILIPPIANS 2:3 (MSG)

INHALE: Help me love others
EXHALE: The way You love me.

The loudest voices in our culture tell us to do what it takes to get ahead, no matter what it costs.

To put ourselves first, always.

But the way of Jesus is to put others *before* ourselves.

The Kingdom of God flips things upside down and shows us a better way:

Culture says: *"It's a dog-eat-dog world."*
The way of Christ says: "Carry each other's burdens, and in this way you will fulfill the law of Christ" (Galatians 6:2, NIV).

Culture says: *"Only the strong survive."*
The way of Christ says: "My grace is sufficient for you, for my power is made perfect in weakness" (2 Corinthians 12:9, NIV).

Culture says: *"Kill or be killed."*
The way of Christ says: "Love your enemies, do good to those who hate you, bless those who curse you, pray for those who mistreat you" (Luke 6:27-28, NIV).

Culture says: *"Everyone for themselves."*
The way of Christ says: "Don't look out only for your own interests, but take an interest in others, too" (Philippians 2:4, NLT).

Culture says: *"Win at all costs."*
The way of Christ says: "What good will it be for someone to gain the whole world, yet forfeit their soul?" (Matthew 16:26, NIV).

Culture says: *"The ends justify the means."*
The way of Christ says: "Learn to do right; seek justice. Defend the oppressed" (Isaiah 1:17, NIV).

Culture says: *"Crush the competition."*
The way of Christ says: "Let's agree to use all our energy in getting along with each other. Help others with encouraging words" (Romans 14:19, MSG).

Jesus invites us to step out of scarcity and competition and into abundance and communal flourishing.

The next time you hear one of these cultural phrases out in the wild, borrow today's breath prayer and reflect on these verses from the New Testament to help you stay rooted in God's Word.

BORROW THIS PRAYER

Help me remember, God,
That You call
Everyone I don't understand,
Anyone I disagree with,
Beloved.
Amen.

FEBRUARY 20

Let's take a good look at the way we're living
and reorder our lives under GOD.

LAMENTATIONS 3:40 (MSG)

INHALE: Search my heart;
EXHALE: Examine my ways.

It's easy to drift through our days until life feels flat. Wake, work, scroll, sleep—repeat. Then, one day, we ask ourselves, *What am I doing? Who am I becoming?*

In a culture of ever-refreshing algorithms that keep us locked in and zoned out, making space for prayer and reflection is something we have to do with intention. We're urged to keep moving, keep working, keep consuming—without ever stopping to breathe.

But what glimmers of God's goodness might we miss because we're already rushing to the next thing? How can we recognize God's voice in our ordinary days if we never pause to listen?

The Examen is an ancient prayer practice that helps us slow down and pay attention. For centuries, Christians have used this rhythm—popularized by Saint Ignatius—to notice where God is present in the everyday flow of life.

When I take a moment to breathe and reflect, I never regret it. I begin to catch glimpses of where God has been there all along—with me in that difficult conversation or in the morning light filtering into the kitchen. I notice patterns in my own behavior and feel more peaceful, even if my day was anything but.

This is the invitation: To take a good look. To ask God to search your heart and examine your ways. To reveal what needs to change so you might reorder your life in love.

PRACTICING THE WAY

Pray the Examen at the end of the day, at the close of a week, or even at the end of a season. Keep it simple and honest.

1. **Become aware of God's presence.** Imagine Jesus beside you on the couch—right there among the unfolded laundry and junk mail—delighting simply to be with you.
2. **Begin with gratitude.** Start your prayer by giving thanks. Recall your day through the lens of thankfulness. Gratitude interrupts our cycles of cynicism or endless problem-solving.
3. **Review the day.** Slowly replay the hours. Where did you notice God? Who showed you love? How did you offer love to others? Were there invitations from God you ignored—or embraced? Pay attention to your emotions.
4. **Get honest.** Bring before God the places where you fell short—whether through your words or thoughts, your actions or inaction. Do this without fear: God meets you with compassion.
5. **Look to tomorrow in grace.** As you close, turn your eyes to what lies ahead. What burdens are you carrying? Where do you need patience, courage, or peace? Ask God to help you reorder your coming days in love.[57]

FEBRUARY 21

If your heart is broken, you'll find GOD right there; if you're kicked in the gut, he'll help you catch your breath.

PSALM 34:18 (MSG)

INHALE: You help me
EXHALE: Catch my breath.

Sometimes grief cuts so deep we can't even breathe. We want to pray but can't because the pain replaces our words with tears.

Jesus is among the brokenhearted, kneeling beside shattered hearts, gathering the shards to make them whole again. He doesn't flinch at the sharp edges. His compassion is greater than any pain. The Hebrew word for "broken-hearted" carries the sense of being crushed or shattered emotionally.[58] It names an ache too heavy for a human heart to hold.

Maybe you've been there—or maybe you're there now. Maybe you've worked so hard only to watch things unravel. Maybe you're tired of having to be the "strong one." Maybe you've been wounded in ways you never deserved. Maybe you're grieving the loss of a loved one or the loss of a dream.

Maybe you're just . . . tired. So. Tired.

Psalm 34 assures us that God isn't scared away by our broken hearts. God isn't waiting until we're healed or whole again to draw near. God is here—*right here*—with you in your exhaustion and your ache.

When your heart is in pieces and you struggle to catch your breath, borrow today's breath prayer. As you breathe, close your eyes and imagine Jesus sitting with you among the fragments of your broken heart. God is near. God will give you your next breath.

And when your breath returns, when your tender heart is pieced back together like stained-glass art telling a new story, you may glimpse something unexpected: hope shining through the panes.

BORROW THIS PRAYER

God, I confess,
It's easy for me
To hold myself
To an unattainable standard.
I'm tired of trying,
Of rushing to do the next thing,
Of feeling like I'm behind.

My side hurts, God.
I don't want to keep running
An endless race
With no end in sight.
I don't even know
What I'm running toward
Or what I'm running from.
Help me catch my breath.
Help me remember life with You
Isn't a race to see how much I can do
Or how far I can get.

Keep me near—
I'm road-weary.
I give my ache to You.

FEBRUARY 22

Come to me, all of you who are weary and carry heavy burdens, and I will give you rest.

MATTHEW 11:28 (NLT)

INHALE: God, I am tired;
EXHALE: You give me rest.

What's holding you back from rest today? Maybe you need to buy groceries or start figuring out your taxes. Perhaps your inbox is overflowing or the snow has been piling up and you need to shovel.

At any given time, endless to-dos clamor for our attention. And often, our culture pats us on the back for being *so busy*. Even in Christian circles, we glorify the hustle. But Jesus never asked us to pile more on our shoulders. He simply said, "Come to me."

Imagine that you're straining at the gym, clutching a heavy medicine ball to your chest. Your arms are shaking. Jesus steps close, extends his hands, and says, "Here. Let Me hold that. You've been carrying it too long. Breathe."

What heavy burdens are you holding right now?

Our bodies and souls need rhythms of rest. One way we enter into rest is by slowing our breath as we pray. Unhurried breathing calms our nervous systems, lowers stress, and tells our bodies that we're safe. Our shoulders drop. Our jaws loosen. And in that stillness, we come to the One who created us for rest.

Rest isn't laziness. And rest isn't earned either. *Rest is God's design.*

As you pray, imagine handing Jesus the heaviest burden you've been carrying. With every exhale, let it go. With every inhale, receive true rest.

SACRED ECHOES

God is closer to us than our own soul, for God is the foundation on which the soul stands. Our soul sits in God and in true rest, and our soul stands in God in sure strength, and our soul is naturally rooted in God's endless love.

Julian of Norwich[59]

FEBRUARY 23

Search for the LORD and for his strength; continually seek him.

1 CHRONICLES 16:11 (NLT)

INHALE: Help me find
EXHALE: My way back to You.

A life with God is an ongoing, ever-unfolding journey. The more we learn, the more we realize how much we're still learning. Our paths bend and curve, and sometimes the turn we thought was wrong becomes the one that leads us home.

For centuries, Christians have walked prayer labyrinths to slow down and pray.

- Labyrinths are winding paths that form a circle you can walk through while praying.
- They look like mazes but have no dead ends—just a single winding path.
- They guide you step by step to the center and then back out again.
- The invitation is simple: Take the next step until you've walked the whole journey.

I first encountered a labyrinth at a Christian retreat center. From the moment I arrived, I felt like I could finally exhale. And when I inhaled, I breathed a deep sense of peacefulness that mingled with the scent of pine.

Later, I learned that women from the Sisters of Mercy had lived on those grounds since the 1960s, faithfully praying for every person who came seeking rest. In their younger years, the women prayed as they walked the labyrinth. As years passed and they became unable to make the walk, they prayed by tracing a finger labyrinth, turning their hearts to God with each gentle movement.

Labyrinths mirror our spiritual lives. We don't have to figure everything out at once. All we need to do is keep seeking God, breath by breath.

PAUSE AND PONDER

Trace the labyrinth slowly with your finger, letting it guide your prayer.

1. **Release:** Offer a prayer of confession. As you move inward, imagine setting down what feels heavy—sins, burdens, or distractions.
2. **Receive:** At the center, pause. Breathe. Borrow today's breath prayer, reflect on today's Scripture, or simply rest in God's presence.
3. **Return:** As you trace outward again, pray for others. Who comes to mind?
4. **Close:** When you lift your finger at the end, give thanks that God was with you at every turn.[60]

FEBRUARY 24

God's various expressions of power are in action everywhere; but God himself is behind it all.

1 CORINTHIANS 12:6 (MSG)

INHALE: In every beautiful thing,
EXHALE: There You are.

The street artist Banksy often leaves art on overlooked walls and buildings. Expressions of work appear in unexpected places—little (and sometimes big) surprises plastered in the middle of everyday life, just waiting to be found.

Sometimes, when the pain of the world is overwhelming, I go on the hunt for expressions of good news tucked into ordinary days. I follow a few online accounts that gather hopeful headlines: The city that unites to find a lost service dog. The medical student who volunteers to treat people living on the streets. The grandma who builds wheelchair ramps out of Legos. The bus driver who has donated blood every two weeks for thirty years.

These news updates aren't particularly rooted in faith, but when I read them, I see glimpses of God's light in a dark world. James reminds us that "every good and perfect gift is from above." All goodness we have in this world reflects the "Father of the heavenly lights."*

As the First Nations Version captures 1 Corinthians 12:6-7,

Creator's power works in different ways through different people, but it is the same Great Spirit who is at work in all of them. It is in these many ways that the Holy Spirit makes himself known in and through each of us, for the good of all.

When the news cycle screams that everything is unraveling, I cling to this hope: God is still working. The expression of Christ is revealed in countless places through countless people in countless ways "for the good of all."

PAUSE AND PONDER

What glimmer of goodness have you heard of recently? How does that point you to hope?

What part of God's goodness is yours to breathe into our weary world this week?

* James 1:17, NIV.

FEBRUARY 25

You've always given me breathing room, a place to get away from it all, a lifetime pass to your safe-house, an open invitation as your guest.

PSALM 61:3-4 (MSG)

INHALE: You've always
EXHALE: Given me breathing room.

I majored in magazine journalism in college. One of my final assignments was to create and design a magazine from scratch. I labored over the clever title and the color palette. But when my professor peeked over my shoulder at what I thought was a *gorgeous* two-page spread, she tapped the computer screen.

"You need more white space," she said. "Increase your margins."

We fill our lives to the brim. Our culture is obsessed with productivity hacks. In two seconds, you can pull up a CEO's minute-by-minute calendar—every block accounted for. "You want to get to the top?" the business coaches ask. "Then work like this."

But our souls need white space.

Our souls need margin.

Our souls need breathing room.

And God offers exactly that. Scripture calls it refuge and rest*—God's invitation to fully exhale.†

When I designed that feature spread, I wanted to cram in every good thing—captivating fonts, clever sidebars, compelling photos. But it was too busy. Too many good things made the whole thing unreadable.

Where do you need more margin today? Where is your soul aching for breathing room? What's one thing you could set down so that what matters comes into focus again?

* See Psalm 91:1-2.
† See Mark 6:31; Psalm 23:2.

BREATHE THIS IN

Breath prayer is a form of Christian mindfulness. One of the first insights you'll experience when you begin a formal practice of mindfulness is how busy your mind is and how much it wanders. That's okay. It's like a muscle—the more you work it, the easier it becomes to clear away the mental chatter and just *be* with God.

FEBRUARY 26

Now you've got my feet on the life path, all radiant from the shining of your face. Ever since you took my hand, I'm on the right way.

PSALM 16:11 (MSG)

INHALE: You will be with me;
EXHALE: I do not go alone.

I'm not *the best* at navigation. When someone gives me directions using "north" or "south," my brain blanks and my eyes glaze over. I have to mark my grocery store parking spot with a pin on my phone so I can find it again. My friend was visiting from out of town, and when I picked her up from the airport, I had my navigation app set.

"Isn't this your hometown?" she asked.

"Yes," I replied, turning the volume up so Siri could get me safely back to my house.

Life doesn't come with turn-by-turn directions. As much as our hearts might yearn for it, no road map exists for the spiritual journey, and no navigation prompts will get us to a faithful end point.

As long as you walk this earth, Jesus is the destination *and* the direction.

A contemplative life isn't a journey toward enlightenment but an opening of the heart to the Spirit of God, the Light of the World who lights your path.

Where in your life do you feel lost—or where do you long for direction? What might it look like today to be mindful of the Light who guides you, illuminating the way, breath by breath?

RHYTHM OF BREATH

The One who dwells
In each breath
Is with you.

The Light
Warms your face—
Can you feel it?
The Presence
Lingers by your side—
Can you sense it?

When the climb
Leaves you gasping for air,
Take heart,
Because the view
Will take your breath away.

FEBRUARY 27

God, the Lord, created the heavens and stretched them out. He created the earth and everything in it. He gives breath to everyone, life to everyone who walks the earth.

ISAIAH 42:5 (NLT)

INHALE: Creator of all,
EXHALE: You give every breath.

It's easy to forget that our breath is a miracle. Our lungs expand and contract without our even thinking about it—an involuntary rhythm that keeps us alive. Just as our bodies can breathe without our awareness, God is sustaining us, breathing life into our every inhale and exhale.

Late winter in the Midwest can feel like hope has gone missing. The skies are gray. The trees are bare. The grass is brown. If I only believed what I could see, I might think new life would never return and that we're stuck in perpetual winter.

But beneath frozen ground, seeds are already stirring. New life is preparing to push through at the hand of the One who "created the earth and everything in it." We just can't see it yet.

Lent—the forty days of reflection and preparation before Easter—mirrors this hidden work. It invites us to sit with the winters of our own hearts while holding out hope that renewal is coming, that there is more than what meets the eye.

God has not forgotten you. Even when you feel undone, God is holding you together, breath by breath.

Take a moment. Place your hand on your chest. Feel the rise and fall. Whisper thanks for this breath, then the next. How might your day change if you received each breath as a gift from the One who gives life to all?

BORROW THIS PRAYER

God of resurrection,
When the world is cold,
When hope is threadbare,
Wrap me in the promise
That there is more
Than what I can see.

When plans fail,
When people disappoint,
When prayers stay unanswered,
Hold me close.
Don't let me go.

When I'm gasping for breath,
When I'm clutching my side,
When I can't run anymore,
Help me fall into You
And trust that You redeem
What feels too far gone.

When I have no words,
When I've seen too much,
When all feels lost,
Bring me back to You,
The One who breathes life
Into the dust.

Whisper into my heart
That You are the God
Of limitless resurrections—
That though the night is dark,
The sun will rise again.

God of resurrection, I believe.
Help me in my unbelief.
Amen.

FEBRUARY 28

The LORD is compassionate and merciful, slow to get angry and filled with unfailing love.

PSALM 103:8 (NLT)

INHALE: God of mercy,
EXHALE: Help me receive Your love.

We are so hard on ourselves. Most of us live with a loud inner critic that whispers, *You're not enough. You should be better by now.*

Here's the truth: Your inner critic is *not* the Holy Spirit.

Psalm 103 reminds us that God is compassionate and merciful, slow to anger and full of unfailing love. If we want to know what God is like, we just have to look at Jesus. Sadly, many of us were introduced to a different God—a vengeful, violent, vindictive God. But that image is a lie, and lies about God don't just wound our souls—they actually harm our brains.

Christian psychiatrist Dr. Timothy Jennings writes that when we believe false ideas about God, fear circuits fire stronger while our capacity for love grows weaker.[61]

The good news? The opposite is also true. Research at the University of Pennsylvania shows that meditating on a God of love literally heals the brain, increasing compassion, empathy, and even memory.[62]

Worshiping the God of love rewires us for mercy.

And mercy begins with how we treat ourselves. Self-compassion is simply alignment with the heart of Christ. As Thomas Keating writes, "Divine love is compassionate, tender, luminous, totally self-giving."[63] When we open our hearts to receive the truth about our loving God, we become more able to extend love to our families, to our neighbors, and even to those we find most difficult to love.

As you pray today's breath prayer, let the truth of God's character soften the voice of your inner critic. Let Christ draw you into mercy toward yourself and toward others.

BREATHE THIS IN

The way we view God really does change us.

A University of Pennsylvania study led by Dr. Andrew Newberg, a pioneer in the field frequently referred to as *neurotheology*, found that "all forms of contemplative meditation were associated with positive brain changes—but the greatest improvements occurred when participants meditated specifically on a God of love."

They showed "growth in the prefrontal cortex (the part of the brain . . . where we reason, make judgments and experience Godlike love)" and had "increased capacity for empathy, sympathy, compassion and altruism."[64]

FEBRUARY 29

LEAP DAY

Rejoice in that day and leap for joy, because great is your reward in heaven.

LUKE 6:23 (NIV)

INHALE: I will consider
EXHALE: It all joy.

My friend Jeremy was born on leap day and proudly identifies as a *leapling*. It's the correct term for people born on February 29, but I can't help but laugh every time I hear that word. It just . . . brings me joy.

We don't have to look long to see that our culture has a real joy deficit. We chase quick hits of happiness on our screens, but the dopamine dissolves as quickly as it arrives.

Joy—true, embodied gladness—is far more rare.

This world is full of sharp edges. Living with integrity is costly. Loving like Jesus is costly. Sometimes loving like Jesus pushes up against cultural norms, and that's costly too.

In His Sermon on the Mount, Jesus blessed the poor, the peacemakers, and the persecuted. Then He told His followers something wild: to *rejoice* when people insulted or mistreated them for choosing His way. Why? Because our truest joy isn't rooted in approval here and now. True joy is rooted in something bigger and wilder than we can imagine. James echoes this idea when he says, "Consider it pure joy . . . whenever you face trials of many kinds."*

That's not easy to do. Say what you will about joy, but it isn't naive. It's forged in struggle.

Even when life leaves us hurt, the story isn't finished. Cruelty and suffering won't get the final say. There is a joy breathed into the future strong enough to sustain us now.

On this rare day—this leap day—pause and remember: Jesus invites us to rejoice, not because the world is easy, but because God's inexhaustible joy is already breaking in. And maybe that's worth leaping for.

RHYTHM OF BREATH

They say look
Before you leap,
But maybe you can't
See much of anything,
And still
You jump.

It'll be terrible,
Maybe
It'll be wonderful.

But I guess you
Won't
Know if your feet
Don't
Leave the ground.

---

* James 1:2, NIV.

MARCH 1

The LORD merely spoke, and the heavens were created.
He breathed the word, and all the stars were born.

PSALM 33:6 (NLT)

INHALE: Your breath breathes
EXHALE: Beauty from chaos.

The same God who painted the sky in a single breath knows your ache.

It can be true that God breathed life into existence—and also true that life feels unbearably hard. People disappoint us. We disappoint others. Dreams collapse and relationships fracture. Daily realities overwhelm, and injustices abound.

Some days, we wonder if our prayers just hang unanswered in the air.

The pain seems so big. We feel so small. This world isn't as it should be. And yet the same God who spoke creation into existence promises that despair is never the end of the story.

Nothing is irredeemable.

No one is too far gone.

As long as we have breath, resurrection is still possible.

Hope doesn't ignore pain. It looks it in the face and refuses to bow. Hope whispers, *God can turn nothing into everything. Chaos into beauty. Death into life.*

In New York City, a bronze statue called *Fearless Girl* stands in a power stance. Tiny but unflinching, she was built to stare down the *Charging Bull* of Wall Street. To me, that's what hope feels like: small but defiant, rooted in a strength bigger than our own.

We can stand firm in hope and look boldly at the groans of creation—not because life isn't frightening, but because we belong to the One whose breath forms galaxies from chaos and sculpts resurrection from death.

God's breath hovers over the earth, big enough to hold our every prayer.

Whatever you're holding today—fear, sorrow, exhaustion—plant your feet. Take a breath. And stand firm in hope.

What would it look like to stand firm in hope right now?

BORROW THIS PRAYER

God of all creation,
I'm in awe of Your artistry.
I marvel at Your power.

In the overwhelm of being human,
It's easy to lose sight of You—
You, who breathes life into existence,
You, who paints galaxies into being,
You, who sculpts life out of dust.

All creation reflects Your love.
Help me to remember
That I bear Your fingerprints
And that every star reflects
Your glory.

When life is overwhelming
And I struggle to catch my breath,
Bring me under Your sky.
Point me to Your glory.

Creator who speaks stars into being,
Who breathes life into dust,
Help me marvel at Your mystery
In every inhale
And every exhale.
Amen.

MARCH 2

You're a tree replanted in Eden, bearing fresh fruit every month, never dropping a leaf, always in blossom.

PSALM 1:3 (MSG)

INHALE: Giver of life,
EXHALE: I trust what I cannot see.

A tree planted by water doesn't worry about where its next drink will come from. It draws what it needs right from the source. It flourishes, bearing fruit at the right time, its roots held steady even in the shifting seasons.

Psalm 1 reminds us that we're nourished when we stay connected to God's presence. We may not always feel strong or see the fruit, but something sacred is happening beneath the surface.

Even in seasons of waiting, even when we feel brittle and bare, we are still held. Still growing. Still sustained.

The very structure of our lungs mirrors a tree, says pulmonologist Michael J. Stephen. He describes how our breath travels down a single airway, then branches into two, and then into smaller and smaller passageways until—deep within us—the exchange of oxygen occurs. This pattern repeats itself throughout creation: tributaries winding into rivers, lightning streaking across the sky, even the way our own limbs extend outward.[65]

What if you saw yourself this way? Designed to receive, to branch out, to be part of something bigger than yourself? What if you trusted that, even when you feel depleted, you are still being nourished by the Giver of life?

BREATHE THIS IN

The lungs tap into something universal in their structure, maximizing uptake of the life force that surrounds all of us.[66]

Michael J. Stephen

MARCH 3

The One who called you is completely dependable. If he said it, he'll do it!

1 THESSALONIANS 5:24 (MSG)

INHALE: Even when I doubt,
EXHALE: You are faithful.

"The One who called you is completely dependable." Paul wrote these words in a letter to a group of early Christians in Thessalonica—a bustling urban center in the Roman Empire—who were facing persecution and needed reassurance in their faith.

We all need to be reminded sometimes: God is faithful, even when our faith is weak. God is trustworthy, even when our trust is wobbly.

So whether you're feeling confident and strong or uncertain and fragile, you can hold on to the promise that the One who calls you into a life of faith remains faithful, now and always.

If you feel like you need to have perfect faith, remember that throughout history, God's people have *never* been perfect. They looked at the world around them and felt discouraged, bereft, and alone. They looked at all the pain, chaos, and suffering and wondered where God was. They made mistakes. They looked inside themselves and wondered if God had ever really called them at all.

Paul reminds us that our faith begins with God's faithfulness. All we need to do is enter into the work that God is doing within us and in the world.

Even the disciples—those closest to Jesus, the ones who saw with their own eyes the Son of God turn water into wine and feed many with a few loaves—struggled with their faith. Doubt is part of being human. Struggling with faith is part of the human experience. But Jesus told his disciples that even a tiny seed of genuine faith can move mountains.

If you're looking around at the pain of the world or looking inward at your shortcomings or looking up and wondering where God is in all of it, take heart.

A mustard seed of faith is still faith. And the One who calls you is faithful.

PAUSE AND PONDER

In what areas of your life are you finding it difficult to trust God right now? Why is it comforting to know that even the early church and those closest to Jesus struggled with their faith?

Reflect on a time in your life when you doubted God's faithfulness. Looking back, how can you see that God was with you all along? How might you carry perspective into what you are struggling with now?

MARCH 4

Clean the slate, God, so we can start the day fresh!

PSALM 19:13 (MSG)

INHALE: God of fresh starts,
EXHALE: Help me to let go.

My third-grade teacher had a special tool for erasing the chalkboard. Only she was allowed to use it. I'd watch, mesmerized, as words and numbers disappeared in smooth, sweeping strokes. Later, I learned it was just a mop head treated with oil. But to me, it seemed like magic.

What was there was gone. A blank space stood ready for new lessons, new stories.

The slate was clean.

We often carry far more than we should. Harsh words echo in our minds. Mistakes play on repeat. Worries about tomorrow abound. We become weighed down by what was never ours to hold, and then we wonder why our souls feel so heavy.

But God is the Author of new beginnings. Even our breath reminds us of this truth. Every inhale brings oxygen that fuels our cells. Every exhale releases carbon dioxide, which our bodies no longer need. Breathing itself is a rhythm of receiving and letting go, of being made new moment by moment.

What if we treated each breath as a fresh start? With every breath, God offers a chance to wipe the slate clean. The chalkboard is erased. The page is blank.

Today, stop holding your breath with what you no longer need. A new story is being written, one breath at a time.

PRACTICING THE WAY

- **Get comfortable.** Relax your shoulders and keep your feet flat on the ground.
- **Breathe in through your nose.** Allow your breath to come from deep in your belly. Inhale for seven seconds, reflecting on the God of fresh starts. Hold for seven seconds.
- **Let it go.** Exhale through your mouth for seven seconds, receiving the forgiveness and renewal of Jesus. Picture the Spirit restoring you. When you release your breath, imagine letting go of any guilt or shame you're holding.
- **Repeat another slow breath.** As you breathe in, receive the grace of God's cleansing Spirit.
- **Give thanks.** When you're ready to return to your day, spend some time in gratitude for every breath that gives you a chance to begin again.

MARCH 5

He himself gives life and breath to everything, and he satisfies every need.

ACTS 17:25 (NLT)

INHALE: You give each breath;
EXHALE: You meet my needs.

It's easy to forget that every inhale is a gift. That this rhythm of life—our lungs automatically expanding and contracting without our having to think about it—is a kindness from the hand of God.

How often do we try to live as if everything depends on us? We live in an era when many of us have access to clean air and water at our fingertips. We convince ourselves we're self-sufficient, forgetting that every breath is evidence of God's nearness and provision. We treat God like an idea instead of the One who gives breath to everything and satisfies every need.

But Scripture reminds us that God is the Giver of life. Breathing is one of the body's automatic functions. We don't even have to think about taking our next breath—our lungs have been formed to do it for us. Even at the cellular level, God is giving us good gifts, breath by breath.

Centering prayer is, as Father Thomas Keating describes it, a prayer that helps us experience God's presence "within us, closer than breathing, closer than thinking . . . closer than consciousness itself."[67]

The practice of centering prayer has been one way I've learned—imperfectly—to receive God's presence. It's not easy for me to slow down. My body and nervous system are geared toward doing. I'm an imperfect practitioner. But I'm trying to, well, stop *trying* at everything and just be still.

Quieting my mind and sitting in this stillness, even for a few minutes, reminds me: *I don't have to hold everything together. God is here, nearer than my next breath.*

Howard Thurman once wrote, "The art of being still must be practiced until development and habit are sure."[68]

Your breath is proof that God is meeting you here. You don't need to do a thing to make that happen.

PRACTICING THE WAY

Centering prayer is a way of sitting in stillness and consenting to God's presence. When practicing this prayer, you don't have to do or say anything at all. Start at five minutes and then move to ten and gradually to twenty. (It gets easier!)

- **Choose a word or phrase.** Let it be a symbol of your desire to rest in God's love.
- **Sit comfortably.** Close your eyes. Take a moment to settle. You're simply practicing receiving God's love with each breath.
- **Be still.** That's it. No list of prayer requests. No thinking about what needs to get done this week. No picking at your cuticles. Each time your mind wanders (and it will!), gently return to your sacred word or breath.
- **End in silence.** When the time is finished, stay quiet for a moment before returning to your day.

MARCH 6

I will both lie down and sleep in peace; for you alone, O LORD, make me lie down in safety.

PSALM 4:8 (NRSV)

INHALE: When the day is done,
EXHALE: Help me rest in You.

For many of us, anxieties creep in at night. Our heads hit the pillow, and we're left with racing minds and restless hearts, replaying the day or rehearsing tomorrow.

If you've felt this way, you're not alone. Nearly a third of adults struggle with insomnia.[69]

When David wrote Psalm 4, nightfall meant vulnerability. No streetlights or security systems guaranteed protection in that ancient culture. To lie down and rest without fear wasn't confidence in circumstances but in the One who holds every moment.[70] Sleep was an act of faith, trusting that God alone gives the deepest sense of safety.

When we truly feel safe, our nervous systems shift out of defense mode (fight, flight, or freeze). Heart rate and blood pressure settle, and cells begin to restore and recharge. Dr. Stephen W. Porges, founding director of the Kinsey Institute Traumatic Stress Research Consortium at Indiana University, explains that in states of safety, digestion and immune function improve, and our brains even become more open to connection with others—and, I would add, with God too.[71]

The outside world may not always be safe, but God is. The One who "never slumbers or sleeps" is holding you.*

Tonight, as you settle into bed, place a hand over your heart. Whisper today's breath prayer. With every inhale, reflect on God's presence. With every exhale, let go of the tension you've been holding throughout the day.

You are safe. You are loved. You can rest.

BORROW THIS PRAYER

God of restoration and renewal,
Breathe rest into my weary heart.
When I can't catch my breath
And my legs can't bear my weight,
Help me fall into Your arms.
When I'm tired of running
And I'm gasping for air,
Give me true rest.
Slow me down,
And let me fall into You.
Amen.

* Psalm 121:4, NLT.

MARCH 7

Those who are peacemakers will plant seeds of peace and reap a harvest of righteousness.

JAMES 3:18 (NLT)

INHALE: Help me plant
EXHALE: Seeds of peace.

Much to the dismay of my white walls, my youngest son comes alive when his hands are elbow deep in soil. He has never met a seed he doesn't want to plant or a sprout he doesn't want to nurture. His potted seedlings line our windowsills, little trails of dirt marking where his enthusiasm has spilled over. And yet when he asks if we can make room for one more, I hear a whisper in my spirit: *Don't despise small beginnings.*[*]

After a horrible act of violence not far from my home, I looked out the window at one of the tiny sprouts, praying for God to right the wrongs of this world. For a few years, I've gathered with others in my community to advocate for gun safety. But news of this fresh nightmare left me reeling. *Does the work we do actually matter?* I wondered. *Why don't we see the fruit?*

James reminds us that planting seeds of peace not only matters, but it's something we're *called to* in God's Kingdom. Peace doesn't happen by accident—it grows when we sow it, even if our efforts seem insignificant. How we spend our time and treat one another, and even the words we use, might feel like a drop of hope in an ocean of pain, but God can do a lot with a little.

Even if all we hold in the palm of our hand is a tiny mustard seed, Jesus says that kind of faith can move a mountain.[†] We may not see mountains shift before our eyes, but that doesn't mean goodness won't grow. We cultivate peace by planting seeds, again and again, even when the soil feels hard and the elements are hostile. It takes all of us to grow and nurture goodness in our weary world.

As you breathe today's prayer, consider what small seeds of peace you might plant with your words and actions.

PRACTICING THE WAY

Plant a small packet of seeds, like herbs or flowers, in a container. Place the pot on a windowsill where you'll see it every day. Each time you see the plants, pause for a breath prayer. As you water them and watch your seedlings grow, remember that even the tiniest acts of peace matter.

[*] See Zechariah 4:10.

[†] See Matthew 17:20.

MARCH 8

Please stand up for the poor, help the children of the needy, come down hard on the cruel tyrants. Outlast the sun, outlive the moon—age after age after age. Be rainfall on cut grass, earth-refreshing rain showers. Let righteousness burst into blossom and peace abound until the moon fades to nothing.

PSALM 72:4-7 (MSG)

INHALE: May peace abound;
EXHALE: Let it begin in me.

God hears our prayers. It's easy to believe the aches of our age are new, but the psalms remind us that humanity has always cried out to God to protect the vulnerable and hold the corrupt accountable.

In today's passage, we're invited to ask God to "be rainfall on cut grass, earth-refreshing rain showers." The thing about rain is that it gives life. It nourishes us from the roots so goodness can flourish. Prayer works the same way. When we seek justice through prayer, the Spirit sustains us—empowering us to bear fruit and become part of the answer to our prayers.

With God's help, we support the poor, advocate for the vulnerable, and speak truth to power. We plant seeds of hope, even if we can't yet see the flourishing to come.

I love standing outside after a spring rain, breathing deep the promise of something new following a long winter. But let's be honest: Even with hope in the air, there are still sidewalks pocked with puddles, worms wriggling on the pavement, and no summer blooms just yet.

Spring is messy—and so is hope. It reminds us of the Kingdom that is both here and still to come.

As we await the future resurrection, we long for renewal in our land, our communities, our own hearts. When you wonder if your prayers matter, remember that prayer is an active posture that joins God's work of restoration.

Ask God to help you breathe in hope and exhale despair. As you breathe, remember that no matter how muddy everything might be, God's justice is like rain, and because of that, we can trust that peace will flourish.

RHYTHM OF BREATH

Breathe into me
A vision of what might be.
Breathe into me
Hope for the weary,
Grace for the lonely,
Peace for the hurting.
Breathe into me
Imagination for a world
Where peace flourishes
Like ivy along a brick wall.
Breathe into me
A vision of what might be.

MARCH 9

Friend, don't go along with evil. Model the good. The person who does good does God's work.

3 JOHN 1:11 (MSG)

INHALE: Loving God,
EXHALE: Guide my work.

As a child, I believed that people in power would always do what was right. As an adult, I've learned how untrue that is. From pulpits to boardrooms to political offices, it's not uncommon to see leaders prioritize greed over generosity, cruelty over kindness, and self-interest over community.

The truth is, sometimes evil isn't just tolerated but celebrated. Standing for love, joy, peace, patience, kindness, goodness, faithfulness, gentleness, and self-control—which we're told is an overflow of Spirit-filled lives—isn't always popular, even among those who claim to be Christians.*

I can still picture the poster above the chalkboard in my middle school classroom: "What is right is not always popular. What is popular is not always right." I rolled my eyes, but the idea lingered, tumbling around in my mind.

It sounded a little cliché, but what if it was . . . actually true?

John begins today's verse with *friend* or, as some translations say, *beloved.* He's giving a tender word specifically to people of faith, knowing the pull to give in, to go along, to stay quiet. But we are called to resist evil, to model what is good, to let our words and work be rooted in love, trusting that God's way is better than the influence of the masses.

Peace cannot be kept. It must be made.

Keeping the peace is easy. It asks for nothing more than silence. Making peace in our warring world may cost something, but it's always worth it. God will be with you in your call to courage when cowardice would feel easier. God will not leave you as you use your voice when shrinking back would cause less tension.

As long as you have breath in your lungs, you have the opportunity to "model the good."

God's people have always been invited beyond popularity into a love that confounds, into a hope that perseveres.

Take a breath. Ask God to breathe courage into you. As you pray, be brave enough to ask, "Where am I keeping peace instead of making it? What would it look like to let goodness fill my words and my work today?"

SACRED ECHOES

If you're standing up for what's right and it feels like no one is standing with you—keep going.

Being courageous has never required a crowd cheering you on.

History is changed by people who had courage in their convictions.[72]

Sharon McMahon

* See Galatians 5:22-23.

MARCH 10

Yet I am confident I will see the LORD's goodness
while I am here in the land of the living.

PSALM 27:13 (NLT)

INHALE: I will see Your goodness
EXHALE: In the land of the living.

When I met my husband, he was a teenager who drove a rusty red pickup. It leaked oil and rattled over every bump, but he loved it. After years of pining for his beloved first truck, he recently found another of the same model—a classic now. It was a bumpy ride that smelled like cigarette smoke and burning oil, but my husband was smitten. He drove his truck home that afternoon, and I took a shower, vowing not to set foot in it again until it was sanitized.

After months of cleaning and repairs, he invited me on a drive. As the sun began to set, he drove along the backroads while the wind blew through my hair. I looked up at the sky, striped with ribbons of pink and gold. "Wow, it's beautiful," I whispered.

"What is? My truck?" he responded, nodding like, *of course*.

"No, the sunset!" I said, gesturing at the gorgeous sun-streaked painting over the field.

"It is?" He cocked his head to the side.

It was then that I realized I was quite literally wearing rose-colored glasses that were tinting my view.

So often, it's easy to look at the world through cynicism-colored glasses, to see the things in our lives through a filter of dismay and despair. What if we put aside both the rose-colored glasses and the doom goggles, and instead asked God for spiritual eyes to recognize goodness amid the everyday chaos?

The ride in my husband's truck wasn't magical because of a social-media-worthy sunset or because he was able to get rid of the smoke smell in the cab. It was meaningful because we were together, hand in hand, driving down prairie backroads.

When you're feeling discouraged, remember that noticing goodness in your daily life is about experiencing life through the lens of *Yes, our world is a mess. And also? There is so much beauty.*

As spring arrives, remember: You don't have to wait for heaven to glimpse God's goodness. You can see it here, in the land of the living.

BORROW THIS PRAYER

When goodness is hard to see,
When I can't remember
What Your voice sounds like,
Whisper into my heart
The laughter of another.
When I've lost sight of You
In the person in front of me,
Show me You are here.
When I've forgotten the way,
Remind me who I am.
Sing me the song of my heart,
Whisper Your melody in my soul.
In every breath,
Reorient the truest parts of me
Back to You.
Amen.

MARCH 11

It's in Christ that we find out who we are and what we are living for. Long before we first heard of Christ and got our hopes up, he had his eye on us, had designs on us for glorious living, part of the overall purpose he is working out in everything and everyone.

EPHESIANS 1:11-12 (MSG)

INHALE: You are working
EXHALE: Everything out.

In my early twenties, I attended my first ever faith retreat. Armed with thick rolls of paper and boxes of markers, our pastor asked us to create a timeline of our lives, highlighting key moments and spiritual milestones.

I sat with my marker hovering over the page. Nothing about my life felt profound. The last timeline I had done was for Martin Luther King Jr. in fifth grade. The only thing I'd done in my life recently was graduate from college. I felt . . . underwhelming.

It's easy to think that if our stories don't have dramatic twists, then God isn't working. But today's Scripture reminds us: God is working things out "in everything and everyone." That means *you*. Even when you don't feel it. Even when your page feels empty.

You might roll your eyes, but here's the truest thing I can write: God has fashioned a profound purpose for *your* life. In Christ, you have meaning. You have a reason to live. And not just to go through the motions, but to live *gloriously*.

When life feels overwhelming and I feel small, that truth gives me hope. As Frederick Buechner writes, our hope "is ultimately hope in Christ . . . The hope that despite the fact that sin and death still rule the world, he somehow conquered them. The hope that in him and through him all of us stand a chance of somehow conquering them too. The hope that at some unforeseeable time and in some unimaginable way he will return with healing in his wings."[73]

We may not always understand how God is working in us and through us, but that doesn't mean it isn't happening. As you move through today's breath prayer, remember that Christ has been there all along, in every moment, in every breath.

PRACTICING THE WAY

Sketch a simple life timeline. (Grab a sheet of paper if you'd like more room.) Add pivotal moments along the way—nothing is too small or too ordinary.

Write whatever comes to mind: hard seasons, times of celebration, special milestones, or complex moments you're still untangling.

This is just for your reflection, so don't worry about making it neat or detailed. Even a single word, abbreviation, or symbol can mark a memory. As you jot each one down, pause and pray through the breath prayer.

BIRTH

TODAY

Note: This practice may evoke some difficult memories. It may be helpful to journal or talk with someone you trust. If trauma is part of your story, consider talking with a trained professional. Find one at emdria.org or psychologytoday.com.

MARCH 12

Be strong and take heart, all you who hope in the LORD.

PSALM 31:24 (NIV)

INHALE: In You, O God,
EXHALE: I find my strength.

We know that God spiritually strengthens us through prayer, but have you ever considered that God also *physically* strengthens us when we practice breath prayer?

According to James Nestor, author of *Breath*, science proves that "prayer heals, especially when it's practiced at 5.5 breaths a minute."[74] When we slow our breathing and pray with intention, syncing our inhale and exhale with our words, we can naturally fall into a rhythm that triggers our body's healing response.

Research confirms this. Dr. MeiLan K. Han, professor of medicine and chief of the division of pulmonary and critical care at the University of Michigan, says that deep, slow breathing lowers heart rate, blood pressure, and stress hormones. It helps us focus and can even reduce pain. She writes, "The act of breathing itself contributes to our day-to-day sense of well-being."[75]

When you enter into breath prayer, you're not only drawing near to God—you're receiving God's built-in gift of restoration too. With each inhale, your cells are nourished, and with every exhale, your body releases what it no longer needs.

The One who formed you designed you so that the very act of praying with your breath would strengthen you in body, mind, and spirit.

Today, let your breath be a reminder of the divine love that surrounds, sustains, and strengthens you.

BREATHE THIS IN

Try a breath prayer with this restorative rhythm:

- Inhale through your nose for four seconds.
- Exhale through your mouth for six seconds.
- Continue this rhythm (about six breaths per minute) for five minutes.

As you breathe, notice how your body responds. Is your pulse slowing? Is your mind settling? Let each breath become a reminder that God's Spirit is sustaining you.

MARCH 13

Oh! May the God of green hope fill you up with joy, fill you up with peace, so that your believing lives, filled with the life-giving energy of the Holy Spirit, will brim over with hope!

ROMANS 15:13 (MSG)

INHALE: God of green hope,
EXHALE: Fill me with joy.

My youngest son stood wide-eyed as the drum lines marched and local groups tossed candy to the crowd. Most people walking the parade handed him a few pieces, but one man came with a five-gallon bucket and practically poured it out. Lollipops and Tootsie Rolls overflowed into my son's arms, tumbling onto the sidewalk. His laughter rang out as the man's eyes sparkled with joy.

God's hope isn't stingy. It's not rationed or scarce. It's poured out abundantly, brimming over and filling us with joy and peace until we can't help but spill hope into the world around us.

The world gives us plenty of reasons why joy and peace are scarce commodities, reserved for only a select few. But the truth is that the hope we have is a gift from the Spirit—a "green hope" that grows even in the coldest corners of our lives, renewing us from the roots up. And it's for everybody. For you. For today. For this very moment, no matter what else is happening in your life.

When you feel drained, whisper today's breath prayer. Let the Spirit fill you until hope brims over into your words and actions. Because God's goodness, sweet and surprising, is enough to spill out into the lives of others.

BORROW THIS PRAYER

God of green hope,
When the darkness closes in,
Whisper the promise
That You are near.

God of new life
And bouquets of second chances,
Help me remember
This ache won't last forever.

God of joy beyond all comprehension,
Encourage the weary,
Lift the downtrodden,
Care for the hopeless,
Protect the vulnerable.

Grow green hope within me—
Crack open my chest
And let it take root,
So that every fiber of my being
And every swirl of my fingerprints
Will brim over with hope,
Extending to all I meet.
Amen.

MARCH 14

GOD made sky and soil, sea and all the fish in it. He always does what he says—he defends the wronged, he feeds the hungry. GOD frees prisoners—he gives sight to the blind, he lifts up the fallen. . . . [He] protects strangers, takes the side of orphans and widows, but makes short work of the wicked.

PSALM 146:6-9 (MSG)

INHALE: There's nothing
EXHALE: You cannot do.

We live in a culture that idolizes independence and self-sufficiency. We're told to muscle through, to stay strong, to carry it all on our own. And when we can't, we wonder what's wrong with us. Sometimes I even catch myself side-eyeing God, asking why I feel so alone in holding everything together.

But Psalm 146 reminds us that it's not all on our shoulders. It's *God* who sculpted the sky and the soil, who painted the world in broad strokes of beauty. It's *God* who defends the wronged, feeds the hungry, and lifts the fallen. We're invited to join in this holy work, but the weight of the world is not ours alone to bear.

The Creator who breathed the world into existence also breathes life into your weary lungs. The One who holds the cosmos cares for it. All of it.

You don't have to be the strong one. Full of power and might, Jesus gazes upon you with tenderness. What would it take for you to receive that? To let go of some of the pressures that have been piling up and instead fully exhale, trusting God to do what God promises to do. Trusting that God sees all that pain, all that suffering, and says, *I see it. I know it. I am here.*

BORROW THIS PRAYER

God who breathed life into being,
God of creation,
Nourisher of souls,
Redeemer of life,
You exist in and beyond all things.
We marvel at who You are
And pray that every breath we take
Would be an overflow of adoration,
Honoring and glorifying You.

We pray that our every breath
Would whisper Your ways
And reflect Your holy name.
Bring the rhythms of Your grace
Into our daily comings and goings.
Amen.

MARCH 15

Do not permit the ways of this world to mold and shape you. Instead, let Creator change you from the inside out, in the way a caterpillar becomes a butterfly. He will do this by giving you a new way of thinking, seeing, and walking. Then you will know for sure what the Great Spirit wants for you, things that are good, that make the heart glad, and that help you walk the path of becoming a mature and true human being.

ROMANS 12:2 (FNV)

INHALE: Change me
EXHALE: From the inside out.

I have dozens of photos of chubby green caterpillars saved on my phone, thanks to my youngest son. He considers them the "before" part of before-and-after photos. We have a pollinator garden, and my son is fascinated by how caterpillars create their chrysalises, waiting in the dark until one day they emerge—completely transformed.

Lent is a season of waiting in the darkness. As much as we may want to jump to the resurrection, these forty days leading up to Easter invite us into the *reflection* that comes before *renewal*, the chrysalis that comes before the butterfly.

The First Nations Version of Romans 12:2 says, "Do not permit the ways of this world to mold and shape you. Instead, let Creator change you from the inside out, in the way a caterpillar becomes a butterfly." Transformation is God's work. All we have to do is make space for the Spirit to reshape us from within.

Spiritual practices, like observing Lent or practicing daily breath prayers, aren't sacred sticker charts to earn gold stars. They're rhythms that keep us open to God's presence, breath by breath, prayer by prayer.

Maybe today you feel stuck in the in-between. Maybe you feel the darkness more than the light. Take a slow breath and pray. Trust that even here in the waiting, God is at work. The One who breathed life into you is still breathing, reshaping you from the inside out into the beloved one you were made to be all along.

To find out more about Lent, see the liturgical calendar in appendix A.

SACRED ECHOES

I cannot transform myself, or anyone else for that matter. What I can do is create the conditions in which spiritual transformation can take place, by developing and maintaining a rhythm of spiritual practices that keep me open and available to God.[76]

Ruth Haley Barton

MARCH 16

Let us press on to know him. He will respond to us as surely as the arrival of dawn or the coming of rains in early spring.

HOSEA 6:3 (NLT)

INHALE: My soul is dry;
EXHALE: You refresh me.

When spring arrives, creation begins to breathe again, transforming the earth from shades of gray to hues of green. Buds appear on bare branches, and daylight starts to linger. The frozen ground softens, preparing to receive the rain, and little by little, winter fades as new life breaks through.

Hosea urged God's people to "press on to know" the One whose presence is as sure as sunrise and as steady as spring rain. Knowing God is not a one-time encounter, but an *ongoing knowing*—a posture of the heart that keeps seeking, even in the driest seasons.

Sometimes I feel like finding God in the midst of real life is a kind of cosmic hide-and-seek. I pray, and silence stretches on. I search, but my efforts come up short. But Hosea's promise stands: When we press on, God responds. Not begrudgingly or eventually, but as surely as morning follows night, as surely as the rains water the earth.

Dry seasons come. Prayers can feel like they hang unanswered in the air. But beneath the surface, our relational God remains close. Our restorative God is at work.

When it seems like your soul is in a never-ending winter, when God feels distant and your spirit feels dry, hold on to this: Spring will come. Rain will fall. God will answer.

Keep pressing on. Because even now, God is closer than you think.

PAUSE AND PONDER

How does the daily certainty of sunrise help you trust God's presence?

When have you kept praying through silence? What helped you keep pressing on?

MARCH 17

SAINT PATRICK'S DAY

May the LORD bless you and protect you. May the LORD smile on you and be gracious to you. May the LORD show you his favor and give you his peace.

NUMBERS 6:24-26 (NLT)

INHALE: You were with me then;
EXHALE: You are with me now.

Green rivers. Parades. "Luck of the Irish." Today's celebrations may be fun, but they barely skim the surface of Saint Patrick's story.

At sixteen, he was kidnapped from his home in Roman Britain by Irish raiders and enslaved across the sea. Alone and desperate, Patrick relied on God's nearness in the fields where he was forced to herd sheep. After six years, he escaped and returned to his homeland—only to sense God calling him back to Ireland years later, not for revenge but to extend Christ's compassion. He returned to the very land of his captivity with a message of hope and justice, even confronting the mistreatment of Irish Christians by British leaders.

Patrick doubted himself. He lacked education and felt unqualified. Yet he trusted Christ's presence—that God went before him and behind him—and stepped into his call anyway.[77]

Maybe you've wondered: Where was God when your life unraveled? Patrick surely asked the same. Maybe you've doubted your ability to step into God's call. Patrick doubted too. But in Christ, he had the compassion to forgive and the courage to bear witness and challenge oppression.

God's presence is with you in your own fields—in both the ordinary ones and the overwhelming ones. Take a breath and remember: The One who was with Saint Patrick is with you now. Open yourself to what God might be whispering into your soul as you reflect on Saint Patrick's legacy.

God's presence surrounds you and goes with you, always.

BORROW THIS PRAYER

Christ, walk with us.
Be present in every step and stumble.
Christ, go before us.
Show us the way to follow in truth.
Christ, walk behind us.
Guide us and protect us.
Christ, linger in the heart
Of everyone who thinks of us.
May we radiate love and compassion.
Christ, be on the lips of everyone
Who speaks of us.
May our hearts beat with
Mercy, compassion, and truth.
Christ, be reflected in every eye that
sees us.
May we show love to all we meet.
Christ, be in every ear that hears us.
May we sing anthems of hope
forevermore.

Adapted from "A Prayer for St. Patrick's Day" from To Light Their Way[78]

MARCH 18

All the broken and dislocated pieces of the universe—people and things, animals and atoms—get properly fixed and fit together in vibrant harmonies, all because of his death.

COLOSSIANS 1:20 (MSG)

INHALE: You take my broken pieces
EXHALE: And make something beautiful.

When I was ten, my grandma took me to the Grotto of Redemption, a little place in rural Iowa that locals have deemed the "Eighth Wonder of the World." It's a collection of grottos—carved-out caves inlaid with stones and minerals—each one shimmering with mosaic scenes of Jesus. I stared in awe, captivated by how bits of quartz and glints of topaz came together to create something breathtaking. Each stone, on its own, looked pretty ordinary. But together, the bits and glints told the best story of all.

At the gift shop, I picked out a geode the size of my fist. On the outside, it was nothing more than a dull gray rock. But cracked open, it revealed crystals that caught the light. The beauty had always been there, hidden inside, waiting to be revealed. But it was only revealed through breaking.

We don't escape the fractures of this world. We all know what it is to carry cracks in our hearts—whether from grief, disappointment, or the long silence of unanswered prayers. Colossians reminds us that Christ holds it all—gathering every fragment, every dislocated piece of creation, and fitting them together in harmony.

The Grotto's builder knew this truth well. After nearly dying from pneumonia, he devoted the rest of his life to telling the gospel story in stone. His brokenness became the offering that shaped his life's work—beauty that continues to whisper hope today.

What looks shattered in your hands is not wasted. In God's hands, the pieces of your heart aren't discarded but become part of a radiant whole. Christ gathers the broken parts and fits them together into a redemptive story more radiant than we can imagine.

As you move through today's breath prayer, imagine holding one fractured part of your life before God. Trust that even here, Christ is piecing you together, breath by breath.

PRACTICING THE WAY

Create a simple mosaic or collage with scraps of paper, bits of nature, or digital images. As you piece them together, reflect on Colossians 1:20 and pray through today's breath prayer, remembering that God's love holds the fragments of your life—and the whole world.

MARCH 19

FEAST DAY OF SAINT JOSEPH

I'll never quit telling the story of your love—how you built the cosmos and guaranteed everything in it. Your love has always been our lives' foundation, your fidelity has been the roof over our world.

PSALM 89:2 (MSG)

INHALE: Your unfailing love
EXHALE: Will last forever.

My husband, Jonny, didn't grow up with a lot of money. With six kids in the house, his parents pinched every penny, and hand-me-downs were just part of life. But one year, he got something brand new: shiny white sneakers. He was thrilled, even if they were just a smidge too big.

Not long after, Jonny was fishing with his dad and brothers. Restless energy bubbled up, and he tore down the riverbank. Sure enough, one shoe flew off . . . straight into the river. His dad, displeased but determined, jumped in after it. When my mother-in-law recounts this story, she adds, "These days, Jonny would just buy new shoes!" And she's probably right.

We live in a fast-fix culture. When something breaks, we replace it. When something wears thin, we move on. Maybe that's why it's so hard for us to grasp the fullness of God's love, so difficult for us to trust that the faithfulness of God isn't temporary. It doesn't wear out or wash away.

The One who breathed life into the world is faithful to hold it together.

Psalm 89 reminds us that God's faithful love is the foundation under our feet and the roof over our heads. That God's promises endure from generation to generation. Today we remember Joseph, a man who modeled that kind of fidelity—standing with Mary, protecting Jesus, and trusting God's promises even when the path was uncertain. Joseph's faithfulness reflected the faithfulness of God.

When worries arise and you wonder if the story of God's love is truly as unshakable as we're told, breathe this truth: God's love is not fleeting. It will hold you. It will steady you. And it will last forever.

PAUSE AND PONDER

When you reflect on your life, where do you see God's faithfulness? What do you think it means that God's love will last forever?

In what ways are you telling the story of God's love with your life right now? If someone were to look in from the outside, what might they see?

MARCH 20

Go after a life of love as if your life depended on it—because it does. Give yourselves to the gifts God gives you. Most of all, try to proclaim his truth.

1 CORINTHIANS 14:1 (MSG)

INHALE: Lead me

EXHALE: Into a life of love.

"Let love be your highest goal."* "Follow the way of love."† "Pursue love."‡ No matter the translation of today's verse, Paul's message remains: Love is our foundation. Love is the soil where everything good grows.

Love is the very air we breathe.

The word *love* can feel a little overused in our culture. We emblazon it on coffee mugs and throw pillows. We pepper song lyrics with it and create reality shows about it. But the *agapē* love Paul describes is anything but cliché. It's selfless and sacrificial, rooted in Christ. It's strong enough to heal divisions, to transform strangers into family.

In Paul's world, love wasn't a commonly held virtue. Power? For sure. Eloquence? Of course. But self-giving love? Not so much. Paul's insistence that love must be the foundation was countercultural. It disrupted the early church's assumptions of what to aspire to.

Without love, Paul warned, the gifts God gives us hang empty in the air. Just like our lungs are ever working to give our bodies breath, love is active too. Love is life-sustaining not just for our souls but for the flourishing of the people around us.

Maybe you feel like you don't have much to offer. Maybe you look around and feel like God breathed gifts into everyone but you. But *you* are uniquely situated to breathe love into the people and places surrounding you in this very moment. Every prayer you whisper, every act of care you extend, every moment you choose patience—they are all exhales of love into a world gasping for breath.

Love is the only oxygen strong enough to revive and sustain us.

When you pursue love, you can trust that the Spirit will do a transformational work within you, stirring love inside you so you might breathe out love (the way only *you* can) into a world running on fumes.

BORROW THIS PRAYER

God, we've lost our way
To one another,
Choosing self-protection
Over the restorative breath
Of communal flourishing.
Wrap us in the tapestry
Of mutuality and hospitality.
Bind us together
In perfect love.
For the only way forward
Is in You.
For the only way through
Is together.
Amen.

* 1 Corinthians 14:1, NLT.
† 1 Corinthians 14:1, NIV.
‡ 1 Corinthians 14:1, NKJV.

MARCH 21

I've kept my feet on the ground, I've cultivated a quiet heart.

PSALM 131:2 (MSG)

INHALE: When my mind is spinning,
EXHALE: Quiet my heart.

When I was a teenager, being grounded meant punishment. Now, I define being grounded as a spiritual rootedness that I long for.

It's easy for me to become untethered by the demands of my personal life and the overwhelming realities of the world's needs. My life is loud. Kids shout, dogs bark, my phone pings me with another notification—it's all too much.

Maybe your noise doesn't sound like mine, but I bet you know the feeling of being inundated with noise. There's always something clamoring for our attention. And it isn't just the outer world that's loud. The inner world is loud too, echoing with lies: *You're not enough. You're falling behind. You're unwanted.*

When life gets this noisy, it's tempting to add to the chaos, tossing in unfiltered words or emotions. But Psalm 131 points us to another way: "I've cultivated a quiet heart." In Scripture, quietness means choosing to rest in God's presence, even when the chaos swirls around us.

Being grounded and getting quiet aren't about blocking out sound with noise-canceling headphones or retreating from the world but letting God quiet us from *within.*

Breath prayer can help us enter that quiet. When we pray with our breath, we remember that stillness cultivates a calm heart, not shutting out the world but being grounded in God's steadying love, right in the midst of the noise.

SACRED ECHOES

We translate dryness in prayer as God's absence until we perceive that God is communicating with us at a deeper level. Silence is God's first language; everything else is a poor translation. In order to hear that language, we must learn to be still and to rest in God."[79]

Thomas Keating

MARCH 22

The Kingdom of God is not just a lot of talk;
it is living by God's power.

1 CORINTHIANS 4:20 (NLT)

INHALE: Your way
EXHALE: Is not just talk.

The best story we tell is the one we live.

When my grandma died, I wanted to put the whole of who she was (and what she meant to me) into words. But no words could hold her legacy of love. What remains is how she showed up—how she loved, day after day. Her life itself was the story.

Paul reminds us that the Kingdom of God isn't "a lot of talk" but living by God's power. In his time—just like today—flashy rhetoric and eloquent words impressed people. But Paul insists that true faith is revealed not in polished speech but in transformed lives: Love that acts and serves. Love that forgives. Love that keeps showing up.

No matter how poetic our words, they're empty if they're not lived out in light of God's love.* Through Christ, we're empowered to live beyond sound bites and into the rhythms of God's Kingdom, where neighbors *and* enemies are loved, where our actions overflow with God's Spirit, equipping us to love in ways we never could on our own.

By the Spirit's power, you can send the apology. You can choose patience when outrage feels easier. You can bring a meal. You can extend grace. You can erase that snarky comment you were about to post.

In Christ, you are empowered to live out an embodied faith that extends beyond yourself. In Christ, your words and actions can align, telling the best story with the life you live.

Choosing the path of Jesus in our loud, divided world isn't easy. But you aren't alone. God is with you, empowering you to live what you say, to embody love beyond words.

Take a slow breath. Inhale God's love for you. Exhale that love into the world.

PAUSE AND PONDER

What does it mean to live an empowered life? Where do you struggle to filter your words and actions through the lens of God's love?

What is the difference between a faith that is talk and a faith that is empowered into action? What example comes to mind?

* See 1 Corinthians 13.

MARCH 23

I live and breathe GOD. . . . God met me more than halfway, he freed me from my anxious fears.

PSALM 34:2,4 (MSG)

INHALE: You meet me
EXHALE: More than halfway.

When we pray alongside our breath—using slow inhales and steady exhales—we give our anxious minds and bodies space to rest in God's care.

I've only experienced one anxiety attack, but I'll never forget it. I woke up in the middle of the night, gasping for air. Tears poured as I tried to catch my breath. My husband was patient and kind, helping me to slow down, connect to my breath, and come back to myself.

Anxiety often takes over our breathing. When we're stressed, we tend to breathe in through our mouths, taking quick, shallow inhales into the chest that actually signal danger to our bodies. But when we switch to deep, slow "belly breathing," our bodies begin to believe we're safe. Studies show this kind of mindful breathing quiets panic and can help us move through anxiety.[80]

Psalm 34 reminds us that God meets us—"more than halfway"—in those overwhelming moments. David wrote these words after barely escaping danger, testifying to a God who draws near, who breathes peace into anxious lungs.

When we practice breath prayer, we participate in God's gift of restoration. The Spirit (whose very name means breath) is with us in every inhale and exhale.

Try this today: Place a hand on your belly. Inhale for four counts, feeling the air expand deep into your lower abdomen, like you're blowing up a balloon. When you're ready, exhale for six counts, releasing your anxiety. With each breath, picture God's peace filling you and fear leaving you.

Even in your anxious nights, you are not alone. Our personal, protective God is attentive to your needs, nearer than the next breath.*

BREATHE THIS IN

The reason diaphragmatic or abdominal breathing is considered an "anti-panic/anxiety" breath is that it helps regulate irregular breathing patterns fairly quickly.[81]

Bob Stahl and Wendy Millstine

* If you're struggling with anxiety, breath prayer is just one tool among many God-given resources. Seek support from a doctor or therapist who can walk with you.

MARCH 24

No word from God will ever fail.

LUKE 1:37 (NIV)

INHALE: You are bigger
EXHALE: Than my doubts.

Somewhere along the way, many of us absorbed the idea that having faith means never doubting. So when our doubts arise—when we wonder if God is truly good or if God even exists—it can feel frightening, as if we're failing (or flailing about) in our faith.

But God isn't afraid of our questions. God doesn't turn away from our wonderings. If you're holding the tension of faith and doubt, you're in good company. The Bible is full of people who lived in this tension: Jacob wrestled.[*] Sarah laughed.[†] David lamented.[‡] Martha agonized.[§] Thomas doubted.[¶]

Even Mary, after hearing the angel's news, asked, "How can this be?"[**]

And through it all, God remained faithful.

Faith has never meant the absence of doubt. Faith is the courage to bring our doubts to the One who holds steady—the One whose word never fails. You have an invitation to bring your whys, what-ifs, and what-abouts to God.

How might your perspective shift if you saw doubt as a doorway into a deeper knowing?

Sarah's laughter turned into joy.[††] Martha's grief turned into resurrection.[‡‡] Mary's question turned into a song of praise.[§§]

[*] See Genesis 32:22-32.
[†] See Genesis 18:12-15.
[‡] See Psalm 13:1.
[§] See John 11:21-22.
[¶] See John 20:24-29.
[**] Luke 1:34, NRSV.
[††] See Genesis 21:6.
[‡‡] See John 11:23-27.
[§§] See Luke 1:46-55.

Life is full of mystery, and we were never meant to fully comprehend the Creator of the cosmos. But even in the unknowing, we're invited to trust the promise: God's word does not fail. Not when the promise feels impossible. Not when grief feels unbearable. Not when questions feel unrelenting.

As you pray, take a slow breath. Breathe in the truth of God's nearness. Breathe out the fear that your questions are too much for God.

Even here, today, in the midst of your wondering, He who promised is faithful.[¶¶]

PAUSE AND PONDER

When life feels out of control, return to the heart of God. Let one or two Scripture references from today's reading lead you back to God's unchanging character. As you read, ask, *What can I learn about who God is from this story?* Learn more about reading the Bible through this lens in Meredith Miller's book *Woven*.[82]

When I doubt, I can remember that even in my wonderings, God is . . .

- ____________________
- ____________________
- ____________________
- ____________________
- ____________________

[¶¶] See Genesis 32:24-32.

MARCH 25

FEAST OF THE ANNUNCIATION

Let it be with me just as you say.

LUKE 1:38 (MSG)

INHALE: I release my life
EXHALE: Into Your hands.

In his now-classic song, Paul McCartney croons, "Mother Mary comes to me, speaking words of wisdom." A mixed bag of lore surrounds what exactly inspired Paul to write these lyrics for the Beatles' hit "Let It Be." Like many artists, he mostly leaves his work open to interpretation.

Today, the church remembers Mary's own "let it be"—words that changed the course of history forever.

On the Feast of the Annunciation, nine months before Christmas, we pause to honor the eternity-altering cosmic shift of God breaking into human history. We reflect on when an angel appeared to an ordinary girl in an unassuming town, inviting her into a story that would reauthor all of humanity forever.

And in that awe-inspiring moment, in the face of infinite unknowns, Mary gave her *yes*. She stepped into the unknown, consenting to bear the weight of mystery. "Let it be to me according to your word," she said.[*] She surrendered control and offered her whole self to God's redemptive work. She couldn't have known that her response would echo forward to Jesus, when he said in Gethsemane, "Not my will, but yours."[†]

Life zigs and zags in ways we don't expect. Saying, "Let it be" is not easy. It takes courage to trust that God's plans won't fail. Sometimes giving our yes means entering into the unknown, but we never do it alone—we go forth with the One we know is good and loving and trustworthy.

Mary didn't know she'd be part of God's redemption story for the whole of humanity. Her yes went beyond human understanding. Her trust was rooted in a God who is faithful.

Where might God be waiting for you to say yes?

As you breathe and pray today, unfurl your hands and leave them open. Ask God to give you a posture of the heart that simply says, "Let it be."

PRACTICING THE WAY

Was there a moment, known only to God, when all the stars held their breath, when the galaxies paused in their dance for a fraction of a second, and the Word, who had called it into being, went with all his love into the womb of a young girl, and the universe started to breathe again, and the ancient harmonies resumed their song, and the angels clapped their hands for joy?[83]

Madeleine L'Engle

[*] Luke 1:38, ESV.
[†] Luke 22:42, ESV.

MARCH 26

I will give thanks to the LORD with my whole heart;
I will tell of all your wonderful deeds.

PSALM 9:1 (NRSV)

INHALE: I will give thanks
EXHALE: With my whole heart.

When we're grateful, something shifts inside us. Gratitude doesn't erase the difficult parts of life, but it does help us refocus on God's goodness.

When we were adopting our son Joseph from West Africa, I browsed through an airline magazine that named Nigeria the happiest country in the world. I had a hard time wrapping my mind around it. At first glance, I saw a lot of income inequality and social inequity. I was equating wealth and power with joy and gratitude. But I couldn't have been more wrong.

As I read through the feature, something stood out to me about every person who was interviewed: I saw joy flowing from a posture of gratitude.

Clinical studies show that intentionally practicing gratitude leads to an improved mood, more positive emotions, and fewer symptoms of anxiety and depression.[84] Gratitude isn't a bandage that fixes all the hurts we hold. But God has formed us to flourish when we remember the goodness and give thanks. (I don't know about you, but I definitely notice the difference between the heaviness of my pity parties and the lightness that comes when I name what I'm grateful for.)

Psalm 9 invites us to give thanks with our whole heart, to remember God's wonders—not only for ourselves but also to encourage others. Gratitude is both personal and communal, a way to strengthen our faith and tell God's story together.

What would it look like to practice gratitude today? To reflect on the goodness of God instead of fixating on what's going wrong?

You don't have to start big. Begin with today's breath prayer. As you inhale, remember God's goodness. As you exhale, release your thanks.

PAUSE AND PONDER

List three things you're thankful for today:

- ______________________
- ______________________
- ______________________

How could you express your appreciation to someone this week? A note, a text, a phone call, a coffee date, a gift? Brainstorm who you could extend a simple thank-you to.

____

____

____

MARCH 27

Since Jesus went through everything you're going through and more, learn to think like him.

1 PETER 4:1 (MSG)

INHALE: You understand
EXHALE: What it's like to be human.

Breath is universal. Just as rain falls on the just and the unjust,* breath fills the lungs of both the kind and the cruel, the forgotten and the powerful.

This is where things get hard. Holding compassion for those on the margins—the ones cast aside, the ones in pain—feels like a natural posture for me. But it is much harder to love those who use their power to harm or oppress others. And yet Jesus tells us to love not only our neighbor but also our enemy.

I don't believe that means condoning evil or excusing injustice. It does not mean staying silent when harm is done. But it does mean remembering—even when it feels impossible—that every breath is a gift from God. And as long as someone has breath, they still bear God's image.

This is the tension of our faith: To resist evil and not lose sight of the humanity of another. To cry out for justice and still remember that God alone is the Giver of breath.

As Peter reminds us, since Jesus went through everything we go through—and more—we can learn to think like Him. That doesn't mean we always get it right. But with every breath, we're learning to reflect how Jesus loves: being tender to another's humanity, even when it's hard to see.

Jesus knows what it's like to see the worst of people and still love them. Not by excusing behavior, but by exhaling a love that refuses to dehumanize.

With every breath, remember: Jesus understands.

PAUSE AND PONDER

Who is hard for you to love right now? Bring their name before God.

____

____

Write a one-sentence prayer asking God to soften your heart toward the person listed above.

____

____

____

* See Matthew 5:45.

MARCH 28

Look to the winged ones who soar on the wind. Do they plant seeds and gather the harvest into a storehouse? No! But your Father from above gives them plenty to eat. Do you not know he cares even more for you?

MATTHEW 6:26 (FNV)

INHALE: I receive Your love;
EXHALE: I release my worry.

"Did you hear that?" My husband tilts his head, squinting into the trees. "Yeah, that's what I thought," he says with a nod. "A white-breasted nuthatch!"

I don't know how it happened, but somehow my husband has gotten *really* into birding. He asked for a pair of binoculars for his birthday and even keeps a little notebook to track his finds. No walk around the block is safe from his eagle eye.

I'm not particularly fond of birds, but I do love how Jesus uses something so ordinary and everyday to remind us of God's care. In the Sermon on the Mount, He points to these winged ones, assuring us that if God cares for them, how much more does God care for us?

It's easy for me to default into worry, to clutch tightly to my fears about tomorrow. But when I notice the sparrows or cardinals flitting through the trees, I remember Jesus' words: If God cares for them, God will care for me too.

As you breathe through today's prayer, ask God to help you trust that the One who cares for the tiniest sparrow cares for you. As you inhale, receive God's love. As you exhale, release your worry.

What are you carrying today that isn't yours to hold?

PRACTICING THE WAY

- **Step outside (or look out a window):** Notice the sky and the trees, and listen for birdsong or the rustle of wings.
- **Plant your feet:** Stand tall, or if seated, press your feet into the floor. Feel yourself grounded and steady.
- **Breathe in slowly:** Name the weight you're carrying today. Pay attention to your body—are your shoulders tight, is your jaw clenched, are your hands gripping?
- **Exhale and release:** Let go of what you're holding and surrender it to God's care. You might open your hands or lift your arms as you breathe out.
- **Keep breathing:** If God feeds the sparrows and watches over the smallest bird, how much more does God care for you? Rest in the truth that you are held.

MARCH 29

As your days are, so will your strength, your rest and security be.

DEUTERONOMY 33:25 (AMP)

INHALE: All that I have

EXHALE: Is a gift from you.

When I was pregnant with my second son, I kept a list of baby names that was a mile long. Our firstborn was Joseph, and I wanted something that complemented it. One Old Testament name stood out: Asher.

Before Moses died, he blessed Asher's tribe with words of strength and protection: "Your gates will be iron and bronze, and your strength will equal your days."* The imagery points to resilience—iron and bronze strong enough to withstand trials—and to God's daily faithfulness: As long as there are days, God will supply the strength to meet them.

Moses' blessing served as a reminder that God's presence would meet Asher's descendants in every season. When we bless each other, we're not trying to change or control outcomes, but we're speaking God's truth over one another—naming God's care and reminding each other that God's presence goes before us and is with us.

Blessings remind us of what's real when the world shouts otherwise. To bless a child, a friend, or even yourself is to whisper: "God is with you. God is faithful. God will not leave you."

Your days may feel overwhelming. The world may feel uncertain. But today's Scripture assures us: As your days are, so shall your strength be.

Who might need you to speak a blessing over them today?

RHYTHM OF BREATH

I am learning
How to breathe
Or rather
How to be.
How to trust
The One
Who gives
Each breath.

* Deuteronomy 33:24-25, NIV.

MARCH 30

What marvelous love the Father has extended to us! Just look at it—we're called children of God! That's who we really are.

1 JOHN 3:1 (MSG)

INHALE: Help me remember
EXHALE: Who I really am.

"The dramatic one." "The athletic one." "The artistic one." "The shy one." Too often, we're labeled from an early age. Those categories can follow us into adulthood, shaping how we see ourselves (and others) today.

There's nothing wrong with gathering with like-minded people or carrying certain roles. Many aspects contribute to the fullness of who we are. But when labels define us more than anything else, we risk losing sight of our truest identity: *children of God.* Nothing else defines us more fully. Not our backgrounds or bloodlines. Not our politics or preferences.

God looks at the whole of who we are and, out of an overflow of the purest love, calls us His own. The world may wear down our sense of worth. We may chase identity in our productivity, performance, or perfectionism. But when we fixate on labels, we miss the bigger, more beautiful reality: that we're named and known by the One who holds the galaxy.

God's love is not abstract. It's not conditional either. We are loved not merely the way a teacher or coach might love us. No, we are given this description: We are loved the way a loving parent delights in their child.

Maybe that imagery feels tender to you—or maybe your relationship with your parents is complicated. Not every parent is kind, loving, nurturing, or even safe. But when we look to Scripture, we find something radical: The marvelous love of our Creator is poured out on us so fully that no role or reputation could ever override it.

Through Christ, this marvelous love defines who you really are. No label, no wound, no achievement defines you more than this.

What label have you carried that God might be inviting you to set down? As you breathe and pray today, remember that being a beloved child of God is the truest thing about you.

PAUSE AND PONDER

Today, remember you are a beloved child of God. In light of that, how will you speak to yourself—and to others—differently?

MARCH 31

He feels the pain of the poor and helpless and sets them free.

PSALM 72:13 (FNV)

INHALE: Help me remember
EXHALE: Your kindness, O God.

It's easy to look around at the sorrow and suffering in this world and wonder where God is. Sometimes I worry that if I ask questions like "Does God really care?" or "Why isn't God intervening?" then I'm doing something wrong.

You don't need to be a scholar or a theologian to understand that the overall story of Scripture is a love story. It's a story of a God who moves toward the hurting, who cares for the downtrodden, who is both kind and just, mighty and merciful.

As we read a few days ago, the rain falls on the just and the unjust.* But we also see—again and again—that God's heart has a place for the down-and-out. Life is a mystery that humanity has sought to unravel across millennia, but our best efforts can't encompass the fullness of who God is or the vastness of a love that extends across the cosmos.

How can it be that we have a God who intricately shapes our DNA and forms entire galaxies? How can it be that we have a God who cares about the health of our souls and feeds the hungry?

Our finite minds cannot fathom the infinite.

When I am overwhelmed by the barrage of distress in the headlines, when I long to fix it and cry out for God to intervene, I remember. I remember God's loving-kindness toward the poor. I remember that the Spirit is our Helper.

In our beautiful yet broken humanity, we often move toward hurt and harm instead of the healing touch of the One who sees. The One who cares. The One who knows. The One who loves.

When headlines break your heart and you long to see restoration and renewal here on earth, remember that our God of mercy and compassion moves toward those who weep, for theirs is the Kingdom of Heaven.

BORROW THIS PRAYER

God, the ache of the world
Feels so big.
And I am so small.
My words
And my actions
Seem like pebbles in the ocean.
Help me do the good
That is mine to do,
Working alongside You
In all I say,
In all I do,
In all I am.
May the words that I speak
And the work of my hands
Echo the beat of Your heart.
Amen.

---

* See Matthew 5:45.

APRIL 1

The LORD God formed the man from the dust of the ground, and breathed into his nostrils the breath of life; and the man became a living being.

GENESIS 2:7 (NRSV)

INHALE: Breathe life
EXHALE: Into me.

I spent my teenage summers lifeguarding at the local water park. But before I could wear the cool blue suit and carry a whistle, I had to pass lifeguard training. To learn CPR, we took turns lying on the ground while others pretended to save us. When it was my turn, my cheeks grew hot and my palms sweaty as classmates leaned over me, checking for breath.

It felt so, well, intimate.

Genesis tells us that God formed humanity from dust and breathed life into us. Unlike other creation stories, the Christian narrative is uniquely personal, introducing us to a God who draws close, bending down and choosing intimacy over distance. God is not only our Creator but also the One who sustains us with every breath we take. This breath isn't just physical—it embodies spiritual life as well, awakening our entire being.

In Hebrew, the word for "living being" is *nephesh,* which is often translated as "soul."[85] From the very beginning, God intentionally and intricately breathed life into the *whole* person: body, mind, spirit—all alive in God's image.

To be human is to be made for relationship with God, entrusted with the responsibility of caring for one another and the earth.

Maybe you're distracted today. Maybe you're feeling discouraged or depleted. Maybe you feel like you're just going through the motions. Let today's breath prayer bring new hope. Take a slow, deep inhale and remember: Nothing God does is accidental. God has breathed life into *you,* here and now, for a reason.

As you exhale, reflect: What is yours to do today? How might you breathe life into others?

LET IT LINGER

You've been formed in love. As sure as the breath in your lungs, your soul has been stirred by the One who made you and sustains you, who longs to know you and be known by you.

APRIL 2

The Lord is near.

PHILIPPIANS 4:5 (NIV)

INHALE: You are nearer
EXHALE: Than my next breath.

It's easy for me to look at the fractures in our world and fall into despair. To wonder where God is in all the pain and heartbreak. To question if God has stepped back, leaving us alone with the messes we've made.

But the truth is, as poet Drew Jackson writes in his poem "Contemplation,"

The world is on fire.
As it always is.
The world is still beautiful.
As it always is.[86]

Paul's world was on fire too. But in the midst of conflict, he offered this assurance: "God is near." Near as in *presence*—Christ with us here and now—and near as in *hope*—Christ will return.

That closeness comes with an invitation. Just before Paul says, "The Lord is near," he writes, "Let your gentleness be evident to all."* Other translations say "graciousness," "reasonableness," or "considerate spirit." However we phrase it, the point is clear: God's people are to be known by our love.

In a world quick to lash out, we're called to extend grace. To embody peace when cynicism seems easier. To meet hostility with humility. To choose mercy over retaliation.

The world has always been on fire. But because the Living Water is within us,† we can show up with hope. God's nearness fills us, sustains us, and allows our presence (even in small, ordinary ways) to whisper peace in a warring world.

Take a breath. As you inhale, notice God's nearness. As you exhale, ask how you might transform the world in love.

SACRED ECHOES

We cannot attain the presence of God because we're already totally in the presence of God. What's absent is awareness. Little do we realize that God is maintaining us in existence with every breath we take. As we take another it means that God is choosing us now and now and now.[87]

Richard Rohr

* Philippians 4:5, NLT.
† See John 7:37-39.

APRIL 3

Christ will make his home in your hearts as you trust in him. Your roots will grow down into God's love and keep you strong.

EPHESIANS 3:17 (NLT)

INHALE: I find my strength
EXHALE: When I'm rooted in love.

In the spring, the trees that line my neighborhood's historic streets come alive. Towering oaks and maples stretch toward the clouds, their new leaves unfurling and bringing color back to our world. The trees' roots reach deep, holding them steady over a century of storms, bearing witness to generations that have come and gone.

Not long ago, neighbors planted some new saplings among the old giants. The tiny trees need stakes to stay upright and frequent watering to help them grow strong. In time, their roots will deepen, and they'll be ready to withstand the elements.

For many of us, "being strong" has meant holding it all together without space to feel or ask for help. That kind of strength may get us through a hard moment, but it won't sustain us for long. Paul reminds us that true strength is found not in self-protection but in being rooted in Christ's love.

Even our lungs carry the reminder to stay rooted. Our airways branch like trees: The trachea is the trunk, branching out into smaller and smaller shoots until, at the edges, alveoli open like leaves. Through them, oxygen enters and carbon dioxide exits.[88]

You were never made to survive on your own. God formed you in love, sustains you in love, and makes you strong in love.

Take a deep breath. Feel the air move through your own "branches."

What might shift today if you let your strength come not from holding it all in but from opening yourself to Christ's love flowing through you?

PAUSE AND PONDER

How do you define strength? Brainstorm words on the branches.

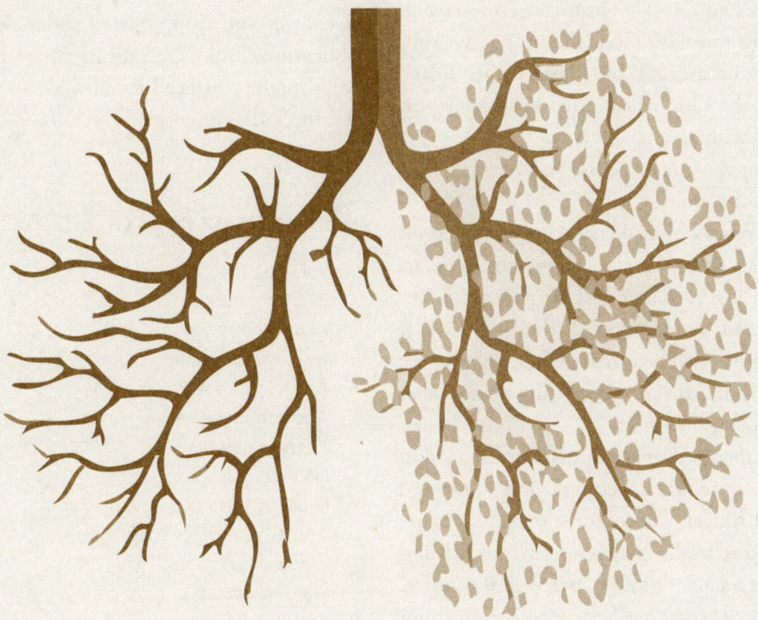

APRIL 4

He gives me rest in fields of tender sweetgrass and guides me near quiet and peaceful waters.

PSALM 23:2 (FNV)

INHALE: You give
EXHALE: Me rest.

Even when life feels crowded and rushed, God offers us soul rest—we just have to receive it. When we rest with God, the protective walls we've built around our hearts can soften because the One who knows each heartbeat holds us with care.

When was the last time you felt rest deep within your soul?

The First Nations Version is an Indigenous Bible translation by storytellers and scholars representing various tribal heritages. Its language slows me down in all the best ways. It weaves truth and beauty together, helping me hear Scripture afresh and inviting me to linger instead of rushing past.

In Psalm 23, David's words become a vision of "fields of tender sweetgrass" and "quiet and peaceful waters." Sweetgrass, sacred in many Indigenous traditions, is often braided and shared as a sign of healing, peace, and courage. In her book *Braiding Sweetgrass*, Potawatomi botanist Dr. Robin Wall Kimmerer notes that sweetgrass flourishes in well-watered meadows and even along disturbed edges.[89]

God's rest meets us in our own worn and weary places.

You don't have to do anything elaborate to simply be with our restorative God. God doesn't promise that the paths we walk with Christ will be easy. But as David goes on to say in verse 4, "Even if my path takes me through the canyon of darkness and gloom, I will fear no evil, for you are close by my side, keeping my eyes straight, my path safe."

Take a breath. Imagine yourself in that sweetgrass meadow beside still waters. Wherever you find yourself today, whatever obligations and expectations you're holding, what might you need to set aside so you can rest in God's presence?

RHYTHM OF BREATH

You lead me
By still waters
And also
By hospital vending machines
And office water coolers
And school hallways.
There is nowhere
I will go
In all my todays
And all my tomorrows
Where You are not.
You are within.
You are beyond
The brick and mortar
Of life.
You bring heaven
To the corners of the earth,
To the passenger seats,
To the desk chairs
And worn couches.
Wherever I go,
You are.

APRIL 5

Then the LORD took Abram outside and said to him, "Look up into the sky and count the stars if you can. That's how many descendants you will have!"

GENESIS 15:5 (NLT)

INHALE: Your promises
EXHALE: Light the way.

When our eldest son was four years old, my husband volunteered with our church's preschool program. He realized that the kids weren't connecting with the old songs, so he wrote one of his own. With a guitar in hand and God's promise to Abram in mind, he sang, "God keeps his promises. And he never, *ever, ever, ever* breaks them!"

The kids loved it. Our son (who was then in speech therapy) sang the words loud and clear. That simple, impromptu song about God's promises became a memory we still carry today. My son may be in high school now, but he can still belt out the chorus.

God keeps his promises.

The angel told Mary the same truth: "Nothing is impossible with respect to any of God's promises."* God promised us a living hope, and in Christ, we have it.

I think of that promise sometimes when I'm outside with our dogs at night. I'll glance up, and the sky sparkles with countless stars—just as Abram saw. The vastness takes my breath away. And I remember: God keeps his promises. Always.

If you can, head outside tonight. Look at the sky. Take a breath and let the stars remind you: God's promises still shine. They can't be broken. No matter what.

RHYTHM OF BREATH

The One who sets
The stars in motion
And breathes life
Into the dust
Is holding us all
In an invisible web
Of grace.

* Luke 1:37, ISV.

APRIL 6

You will keep in perfect peace all who trust in you, all whose thoughts are fixed on you!

ISAIAH 26:3 (NLT)

INHALE: You keep me
EXHALE: In perfect peace.

When we pray alongside our breath, we practice noticing God in the ins and outs of our everyday lives. Each inhale and exhale relaxes our grip on control, reminding us that every breath is a gift—and that we can focus our thoughts not on what's unraveling but on the One who holds us steady.

But when my phone is pinging from ten different apps, I find myself fixing my thoughts on everything *but* God. *What's for dinner? What political crisis is exploding now? What video did a friend just send?* My thoughts gather into a giant tumbleweed of anxiety. My brain isn't always a peaceful place.

The prophet Isaiah spoke into the chaos of his time. The kingdom of Judah was constantly threatened by surrounding nations, caught in political turmoil and spiritual crisis. Yet Isaiah reminded them that God was the true foundation of peace. The Hebrew term for "perfect peace" is *shalom shalom*—peace upon peace.[90] The peace we find in God isn't a passing calm or a momentary pause but a deep, whole peace that covers us, mind, body, and soul.

That promise didn't end with Isaiah. It rippled forward, finding its fullest expression in Jesus. Centuries later, God sent Christ to embody this perfect peace and extend it to all people. "Peace I leave with you," Jesus said, "my peace I give you."*

Take a slow breath. Ask God to calm the tumbleweeds in your mind. What would it look like to focus your thoughts on God today, even in the middle of the noise?

PAUSE AND PONDER

What is making up your tumbleweed of anxiety? Write down a few directions your thoughts are being pulled in today.

____

____

____

Fill in the blank: When my mind races with ______________________________, I will fix my thoughts on God.

* John 14:27, NLT.

APRIL 7

Didn't our hearts burn within us as he talked with us on the road and explained the Scriptures to us?

LUKE 24:32 (NLT)

INHALE: Open my heart
EXHALE: To Your presence.

My family loves gathering around a bonfire among the crackling logs and warm glow. My husband has been teaching our sons how to build a fire. "If it starts but doesn't keep going," he says, "blow gently on the glowing pieces." The breath feeds the flame until it sparks back to life.

On the road to Emmaus, two followers of Jesus walked with heavy hearts. Their words dripped with disappointment as they processed the recent events: Jesus' death and the mystery of His missing body. Then a stranger joined them. They didn't recognize Him, but He walked beside them, listening as they poured out their lament. "We had hoped . . ." they told Him.* They'd believed Jesus was the One who would redeem Israel, but now He was gone. Their hope felt foolish.

The stranger reminded them of God's story—that suffering was not the end, that redemption was still unfolding. With each step, He unraveled truths from Scripture. Captivated, the two invited Him to stay and share a meal. At the table, He broke bread, blessed it, and gave it to them. In that moment, it dawned on them—it was Jesus! And then, in a split second, He vanished.

Stunned, they turned to one another: "Didn't our hearts burn within us as he talked?" Jesus transformed the cold embers of their hearts into a rekindled flame. Jesus had breathed hope back into what they thought was lost.

Like those followers of Jesus, we may not always notice Jesus walking with us. But Christ comes alongside us in our confusion and grief, gently breathing onto the embers of our hearts until they burn again with hope.

Where do you need Jesus to rekindle your hope today?

PRACTICING THE WAY

Light a candle. As you sit in its glow, say today's breath prayer. Remember: Christ is near, even when you don't realize it. As the flame steadies, imagine Jesus breathing on the embers of your heart, rekindling hope.

* Luke 24:21, NLT.

APRIL 8

Blessed are those who trust in the LORD, whose trust is the LORD. They shall be like a tree planted by water, sending out its roots by the stream.

JEREMIAH 17:7-8 (NRSV)

INHALE: My roots are in You;
EXHALE: My trust is in You.

When Jeremiah wrote today's verses, the world felt unsteady.

The people of Judah were tempted to lean on political alliances, idolizing power and prestige instead of trusting God. So Jeremiah gave them a picture to hold on to: a tree planted by water, with roots stretching toward the stream.

In a dry land where water was precious, a tree by water would thrive—its leaves green even in heat, its fruit healthy even in drought. Trees rooted near water grow stronger and more resilient.

This is what trusting God is like. When our roots are deep in God's presence, we're not easily swayed by the whispers that our worth lies in what we have or who we know. Centuries later, Jesus echoed this image, calling Himself the giver of living water, reminding us that it's God alone who sustains us.*

This spring, as fresh leaves unfurl, let the trees remind you that life with God at the center is not a colorless survival but a vibrant flourishing. God brings new life, splashing Technicolor across our weary world.

When headlines dishearten you, when turmoil tempts you to despair, pause and breathe. Imagine your roots reaching deep into the stream of God's love.

Where do you need God to steady and nourish you today?

LET IT LINGER

A life grounded in God's love bears fruit that nourishes the world. Just like trees release oxygen to help clean our air, lives rooted in God help goodness grow all around us. Peace begets peace. Faithfulness begets faithfulness. God's life in us becomes hope for a hungry world.

* See John 7:37-39.

APRIL 9

Don't tolerate people who try to run your life, ordering you to bow and scrape. . . . They're completely out of touch with the source of life, Christ, who puts us together in one piece, whose very breath and blood flow through us. He is the Head and we are the body. We can grow up healthy in God only as he nourishes us.

COLOSSIANS 2:18-19 (MSG)

INHALE: Your breath
EXHALE: Nourishes me.

When my kids tattle on each other, they like to add their opinions about why exactly their sibling was in the wrong, adding some extra color to the story.

"We don't need your commentary" is usually my response.

Talking heads and hot takes flood our feeds. Opinions come at us loud and fast. *You care too much. You care too little. This person is terrible. This person is perfect.* It's easy to let those voices loop endlessly in our minds.

Paul's message to the Colossians cuts through the noise: Don't let others define your worth or your faith. Don't lose touch with the Source of life. The very breath and blood of Christ flow through us. He's the One who nourishes us, holding us together and empowering us to grow.

Slow down for a moment. Feel your breath moving in and out. The breath of Christ flows through you. *That* is your source of life—not the demands, opinions, or judgments of others.

With Christ at the center, step into your day free to let love flow through you into a world gasping for breath.

BREATHE THIS IN

With every breath, your body keeps blood moving. Negative pressure pulls blood into your heart when you inhale. The blood is pushed back out to your lungs and body when you exhale, ebbing and then flowing like the tide.[91] The breath of Christ sustains life at every moment.

APRIL 10

I am leaving you with a gift—peace of mind and heart. And the peace I give is a gift the world cannot give.

JOHN 14:27 (NLT)

INHALE: Help me receive
EXHALE: The gift of Your peace.

If you've flown on an airplane, you've likely heard the safety spiel: "Put on your oxygen mask before helping someone else." It's become a bit of a cliché now, repeated in countless self-help books and inspirational keynotes. But it's a popular saying for a reason.

You can't help others breathe if you're gasping for air yourself.

In turbulent times, I'm reminded how much I need to draw near to Christ, to breathe in the presence of God before I can breathe peace into my corner of the world.

We seek peace for ourselves in many ways—through reading, exercise, volunteering, even naps. These can help, but they'll never sustain us in the long run. True peace isn't something we create or earn. True peace is a gift. And it's a gift the world can never give.

On the night before His death, Jesus promised His disciples a peace that would endure through every bit of fear and loss. The promise stands for us too. When we open our hearts and minds to the Spirit, a peace that passes understanding settles our souls. The peace of the Spirit flows through us like breath, restoring our clarity and renewing our strength.

Just as oxygen on an airplane gives us the ability to help someone who needs it, Christ's peace gives us what we need to be peacemakers in a world bent on war.

As you pray today's breath prayer, remember: Christ's peace is already yours. Breathe it in—and then breathe it out for the sake of the world.

BORROW THIS PRAYER

You've been with me all along.
All those tears, all those hopes,
All those late-night wonderings—
You were with me then,
You are with me now.

Your mercies never fail.
Your compassion never falters.
Though I don't know
Where You are right now,
Help me believe
That You, O God,
Will never leave me.
That You are closer
Than my every breath.
Amen.

APRIL 11

Now we also may live new lives.

ROMANS 6:4 (NLT)

INHALE: In every breath,
EXHALE: I am made new.

No matter where you've been or where you're going, with each breath you take, God is inviting you into a new story. As long as you have breath in your lungs, God is not done working within you or alongside you.

Transformation is the slow work of the heart.

When we inhale, our heart rate increases. When we exhale, it slows. Each breath we take is connected to the rhythm of our heartbeats. When this rhythm is balanced, we're more regulated, more able to respond wisely to frustration and disappointment, more able to calmly discern what's happening when we feel left out or unseen.[92]

In Christ, we're drawn into a rhythm of renewal. With each breath, we're restored, reflecting resurrection not just in what we do or say but at the heart of who we are.

With each breath, God reauthors us in resurrection hope—a hope that changes us from the inside out.

Just as death could not hold Christ, we're invited to live new lives. We have a future hope, yes, but also a right-now kind of hope that breaks into the mess of our ordinary days.

Maybe you feel like you're just trying to make it through the day. Maybe you feel like you have no breathing room in your life to figure out what you believe. Maybe you have more questions than answers, more doubt than faith. No matter how chaotic life feels or how flawed you think you are, as sure as you have breath in your lungs, God is offering, over and over again, the chance to begin anew.

Jesus, in a cosmic reordering, has created a new story for you—and He is still writing it today. Right here, right now. Place your hand on your heart. As you breathe, ask God to help you trust that your story isn't over.

BREATHE THIS IN

The average person takes about around twenty thousand breaths every day. Every one of those breaths is a chance to begin again—an invitation to receive God's renewing love.

APRIL 12

What happens when we live God's way? He brings gifts into our lives . . . things like affection for others, exuberance about life, serenity.

GALATIANS 5:22 (MSG)

INHALE: Help me live

EXHALE: Your way, O God.

We live in a moment when people with large platforms often claim the name "Christian," but their actions look less like Jesus and more like greed, rage, impatience, and cruelty.

Jesus told us we'd recognize a tree by its fruit*—and that's true of public leaders *and* all of us.

Following the way of Christ doesn't make us perfect. But "if we follow the guidance of the Spirit, our lives will bear good spiritual fruit. The Spirit will grow in us the fruit of love and joy, peace and patience, kindness and goodness, faithful hearts, gentle ways, and self-control."† This isn't something that happens overnight. Fruit trees grow slowly, season after season.

What voices are you most influenced by (online, in your community, politically)? What kind of fruit do their words and actions produce?

When we live God's way, we become more like Christ.

When we insist on our own way, our lives shrink around our egos. *The Message* says that living God's way grows "a willingness to stick with things, a sense of compassion in the heart, and a conviction that a basic holiness permeates things and people."‡ When we open our hearts so the Spirit can work inside us, "we find ourselves involved in loyal commitments, not needing to force our way in life, able to marshal and direct our energies wisely."§

This is the fruit that lasts. This is the evidence of a life rooted in God.

PAUSE AND PONDER

Which of the Spirit's fruit do you notice growing most naturally in you right now?

Which feels hardest to embody in this season?

* See Matthew 7:16.

† Galatians 5:22-23, FNV.

‡ Galatians 5:23, MSG.

§ Galatians 5:23, MSG.

APRIL 13

Christ himself has brought peace to us.

EPHESIANS 2:14 (NLT)

INHALE: Tear down
EXHALE: The walls of my heart.

When my kids were younger, I loved finding secondhand treasures to keep them busy. One day at an estate sale, I scored a giant tote bursting with large, colorful cardboard bricks. They were an immediate hit with my kids, who built towers, forts, and whole living-room kingdoms. After an epic brotherly dispute, the boys even built a wall in an attempt to split their bedroom in half. They swore it would stand forever—until a dog plowed through and they reconciled.

On a broader scale, we're a people divided. While unity in diversity is possible, too often we weaponize our differences, building walls instead of bridges. When I was catching up on the news one day, my first grader heard a politician's chant to "build that wall!" My son had just learned in Sunday school how Jesus breaks down barriers, and he was confused about why people would cheer for bigger walls to divide us.

When Paul wrote to the church in Ephesus, he was speaking into a similar reality. There were significant cultural and religious differences that divided Jews and Gentiles, but Paul proclaimed that Jesus made "them into one new people,"* breaking down the barriers between them.

Christ reconciles us to God and to one another. Jesus doesn't just bring peace but *is* the fullest embodiment of peace. In Christ, all of us are invited into a peace that is more than the absence of conflict; it is the restoration of relationship.[93]

My kids are older now, but sometimes the old cardboard bricks reappear, this time for laser-tag obstacles. Gone are the days of petty walls. With Jesus as our peace, we're invited to destroy hostility and celebrate diversity. We're called to live alongside one another, uniting despite our differences and reflecting Christ's peace to a watching world.

As you borrow today's breath prayer, ask the Prince of Peace to show you where to tear down the walls in your life.

SACRED ECHOES

For Jesus, peace seems to have meant not the absence of struggle, but the presence of love.[94]

Frederick Buechner

* Ephesians 2:14, FNV.

APRIL 14

Good fruit grows along this path as you walk in a sacred manner on the road that leads to the life of the world to come that never fades away, full of beauty and harmony.

ROMANS 6:22 (FNV)

INHALE: You meet me here;
EXHALE: I do not go alone.

As you journey the hills and valleys of life, you don't go alone. In Christ, you're set free from the way of self and invited into a new way—one that bears "good fruit."

God meets you on the path and walks alongside you, shaping your inner life so you can breathe out goodness into the world.

We have a hope that's not just for someday but for right now, right here in the middle of tax season and grocery runs and getting to that meeting on time. Paul often uses "fruit" to describe the Spirit inside us, who shows up in our words, choices, and relationships.

When we're in step with the Holy Spirit, patience grows where we once rushed, gentleness blooms where we once snapped, and grace flows where we once withheld.

Spring's rains and blooms echo this reality: God brings life out of hidden roots. The way of Jesus is not just a path but a *posture*—a way of becoming. Left to only ourselves, it's easy to default to paths that only lead to hurt or harm. With the Spirit, we're free to go another way—into fields of freedom, into the fullness of God.

Take a deep breath through your nose. Hold for five seconds and then slowly exhale through your mouth. Remember that God meets you along the path that never fades away, and He goes with you today.

PAUSE AND PONDER

As you picture yourself journeying with Christ, what does the path look like right now? Smooth, rocky, uphill, full of twists and turns?

Which part of your daily routine feels most like "the way of self"? How might you invite the Spirit to show you a new way?

APRIL 15

His Holy Spirit, moving and breathing in you,
is the most intimate part of your life.

EPHESIANS 4:30 (MSG)

INHALE: Spirit of God,
EXHALE: Breathe life into me.

God gives us the very breath we're breathing right now.

In the New Testament, the Greek word for "breath" (*pneuma*) also refers to "wind" and "spirit."[95] With every breath, the Spirit moves in you, shaping you into who you were meant to be all along. With every breath, you are becoming.

Paul urges us not to take the Spirit for granted. It's easy to take our breath for granted too. We don't have to think about it—we've been formed in such a way that our bodies just do it for us. But every breath is a gift of God's design and presence. In Christ, God's Spirit fills every part of you. God knows you better than you know yourself. God is not an abstract being but a Spirit who moves within us and gives us life.

Science echoes this mystery. Researcher James Nestor says that breathing is more than a physical reflex. The tens of billions of molecules you draw in with each breath reach nearly every organ in your body, influencing almost every part of you—your heart rate, your digestion, and even your mood.[96]

When we pray with our breath, we remember the One who fills our lungs, who created us intricately and knows us intimately. It helps us resist the temptation to take God for granted.

As you breathe today, imagine God's breath filling you and transforming you. Take a slow inhale. Pause. Slowly exhale. Allow the Spirit to quiet your heart and bring you peace.

BREATHE THIS IN

Deep, prayerful breaths do more than fill your lungs. Research shows that slowing your inhale and extending your exhale lowers your heartbeat and brings your body a sense of calm.[97] With every breath, your body makes space for God's peace.

APRIL 16

I'll refresh tired bodies; I'll restore tired souls.

JEREMIAH 31:25 (MSG)

INHALE: Refresh my tired body;
EXHALE: Restore my tired soul.

Not long ago, in the midst of an intense season of parenting and writing, my grandma passed away. What I wasn't expecting at the time but now know deep in my bones is how *exhausting* grief can be. It leaves you bone-tired and mentally and emotionally depleted.

Maybe right now you're grieving not the loss of a loved one but the death of a dream. Maybe you're mourning how life turned out, holding the broken pieces of a relationship or a career. Maybe you're saying goodbye to a past version of yourself or a future that isn't unfolding the way you imagined.

Or maybe you're simply burned out by the endless demands of daily life. Maybe your soul is tired from working so hard to be everything to everyone.

Despite how you might feel, rest is not for everyone else but you. God is for you. Rest is for you.

Grief and exhaustion are part of the human experience. From the very beginning, God has offered restoration for weary souls. In Jeremiah 31:25, God promises to "refresh tired bodies" and "restore tired souls." And that promise still stands.

When your soul is tired, when your heart is so heavy you can barely get out of bed, borrow this breath prayer. You don't have to do anything to earn rest and renewal—it's a gift freely given.

Where do you need God to refresh your spirit today? Be gentle with yourself, and rest in the love God has for you.

Take a slow breath. Inhale God's presence. Exhale your exhaustion. Let yourself be held.

BORROW THIS PRAYER

In the hard edges
And harsh corners,
You are a soft place to land—
A willow swaying in the breeze,
A wave rolling on the waters,
A wind rushing over the field,
A wing of a robin,
A wisp of a promise.

APRIL 17

In Christ you have been brought to fullness.

COLOSSIANS 2:10 (NIV)

INHALE: In You, O God,
EXHALE: I am made whole.

I'm not a huge fan of puzzles. I know many friends find them peaceful, but I find them frustrating. *Do I start with the corners? What kind of shape is this, anyway? Why are there so many shades of blue?* Inevitably, I end up declaring, "This box is missing a piece!" as I dramatically exit the room.

People aren't puzzles. We don't need to be pieced together, bit by bit. In Christ, there are no missing pieces. Nothing is left out. You're already whole and wholly loved.

"God has already completed us, brought us to fullness, and made us whole," Whitney R. Simpson writes in her book *With God in Every Breath*. "The Creator has made us whole. Scripture teaches us that *because of Christ, we have everything we need within us to be whole and complete*."[98]

You don't have to work your way into wholeness.

You don't have to be anything other than who you already are.

Because of the fullness of Christ, you are made whole. God looks at the entire picture of you—who you've been, who you are, who you'll be someday—and breathes a restorative breath over you, saying, *It is good.*

What might change in your day if you lived from that wholeness instead of striving for it? What is preventing you from living in wholeness today?

PRACTICING THE WAY

- **Gather your pieces.** On a sheet of paper or in a journal, list pieces of your life that come to mind—relationships, jobs, hobbies, personality traits, seasons of joy or pain, dreams, fears, regrets. Don't edit or overthink. Just write.
- **Pause and pray.** Pray over each item on your list. As you inhale, pray: *You see this part of me.* On your exhale, pray: *You're making me whole.*
- **Rest in wholeness.** When you've finished, close your eyes and sit with your hands open. Picture all those pieces held in God's hands, forming a whole *you*. Thank God for who you are in the fullness of Christ.

APRIL 18

Look, I am making everything new!
REVELATION 21:5 (NLT)

INHALE: You are making
EXHALE: All things new.

Life is not as it should be. Injustice abounds. People disappoint. Poverty, violence, and cruelty flood the headlines. Sometimes it's hard to hold on to hope.

When I'm overwhelmed by the world's suffering, when I'm discouraged by the way things are, I think about the new hope of spring. Yes, winter can be so dark, so discouraging. Outside, life looks bleak; trees stand bare and brittle in the wind. Yet year after year, spring returns—even when it feels like we're stuck in an endless winter. Even when it feels like spring will never come.

New life breaks forth in the spring. As sure as the weather warms and the sun lingers in the evening, as sure as bright green leaves appear and robins return, we can hold on to hope—stubbornly, like tulips pushing through hard earth—in the One who is making everything new.

Hope comes back. It always does.

Our restorative God doesn't leave things dead.

God renews. God restores. God redeems.

When you feel discouraged, like you're standing on the verge of despair, let the tangible promise of spring remind you of the transformative nature of God—the One who is making all things new, even you.

BORROW THIS PRAYER

Breath of life,
Restorer of lost causes,
Repair what feels too broken.
Renew within me
Hope when I cannot feel it,
Love when I cannot sense it,
Grace when I cannot grasp it.
You are doing a new thing
Even when I don't know it.
Amen.

APRIL 19

Chosen by God for this new life of love, dress in the wardrobe God picked out for you: compassion, kindness, humility, quiet strength, discipline.

COLOSSIANS 3:12 (MSG)

INHALE: Loving God,
EXHALE: Wrap me in Your way.

The world tells us to armor up. To protect ourselves and harden our hearts. But God calls us to something different. We are chosen for a life of love, and this love has a shape: compassion, kindness, humility, quiet strength, and discipline.

A life away from God pulls us toward fear and self-protection. It can feel like wearing a heavy coat that makes it harder to breathe.

But God invites us to shrug off that weight and wear something new:

- Compassion, not cynicism.
- Kindness, not indifference.
- Humility, not self-preservation.
- Strength, not striving.
- Discipline, not distraction.

When we try on these ways of Christlike living, it can feel awkward at first. Kindness in a cynical world? Humility when everyone is promoting themselves? Compassion when you're already running on empty? It may feel uncomfortable because your nervous system has been wired for defense. But these are the clothes Christ gives us, and they're tailored to fit the true you.

The storms of life tempt us to shield ourselves. But what if, instead, you wrapped yourself in the comfort of God's love? To be clothed in love is to mirror the One who is perfect love, the One who calls *you* beloved.

What would it look like to be gentle with yourself, the way God is gentle with you? How might this new life of love affect how you treat others?

Take a breath. As you exhale, let the heavy coat of self-protection fall away. Let yourself be wrapped in what is real and true.

PRACTICING THE WAY

In her book *Try Softer*, therapist Aundi Kolber invites us into what she calls a "loving-kindness" meditation:

1. **Sit comfortably, either in a chair or on the floor.** Notice your breathing and focus your attention on your heart. Visualize your breathing coming in and out of this area. Try picturing a beam of calming light shining directly into this area of your body.
2. **Now recite the following to yourself as you breathe from your heart's center:** "May I experience Christ's love. May I experience Christ's peace. . . . May I experience Christ's compassion."
3. **Now think of someone toward whom it is easy to direct feelings of loving-kindness.** Recite those words again, this time inserting the person's name: "May ____________________ experience . . ."
4. **Finally, as you feel comfortable, extend this blessing to all the earth and its inhabitants:** "May all creation experience . . ."[99]

APRIL 20

You will go out in joy and be led forth in peace; the mountains and hills will burst into song before you.

ISAIAH 55:12 (NIV)

INHALE: Joy is for all of us;
EXHALE: Lead us in peace.

I sometimes feel guilty about feeling joy. How can I delight in the way the sun filters through the clouds when wars rage around the world and families go hungry in my own community?

Is it okay to hold both the ache and the delight?

Isaiah's words break in like birdsong after winter: "You will go out in joy and be led forth in peace." When the prophet wrote these words, the Israelites were waiting for release from Babylonian exile.

The joy Isaiah spoke of wasn't shallow or naive. It was the joy of people who were anticipating liberation. The peace he foretold meant *shalom*—complete wholeness and harmony with God. In Christ, that promise reaches its fullness with a joy and peace rooted not in our circumstances but in God's covenantal love.

Following Jesus draws us toward the weary and overlooked. It propels us to work for the flourishing of our world. But when we *only* focus on the hard parts of humanity without also holding on to hope, we become drained. Relying on our own reserves and strength is depleting.

Care without replenishment leads to cynicism.

God offers a vision of joy and shalom big enough to hold our heartbreak *and* our heart songs. In Christ, we hold the hard and the holy, the laughter and the tears, the work and the rest. We neither avoid pain nor become consumed by it.

In her poem "Don't Hesitate," Mary Oliver famously wrote that "joy is not made to be a crumb"[100]—and she was right. Joy is God's limitless gift to sustain us in the work of love.

As you breathe through today's prayer, name one joy and one sorrow you're holding. As you exhale, release your prayers into the heart of God.

SACRED ECHOES

If you suddenly and unexpectedly feel joy, don't hesitate.[101]

Mary Oliver

APRIL 21

Steadfast love and faithfulness will meet;
righteousness and peace will kiss each other.

PSALM 85:10 (NRSV)

INHALE: I give my troubled heart
EXHALE: To You, O God.

"Do not let your hearts be troubled."* Jesus said this to His friends on the eve of His death, looking into their fearful faces, tending to their hearts even as His own was breaking.

Centuries earlier, the psalmist wrote of steadfast love meeting faithfulness, of righteousness kissing peace. Jesus embodies this vision. In Jesus, God's faithful love steps into the world. In Jesus, justice and peace meet in a person. Wholeness is no longer just a future hope but a present reality breaking in.

Righteousness here points to God's justice, to setting things right. *Peace* points to shalom—wholeness and well-being found in the fullness of God.[102] In Christ, righteousness and peace are intertwined. Even in our messy, ordinary lives, we're invited to live this way: practicing peace through just action and embodying justice with a peacemaking spirit.

We live in the tension of the now and not yet. We glimpse God's Kingdom while still experiencing violence, division, and heartbreak. "Do not let your hearts be troubled" isn't a command to toughen up but an invitation to breathe and rest your heart in the fullness of Christ.

When the horrors of the day are crushing, when cruelty seems louder than compassion, remember the One who gives every breath. He is justice and peace, holding your fractured heart together.

Take a slow, deep breath. Place your hand over your heart. Breathe in the promises of God's steadfast love. Picture righteousness and peace swirling inside you, making you whole. This is how Christ heals our hearts—and through us, our world.

PAUSE AND PONDER

What is one thing happening right now that is troubling your heart?

____

____

____

Write a one-sentence prayer asking for God's steadfast love, faithfulness, justice, and peace to surround that situation.

____

____

____

* John 14:1, NIV.

APRIL 22

EARTH DAY

The earth is the LORD's, and everything in it. The world and all its people belong to him. For he laid the earth's foundation on the seas and built it on the ocean depths.

PSALM 24:1-2 (NLT)

INHALE: Creator God,
EXHALE: Everything belongs to You.

Today, millions of people celebrate Earth Day, a reminder of our lifelong calling to care for the world that God so loves.* Our Creator breathed it all into being: the soil beneath our feet, the air in our lungs, the water that sustains us all.

From the beginning, humanity was invited to work and keep the garden—to tend creation, not exploit it.† When God transforms us from the inside out, we begin to move differently in the world. We start to see creation not as something to use up but as something to honor and nurture. No longer are we just serving ourselves, but we are working for the good of the whole, for the flourishing of the earth and everything in it. It's all God's. And we honor God when we honor His handiwork.

Almost half of the US population is exposed to unhealthy levels of air pollution, as reported by the American Lung Association.[103] Researchers estimate that around fifteen *billion* trees are cut down worldwide each year.[104]

Those numbers can feel overwhelming. But they also serve as a reminder that every small act of creation care matters, whether it's planting a tree, tending a garden, or walking instead of driving. Every day, we can do what we can to participate in *restoration* instead of *resignation*.

We're called to care for creation—not just today, but for all the days to come. To do what we can to cultivate goodness with the work of our hands. The earth is the Lord's, and everything in it. When you care for the earth, you're living your worship in real time, joining God's work of renewing all things.

PRACTICING THE WAY

If you're able, head outside today. Smell the fresh scent of an afternoon rain. Notice the flowers bursting forth. Listen for the birds trilling in the trees. Take a deep breath of fresh air. As you feel it flow through you, name an aspect of creation you're grateful for and one way you can tend it this week. Maybe this will look like picking up litter at a local park, planting a tree, or clearing brush from a neighbor's yard.

---

* See John 3:16.
† See Genesis 2:15.

APRIL 23

Live in a sacred way by walking the road of peace with all people.

HEBREWS 12:14 (FNV)

INHALE: With your help,

EXHALE: May I walk the road of peace.

The path of peace is narrow. And often misunderstood.

In our polarized world, we're told to pick a side, plant a flag, and stay there. Walking the road of peace with Jesus isn't just a "third way" between extremes but an entirely different existence. One that transcends division, breaks down barriers, and breathes a new way of being into our lives.

Embodying peace in a culture that runs on outrage isn't easy. The opinions and demands of others press in on us all the time. But every word you speak and every action you take carries the power to purify the air around you.

Living God's way doesn't mean we agree with everyone or stay silent on important issues. We can stand up for ourselves and others. We can work for justice and speak truth to power. In Christ's upside-down Kingdom, we're even called to love both the oppressed and the oppressor—seeking restoration without excusing harm. But whatever we do, we're called to act from a posture of peace, with God at the center.

Practicing the Way costs something. But we do not go alone.

As you pray, picture yourself stepping onto a quiet path, with Jesus by your side.

LET IT LINGER

Peace isn't passive. Walking the road of peace doesn't mean we appease others or take the path of least resistance. Choosing peace means actively moving toward reshaping the world in God's love.

APRIL 24

Don't worry about anything; instead, pray about everything. Tell God what you need, and thank him for all he has done.

PHILIPPIANS 4:6-7 (NLT)

INHALE: I give You my worries;
EXHALE: You give me Your peace.

God doesn't dismiss your worry.

I used to think that when Paul told the Philippians, "Don't worry about anything," he was being dismissive. As someone who has struggled with the inner noise of anxiety throughout my life, I've often been told to "just stop." When I was a child, my parents didn't know what to do with my catastrophizing, so they gave me a "worry rock" to rub when I felt anxious.

I now see Paul's words in a new light. Instead of dismissing our worries, he reminds us that God cares. That God listens to *everything* we share and holds our prayers with compassion and tenderness. Paul isn't downplaying or trivializing our anxieties but acknowledging that feeling anxious is just part of being human. Paul wrote his words while under arrest, facing an uncertain future. (Who *wouldn't* feel uneasy in that situation?) He wasn't minimizing our worries but pointing to a safe place to lay them down.

It's normal to worry. We're stressed because life is stressful. We're alarmed because alarming things happen. But we're not alone in our anxieties—in our concerns about today or our fears about tomorrow.*

God meets us in every *what-if* and holds our fears with compassion.

When I start to spiral into anxiety, prayer calms my soul. I tell God my worries and turn my breath into prayer. Then, as Paul encourages, I end my prayer with gratitude. This practice doesn't erase anxiety, but it soothes my nervous system and shifts my focus. (Science confirms that both intentional breathwork and practicing gratitude are good for our bodies!)[105]

Take a slow breath. Inhale for four counts as you pray the first part of the breath prayer. Exhale for six counts, releasing one worry you've been holding into God's hands. Let Christ's peace guard your heart and mind.

LET IT LINGER

When anxiety rises, small grounding actions help:

- Step outside to breathe fresh air.
- Drink a glass of cold water.
- Move your body—walk, stretch, run.
- Create art or write in a journal.
- Hug someone.
- Smell your favorite scent.

* Anxiety can be chronic and complex. If you're facing worry that won't go away, I encourage you to seek professional support. God can use various methods and people to help us break a cycle of anxiety.

APRIL 25

SAINT MARK'S DAY

Go into the world. Go everywhere and announce the Message of God's good news to one and all.

MARK 16:15 (MSG)

INHALE: Help me embody
EXHALE: Your love for all.

Today we remember Jesus' call to "go into all the world."* We aren't meant to live in bubbles with only those who look, think, and believe like us. We're invited into the wide, wild work God is already doing.

Our limited vocabulary can't capture God's goodness. Whether or not Saint Francis actually said "Preach the gospel at all times. Use words if necessary," the truth stands: Our lives can be living messages of God's love—no soapbox needed.

We can reflect Jesus in what we do, what we say, and who we are. God's transformational love is always on the move, with or without us. But God is gracious to invite us to join in.

I think of my husband at the grill, spatula in hand, as the smoke rises. He calls our son over to "help," even though it's messier and slower that way. He doesn't need assistance with flipping burgers, but he delights in including him and passing on the goodness. That's how God welcomes us into the work of Christ's love.

God writes love on our hearts. Living openheartedly, letting down our guard, and sharing our hearts with others feels vulnerable. But it's also where renewal and redemption happen, where another heart can catch a glimpse of the story God is writing in their own lives.

Where might God be inviting you to move beyond your usual circle to join in the wild, wonderful work of love?

BORROW THIS PRAYER

Replace the armor of my heart
With humility of the soul.
Give me bravery
To stay vulnerable.
Give me courage
To go forth
In love.
It's easier to stay guarded,
But the shields
And the masks
Guard us
From the beauty of loving
And being loved.
Amen.

* Mark 16:15, NIV.

APRIL 26

Let everything that has breath praise the LORD.

PSALM 150:6 (NIV)

INHALE: Let my every breath
EXHALE: Be an offering of love.

Praise is more than any worship song we could sing. (That's good news for those of us who can barely carry a tune!) Praise is the posture of our very lives.

As we have breath, we can exhale praise through the songs of our lives. We can offer up our bodies "as a living sacrifice"*—our ordinary, everyday lives as worship to God.

You praise God with your life when you

- **Bring a meal to someone.** "I was hungry, and you fed me" (Matthew 25:35).
- **Extend forgiveness.** "Make allowance for each other's faults, and forgive anyone who offends you" (Colossians 3:13).
- **Hold back a heated response.** "Understand this, my dear brothers and sisters: You must all be quick to listen, slow to speak, and slow to get angry" (James 1:19).
- **Sit with someone as they cry.** "Share each other's burdens, and in this way obey the law of Christ" (Galatians 6:2).
- **Refuse to ignore injustice.** "Learn to do good. Seek justice. Help the oppressed" (Isaiah 1:17).
- **Defend the vulnerable.** "Speak up for those who cannot speak for themselves; ensure justice for those being crushed" (Proverbs 31:8).
- **Welcome the stranger.** "I was a stranger, and you invited me into your home" (Matthew 25:35).
- **Donate to the food pantry.** "He gives . . . food to the hungry" (Psalm 146:7).†

God has given you breath in your lungs for a reason. Let your life be a psalm of praise. Which of these invitations might you live out this week?

BREATHE THIS IN

Lungs circulate roughly eleven thousand liters of air in and out daily.[106] Think about how many liters of mercy or justice we might circulate into the world if every follower of Jesus let their life be a psalm of praise!

* Romans 12:1, NIV.

† All verses in this list are taken from the New Living Translation.

APRIL 27

You're here to be light, bringing out the God-colors in the world.

MATTHEW 5:14 (MSG)

INHALE: Color my life
EXHALE: With Your brilliant love.

When my daughter was three, she spent nearly a month on a ventilator in an intensive care unit. It was agonizing. There was nothing I could do but sit by her hospital bed and pray. I could barely even muster that.

Our community supported us with visits and meals, and at some point, someone dropped off a coloring book and colored pencils. I left them untouched for days, along with the food I couldn't stomach. But one night, as the machine's beeps filled the room, I couldn't take the buzzing in my mind anymore. I picked up a pencil. As I filled in the tiny shapes with color, I realized I'd been holding my breath. I finally *exhaled.* The simple act of coloring became a quiet (and unexpected) form of prayer.

Professor Susan Forshey shares a similar experience from the seminary where she teaches. She created a Sabbath space, with the idea that students could go there to pray and rest. Initially, the art supplies she provided went unused, so she printed simple mandalas (geometric circles filled with patterns). Sure enough, everything changed. Coloring the mandalas became the students' favorite activity. Soon they started hanging their art on bulletin boards. Splashes of color covered the hallways.

"Some students prayed for people while they colored and then gave the finished mandala to the person with a note," Forshey writes. "Others simply let their brains breathe in color and shapes for a time, taking a break from words."[107]

Christians throughout history have used shape and color to connect with God. Celtic monks illustrated Scripture with intricate geometric designs.[108] Patterned circular rose windows were included in cathedrals like Notre-Dame, scattering light into dazzling colors.

When Jesus tells us to bring out "the God-colors in the world," He's inviting us to let God's light pass through us like sunbeams through stained glass.

As you breathe and pray, stay awake to the colors around you today.

PRACTICING THE WAY

Grab some pencils, crayons, or markers. Practice today's breath prayer as you color this mandala.

APRIL 28

A new heart I will give you, and a new spirit I will put within you.

EZEKIEL 36:26 (NRSV)

INHALE: Restore my heart;
EXHALE: Renew my spirit.

When we let go of the idea that prayer must be a beautiful string of words used to inform or impress God and instead approach prayer as a way to be fully *present* with God, the harsh edges around our hearts begin to soften. The armored walls we've built start to crack.

It's tempting to believe that spiritual growth depends on sheer willpower—that we can force ourselves into something new. But true transformation is a slow, steady work of the Spirit.

God isn't waiting for you to get everything right before offering renewal. God isn't waiting for perfect words or an ideal, quiet morning while the sun rises. Ezekiel records the sacred promise that it's *God alone* who will give you "a tender, responsive heart."*

You don't have to do anything for our restorative God to work in your heart. All you need is to be open to being with God. Allow all the armor of what you *think* you should do fall away. Bring yourself fully to the One who already knows your every ache and every delight.

Today, give yourself five minutes simply to be with God. Silence your phone. Sit with your feet flat on the floor. Notice the rhythm of your breath. When your mind wanders, use the word *restore* to prayerfully return to Christ at the center.

How did your heart respond to the One who restores?

SACRED ECHOES

Prayer is not designed to change God but to change us.[109]

Thomas Keating

---

* Ezekiel 36:26, NLT.

APRIL 29

We all stumble on the path in many ways. But if we could keep our words from hurting others, we would be mature human beings, able to aim our whole lives in the right direction.

JAMES 3:2 (FNV)

INHALE: May my words
EXHALE: Heal instead of harm.

As a child, I had *a lot* to say. My teachers wrote that I was a "pleasure to have in class" but also "quite chatty." For better or worse, I always had a quip to share.

Our words possess the power to heal or to harm.

Our minds are like banks, filled with words, and we should spend them wisely. James offers another image, comparing the tongue to a rudder steering a ship.*

Small words have the power to set an entire course.

None of us get it right all the time. Spiritual maturity takes time. There are countless moments I wish I had a vacuum to suck in the hurtful words I've spoken. Even though we can't take our words back, we can apologize when we get it wrong, using our words to repair and set things right.

With the Spirit's help, we can become slower to speak. And when we do share, we can remain open to God working within us so our words reflect a transformed heart.

The same Spirit who is breathing life into you can shape your speech and guide your direction. With an open heart and God's help, your words can direct others toward healing and wholeness rather than inflicting hurt or harm.

Even one Spirit-led sentence can reorient the course of a conversation. It costs us nothing to treat people with the kind of goodness that God lavishes upon us.

BORROW THIS PRAYER

Breathe in me
A gentle spirit
That propels me
To move toward
The ones who
You call beloved.

* See James 3:4.

APRIL 30

You make known to me the path of life; you will fill me with joy in your presence.

PSALM 16:11 (NIV)

INHALE: I'm not alone
EXHALE: On this path with You.

If you've had to be "the strong one," scanning for danger and caring for yourself because no one else did, that past vigilance doesn't just vanish in another life stage. It can live on in your nervous system, keeping you alert even when you're safe, whispering, *You're on your own.*

When people from your past didn't show up for you, it can be hard to believe that God is really with you and taking care of you *now.* It's terrible to feel so alone. If you weren't raised by kind and present parents, it can be confusing to hear that God cares for us as beloved children, that God is like a protective father or a nurturing mother.

People can hurt us and disappoint us in this life. They can inflict very real harm and hurt, and sometimes those deep wounds seem like they'll last forever.

Healing takes time. Trust takes time too.

But Dr. Curt Thompson writes that God works through the very networks of our minds and memories, healing and renewing them.[110] God doesn't shame your survival skills or bypass your story. Jesus enters it, bringing presence into places once marked by absence.

Throughout Scripture, we're reassured that God is with us on the path of life. God's presence is safe, and in the presence of God, you are secure. Christ goes before you, behind you, and beside you. You are never alone.

PRACTICING THE WAY

Try practicing today's breath prayer at a gentle pace of about six breaths per minute, inhaling for four to five seconds and then exhaling for five to six seconds. Notice how each breath feels in your body.

Dr. Bessel van der Kolk says, "Erasing awareness and cultivating denial are often essential to survival, but the price is that you lose track of who you are, of what you are feeling, and of what and whom you can trust."[111]

Use this moment to jot down (or simply hold in your heart) responses to these prompts:

- One thing that's true about me:
- What I'm feeling right now:
- Someone I can trust:

If today's topic brings up past trauma, please know you are not alone. Find someone to talk to at psychologytoday.com.

MAY 1

With your very own hands you formed me; now breathe your wisdom over me so I can understand you.

PSALM 119:73 (MSG)

INHALE: God who formed me,
EXHALE: Breathe wisdom over me.

God isn't asking you to be anything other than *in this present moment.*

You don't have to dwell on the past. You don't have to focus on the future. You only need to be *here*, awake to the presence of God breaking through among the dishes piling in the sink, the laundry still lingering in the dryer, the inbox that's overflowing.

"Christian mindfulness is about making time to turn our whole attention to God so that we can hear and abide in his voice above the chatter and stress of our lives," write therapists Regina Chow Trammel and John Trent.[112]

The One who formed you is with you now, breathing wisdom over you in the comings and goings of your days. The question is: Are you paying attention?

SACRED ECHOES

Instructions for living a life:

Pay attention.
Be astonished.
Tell about it.[113]

Mary Oliver

MAY 2

The law indeed was given through Moses;
grace and truth came through Jesus Christ.

JOHN 1:17 (NRSV)

INHALE: By Your grace,
EXHALE: I am free.

I wonder what we lose when we turn faith into a list of rules to be obeyed instead of an invitation to know and be known by God.

In Christ, we're free from a checklist of demands. Instead, we're transformed from the inside out. Our lives become an overflow of God's presence within us, spilling into our work, our homes, our relationships, and even what we buy and consume.

Still, a faith drenched in grace can feel scary. Our tidy to-do lists, complete with faith-related checkboxes, create the illusion of safety and control. In the Old Testament, the law was a gift—God's way of caring for Israel and setting God's people apart in covenant love. But Jesus fulfilled the law and opened a new way of life in the Spirit, breaking down our boxes of how we think things should be:

God born in a barn. A King riding a donkey. The Savior with nowhere to lay his head.

The grace of God gives breathing room for tired souls. Where do you most need that breathing room today? The Bible is not an instruction manual but an invitation to a new way of being. No matter what you've been told, grace is yours for the taking, right here in your everyday life.

God is not piling on rules but inviting you into an ongoing relationship.

Let go of that breath you've been holding.

PAUSE AND PONDER

Does faith feel constraining or free to you? Why might that be?

What messages have you received from others about what it looks like to live in Christ?

MAY 3

I yell out to my God, I yell with all my might,
I yell at the top of my lungs. He listens.

PSALM 77:1 (MSG)

INHALE: I release my anger
EXHALE: To the One who listens.

It's okay to be angry.

In fact, it's healthy to be able to name your anger and move through it.

Anger is not a feeling I struggle to access, especially when I see the vulnerable mistreated or justice ignored. God's ways are truth and peace, and when I don't see that lived out, my heart starts racing and my breathing becomes shallow. And as the Incredible Hulk says, "You wouldn't like me when I'm angry."

Sometimes my anger isn't so righteous. We all like to picture ourselves flipping over tables, like Jesus did with the money changers in the Temple. But sometimes I'm just heated that my kids keep leaving their snack wrappers on the floor, in the couch cushions, and dangerously close to the fireplace. Annoyance can easily veer into anger if I'm not paying attention.

If you've ever flown off the handle and without really knowing why, it might be because there are underlying triggers or anxieties you're holding. Flora Slosson Wuellner writes, "If we suspect that much of our 'righteous anger' is really a disguised desire to punish or a mask for our hurts and unexpressed needs, then we need (perhaps with the help of a counselor) to face our deep feelings in the presence of God's compassion and allow ourselves to be healed."[114]

Anger in itself is not destructive. (If we never feel anger, it's probably a cue that we're a bit out of touch with our feelings.[115]) It's what we *do* with our anger (Let it fester? Disguise it? Hand it back to God?) that can be either productive or problematic.

Take a deep breath for five counts. Hold it for five counts. Release it for five counts. As you breathe and pray, remember that the One who gives each breath is also the One who listens.

PRACTICING THE WAY

Noticing and naming our anger helps us move through it. Read these questions aloud.[116] As you do, pay attention to the ones that your body reacts to. Pick one or two to reflect on today.

- Is anger my typical response to difficult situations or circumstances?
- Am I directing my anger toward people who have nothing to do with why I'm upset?
- Do I say "You are . . ." instead of "I feel . . ." when I'm upset?
- How do I feel about myself after I express anger?
- Does anything creative or constructive come from my anger?
- Am I avoiding deeper wounds that might be behind my anger?
- Do I sometimes feel anger, or have I become an angry person?

When you're done reflecting, say today's breath prayer as you release your anger to the One who is making you whole.

MAY 4

Walk out into the fields and look at the wildflowers. They never primp or shop, but have you ever seen color and design quite like it?

MATTHEW 6:28 (MSG)

INHALE: I release my worry
EXHALE: To the Creator of all things.

My friend Debbie often asks her husband to pull over during road trips. Not because he's a bad driver or because she's getting carsick but because she's captivated by wildflowers blooming in roadside ditches. She jumps out and takes a picture, reminding herself of God's care in her everyday life.

God's fingerprints are all around us. We just need an open spirit to notice them.

When we're worried, Jesus encourages us to shift our focus, to redirect our gaze. He tells us to "look at the wildflowers." Jesus was pointing to God's provision and trustworthiness: "If God cares so wonderfully for wildflowers . . . , he will certainly care for you."*

This poetic invitation from Jesus actually points us to a clinically proven way to calm both our bodies and our racing minds. When we notice what's happening around us, engaging our senses of smell, touch, and sight, we're participating in *sensory grounding*. This signals safety to our brains, slowing our breath and heart rate. Looking at the wildflowers really *can* help us move out of the worry we hold.

When was the last time you breathed in the sweet scent of honeysuckle? When was the last time you watched a bee dance in the breeze or marveled at colorful bursts of wildflowers?

Wildflowers thrive because they're held in God's care, not because they're striving. We often think our worry is what keeps the world spinning, but we're not the ones who keep our hearts beating and our lungs breathing.

The breath of God holds us together.

The One who whispers life into every bloom, who splashes color even on roadside flowers, cares so much more for *you*. As you breathe and pray today, picture blowing on a dandelion and watching its wisps float free on the spring wind.

SACRED ECHOES

Come and rest,
Don't waste today
Being scared of tomorrow.

Jess Ray

Listen to "Lilies and Sparrows" by Jess Ray.

* Matthew 6:30, NLT.

MAY 5

He is the Rock, his works are perfect, and all his ways are just.
A faithful God who does no wrong, upright and just is he.

DEUTERONOMY 32:4 (NIV)

INHALE: You are shelter
EXHALE: From the storm.

Waves may rise and the ground may shift, but the One who gives each breath offers safety for your soul.

When the foundation beneath you feels like it's crumbling—when bad news breaks, when relationships fall apart, when life feels its most unstable—Christ offers refuge.

God's works are perfect. God's ways are just. Sometimes it feels like fault lines have fractured our culture so profoundly that the ground won't ever be solid again. But God's stability isn't dependent on our own. Empires rise and fall like crashing waves, but we can trust the One who endures, who remains the shelter in every storm.

Because of the love our unshakable God breathes upon the earth, we too are called to exhale the works and ways of Christ, our solid Rock. Jesus gave us an example to follow.* And we become more like Him by walking His ways with all that we say, all that we do, and all that we are.

How might the Spirit be uniquely transforming *you* into Christ's likeness, shaping your words, actions, and posture toward others so you can extend safety in life's storms?

As you breathe and pray today, feel your feet on the floor. Even when things seem unsteady, trust that you are supported by the Rock of Ages.

SACRED ECHOES

On Christ, the solid Rock, I stand:
all other ground is sinking sand.

"My Hope Is Built on Nothing Less" by Edward Mote

* See 1 Peter 2:21.

MAY 6

You know the saying, "We live in God; we move in God; we exist in God." And still another said, "We are indeed God's children."

ACTS 17:28 (THE VOICE)

INHALE: I live and move
EXHALE: And exist in You.

"You have her smile." I heard the refrain over and over at my grandmother's funeral. I was taken aback. I had never thought about it before, but as I looked at the pictures on display, snapshots of her life through the years, I saw it was true.

Even when we don't realize it, children carry traces of those who came before. In the same way, you reflect the image of God.* You are a child of God, bearing divine fingerprints on your very being. Your belovedness isn't something you earn. It's who you already are.

When you doubt yourself, when discouragement covers your heart and disappointment clouds your mind, pause and breathe. Remember that God calls you a beloved child. And because of that, you are empowered to live in God. To move in God. To exist in God.

Even when it doesn't feel like it. Even when you forget.

As you inhale today, picture God's life-giving breath filling you.

As you exhale, imagine letting go of your self-doubt.

Let every breath you take remind you that you are seen and cared for. That you are God's very own.

* See Genesis 1:27.

BORROW THIS PRAYER

God, sometimes the suffering
Feels like too much to hold.
I'm overwhelmed by the need
And by my lack.
It's so hard in this big world
To feel so small.
Help me remember,
Gracious and loving God,
That small things are held.
Amen.

MAY 7

I have told you these things, so that in me you may have peace. In this world you will have trouble. But take heart! I have overcome the world.

JOHN 16:33 (NIV)

INHALE: I will take heart;

EXHALE: You have overcome the world.

Your chest tightens. Your heart somersaults. You can barely catch your breath.

Maybe it's an unexpected diagnosis that takes your breath away or a news alert too overwhelming to process. And yet the car still needs gas. The work deadline still looms. Someone at home is calling your name.

It feels like too much because sometimes it really is too much for one human heart to hold.

How do we hold on to hope when our hearts are heavy?

Jesus' words in John 16 land in this very place. On the night before His death, Jesus didn't tell His friends everything would be fine. He told them the truth: "In this world you will have trouble." But He also gave them a tenderness and a hope that transcends this reality. "Take heart," He said. "I have overcome the world."

Trouble is real—and so is Christ's overcoming. In the middle of headlines and heartaches, in the ordinariness of errands and emails, this hope for the now and not yet is the larger reality God invites us into.

Take heart.

This is not the end of the story.

Put your hope in the One who has overcome the world.

Put your hand on your heart. Take a deep breath over five counts as you pray. Slowly release your breath for seven counts. Let each breath be a small act of resistance to despair, a quiet "yes" to the One who gives peace even here.

BORROW THIS PRAYER

God, I hold the tension
Of wanting to be informed
And being overwhelmed
By the barrage of news.
I don't know how to absorb
And understand the
Breaking apart of humanity.
I ache for Your presence,
But You are hard to see
In headline after headline.
I'm squinting after the storm,
Trying to make out a rainbow.
Remind me that You are bigger
Than my worry,
That You hold every tear.
May all I read
Bring me to greater compassion
For others
And for myself, Lord.
Amen.

MAY 8

Praise be to the God and Father of our Lord Jesus Christ, the Father of compassion and the God of all comfort, who comforts us in all our troubles, so that we can comfort those in any trouble with the comfort we ourselves receive from God.

2 CORINTHIANS 1:3-4 (NIV)

INHALE: As you comfort me,
EXHALE: Help me comfort others.

I imagine sitting across from Jesus while He breaks bread and pours wine as the candles melt down. I can almost *hear* myself laughing with Him when my kids do something completely bonkers. I can almost *feel* what it's like to sit with Him on my porch swing, swaying in the breeze and saying nothing at all.

After the resurrection, Jesus told His disciples that He was leaving them but sending them something even better—His very Spirit, alive in the world in every single follower.[*]

In some way, I *do* get to experience those things I dream of. We are called the body of Christ,[†] so when I'm comforted by someone who is in Christ, in some cosmic way I am being cared for by Jesus. Every time we gather around the table to share and retell our stories, laugh so hard we cry, or wipe away each other's tears, we experience the care and comfort of Jesus.

God broke into our world and experienced life the way we do.

Our compassionate God cares deeply for us and desires to make His home among us.[‡] The Spirit, called the Comforter,[§] cares for us with compassion.

Sometimes it's impossible to make meaning out of the awful things in our lives and in the wider world. While healing takes time, we can trust that God will comfort us. And we can extend that comfort from God into the compassion we have for others. The pain you've carried can be used for a purpose.

Out of scars, compassion overflows.

PAUSE AND PONDER

God of all comfort, I come to You feeling ______________________.

Thank You for being with me when ______________________.

When I felt ______________________ ______________, You held me.

When I was ______________________ __________, You comforted me.

Help my pain to have a purpose.

Help me extend Your compassion to ______________________.

As You comfort me, help me comfort others. Amen.

[*] See John 16:7.
[†] See 1 Corinthians 12:12-27.
[‡] See John 1:14.
[§] See John 14:26.

MAY 9

How often I have wanted to gather your children together as a hen protects her chicks beneath her wings.

LUKE 13:34 (NLT)

INHALE: You protect me
EXHALE: With Your love.

When I was in the thick of parenting four young kids, I was asked to write a poem for my church. My assigned reading: Luke 13:34. Never in my life had I heard (or paid attention to) the maternal way Jesus described His sacrificial love.

Using the picture of a mother hen, Christ shows us a love that is protective and patient: When a fox attacks, a mother hen stands bravely, opening her wings in courageous concern, wanting to tuck her babies close.

"How often I have longed to gather your children together, as a hen gathers her chicks under her wings,"* Jesus shares, the grief of His love palpable.

Because of a love so big it covers us like the wings of a mother hen, the evil in this world doesn't have the final word. God's encompassing love and protection do, even when we wander away.

"I've seen mother hens gather their chicks under their wings when a predator approaches. The way they swell with indignation, fear, and courage. The way they stand their ground. The way they prepare to die if they have to, their children tucked securely beneath their soft, vulnerable bodies," Debie Thomas writes. "I can't imagine a more profound or radical picture of our God. Can you?"[117]

Have you ever thought about Jesus yearning to protect you in this way? What does this metaphor tell us about God's character?

RHYTHM OF BREATH

The fox is weak
In its strength,
Not knowing
True power
Comes in the form
Of a mother hen,
Wings stretched wide—
Wide enough
For the pain
Of the whole world,
For the babies
Who ran astray,
Warm enough
To cover them all—
Sweeping her flock
Under her feathers,
Aching to
Absorb the agony.

But her grace is
Offered,
Never forced.

So she watches,
She waits,
And she weeps,
Longing for her
Lost little ones
To return home.

* Luke 13:34, NIV.

MAY 10

His mercy flows in wave after wave on those who are in awe before him.

LUKE 1:50 (MSG)

INHALE: Your mercy
EXHALE: Crashes over me.

I stand hand in hand with my husband on the beach, watching him watch the waves ebb and flow. It's his first time experiencing the ocean. Before I know it, he slips off his shoes and runs into the surf, laughing like a child as he breathes the salt air and the waves crash over him. I laugh too, and I know deep in my bones that I'm bearing witness to a sacred moment.

God breathes, and wave after wave of mercy washes over us with love so much bigger and fuller than we could even ask for.

I've never met anyone who could stand in front of the ocean and not fall, at least a little, into awe. The sea has a way of shrinking our egos and expanding our wonder. When we stand before it, we sense how small we are and how vast the world really is. Awe before the One who formed the waters opens us up to what's already flowing—streams of mercy, never ceasing.

When your brain and body ache for God's mercy, try "ocean breathing":[118]

Inhale for a count of four.
Imagine that each inhale draws in God's mercy like a tide coming into the beach.
Exhale for a count of six.
Picture the outgoing tide carrying away your fear.
Repeat for a minute or two, letting your breath move like the waves.

When you practice this form of mindful breathing, your nervous system begins to settle as your breath matches the rhythm of the ocean's swell.

In . . . and out. In . . . and out.

Let your breath become prayer as the rhythm of God's steadfast love washes over you, wave after wave.

BORROW THIS PRAYER

God, You breathe,
And the waves crash like thunder.
God, You breathe,
And the ocean splits in two.
God, You breathe,
And Your mercy crashes over me.

MAY 11

GOD's not finished. He's waiting around to be gracious to you.
He's gathering strength to show mercy to you.

ISAIAH 30:18 (MSG)

INHALE: God of mercy,
EXHALE: You're not finished with me.

The voice of shame often disguises itself as the voice of God. *You're a failure*, it whispers. *You're not good enough. You never will be.*

But the One who gives each breath doesn't shame you. God desires to give you grace.

We all get it wrong sometimes. And when we harm someone with our words and actions, or our silence and inaction, we are called to repent, repair, and reconcile. But our mistakes don't define us. God doesn't leave us in our worst selves.

God breathes mercy over us, again and again. The Israelites were often rebellious, continually choosing everything *except* what God told them was best for them. The allure of power, self-preservation, and platform was as alive and well then as it is today. But even with their failures, God was ready to offer restoration.

The people of Israel often faced the natural consequences of their choices—but God's justice *always* came with an open invitation into wholeness.

God doesn't give up on us, even when we've given up on ourselves.

God's intentional, incarnational love is alive and active. We don't have a passive God, just waiting to punish us. We have a compassionate God who moves toward us, yearning to be gracious to us and set things right.

When shame begins to speak into your soul, borrow today's breath prayer. Let each breath remind you that God's mercy is still moving toward you, right now in this moment.

PAUSE AND PONDER

What is at stake if you imagine God's mercy being passive instead of active?

Where in your life are you struggling to trust God's willingness to forgive and restore?

MAY 12

I will comfort you there in Jerusalem as a mother comforts her child.

ISAIAH 66:13 (NLT)

INHALE: I find comfort
EXHALE: In Your arms.

Strong as a rock. Faithful as a shepherd. Steady as each new morning. Scripture uses countless everyday word pictures to describe God's love.

In today's verse, Isaiah paints us a picture of God's protective love by showing us a mother holding her child. It's an intimate image: a mother cupping her child's face, feeling the beat of their heart as she soothes their cries, wipes their tears, and feels their breath on her skin. The Hebrew word used for "comfort" in this verse also means "to sigh" or "to breathe strongly."[119]

As I raise my kids, I've come to realize that while they have to go their own way, and sometimes that leads to incredible heartache, I will do everything I can to be there for them. To hold them in my arms, no matter how much taller they get than me, to whisper, *I'm here, I'm here, I'm here.*

God offers you the kind of embodied love that breathes alongside your sighs.

Maybe you've known what it feels like to long for someone simply to be with you, to breathe with you when the ache is too much. Isaiah's words remind us that God comes close like a mother who knows her child's cry and would move heaven and earth to hold them in her arms and keep them safe.

As you inhale, imagine being gathered in God's arms. As you exhale, trust that in this moment, you are safe and secure in God's love.

PAUSE AND PONDER

What comfort from God do you need most right now?

How does it make you feel to know that God loves you the way a mother comforts her child?

MAY 13

God's glory is on tour in the skies, God-craft on exhibit across the horizon.

PSALM 19:1 (MSG)

INHALE: You paint the skies
EXHALE: With glory.

If you've ever tried to take a picture of a stunning sunset or a starlit night, you know how the feeling of awe is quickly replaced by disappointment as you glance down and realize how terrible the photo turned out. It's almost impossible to capture the fullness of the splendor God spins into the sky. Creation refuses to be contained.

No matter who you are or where you live, we all share the same sky. Every shimmer of a star and each golden glow of a sunset sings the song of the One who made it. Creation reflects the Creator to every one of us.[120]

It's easy to look down at our phones so much that we forget to look up.

How might you stay awake to God's glory today? How can you cultivate a sense of wonder and gratitude for the world God has breathed into being, allowing it to draw you closer to the Creator?

Let today's breath prayer remind you:
Stay curious.
Look up.
Stand in awe.
Worship with wonder.

PRACTICING THE WAY

Give yourself a few minutes this week to look up. Whether you watch the sunrise or the sunset, or you set some time to marvel at the stars, let yourself be fully present and open to wonder.

What colors do you see? How is the light shifting? How do you feel as you breathe in the moment?

Let the fading or emerging light remind you that the One who paints the heavens is near, filling every in-between with presence. Offer a prayer of gratitude before you head back inside.

MAY 14

Open up your lives. Live openly and expansively!

2 CORINTHIANS 6:13 (MSG)

INHALE: Open my heart,
EXHALE: Open my hands.

Relationships get messy because, well, we're messy people. When we bring our whole selves into relationship with someone else, tension and conflict arise—that's just what it is to be human. But what matters most isn't avoiding disagreement but living openheartedly and caring for each other.

Relationships—whether with your friends, your children, your parents, your spouse, or your neighbors—flourish in mutuality. Our connections with others grow when both people open their hearts to give and receive care. (Living openheartedly doesn't mean tolerating harm but choosing courage and compassion where safety and trust are present.)

Where in your relationships do you feel safe enough to be open?

In today's verse, the Corinthian church was influenced by false faith leaders, fracturing their relationship with Paul. By writing to them and urging them to open their hearts, Paul is calling them back to reconciliation and restored trust—a call for vulnerability that still speaks to us today.

It's vulnerable to live openheartedly. To crack open the protective shell that guards you. To open yourself up to someone else's care.

Living expansively begins with prayer and moves into action. Prayer softens our hearts, and the work of our hands extends that openness outward.

As you let your breath settle, open your hands as you read Anthony de Mello's prayer. Notice the words or phrases that stand out to you. Consider underlining them, or jot them down in your journal. Notice where your heart feels guarded, and bring those places into God's hands.

BORROW THIS PRAYER

I seek the depth that silence brings,
for prayer that springs from silence
is powerful and effective.

From "The Benediction"
by Anthony de Mello[121]

MAY 15

A friend loves at all times, and a brother is born for a time of adversity.

PROVERBS 17:17 (NIV)

INHALE: Help me love

EXHALE: The ones in front of me.

When life cracks open, we start to see who's really in our corner. Who shows up when there's a death in the family? Who comes over with a meal when you receive a difficult diagnosis? Hardship often reveals the depth of our relationships.

In the world of the Bible, family ties meant *survival.* Your people were your provision and protection—the ones who stood between you and hunger or danger. The term *brother* didn't just mean a sibling but anyone who was fiercely loyal, who wouldn't jump ship at the first sight of adversity.

The First Nations Version puts it this way: "A friend's love always remains true" and relatives are "born to share heartache and trouble." *This* is the kind of love Jesus talks about in John 15:13 that lays itself down for friends. And in the upside-down way of Christ, we can even extend this love to our *enemies.*

The song "Brother" by the Brilliance reminds me that when I look into the face of my enemy, "I see my brother." That lyric takes my breath away. God's love opens our eyes and moves us to honor not just their humanity but their inherent belovedness, seeing an enemy as a brother.

Hebrews 2 tells us that Christ Himself is our brother, entering our suffering and standing with us in need. As Christians, we are called to love others as Christ loves us. This means being present and supportive, especially when others face trials.[122]

Who has been there for you in a time of adversity? Where might God be inviting you to show up for someone else?

Treating everyone whose paths we cross with the same care we'd give our closest family members glorifies God and makes space for God's Kingdom to break through in our ordinary lives.

BORROW THIS PRAYER

In a world that
Chooses enemies,
Help me to choose love.
Cleanse me of any desire
To worship at the altar of self.
Make new my heart
So I may stop
Bowing at the feet
Of the idol that reflects
My image.
You have made us
To dwell in the womb
Of communal flourishing.
Every morning
Is a chance to be reborn
So I might love You,
And in turn
Love my neighbor,
More fully.
Amen.

MAY 16

Love the LORD your God with all your heart and with all your soul and with all your strength.

DEUTERONOMY 6:5 (NIV)

INHALE: God, help me live out love
EXHALE: With every breath I take.

At a leadership training years ago, I was handed a sheet of paper. On it was a neat little pie chart dividing life into slices: work, family, health, finances, hobbies, relationships, faith. It was meant to help people balance everything, but it felt too small. It didn't capture the fullness of who we are.

Faith isn't just one slice of life. God calls the *whole of who we are* into love. Imagine transparent circles laid over one another, with love shining through every layer until they blend in the center.

In Deuteronomy 6, God's people are taught to pray the *Shema*. This declaration of God's oneness—this call to love God with your whole being—was prayed every morning and evening, shaping everyday life. Centuries later, Jesus recited this prayer, naming the command to love God with your full self as the "greatest" one, and then He paired it with a command to "love your neighbor as yourself."*

What if every word you spoke and every choice you made flowed from this center of loving God and others? How might it change your spending, your scheduling, your scrolling? How might it transform the way you speak with a difficult coworker or choose which media you let shape your imagination?

We don't break up our minds or our hearts into slices, divvying out a limited amount of love. God lavishes limitless love upon you so you can reflect it back with your life. Father M. Basil Pennington writes, "Growth in the Christian life is a matter of intensification, of growing toward loving God in Christ with one's *whole* mind, *whole* heart, *whole* soul, and *whole* strength."[123]

Loving God isn't one slice of your life—it's the whole of who you are. Every moment of every day, you're invited to love God in the wholeness of what makes you, well, *you*. Consider praying the *Shema* every morning or evening this week, and imagine loving with the fullness of your life as a door to walk through, day after day, until loving God and others is as natural as breathing.

As the circles of your world overlap, may Christ's love be the center and spill over into your every breath.

* Matthew 22:36-39, NIV.

PRACTICING THE WAY

Picture a few transparent circles representing different areas of your life—work, relationships, inner life, health, finances, downtime. Watch them overlap until they form one space in the center. In that center, imagine love radiating out.

Ask yourself:

- Which circle feels easiest to offer to God right now?
- Which circle feels most private or hardest to let go of?
- Where might God be inviting more wholeness today?

MAY 17

Let me hear what God the LORD will speak, for he will speak peace to his people, to his faithful, to those who turn to him in their hearts.

PSALM 85:8 (NRSV)

INHALE: Speak peace
EXHALE: Into my heart.

Psalm 85 is a prayer of restoration, introducing us to a God who turns toward us with steadfast love and *shalom*—wholeness, well-being, and peace.

And yet, throughout history, entire wars have been waged and atrocities justified by people who sincerely believed God was calling them to death and destruction. How do we reconcile this reality with the psalmist's promise that God speaks peace?

If we're not careful, we can begin to believe our egos are actually God's voice. We hear whispers of greed, violence, selfishness, pride—and, without even realizing it, sanctify our thoughts with a God-stamp over them.

If the voice you're hearing isn't speaking peace, it's not God.

Jesus, the Prince of Peace, says, "Peace I leave with you; my peace I give to you."* God's peace is a current that flows into us and out of us, into the thoughts we have and the choices we make. When you have peace like a river in your soul, it's *God* who is sanctifying your thoughts, your words, your actions.

As you breathe, ask God to reveal where you may have mistaken your own ego or fear for God's voice. Ask yourself,

- Does this inner voice move me toward love, humility, and mercy?
- Where might God be inviting me to embody peace today—in my words, my social media habits, my relationships?

We have countless reasons to fight, to defend, to conquer. But when we turn our hearts to God, God will speak peace into our souls, transforming us from the inside out. As you breathe through today's prayer, let God's voice—not mine, not yours, not the loudest people shouting on the Internet—move you toward *shalom*.

May the peace of Christ become the truest sound in your soul.

BORROW THIS PRAYER

God of all that was and is,
I come to You with all of me,
Emptied of words to pray,
Lost in my overwhelm.
Help me find my way back to You.
Stay with me in the silence;
Be near in the unknowing.
When I don't know what to say,
Whisper into my wondering.
Breathe peace into the
Noise of my mind
And the chaos of my soul.
Amen.

---

* John 14:27, NLT.

MAY 18

Don't be obsessed with getting your own advantage. . . .
Think of yourselves the way Christ Jesus thought of himself.

PHILIPPIANS 2:4-5 (MSG)

INHALE: Help me care for others
EXHALE: The way You care for me.

My social media algorithms keep feeding me a message packaged in cute, designed videos: *Put yourself first.* Caring for ourselves is healthy—even Jesus withdrew to pray and rest. But when self-care becomes self-rule, we drift from the way of Christ's humility.

In his letter to the Philippians, Paul urges them to have the same mindset as Jesus, who had every right to cling to privilege but humbled Himself for the good of humanity. In the Roman Empire, which Philippi was part of, people were obsessed with personal achievement and advancement (not unlike today). And it was leaking into the church. (Also not unlike today.) But Paul tells them not to look to their own interests "but also to the interests of others."* Paul casts a radically different vision from what people were used to. He wasn't calling people to erase their needs but to expand their vision to care for others.

Philippians 2 pushes against the ever-popular "liturgy of self" we're bombarded by. Wrapped in a message of empowerment, it goes something like this:

> "Work obsessively for your own advantage.
> Remember yourself before anyone else.
> Think of yourself as your own god. Look
> to your own interests. Put yourself first,
> always. You are so worth it."

We've seen the damage of using Scripture to demand self-erasure. Too many abusive churches and manipulative ministry leaders have twisted Paul's call to be Christlike to hold power over people. This has led to an overcorrection, where the pendulum swings too far the other way—urging us to create Christ in our own image and elevate ourselves above all.

By intentionally looking to the good of others, you reflect Christ's sacrificial love and live into a counterliturgy that follows the way of Jesus, who had every right to cling to privilege but humbled himself for our sake. Philippians 2 sings of Jesus' self-emptying love and shows us a new way to be in the world.

Where is Christ inviting you to tend your own soul *and* extend care to others? Imagine Christ's humility washing over you, expanding your heart without diminishing your worth.

PAUSE AND PONDER

Where are you tempted to erase yourself?

Where are you tempted to worship yourself?

* Philippians 2:4, ESV.

MAY 19

True to your word, you let me catch my breath
and send me in the right direction.

PSALM 23:3 (MSG)

INHALE: Help me catch my breath;
EXHALE: Send me in the right direction.

When the pain of the world threatens to take our breath away, the psalms give us language for our longing. When we don't know how to pray, we can let these ancient prayers become our own.

The psalms give us a front-row seat to hearts cracked open, praying to a God who is present to the pain of His people. In Psalm 23, David doesn't claim, "Life with You is without pain." Instead, he writes, "You let me catch my breath." Other translations say, "He restores my soul."* David's words remind us of the fullness of our humanity and the all-encompassing presence of God in our lives. He reminds us that having faith doesn't mean you have to pretend that everything is okay. God already knows that sometimes, *it's really not.*

When we return to the center of who we are in Christ, our minds and souls find breathing room. We can receive the gift God is giving us with each breath. As Flora Slosson Wuellner writes, "Just as God breathed the breath of life into the first living being, so our deep, instinctive taking of breath is receiving again the gift of life from God for each moment."[124]

God has always been the One who restores the weary, resetting our hearts and minds in love. God knows the exhaustion in our bones. God feels the weight we carry in our hearts.

In her song "Breathe Again," Joy Oladokun offers her own psalm: "Hold my breath until I'm honest/Will I ever breathe again?"

These lyrics remind us that breathing is a form of beginning again.

You're not less than for being on the brink of burnout. God meets you in your exhaustion and doesn't leave you alone in your worry or stress. Each breath is a gift from God to reset—to bend without breaking when the weight of the world feels too heavy.

With every breath, the Spirit offers restoration and direction.

As you breathe today, may God help you catch your breath and send you on the right path.

PRACTICING THE WAY

1. Place your hands on your stomach.
2. Inhale deeply, letting your abdomen rise like a balloon.[125]
3. As you inhale, pray, "Help me catch my breath."
4. Exhale slowly, feeling your belly soften. Pray, "Send me in the right direction."
5. Continue for several rounds, noticing how you feel as you become present to God's restorative presence.

Why it helps: Diaphragmatic or abdominal breathing calms your nervous system and regulates irregular breathing patterns. This "anti-anxiety" breath helps you feel more balanced and receptive to God's presence.[126]

---

* Psalm 23:3, NRSV.

MAY 20

In peace I will lie down and sleep,
for you alone, O LORD, will keep me safe.

PSALM 4:8 (NLT)

INHALE: When the day is done,
EXHALE: My peace comes from You.

Tonight, when your head hits the pillow, let yourself be still.

Feel the weight of gravity holding you. Notice the rhythm of your breath, letting every inhale and exhale become a prayer of its own.

In a world that shouts for your attention, seeking the presence of God is an act of resistance.

Resist the pull to let your mind wander toward tomorrow.

Resist the urgency that asks you to do more. To be more.

Just be.

Begin to breathe deeply through your nose. Exhale gently through your mouth. Notice the noise of the world fading into the background. Remember: You are not alone in the quiet of the night. The Spirit of God is with You.

As you breathe in, pray, "When the day is done," and as you breathe out, pray, "My peace comes from You."

Turn from the frenzy of the day. Turn from the fears about tomorrow, just for this moment. Let your breath open your heart to the peace that passes all understanding.

You don't have to hold the world together. Here in this moment, you don't have to hold anything at all. Let God hold *you* now, as night comes.

The world shouts. But God whispers peace.

All you have to do is listen.

SACRED ECHOES

Breath prayer does not replace other ways of praying; rather it is foundational to our whole prayer life, supporting it and making it possible for us to pray without ceasing.[127]

Ruth Haley Barton

MAY 21

When God lives and breathes in you (and he does, as surely as he did in Jesus), you are delivered from that dead life.

ROMANS 8:11 (MSG)

INHALE: You live in me;
EXHALE: You breathe in me.

You don't have to escape your life to meet God. Even now, God's Spirit is breathing in you, sustaining your every moment.

Romans 8 reminds us that we don't have a distant God but a present God who dwells within us.

What a beautiful mystery that we're given the Holy Spirit and welcomed into a transformative, life-giving relationship that does not leave us as we were but continually shapes us into who we *really* are.

The same power that raised Jesus from the dead is alive in you right now. Yet in the noise and demands of our everyday realities, the gravity of this gift is so easy to forget.

We pray to remember.

We often put a lot of pressure on ourselves for prayer to look a certain way. But prayer isn't another box to check or a performance to perfect. We're already in God's presence, and God's presence is already in us. Prayer can happen whenever we find ourselves drawn out of our ordinary awareness and toward a sense of "awe of the Holy," as Caroline Oakes points out.[128]

Prayer is so much more than any words we can string together.

Prayer is an awakened awareness of God's extraordinary Spirit breathing into every ordinary moment of our messy, holy lives.

Oakes puts it this way: "Prayer is being aware of the power of this Great Mystery, this great Love, right in the midst of our 'ordinary' lives—catching sight of the full moon, watching a baby being born, being captivated by a glorious sunset or by the eyes of someone you adore gazing into your own."[129]

Today, how might you open your life to be awake to God right here in your every breath?

BREATHE THIS IN

The Hebrew word *ruach* and the Greek word *pneuma* both mean "spirit," "breath," and "wind."[130]

MAY 22

Cast your cares on the LORD and he will sustain you.

PSALM 55:22 (NIV)

INHALE: You sustain

EXHALE: My every breath.

Take a deep breath. Let yourself name, without judgment, what you're carrying today. Are you angry? Grateful? Frustrated? Curious? Numb?

You don't have to shine up how you're feeling. You can bring your full self—your joys and your struggles—to God right here, right now. Psalm 55 reminds us that we can be honest in our prayers. God doesn't just tolerate your emotions, your worries, and your thoughts, but *welcomes* them.

Your burdens are not too much.

You are not too much.

Not only can we cast our cares on God, but we're given a promise too: God will *sustain* us. God doesn't just hear your prayer but promises to be with you. To sustain you. To give you the strength you need to keep breathing, to keep going. The One who gives each breath is faithful. You can trust that all that you're holding will be held with care.

Give yourself some time and space today to work out how you're feeling so you can release your emotions into God's hands as you pray today's breath prayer.

PAUSE AND PONDER

What feels heavy on your shoulders?

What are you holding that no one knows?

What burdens are you tired of managing?

What do you long to hand over to God?

MAY 23

Guide me on your road of truth and instruct my heart. You are my Creator and the One Who Sets Me Free. From sunrise to sunset, I think deeply about your ways and put my hope in you.

PSALM 25:5 (FNV)

INHALE: Guide me on
EXHALE: Your road of truth.

"I just . . . don't . . . know!" my friend confided, her exasperation and exhaustion spilling out over the phone. Her job search had been full of twists and turns, and after sleepless nights and countless interviews, she now faced a fork in the road: two job offers, each with its own benefits and setbacks.

For so long, she'd prayed for a way to provide for her family, but now she felt stuck. Afraid of making the "wrong" choice, she wanted to follow God's will, but she was unsure of which path to take.

"Will one wrong move derail *everything*?" she whispered.

I know that feeling of being pressed in and pressured to make the "right" call.

When I was researching seminaries for a spiritual direction program, I prayed, talked with friends, memorized course descriptions—and *still* agonized over the decision. Later, sitting in Julie Saad's class session on contemplative discernment at Columbia Theological Seminary, I thought, *How I wish I'd had this process then!* Yet even that realization was its own confirmation that I was where I needed to be.

Discernment doesn't mean every decision becomes easy or that every outcome will be perfect, but it's a prayerful way of staying with God in uncertain times. When we have a listening heart and a willing spirit, God meets us where we are. And when we're with God, we're already on the good road.

Discernment invites God into our wrestling until our wrestling feels more like resting. Julie puts it this way: "When discernment starts with going to God with our questions and desires, the answers will find us."[131] What crossroads are you at today? Hold it all with open hands as you learn to listen to the Spirit. As you walk this road of truth, place your hope in the One who gives each breath.

PAUSE AND PONDER

Use this space to help you open your heart (without an agenda) to what the Spirit might be speaking to you.

As you prayerfully reflect on the advantages and disadvantages of each path in front of you, notice recurring themes in your answers.

What are the advantages of taking this path? What are the disadvantages of taking this path?

Further Reading: Read *Contemplative Life: Discovering Our Path into the Heart of God* by Julie Saad.

MAY 24

We look at this Son and see the God who cannot be seen. We look at this Son and see God's original purpose in everything created.

COLOSSIANS 1:15 (MSG)

INHALE: Fix my eyes
EXHALE: On You.

God is a great mystery. (Understatement of the year!) But if we want to know what God is like and how God loves us, we have to look no farther than Jesus.

When we fix our eyes on Jesus, it's not like staring at a painting in a museum, static and one-directional. Jesus looks back at us.

Have you ever been looked at with so much love—maybe by a relative or a child or a spouse—that you felt completely and wholly held in that moment?

Can you see Jesus looking at you like that? Can you sense His gaze meeting yours?

Saint Teresa of Avila, a sixteenth-century Spanish nun, recommended an imaginative prayer summarized as *mira que te mira*—"see that you are seen." It's said that she encouraged people to notice Jesus looking at them *lovingly* and *humbly*.[132]

Maybe you struggle to imagine Jesus looking at you lovingly, especially if you've been given an image of Him that is harsh or demanding. Or maybe it feels even more impossible to imagine Jesus looking at you humbly, especially if you've been told that His biggest concern is if you check all the religious boxes.[133]

But the Jesus we see throughout the New Testament is marked by humility and unconditional love. He's the One who *truly* saw the woman at the well, who noticed Zacchaeus in the tree,[†] who stopped for the blind man on the road.[‡]

The more you look at Jesus, the more you see the invisible made visible.

If picturing Jesus feels awkward or even difficult, that's okay. We've been given a lot of pictures of Jesus that are simply untrue. In a world where it's hard to see clearly, ask the Holy Spirit to give you a sacred imagination so you can see—and be seen—by the One who reveals the heart of God.

Will you allow yourself to be loved today?

PRACTICING THE WAY

Set aside a few minutes to move through this guided prayer.

- Find a quiet moment to pause. Intentionally welcome God's presence.
- Let your shoulders soften and the noise of the day grow faint.
- Close your eyes, if you'd like, and imagine Jesus standing before you.
- On your inhale, pray, "Fix my eyes." As you slowly exhale, pray, "On You."
- Allow yourself to be seen. Allow yourself to be held.
- Notice the gaze of Jesus. Let the love in His eyes meet the ache in yours.
- Stay here for a few slow breaths.
- How do you feel? Carry that reflection with you into whatever comes next today.

[*] See John 4:1-26.
[†] See Luke 19:1-10.
[‡] See Mark 10:46-52.

MAY 25

Still, God, you are our Father. We're the clay and you're our potter: All of us are what you made us.

ISAIAH 64:8 (MSG)

INHALE: Shape me
EXHALE: Into Your image.

Spiritual formation isn't something that happens to a transcendent few—it's available to *all* of us, *all* the time. Maybe that's why the Bible includes so many references to people being like clay.

It's up to us, though, whether we'll be formed by God's hand.

As followers of Jesus, we're invited to be formed by His ways. But in our distracted world, it's easy to be shaped by other forces: achievements, politics, even the media we consume. Whatever forms us leaves its fingerprints on our hearts—and inevitably touches our families, neighbors, and coworkers too.

In his book *The Deeply Formed Life*, Rich Villodas explores how being rooted in Christ can help us to live more robust lives, formed by God.

"Whether we know it or not, see it or not, or understand it or not, we are always at risk of being shallowly formed," he writes. "We are formed by our false selves, our families of origin, the highly manipulated presentations of social media, and the value system of a world that determines worth based on accomplishments, possessions, efficiency, intellectual acumen, and gifts. So we need to be regularly called back to the essence of our lives in God."[134]

Those words are a gentle reminder that we all need regular nudges to return to the hands of the One who loves us. The more we open ourselves to being deeply formed in goodness and truth, the more our lives reflect the One who created us in love.

Today, how might God be calling you back to who you *really* are? As you breathe today's breath prayer, remember that you are a creation held in the loving hands of your Creator.[135]

BORROW THIS PRAYER

Creator God,
You breathed us into being
Out of dirt and dust.
You are not done with
The forming and fashioning
Of who we are
And who we are becoming.

God, we know You are
Forever speaking into
The contours and crevices
Of our lives.
Carve mirrors into our hearts
So we might examine
And reflect on who and what
We have allowed
To form our days
And our lives.

Soften our harsh edges,
And form us into Your image,
Through Christ alone.
Amen.[136]

MAY 26

I will praise the LORD as long as I live. I will sing praises to my God with my dying breath.

PSALM 146:2 (NLT)

INHALE: May my every breath
EXHALE: Echo Your love.

We sing praises to God with the songs of our lives.

Every moment of every day can become an offering of worship.

With the art we create, the children we raise, the meals we serve.

With the help we extend, the words we speak, the money we steward.

With the way we listen, the gardens we plant, the justice we sow.

With the grace we share, the bathrooms we clean, the kindness we offer.

With the silence we hold, the apologies we give, the spaces we make safe.

Each of these small, everyday acts can become a psalm of praise.

Thinking about our mortality can feel uncomfortable. Yet Psalm 146 invites us to imagine a life so drenched in gratitude that even our final breath becomes praise. Sometimes we just need a little perspective to notice that the small parts of our days that make up our lives can be an overflow of praise to the One who has been with us all along.

Take a slow, deep breath. Place a hand over your heart as you whisper, "May my every breath." Recall the people you've loved and those who have loved you. As you let your breath go, whisper, "Echo Your love." Ask God to reveal how your time, gifts, and words might tell a story of praise.

What praise will your breath offer today? How might God's love meet you in the ordinary moments today?

PAUSE AND PONDER

God, let my every inhale and every exhale be a song of gratitude.

Today, I praise You for ______________________ ______________________.

When I am tired, I know that You are ______ ______________________.

Let my breath carry Your goodness into the world. Amen.

MAY 27

We take our lead from Christ, who is the source of everything we do. He keeps us in step with each other. His very breath and blood flow through us, nourishing us so that we will grow up healthy in God, robust in love.

EPHESIANS 4:16 (MSG)

INHALE: Your breath
EXHALE: Flows through me.

Christ is the source of the breath in our lungs and the blood in our veins. The very fibers of our being are God-breathed. And this truth empowers us to have an embodied faith in a chaotic world.

Because Jesus breathes peace, so can you.
Because Jesus breathes compassion, so can you.
Because Jesus breathes hope, so can you.
Because Jesus breathes strength, so can you.
Because Jesus breathes justice, so can you.
Because Jesus breathes restoration, so can you.
Because Jesus breathes mercy, so can you.
Because Jesus breathes power, so can you.
Because Jesus breathes forgiveness, so can you.
Because Jesus breathes truth, so can you.

When we rely on our own reserves, we burn out. Cynicism creeps in. We feel exhaustion deep in our bones from all the ways the world isn't as it should be.

But the breath of God nourishes us, restores us, and sustains us. Christ is the breath in our lungs, strengthening us so we might love God with all our heart, soul, mind, and strength—and love our neighbor as ourselves.

Spiritual director Nancy S. Wiens notes that breath prayer can "bring calm and spiritual awareness of God's healing power into the emotionally fraught world of prior distress and trauma." Some of her clients initially think breath prayer sounds touchy-feely or disconnected from faith. Others welcome it but don't see the link to science. Wiens explains that exploring "the science-spirituality intersection offers both permission and inspiration for practicing Breath Prayer in distressing situations."[137]

Because Jesus breathes, so can you.

Take a deep breath through your nose. As you inhale, place your hand on your lower stomach and feel it expand.

Hold your breath for a few counts, noticing your heartbeat in the stillness.

Exhale slowly for as long as you can, extending the breath as you feel comfortable.

With each inhale, pray, "Your breath."

With each exhale, pray, "Flows through me."

BREATHE THIS IN

God is actively renewing you, right here, right now. In fact, about 330 billion cells are replaced in our bodies every day.[138] The same God who renews your cells is renewing your soul. Turns out, mercies really are new each morning.

MAY 28

GOD holds the high center, he sees and sets the world's mess right.

PSALM 9:7 (MSG)

INHALE: In You, O God,
EXHALE: The center holds.

With the swipe of a finger, we have access to unlimited anxiety. Endless news cycles flood our ever-updating screens, delivering heartbreaking headlines and traumatic triggers faster than our brains can metabolize the pain.

If you're feeling anxious today, know this: You're not broken. Your body is doing exactly what it was divinely designed to do, and your brain is working to keep you safe.

Though we live in a world drenched in hope and full of beauty, and though we seek to hold on to the promise that the love of God has the final say, the truth is that the bad often outweighs the good in the way our brains and bodies respond—and that's not our fault.

Psychologists and neuroscientists call this our *negativity bias*,[139] a survival instinct that helped our ancestors focus on threats to stay alive. Historically, this meant paying attention to danger at a ratio of 250:1—one bad thing could override 250 good things.[140] The more stress and danger our brain perceives, the more it's prone to stay on high alert.

Fast-forward to today: Our negativity bias collides with the age of endless scrolling, turning a survival instinct into a daily source of overwhelm. Tech companies know how our brains work—and they profit from it. They design platforms to exploit our fear, anger, and sadness, pushing that 250:1 ratio to 500–750:1.[141] Our shallow, rapid breaths are physiological signals that we're living in a constant state of survival. It's exhausting to live this way, isn't it?

God made you for connection, not for internal combustion.

You may feel stuck in stress, but you don't have to stay there. With intentional community and prayer, we can disrupt the stress cycle, cling to what is good, and find space to breathe again.

The world's pain is real, but so is its beauty. What would it look like for you to embrace both as you step into hope and create space for the peace of your Creator to hold the center?

PRACTICING THE WAY

Box breathing is a rhythm of breath that helps us reset. It's a simple practice you can pair with your prayers and come back to anytime you're feeling anxious or stressed.

Breathe in for four counts.
Hold for four counts.
Breathe out for four counts.
Hold for four counts.

As you work your way around the box, imagine God in the center, holding it all together.

MAY 29

Never stop praying.

1 THESSALONIANS 5:17 (NLT)

INHALE: May all my life
EXHALE: Be a prayer.

God is in conversation with you. Every moment of every day, the One who gives each breath is speaking. And listening too.

Prayer is entering into that ongoing conversation, with each breath anchoring us in God's nearness as we move through the day.

Paul's simple call to the church in Thessalonica—a small community trying to follow Jesus in a culture that rewarded the opposite—points to a way to hold on to hope even in hardship: Pray without ceasing.

Different translations highlight the fullness of this call:

Pray continually (NIV).
Never stop praying (NLT).
Pray without ceasing (ESV).
Pray at all times (GNT).
Be unceasing and persistent in prayer (AMP).
Continually be prayerful (ISV).
Constantly pray (NET).

Breath prayer is one way to begin living into this call. Praying alongside our inhales and exhales awakens us to God's sustaining presence.

In his book *Everything Could Be a Prayer*, artist and writer Kreg Yingst describes how the nineteenth-century Russian spiritual classic *The Way of a Pilgrim* inspired him. Yingst writes that the book recounts the journey of "a pilgrim [who] travels throughout Ukraine, Russia, and Siberia . . . [asking,] How is it possible to pray without stopping?"[142]

Along the way, the pilgrim discovers the ancient Jesus Prayer:

Inhale: Lord Jesus Christ,
Exhale: Have mercy on me.

The first part of the prayer "marks the authority of God," Yingst explains, and the second "acknowledges our need for forgiveness."[143]

Over time, the pilgrim's repetition of this simple prayer saturates his life until listening and talking with God becomes as natural as breathing.

Entering into the rhythms of Christlike love in our everyday lives isn't always popular. To love God and love your neighbor as yourself is quite countercultural. When you're overwhelmed, take a breath. Keep your thoughts on what is true: You don't have to rely on your own reserves to get through the day. Our merciful God will be with you wherever you go.

As Yingst says, "To *pray without ceasing* is to make our life a prayer."[144]

BREATHE THIS IN

"The average person takes approximately 960 breaths per hour. In thirteen hours, one would have taken roughly 12,000 breaths. To pray without ceasing is to breathe in God and to maintain an attentive focus on the Divine at all times."[145]

MAY 30

God's Way is not a matter of mere talk; it's an empowered life.

1 CORINTHIANS 4:20 (MSG)

INHALE: Turn my words
EXHALE: Into actions.

I'm exhausted by empty words. I scroll past them in my feeds, hear them on TV, see them splashed on stickers and stitched onto T-shirts. Everyone claims to care. Everyone claims to stand for something. Yet so often the words don't match reality.

In a culture that prized flashy rhetoric and public status, Paul urged the believers in Corinth, a city brimming with rival philosophies and endless distractions, to embody a deeper reality: God's way "is not a matter of mere talk; it's an empowered life."

Paul said that works don't earn us God's love, but he never said that words don't matter. Right after proclaiming salvation by faith, Paul writes: "We are God's handiwork, created in Christ Jesus to do good works, which God prepared in advance for us to do."*

James picks up the same thread when he says that faith without works is dead.†

Think of it this way: Paul speaks to how we enter God's family—by grace, not by how many Bible verses we memorize or how hard we strive.

James speaks to how we live as transformed people who belong to God's family—embodying Christ's way by showing compassion, doing justice, showing mercy, and loving our neighbors.

James describes what grace looks like when it comes alive. Grace comes first.[146] But God's grace reshapes us from the inside out, leading to acts of mercy and love, courage and generosity.

What we *do* is a result of who we *are* in Christ.

Anyone can say "I'm a Christian," but words ring hollow without a life that reflects the heart of God. Anyone can recite creeds or doctrines, but if those truths don't overflow into our choices, they're as thin as the paper they're written on.

God's Kingdom moves not through empty rhetoric but through real lives alive in Christ.

God is changing the world through transformed people, including you.

LET IT LINGER

God is inviting you to breathe in grace so you can breathe it out into the world. To let the Spirit work within you so that the work of your hands reflects the overflow of your heart.

* Ephesians 2:10, NIV.
† See James 2:17.

MAY 31

Wilderness and desert will sing joyously, the badlands will celebrate and flower . . . a symphony of song and color.

ISAIAH 35:1-2 (MSG)

INHALE: In You, O God,
EXHALE: New life bursts forth.

Born and raised in the Midwest, I wasn't sure *what* to think the first time I found myself in a desert. As my friends and I drove the long stretch into Joshua Tree National Park, I watched the tumbleweeds meander down the road, feeling a quiet panic rise within me. The green cornfields I was used to were replaced by vast stretches of, well . . . *nothing*. I shifted in my seat as I watched the desert views blur past the window. I glanced at my phone and realized I had no reception. *What would happen if our car broke down? Who would help us out here?*

We all go through seasons when our souls feel dry or desolate—when it seems like all hope has dried up. We imagine our spiritual lives will always be lush landscapes, but sometimes we find ourselves on barren ground. Will God hear our prayer?

A life rooted in Jesus doesn't mean we won't have disappointments or doubts. It doesn't mean there won't be long stretches when we feel like we've been swallowed by shifting sands, left alone in our wandering and wondering.

Scripture acknowledges this ache. There is so much we cannot control—the dryness of the season, the slow blooming of the desert rose. Isaiah's words were for people in exile who were displaced and disoriented. But the promise held: Even here, life will rise. Even now, joy will sing.

Isaiah 43:19 says, "I am about to do a new thing; now it springs forth; do you not perceive it? I will make a way in the wilderness and rivers in the desert."*

After traveling the dry Southern California roads, my friends and I finally entered Joshua Tree. As we hiked, I began to see that the desert has its own kind of beauty. Stunning rock formations, vast vistas, sculpted boulders, and the park's iconic namesake trees revealed a surprising symphony of life. There were even unexpected pops of color from wildflowers.

If you're finding your own way in the wilds of working out your faith, take heart: You do not go alone.

If your soul feels cracked with weariness or scorched by grief, remember that the God who brings beauty from barrenness has not forgotten how to breathe life into dust. As you borrow today's breath prayer, may you sense new life bursting forth within and around you—again and again.

RHYTHM OF BREATH

I cannot control the sunset
Or the rolling thunder on a summer night.
I cannot control the way the wind blows
Or when a desert rose will bloom.
I cannot control the rhythms of creation
Or the heartbeats of another.
I cannot control the wild earth
Or all that stirs within it.
But I can sing.

* NRSV.

JUNE 1

At the command of the LORD, at the blast of his breath, the bottom of the sea could be seen, and the foundations of the earth were laid bare.

2 SAMUEL 22:16 (NLT)

INHALE: There is power
EXHALE: In Your breath.

The One who split the sea is still breathing today.

Right here, right now, with you.

God's power is unmatched . . . but it's also never distant. The divine love of Christ is so powerful that it holds every element on this earth together. Maybe you've glimpsed this power when you stood on the edge of a canyon or when you dipped your toes in the sea or when you bore witness to thunder rolling across the summer sky. A mighty wind, a rushing breath—*this* is God's presence drawing near.

The One who breathed life into being and divided the waters for the Israelites still makes a way for you.

Jesus said, "I AM."* And we breathe because He is. God's breath is the fierce love that creates us and sustains us.

Have you ever stopped to think that the same breath that parted the sea still hovers over the earth, filling your lungs even now?

It's a mystery of power and tenderness: The God who speaks so that the sea listens also draws close enough to speak to *you*, to listen to *you*.

Artist and poet Morgan Harper Nichols captures this captivating glory, writing that "as you breathe / in the subtle, sweet scent . . . / of the ponderosa pines," you are invited to do nothing except to "notice what's before you."[147]

God-breathed wonder isn't limited to grand vistas or crashing waves. It's nestled in the ordinary too: in the rhythm of breath as a baby sleeps on your chest, in the hush after rain breaks a June heat wave, in the quiet surrender of your own inhale and exhale.

As you pray today, trust that the same power that split the sea and carved the canyon is nearer than your next breath.

BREATHE THIS IN

Regularly practicing "coherent breathing"—as we do in breath prayer—at a rate of five to six breaths per minute has been shown to relieve stress, tension, anxiety, and insomnia. This type of breathing balances and stabilizes your stress-response system, helping you react at an appropriate level instead of with excess fear, anger, or helplessness.[148]

---

* John 8:58, NLT.

JUNE 2

Real religion, the kind that passes muster before God the Father, is this: Reach out to the homeless and loveless in their plight, and guard against corruption from the godless world.

JAMES 1:27 (MSG)

INHALE: Give me courage
EXHALE: To love like You.

We're bombarded by messaging about what Christians should do, think, and say. We're urged to care for *this* cause, not *that* one—or the other way around. Lines are drawn. If you're on this side, you're in. If you're on that side, well . . . good luck to you.

But Jesus challenges our boundaries. He cares for the whole of humanity. No one is outside the reach of God's care or God's justice.

Real religion braids justice and care with the unifying thread of Jesus.

James wrote to believers who—like us—were getting distracted by religious debates and political arguments instead of simply loving and helping the people right in front of them. His words cast a vision of a religion free from corruption or hypocrisy, a life disentangled from the lure of power and platform. He invites people to a kind of faith that goes beyond semantics, a faith that practices compassion and justice instead of judgment and self-interest.

The message of James 1:27 is simple: We are to care for the vulnerable in their suffering *and* resist letting the world corrupt us. True religion, he says, is this: (1) Practical love for the most vulnerable (2) Christ-centered integrity in a world full of compromise.

Without this dual approach—justice paired with holiness—our faith becomes dull and hollow. "We cannot separate justice from caring—they go together just like peanut butter and jelly," writes Shawn A. Ginwright in his book *The Four Pivots*.[149]

When we follow Jesus, we align with the rhythms of His life: caring for the marginalized, moving toward the most vulnerable in a practical expression of love. Social action and personal integrity are connected. Belief and behavior are inseparable in the Christian life.[150]

"Our movements for justice are fundamentally about how we collectively have concern and empathy for one another," Ginwright says.[151]

We all breathe the same air. With every exhale, we can join God in making that air less polluted by moving toward care and justice through the love of Jesus, allowing our faith and our actions to intertwine for the sake of the world God so loves.

BORROW THIS PRAYER

O cosmic Christ,
Give us this day
Our daily breath.
Spirit, remind us that
You dwell deep inside us
And that each inhalation,
Each exhalation,
Is a sacred gift from You alone.
Amen.

JUNE 3

The creation all around us is waiting on tiptoe for Creator's sons and daughters to be revealed in the full beauty of who he has created them to be.

ROMANS 8:19 (FNV)

INHALE: I am becoming
EXHALE: Who You created me to be.

The first time I saw a flower unfurl in a time-lapse video, I was enchanted. In an instant, a tiny bud blossomed into a rose, bursting with life. As a ten-year-old, I couldn't imagine anything more captivating.

But in real life, change is rarely instant. True transformation doesn't happen all at once; it's a slow unfurling as we grow into the fullness of who God has created us to be.

Most days, we don't notice our own renewal. It's like watching a child grow taller—you only register the change when the height is measured at the yearly doctor's visit or from the way their pants no longer fit. Spiritual growth surprises us in the same way. It's quiet. Gradual. Until one day, it's obvious how much has truly changed.

God is not in a hurry. We can trust that *God's Spirit* is revealing beauty in *God's time*, even when we can't yet see it.

We hold imagination in one hand and expectation in the other, trusting that God is working behind the scenes and will reveal the fullness of beauty in the fullness of His time. Romans 8 describes creation holding its breath, waiting for each of God's beloveds to flourish into the fullness of who they were always meant to be, before the pain of the world left its mark.

We wait with active hope, imagining a world made right because we trust the One who will make it so. Can you see it? *Wildflowers bursting forth. Weapons laid down. Tables filled with abundance. Justice rolling like a river. Compassion overflowing.*

Having imagination for a redeemed reality isn't wishful thinking. Every small act of mercy you extend and every prayer you offer help bring God's vision into the present, right in the midst of your everyday life.

When it seems like nothing is changing, take heart: The Spirit is working. With each breath, you are part of creation's long, slow unfolding toward wholeness.

On your inhale, picture a flower lovingly planted into the earth. On your exhale, watch it burst forth into life. Trust that the Spirit is doing this work in you—right here, right now.

BORROW THIS PRAYER

God of creation,
Create in me
A spirit of imagination
To see things not just as they are
But as they could be.
Breathe in me
Tenacious tenderness
And stubborn hope
To cocreate alongside You,
To paint a future of flourishing
On earth as it is in heaven.
Amen.

JUNE 4

Walk with me and work with me—watch how I do it.
Learn the unforced rhythms of grace.

MATTHEW 11:29 (MSG)

INHALE: Help me learn
EXHALE: The unforced rhythms of grace.

"Come on out here," he says, rolling up his sleeves as he heads to our garage. My son follows his dad out to where his lopsided blue bike is balanced in the driveway. "This," my husband explains, "is how you fix a flat tire. Watch me first—and then you'll do it yourself."

Flat tires are inevitable for a cyclist. The fix is simple: You just need some basic tools and plenty of practice. The more you do it, the more natural it becomes.[152]

Life is full of stressors vying for our attention: a family text thread gone awry, a misunderstanding with your spouse, a train blocking your path to work when you're already running late. We live demanding lives that ask a lot from us. On and on we go until it feels like we've hit a flat tire. We keep going through the motions, spinning our wheels, but the tire is bumping along, deflated.

In Matthew 11, Jesus extends this invitation: *Walk with Me. Work with Me. Watch Me.* This threefold rhythm of rest isn't automatic. Like fixing a flat tire, it has to be learned, practiced, and repeated until it becomes part of us. Just as tires inevitably wear down, no matter how skilled a bicyclist you are, you'll wear out too if you don't incorporate rhythms of rest into your life.

One of the first steps to fixing a flat tire is finding the leak. What is taking the air out of your lungs today? What might it look like to get away with Jesus, to work with Him and watch Him so you might learn to bring rhythms of rest into your days?

Rest isn't for the weak. It's not reserved for those who earn it either. Rest isn't a sign of laziness or a luxury—it's a core part of how God designed life with Him. We do not have a distant god—we have Jesus, who knew what it was like to need regular breaks in His own life. If even Jesus rested, how much more do *we* need it in our everyday lives?

Just as my husband taught my son to repair and change a flat tire, Jesus knows that rest isn't something that comes naturally; it's something that must be learned through practice until rest in Christ becomes a rhythm that matches the beat of our hearts.

My son didn't *have* to fix anything, but he wanted to spend time with his dad, to learn, to know and be known. Rest is what keeps us going, keeps us moving. By the grace of God, we're invited into rhythms of work and rest. We don't have to strive; we can just *be* with the One who is teaching us a better way.

Today, let your breath be unforced. Watch how it comes and goes. Let every inhale and every exhale be a rhythm of grace.

RHYTHM OF BREATH

When it feels like too much,
When your shoulders are heavy
With the weight of your world,
There's nothing you have to do
Nowhere you have to be.

JUNE 5

Where you are right now is God's place for you. Live and obey and love and believe right there.

1 CORINTHIANS 7:17 (MSG)

INHALE: Right here, right now,
EXHALE: You are with me.

When my kids were young, I'd go for walks pushing a double stroller while one rode a bike and another insisted on taking a scooter—only to have me carrying it by the end. We used to walk by a tall wooden fence painted with the words, "Bloom where you're planted."

I kind of hated it. I felt stuck in a small town where I didn't fit the culture. The phrase sounded like a command to stay small, to be quietly content without rocking the boat, to accept things as they were without any hope of change.

Paul wrote his letter to the Corinthians who were discontented in their own realities. They imagined that their circumstances—their relationships, their jobs, their homes—would look different. Yet Paul reminded them that they didn't have to wait for *someday* to cocreate with God, because God was dwelling in and among them. Right there. Right then. This pushes against how I perceived that fence décor. Paul wasn't calling the church into passivity but inviting them into presence.

The Holy Spirit doesn't demand you bloom in silence. No, as Paul reminds us, God breathes life into your current reality so you can live faithfully, love deeply, and act courageously *now*.

Live now, Paul says. Obey now. Love now. Believe now. Don't get distracted. Live on purpose.

Living in the present doesn't mean you're stuck forever. It means you're empowered to experience God's presence *where you are*. You don't have to wait for a promotion, move to a new city, or find your soulmate to encounter God.

Right here, where you're breathing, is where God is—even in and among your wonderings, frustrations, and doubts. Yes, there's much more life in store for you in the future, but you don't have to wait to encounter God-breathed life now.

God entrusts us with our current circumstances.* When Paul encouraged believers to remain faithful in their present situation, he wasn't limiting them; he was empowering them to live fully and serve faithfully in whatever place or season they found themselves.

How might you awaken to that presence today—one that says you're not stuck but breathed into?

Take a slow breath. On your inhale, picture roots reaching into nourishing soil. On your exhale, imagine new leaves unfurling toward the sun. Let the Spirit fill your present moment with life.

SACRED ECHOES

Tell me, what is it you plan to do
with your one wild and precious life?[153]

Mary Oliver

---

* See Jeremiah 29:11; 1 Peter 4:10.

JUNE 6

Love never gives up, never loses faith, is always hopeful, and endures through every circumstance.

1 CORINTHIANS 13:7 (NLT)

INHALE: Love endures
EXHALE: Through it all.

I glanced out the window to see my youngest son and his friend knee-deep in a rough patch of unlandscaped yard. "We're planting sunflowers!" he proclaimed, dirt under his nails and a proud grin planted on his face.

I smiled back, quietly doubting that anything would take root in that weed-filled corner. But through the summer, those small seeds sent roots deep into the earth, and tall stalks began to rise until, finally, in late summer, they bloomed, boasting ten feet of glory with their faces turned toward the sun.

When my husband and I got married in our early twenties, plenty of people doubted us. *Too young*, they said. *Too untested, too many storms ahead!* But like those hidden seeds, our love continued to grow. *We* kept growing. We didn't always know what we were doing, but we kept turning toward each other and toward the Light, rooted in something bigger than ourselves.

Sunflowers thrive when they can stretch their roots deep into the earth. They must be strong enough to withstand the weather and compete with pesky weeds. They require sunlight and sometimes need pruning.

Love works the same way. Paul's words in 1 Corinthians 13 are often read at weddings, but they describe not only romantic love but also God's covenant love, which is faithful, enduring, and self-giving. A love that holds us in the storms, makes space for hope, and keeps drawing us toward the Light.

Where do you sense God inviting your roots to go deeper today? What weeds or old leaves might you clear out so hope can grow?

Take a slow breath. As you inhale, picture a seed settling into dark soil. As you exhale, envision it growing and reaching toward the sun. Trust that the Spirit who never gives up is doing this same work in you.

PRACTICING THE WAY

Love is patient and kind. Love is not jealous or boastful or proud or rude. It does not demand its own way. It is not irritable, and it keeps no record of being wronged. It does not rejoice about injustice but rejoices whenever the truth wins out. Love never gives up, never loses faith, is always hopeful, and endures through every circumstance.

1 Corinthians 13:4-7

Read through the passage slowly, letting the words take root. On a blank page, sketch a circle with lines or simple petals radiating outward, like a sunflower. In the center, write *LOVE*. On each line, write a word or phrase from (or inspired by) the passage. As you write each word, pause and pray through today's breath prayer. Slow your breathing as you inhale and exhale. Notice which word or phrase draws you in. Sit quietly with this image, trusting that the Spirit is planting and growing love deep within you.

JUNE 7

In the morning, LORD, you hear my voice; in the morning I lay my requests before you and wait expectantly.

PSALM 5:3 (NIV)

INHALE: Each breath
EXHALE: Is a new beginning.

I'm not a morning person. In college, my roommates (rightfully) lost patience with how many times I'd snooze my alarm before class. Even now, I need a mild to moderate amount of coffee before I can interact with my kids or my husband. I've run out of the house with wet hair more times than I can count, paying the price for yearning for *just five more minutes* of sleep.

Over the years, I've tried everything to greet mornings with less animosity: early alarms, exercise routines, even an alarm clock light that mimicked the sunrise.

Over time, I've realized that two practices help me start the day well, whether I'm waking up in a hotel room while traveling for work or being jolted awake by a child needing help packing a school lunch: Begin with prayer, and pray before looking at your phone.

This anchors our hearts with the One who gives each breath and recenters us to face the joys and challenges ahead. Here are four simple ideas:

- **Breath prayer:** Take a few slow breaths before you even get out of bed. On your inhale, pray, "Each breath," and on your exhale, "Is a new beginning." Need a reminder? Write your favorite breath prayer on a sticky note to keep by your bed.
- **Jesus Creed:** Scot McKnight says praying the "Jesus Creed" every morning is spiritually transformational.[154] "'Hear, O Israel: The Lord our God, the Lord is one. And you shall love the Lord your God with all your heart and with all your soul and with all your mind and with all your strength.' The second is this: 'You shall love your neighbor as yourself.'"*
- **Examen:** As you're making breakfast or brushing your teeth, ask: *What do I need to name before God, honestly and without editing? What thoughts or worries did I wake up with? Are there burdens I'm tempted to carry on my own?*
- **Liturgy:** If you're like me and struggle to find your words in the morning, consider borrowing the following prayer, "A Prayer for Morning." Bookmark this page so you can have it close.

You don't have to be a "morning person" to be a praying person. Whether you whisper a breath prayer as you brush your hair or pray the Jesus Creed on your commute, God will meet you there.

BORROW THIS PRAYER

Be with each of us
As we go about the day.
And when the day is done,
Bring us home safely
Under the shelter of Your wings.
Amen.

From "A Prayer for Morning"
in Every Season Sacred[155]

---

* Mark 12:29-31, ESV.

JUNE 8

Is there anyplace I can go to avoid your Spirit? to be out of your sight?

PSALM 139:7 (MSG)

INHALE: Wherever I go,
EXHALE: There You are.

I adore wedding reception speeches. I'm here for every single sentimental story from a tearful bridesmaid. I laugh along with every inside joke shared by the best man.

At one reception, as the candles flickered and the room quieted, the father of the bride tapped his glass to give a speech. We all expected some profound wisdom. He lifted his glass, looked at his daughter, and said, "Wherever you go . . ."—pausing like he was about to reveal the secret to life—"there you are."

Everyone laughed.

In their own dad-joke way, his words reminded me of something Psalm 139 whispers: *No matter where we go, God is already there.*

Our God is so expansive and so intimate that there is nowhere we can go where God isn't already.

No matter who we are, what we've done, or where we've been, God promises never to leave or forsake us. I was reminded of this during a Bible conference when we opened the floor for prayer. People shared heavy and holy requests—prayers about restored relationships, infertility, mental health. One woman prayed, "God in schools!" I nodded, but a question flashed through my mind: *Isn't God already there?*

Her request nudged me to remember what is always true: God is with you in the hospital waiting room. God is with children in the school cafeteria. God is in the cross fire of a war zone. God is downtown and in the quiet cornfields too. God is in the gas station and the grocery store. God is in the room where you cried yourself to sleep, in the barbershop, in the parking lot where you couldn't find a spot.

God is *everywhere*, and this is the heartbeat of Psalm 139: Wherever we go, God is already there, surrounding and sustaining us.

Today, right here in this moment, God is with you. Pause. Take a slow, deep breath. Inhale and exhale the air God gives you with the lungs God gave you. Name the place where you are right now—your kitchen, your car, your office—and whisper, "You are here."

Wherever we are, we have a direct line to the One who holds it all together and draws near to us. Trust that the Spirit who never leaves is with you in every space you inhabit.

Even in the most overwhelming or ordinary moments, God is present and expansive enough to hold the whole world and close enough to feel your every breath.

SACRED ECHOES

You speak peace in every breath
For you are always, always with me.

"Always with Me," by Paul Zach and Jessica Fox

JUNE 9

The heart regulates the hands.

2 CORINTHIANS 8:12 (MSG)

INHALE: Guide the work
EXHALE: Of my hands.

At some point or another, every writer learns the phrase, "Show, don't tell." We don't just write, "She was angry." We show her hands shaking, her face flushing, her breath growing shallow.

This rule also works in faith.

If we claim to love our neighbors but treat them with suspicion, what story do our actions tell? If we read Scripture about God welcoming the stranger in church but we withhold kindness from people who look or live differently from us, what are we *showing*?

Paul writes that without love, our words are just noise.*

He also tells the church in Corinth that generosity flows not from pressure but from the willingness of the heart.† The point isn't that God is tallying our failures—it's that the Spirit is constantly reshaping us from the inside out.

We don't pour out patience because we're naturally patient. We don't forgive because it's easy. *We love because God first loved us.* As the Spirit works within us, the work of our hands becomes an overflow of worship.

What would it look like to start every day with a prayer that the work of your hands would reflect the best of your heart, rooted in God's love?

If your life were a movie and someone watched only your actions, how would they describe your character?

Jesus said people would know His followers by their love.‡

What we do and how we live flows from what we hold inside. This is true in every area of our lives: At work. In our homes. In our relationships. In our communities.

Today, pause and notice: Where do your hands and your heart feel out of alignment? Where might you invite God's Spirit to bring them together?

BORROW THIS PRAYER

Be in the work of my hands
And the beat of my heart.
Be in the breath of my body
And the sweat of my brow.
Be in my wonderings,
Be in my doubt.
And as I start this new day,
Be here in the people I see
And in the ones I do not understand.
Amen.

* See 1 Corinthians 13:1.

† See 2 Corinthians 8:12.

‡ See John 13:35.

JUNE 10

O LORD, what a variety of things you have made! In wisdom you have made them all. The earth is full of your creatures.

PSALM 104:24 (NLT)

INHALE: I stand in wonder
EXHALE: At Your wisdom.

The golden hour wrapped everything in light as my youngest came sprinting toward me, wild and barefoot, blond curls bouncing, with fists full of orange lilies yanked from the yard. He proudly extended a lopsided, dirt-flecked bouquet picked just for me.

Up until then, when I looked at the lilies stubbornly sprouting along our back fence, I usually felt more annoyance than awe. But my son's backyard bouquet reminded me of the sacred hiding in the ordinary, if only I'd change the posture of my heart to be more open to the everyday wonder I often overlook.

My husband has started dabbling in bird-watching. He now has binoculars, a notebook, and even a little identification booklet. It's kind of funny, but I've learned from him how much beauty we miss when we're rushing.

Jesus told His disciples to look at the lilies and to notice the sparrows. He prayed on mountainsides, taught from a boat on the water, and sought solitude in the wilderness.* Scripture is full of moments where Jesus was attuned to God's presence in the natural world, showing us how creation can become a sanctuary.

Creation comes alive in the summer. What was once barren is now lush and green, teeming with life abundant. When we spend time in nature, it slows our heart rate, regulates our breathing, and calms our nervous system.

Something in us exhales when we step outside.

In one study, people spent five days immersed in the wild while researchers measured their heart rhythms and mood. Instead of simply relaxing, their bodies showed increased alertness alongside improved mood.[156]

Experiencing the Creator by noticing creation doesn't just *calm* us—it *awakens* us.

When we pause to notice creation, we're welcomed into wonder. And that wonder draws us closer to the One who made it all. Just as I understand my kids a bit more when they explain the meaning behind their artwork, holding Scripture in one hand and prayerfully noticing creation with the other gives us a fuller glimpse into God's heart.

If you're able to, spend time outside, even if just for a few minutes, practicing today's breath prayer. Ask yourself: *How might I awaken to the presence of God right in front of me?*

Let your breath whisper your wonder as you worship the One who made all things. As you breathe and pray, remember that you're part of a living, breathing world shaped by a loving, living God.

SACRED ECHOES

Every corner of this wild earth, peace.

"This Wild Earth" by Young Oceans

* See Luke 12:27; Matthew 10:29-31; Luke 6:12; Luke 5:3; Mark 1:35.

JUNE 11

Since Jesus went through everything you're going through and more, learn to think like him.

1 PETER 4:1 (MSG)

INHALE: You understand
EXHALE: What I'm going through.

Sometimes the ache of humanity feels too heavy to hold. We read hateful words. We see unjust systems. We carry our own private sorrows.

In all the heartbreak, we have hope: We have a God who became one of us, who draws near, who *understands*.

Peter wrote to believers facing opposition and weariness, reminding them that Christ Himself endured suffering so they could live with His mindset. Some people imagine a God who observes but never enters in, but Jesus gives us a faith so much more expansive—and personal too.

The Christian story is radically different from other religions because God didn't simply send instructions; God entered in as a baby—fully human, fully divine—and changed the course of history forever.

Jesus knows what it is like to exist on this complicated earth, with complicated people. He cried. He laughed. He felt hunger pangs. He was a helpless baby and a curious teen. He knew joy and sorrow, tenderness and tension.

When you're at your tipping point, when you feel most misunderstood, take heart: Each breath you take is a gift from a God who truly gets it.

Because Jesus entered our human life, we can trust Him with our own. And because Jesus understands, He will help us to follow His ways of being in the world. Jesus is at home in your mess of emotions too. He doesn't ask you to clean up your soul before He comes close. He meets you in the realness of your life—in your disarray, in your discouragement, in your doubt.

Take a moment to step outside today. Feel the warmth of the sun on your skin or the evening breeze across your face. Inhale slowly: "You understand." Exhale: "What I'm going through."

As you breathe, imagine handing over to Jesus what you're holding—in complete honesty. Picture Him placing a steady, kind hand on your shoulder, looking you in the eyes, and whispering, "I know, dear one. I know."

Stay there for a few breaths. Let your shoulders drop. Trust that the One who lived the life we live goes with you on the path today.

SACRED ECHOES

Christ came to us as Jesus of Nazareth, wholly human and wholly divine, to show us what it means to be made in God's image.[157]

Madeleine L'Engle

JUNE 12

It is the spirit in a person, the breath of the Almighty, that gives them understanding.

JOB 32:8 (NIV)

INHALE: Breath of God,
EXHALE: Show me the way.

Job knew what it was to lose everything. (He lived a long time ago, but his struggles feel surprisingly relatable. After all, there's a whole book in the Old Testament dedicated to his woes.)

The blows kept coming until he could barely catch his breath. Friends surrounded him with words they thought were wise, but they landed like stones. He was desperate for someone to tell him where God had gone, for someone—*anyone*—to help him make sense of his pain.

Then a younger man spoke: "It is the spirit in a person, the breath of the Almighty, that gives them understanding."

Our wisdom, our spiritual understanding, comes from God alone. God's breath inside of us is a thread that moves through Scripture. In the Old Testament, the Hebrew word *ruach* means "breath," "wind," and "spirit" all at once. In the New Testament, the Greek word *pneuma* carries the same layered meaning.[158] From the garden to the upper room, God's breath is always moving and guiding.

God breathed life into Adam's nostrils. God's breath filled dry bones, and they came alive. Jesus breathed on His disciples, saying, "Receive the Holy Spirit." At Pentecost, the Spirit rushed in like wind.*

We don't always have answers for our pain. All too often, the awful things we've walked through can't be excused or explained. But even in the mystery, even in our deepest questions and widest unknowns, the breath of God meets us and whispers wisdom into our listening hearts.

Douglas Scott Dent writes, "Each person breathes with God in a distinctive way because each person is a unique creation of God."[159]

God's wisdom is personal and particular, attuned to who you are and what you're facing.

Where do you need to hear the Spirit's voice today? Where might you be willing to pause and listen, trusting that God's breath can whisper wisdom in your lungs?

Take a deep, slow breath for six counts. Let your shoulders drop. Imagine handing your honest questions to Jesus. As you release your breath, let the Spirit fill the space inside you where anxiety or confusion once lived. Trust that understanding is a gift, breathed into you by the God who knows and loves you, right here, right now.

To find out more about Pentecost, see the liturgical calendar in appendix A.

SACRED ECHOES

[God's] message is not written out in starlight, which in the long run would make no difference; rather it is written out for each of us in the humdrum, helter-skelter events of each day; it is a message that in the long run might just make all the difference.[160]

Frederick Buechner

* See Genesis 2:7; Ezekiel 37:1-10; John 20:22, NLT; Acts 2:2.

JUNE 13

God's love has been poured out into our hearts through the Holy Spirit, who has been given to us.

ROMANS 5:5 (NIV)

INHALE: You pour love
EXHALE: Into me.

You pour yourself out at work and at home, in your relationships and in your community.

But what is filling you back up?

If we rely only on our own reserves, our energy and our hope will run dry. Thankfully, the Holy Spirit doesn't stand at a distance: God breathes love into our hearts. And this love is like a living stream,* flowing and replenishing us so that even in hardship, hope rises.

In Romans 5, Paul writes to a community under pressure. He tells them that "suffering produces endurance, and endurance produces character, and character produces hope."† And "hope does not disappoint us," he says, "because God's love has been poured out into our hearts."‡

What might it look like to let yourself be cared for? To be gentle with yourself instead of overscheduling? To pause and marvel that the very essence of God dwells within you?

When we view God as a taskmaster, we often end up being overly critical of ourselves—and, in turn, hard on others. But the Spirit is a life-giver. God meets your thirst and says, "Come, drink."§

Sometimes the bravest thing we can do is step away and allow God to replenish us.

You are not a worker bee. You are not a "yes" machine. You don't have to be everything to everyone. You don't have to push yourself to exhaustion. You are chosen and beloved. You are poured into.

When you live from that fullness, your heart overflows with hope, and you are more positioned to cultivate peace in a land that is dry and weary.

Release that breath you've been holding as you ask God to help you live from a place of continual renewal. As you inhale and exhale, trust that even through exhausting expectations and difficult circumstances, God's heart toward you is gentle and kind, not harsh or withholding.

PAUSE AND PONDER

Where do you feel most depleted today (work, family, health, church, world news)? Who or what genuinely replenishes you?

How does the image of God being full of loving-kindness affect the way you treat yourself? How might being kind to yourself spill over into kindness toward others?

---

* See John 4:10-14.
† Romans 5:3-4, ESV.
‡ Romans 5:5, ISV.
§ See Isaiah 55:1; John 7:37.

JUNE 14

Don't hit back; discover beauty in everyone.

ROMANS 12:17 (MSG)

INHALE: When I want to fight,

EXHALE: Help me see the good.

"What they don't understand," I confide in my husband, "is how much power it takes *not* to say the thing I'm thinking."

He nods, equal parts impressed and terrified.

Lately I've been asking God not only to keep my mouth from harsh words but also to transform my inner commentary, to help me hold on to grace for people even when I'd rather read them the riot act.[161]

The truth is, some people push my buttons. Sometimes I *do* want to hit back. But Romans 12 calls us to a different way—the way of Jesus. Paul urges the Roman church not only to refrain from revenge but to discover the beauty in everyone, not to check *if* beauty exists but to recognize what's *already* there.

All God's ways are peace, and Jesus is the Prince of Peace.*

Following Jesus means extending the peace God gives us to others. (This doesn't mean tolerating harm or ignoring injustice. Boundaries and courage still matter.) When we follow Jesus' way, it affects how we spend our energy. We refuse to take cheap shots. We pause before shooting a scathing reply. We honor the inherent worth of another human being who, too, was made in God's image.†

Paul doesn't write, "Discover to see *if* beauty exists," but instead he urges us to recognize that it's *already there*, just waiting to be noticed.

We live in a culture of hot takes and clapbacks, where "dumpster fire" has become shorthand for the whole world since 2020. But we don't have to add fuel to the fire (or erupt into flames ourselves). Life in Christ is a call to humility and restraint—a countercultural invitation to intentionally seek the beauty that's already present in others.

Yes, even *that* person.

The next time you're triggered and you feel your heart racing and your breath getting shallow, borrow today's breath prayer. Inhale as deeply as you can, hold for a few counts, and then exhale for as long as you can. (Aim for about five breath prayers per minute.) A breath prayer is quick enough to do in a meeting, a car line, or a grocery aisle—just long enough to reset and remind you that sometimes what's "right" may not be the right thing to say.

PAUSE AND PONDER

Write a one-sentence prayer you can turn to when someone is pushing your buttons.

____

____

____

* See Isaiah 9:6.

† See Genesis 1:27.

JUNE 15

He gives power to the weak and strength to the powerless.

ISAIAH 40:29 (NLT)

INHALE: You give strength
EXHALE: To the powerless.

I used to believe strength was pushing yourself to the limit and never asking for help. Then I began raising a child whose every milestone came through perseverance and grace. Parenting a child with significant disabilities has taught me that God's power often shows up in unexpected ways.

In a world that celebrates hustle and filters out weakness, Isaiah 40:29 introduces us to the One who delights in strengthening the worn-out and weary—who gives power to the weak and strength to the powerless. Isaiah 40 was written to people in exile who were convinced that God had forgotten them. But into their exhaustion, God breathed this promise: "Those who hope in the LORD will renew their strength."* From the beginning, God has been breathing strength into those who need it.

I see this every day as I raise my daughter, Eliza. She has Down syndrome and lives with physical challenges stemming from a seizure disorder as a baby. She has spent countless hours in therapy learning to walk. It hasn't been easy, and she still often needs a hand to hold, but step-by-step, she's doing it. She perseveres. Her body holds limits, but she is resilient. I have no doubt God looks at her and calls her strong.

That's just God's way: Power where the world sees weakness. Strength where the world sees powerlessness. Hope when it feels like none should be left.

A quick look at the news shows the places where creation aches for God's power to breathe life again—videos and images of war zones and starving children, people in power mocking kids with disabilities, the elderly scammed out of their savings, neighbors maligned because of race or nationality. But God is near—and always has been. This is why we don't shrug and say, "Oh well," when we see hard things. Instead, we let hope propel us to keep caring and moving forward in love. As the body of Christ, we're called to create a world where even "the parts of the body that seem to be weaker are indispensable."†

Joining God in the "renewal of all things"‡ may look like small, faithful steps—befriending a neighbor, advocating for someone vulnerable, mentoring a teen, praying through the headlines.

How is the Spirit of our living God empowering you so you might empower others?

PRACTICING THE WAY

One way to enter the reshaping of our world, no matter who you are or where you are, is to pray through the news:

- Grab a newspaper or open a trusted news app.
- As you read each headline, pray for those in the story who hold less power.
- Ask God to strengthen and comfort them, to surround them with advocates, and to show you one small way you can be part of Christ's renewing work.

* Isaiah 40:31, NIV.
† 1 Corinthians 12:22, NIV.
‡ Matthew 19:28, NIV.

JUNE 16

Attention, all! See the marvels of GOD! He plants flowers and trees all over the earth, bans war from pole to pole, breaks all the weapons across his knee.

PSALM 46:8-9 (MSG)

INHALE: Fill the earth
EXHALE: With Your flourishing.

When I was in fifth grade, I ripped my favorite pair of flared jeans while playing tag at recess. I was bereft. The fashion trends of the 1970s were experiencing a bit of a renaissance, so my mom saved the day with an iron-on patch of a groovy flower, turning damage into delight.

In Psalm 46, we encounter a God who transforms war zones into fields of flowers and turns weapons into gardening tools. God's heart beats for new life. In one breath, the psalmist praises God for flowers and trees *and* for banning war. Beauty and justice are not separate. God's peace is as tangible as creation. We just have to notice.

War is not God's plan but humanity's fallback when everything else has failed. Throughout history, people have waged wars in God's name—an attempt to shape God into our image rather than letting God shape us. Anne Lamott talks about the time a pastor shared this wisdom: "You can safely assume you've created God in your own image," he told her, "when it turns out that God hates all the same people you do."[162]

The psalmist in today's verse invites us to pay attention as a way to move toward love instead of hate, to experience the God who pushes flowers through cracks in concrete and plants peace in unexpected soil.

Noticing beauty is an act of defiance against despair. It retrains our hearts to rest in the awe of God's way breaking through in our weary world. Even in times of turmoil, even amid devastation and destruction, God is bringing beauty.

Kingdom imagination gives us eyes to see weapons turned into tools, war zones turned into gardens, and a desire for control turned into Christ-centered creativity. God's heart for peace runs through Scripture and comes to full expression in Christ, our Prince of Peace.*

Which of your weapons (defensiveness, cynicism, harsh words) might Jesus want to break across His knee?

PRACTICING THE WAY

RAWtools leads a "Guns to Gardens" movement that turns unwanted firearms into garden tools. Each gun is safely and permanently disabled before it's forged into a new tool. With more than one hundred Americans killed by gun violence each day,[163] RAWtools offers a way to live into the biblical vision of swords beaten into plowshares. Learn more at rawtools.org/swords-to-plowshares.

* See Ephesians 2:14.

JUNE 17

This is what the Sovereign LORD says: Look! I am going to put breath into you and make you live again!

EZEKIEL 37:5 (NLT)

INHALE: You breathe life
EXHALE: Into dry bones.

Getting tired is not a moral failure. If even the One who breathed life into the universe—animating the twinkling stars and roaring seas—took time to rest, why do we so often think that we can just push through our exhaustion?

I once watched a detective in a TV drama stay late on a case, rifling the same files as his eyelids drooped and his mind grew fuzzy. He sent his team home but stubbornly tried to work through the night, convinced that sheer effort would solve what fresh eyes could not.

How many times have you done the same—working and powering through, as though depletion will deliver you?

God doesn't tell us to rest because it's a nice idea; God tells us to rest because we need it.

Like those dry bones in Ezekiel's vision, we come to the end of our own strength. We're only human, and we all have limitations. But God breathes where we've run dry. And God doesn't just *repair* us but *reanimates* us.

God breathes and life bursts forth.

Ezekiel 37 describes the valley of dry bones—an image of literal hopelessness. God doesn't tell Ezekiel to glue the bones back together but tells him to speak, and then God breathes. Breath rattles the bones into bodies, and hearts pulse again. This is the same breath that formed Adam's lungs in Genesis. This is the same wind that filled the upper room at Pentecost. This is the same Spirit who does more with breath than we can ever do with our own striving.

Even when we're depleted, even amid devastation and disillusionment, God promises renewal. And not just for someday but for now. "Just as God breathed the breath of life into the first living being, so our deep, instinctive taking of breath is receiving again the gift of life from God for each moment," Flora Slosson Wuellner writes.[164]

Sometimes the strongest, most sacred thing we can do is to set aside our own labors and trust the breath of God to do what only God can do.

Breathe in through your nose and then slowly exhale as you borrow today's breath prayer. As you breathe and pray, reflect on where you feel like "dry bones" in your life. What would it look like to receive God's breath there?

BREATHE THIS IN

Even science points to breath as a hidden source of renewal. Studies show that slowing your breathing to about six breaths a minute can slow your racing heart, quiet your brain activity, and ease stress.[165]

JUNE 18

Fix your thoughts on what is true, and honorable, and right, and pure, and lovely, and admirable.

PHILIPPIANS 4:8 (NLT)

INHALE: Fix my thoughts
EXHALE: On what is true.

One morning after my kids left for school, I caught up on the news and felt a stress spiral pulling me under. As discouraged as I was, I'd signed up to volunteer at a downtown fun run for local elementary students, so I stashed my phone and took a deep breath, asking God to give me hope in our weary world. Seeing more than a thousand fourth graders running and cheering began to shake me out of my "everything is terrible" stupor.

Community members lined the streets, and my daughter, who has been working hard in physical therapy to strengthen her walking skills, crossed the finish line to a roaring crowd. It felt like a glimpse of heaven—watching people on both sides of her clap and cheer as she stepped across. It was a Philippians 4:8 moment: something lovely, admirable, and true right in front of me to fix my thoughts on.

Yes, horrible things are happening in our world, *and* that's not the whole story.

At any given time, children are laughing, communities are gathering, and moments of joy are happening, just waiting to be noticed. Sometimes we need a reset—to go outside, breathe in the fresh air, feel the sun on our faces, and look into another person's eyes, letting encouragement replace dread and community replace algorithms.

The heartbreaking parts of life don't tell the whole story.

Focusing our thoughts on what is good and true doesn't mean ignoring injustice or suffering but rooting ourselves in God's reality so we have the strength to face difficult situations with fresh courage.

Anchoring your soul in God's goodness builds the resilience to walk into life's difficulties with hope that surpasses all understanding.

Breath prayer is one way to "fix your thoughts on what is true, and honorable, and right, and pure, and lovely, and admirable." The next time you feel an anxiety spiral pulling you into inner stories that stray from God's truth, return to today's breath prayer.

PAUSE AND PONDER

Where do your thoughts automatically drift—to what's broken or what's beautiful?

____

____

____

What's one lovely or admirable thing you can focus on when you start to write a story in your mind that's only focused on the bad?

____

____

____

JUNE 19

JUNETEENTH

Do you know what I want? I want justice—
oceans of it. I want fairness—rivers of it.

AMOS 5:24 (MSG)

INHALE: Flood the world
EXHALE: With Your justice.

No matter who we are, God calls and empowers us to treat others fairly and to advocate for the oppressed.

Juneteenth marks the day in 1865 when enslaved Black people in Texas were finally told they were free—two and a half years *after* the signing of the Emancipation Proclamation. Today, we hold in our hearts that freedom was both announced *and* delayed.

Though there were many Christian abolitionists, slavery is a sinful part of US history that Christians were too often on the wrong side of. Thousands of years before the horrific, long years of slavery in the States, Amos wrote to God's people who were living in ways that betrayed God's character. His words about "oceans of justice" and "rivers of fairness" rebuke a faith that follows religious practices but doesn't demonstrate a changed life.

Amos was calling people back to God's life-giving vision for justice as an unstoppable, mighty stream. Righteousness is a way of being and breathing that aligns with God's call to do justice, act mercifully, and care for the marginalized.[166]

In the face of oppression, the church can offer an exhale. Jasmine Marie, author of *Black Girl Breathing*, recalls first experiencing the idea of intentional breathing at her church: "My chest didn't feel so tight. My face relaxed. I was able to be more present."[167] That quiet exhale evolved into "Black Girls Breathing," a movement she founded to give Black women space to rest and use breathwork as a form of renewal.

"Just as I inherited trauma from my predecessors," Jasmine says, "I also inherited resilience and hope that affirmed to me that despite occasional moments of hopelessness, I am not toiling in vain."[168]

Where do you need to be gentle with yourself—to seek resources and enter regular rhythms of rest? And where might Christ be calling you to compassionate courage—to confront unjust systems today and stand with those harmed by history's sins?

Let today's breath anchor you in remembrance and restorative action. As you inhale, imagine yourself receiving the Holy Spirit's healing presence. As you exhale, imagine your breath flowing like a rushing stream and extending Christ's compassion to all.

BORROW THIS PRAYER

Mighty God, only You
Can bring songs of freedom
In a strange land.
Help us—the oppressed
And the oppressor—
To humbly seek Your face.[169]

Dorena Williamson, author of The Story of Juneteenth

JUNE 20

From the rising of the sun to the place where it sets, the name of the LORD is to be praised.

PSALM 113:3 (NIV)

INHALE: I trust You, God;
EXHALE: I don't have to figure it out.

The longest days of the year have arrived. Light stretches toward the edges of the evening, whispering that after every dark season, daylight awaits. As sure as the sun rises, God holds the seasons in rhythm—and God holds you too.

Summer invites us into a sacred slowing. To bask in the warm glow of possibility, to breathe in the scent of honeysuckle carried on a breeze. The summer solstice—brimming with light—whispers, *The old is gone. The new is here.*

This week, stand in awe at the sunrise. Sit in wonder at the sunset. You don't have to figure it all out. You don't have to pack this season full of things to do and places to be. Be still. Know that God is near as you rest your bare feet in the grass and watch water ripple over stones, as you let yourself exhale.

You don't have to go on a fancy vacation to enter into wonder. The fingerprints of our Creator are already here with you, right now, nestled in the wildflowers that bloom along your back fence or the weeping willow that sways in the breeze at your local park.

"When I speak of wonder, I mean the practice of beholding the beautiful. Beholding the majestic . . . the sun setting on the sea—but also the perfectly mundane—that soap bubble reflecting your kitchen, the oxidized underbelly of that stainless steel pan," Cole Arthur Riley writes. "More than the grand beauties of our lives, wonder is about having the presence to pay attention to the commonplace. It could be said that to find beauty in the ordinary is a deeper exercise than climbing to the mountaintop."[170]

Slow down. Stop worrying about tomorrow, just for a moment.

Let your shoulders loosen. Unlock your jaw.

Breathe.

As sure as the sun rises and sets, God is with you.

Always has been. And always will be.

RHYTHM OF BREATH

As sunlight floods in,
God is beaming,
Calling you beloved,
Beckoning you home.

JUNE 21

The LORD will guide you continually, giving you water when you are dry and restoring your strength. You will be like a well-watered garden, like an ever-flowing spring.

ISAIAH 58:11 (NLT)

INHALE: Giver of life,
EXHALE: I receive what You restore.

Imagine your heart as a garden. Is the soil rocky or rich? Is the landscape overgrown or neat and tidy? What's flourishing? What's fading? Where do you ache for new growth? What needs pruning for life to return?

The prophet Isaiah spoke this hopeful promise to God's people, casting a vision for restored strength, well-watered gardens, ever-flowing springs, rebuilt cities, and restored homes.* What an exhale, right? But if we camp out on these words alone, we risk missing the broader picture.

Isaiah's promise of a well-watered garden arrives only *after* a call to mercy and justice. He warns against performative religion—those who make a big deal about fasting but exploit their workers, pray but are constantly picking fights, act pious but conveniently ignore the oppressed. The promise comes after the call.

God's grace doesn't fill the gardens of our hearts with living water just so we can store it up and check "Christian" off our to-do list. God restores us so *we* can be restorers—a people set apart—embodying mercy and moving against the grain of our culture to loosen chains and extend grace, even when it costs us.

As you exhale, let God's restorative love saturate your heart and overflow into our weary world.

* See Isaiah 58:11-12.

PRACTICING THE WAY

Ask God to guide you as you read. Then slowly read Isaiah 58:6-12 aloud. Notice any words or phrases that catch your attention.

Now, practice some prayerful imagination, inspired by Saint Ignatius:[171]

- **Breathe.** Take a slow and deep inhale. As you exhale, ask God to be with you.
- **Picture it.** Picture Isaiah writing this passage today. What setting is he in? A bustling city? A crowded church? A refugee camp?
- **Look.** As you hear his words, who comes to mind? Who are the "imprisoned" in your community? Who is burdened? Who is hungry or without shelter?
- **Imagine.** Ask God to help you envision the oppressed, the unhoused, the unjustly accused. Hold them in your heart.
- **Stay open.** Let the Spirit reveal the chains that burden people around you. Are they under the weight of addiction? Loneliness? Injustice? Fear?
- **Listen.** Hear God's invitation to you: What does it mean to share your food, your time, your heart?
- **Read.** Return to Isaiah 58:11. As you read, visualize a parched, cracked desert. Now see the living water flowing into the ground, turning it into a lush garden.
- **Notice.** How does your heart feel as the land fills with life?
- **Pray.** Close with a short prayer.

JUNE 22

The Spirit gives life.

2 CORINTHIANS 3:6 (NLT)

INHALE: I release my striving;
EXHALE: Fill me with new life.

Sometimes what looks nourishing on the surface leaves us emptier than before, while what feels costly at first actually restores our soul.

What's giving you life these days? What's draining you?

I don't always feel renewed after an evening spent watching another obnoxious (yet compelling) reality TV series. And yet showing up for a neighbor—even when it feels inconvenient—often leaves me more alive and more awake to God's presence.

The most life-giving way we can spend our time is to walk—and rest—in step with the Spirit.

The Spirit alone gives life. Paul calls the Corinthians living "letters" of God's work* because the Spirit has written transformation upon their hearts—a fulfillment of God's promise to give a new heart and new spirit.†

With every breath we take, the Spirit remakes us from the inside out, leading us into rhythms of love in our everyday realities. We rest with our inhale, and then we move out into the world with our exhale, trusting that each time our lungs fill with air, the Spirit is giving us life.

The word *inhale* comes from the Latin word *inspirare*, which means to "take in the spirit."[172] With each breath, God brings life through the Holy Spirit. And because the Spirit is alive within us, we can enter a deep soul-rest, trusting that God's transforming work is already underway within us. We can breathe with the Spirit, exhaling love, joy, peace, patience, kindness, goodness, faithfulness, gentleness, and self-control into our weary world.‡

Ask the Spirit to show you one place you can stop striving today. Be gentle with yourself. Sometimes life-giving moments look like quiet solitude; sometimes they look like showing up for someone else.

Either way, the Spirit is already with you.

How might you embrace the Spirit's life-giving work in your life today?

SACRED ECHOES

Love is the language of the Holy Spirit; and through love, the Spirit guides us.[173]

Makoto Fujimura

* 2 Corinthians 3:3, MSG.
† See Ezekiel 36:26-27.
‡ See Galatians 5:22-23.

JUNE 23

You have made my life no longer than the width of my hand. My entire lifetime is just a moment to you; at best, each of us is but a breath.

PSALM 39:5 (NLT)

INHALE: I am small,
EXHALE: But I am held.

Under the darkened dome of the planetarium, my son and I leaned back, the ceiling above us alive with glittering galaxies. We gazed up at the scattered stars, no longer at a science center in the middle of Iowa, but floating among the cosmos. Liam Neeson's deep voice boomed through the speakers, his narration guiding us on a ride through the galaxy.

It was breathtaking—and, I'll be honest, more than a little terrifying. Black holes, the bending of space and time, galaxies swallowed whole. It felt so big, and I felt so small. A question popped into my mind and wouldn't let me go: *Where is God in all this?*

Scripture reminds us that our lives are "but a breath." That's not meant to scare us but to center us. Life's brevity and the cosmos's immensity are not proof of our insignificance but of God's vast love.

The truth is that our life is a mystery and our life is but a vapor. We can find comfort in this, letting the mystery draw us closer to the One who holds it all in existence, or we can let it scare us and harden our hearts so we don't have to think about it.

One of my all-time favorite authors is Madeleine L'Engle. She's well-known for her award-winning novel *A Wrinkle in Time*, but I adore her nonfiction too. The mysteries of space and time *and* the mystery of Christ are common threads in her work. She asks questions that make me feel like my questions are okay too. L'Engle poses this question: "Could we be fascinated by a Maker who was completely explained and understood?"

Step outside tonight. Look up. Consider L'Engle's question about our mysterious Maker as you soak in the way the moon illuminates the night, as you notice how the stars sparkle over the streetlights. Borrow today's breath prayer as you let the night sky remind you that your smallness is an invitation to draw near to the One who holds it all.

The Maker who holds the cosmos in existence wants to hold you too.

LET IT LINGER

If you are small:
You're small enough to be held.

If you are overwhelmed:
You can rest in the hope that there is more than what you can see.

If you are doubting:
You can trust the divine promise that the One who creates at a cosmic scale designed every strand of DNA in your body too.

If you are burdened:
You can take heart because there is more coming, a vastness rich in love that we can barely even fathom but someday will taste and see and feel, forevermore.

JUNE 24

I've kept my feet on the ground, I've cultivated a quiet heart.

PSALM 131:2 (MSG)

INHALE: Quiet my heart;
EXHALE: Help me hear You.

A siren blares in the distance. One son argues with his brother. The dog barks. Cartoons chatter in the background. My phone and the doorbell ring *at the same time*.

I used to think that cultivating a quiet heart meant escaping the noise. But the loudness of our lives has no bearing on the posture of our hearts. A quiet heart welcomes God's presence in every nook and cranny of our ordinary lives. When we quiet our hearts, we're more likely to hear the divine whisper beneath the sound of the bird's song and, yes, maybe even the neighbor's leaf blower. (God really *can* do anything.)

Keeping our feet on the ground and quieting our hearts helps us stay awake to experiencing God's grounding presence in, well, the present.

I began my studies in contemplative spiritual formation during a very loud season of parenting four children. Even when I tried to sneak away to pray in silence, I could still hear a child playing or yelling or singing or crying. I started to feel like I had failed in my practice of cultivating a quiet heart.

In one of my final papers, I shared my experience of feeling like a failure with my instructor Julie Saad. She replied, "Most people who are busy crave quiet and stillness sometimes, but they never realize that we can have it in every moment, when we give our time and attention to the divine in each moment. I can't tell you how many times I have heard people say, 'I don't know what I would do or how I would have gotten through this without my practice.' And what they are really saying is 'without the invincible conviction of the presence of God in every moment.'"

What would it look like to let God quiet the noise within your heart so you can notice God's nearness today?

PRACTICING THE WAY

"Centering prayer" is one way to simply be with God and let your heart get quiet. (No perfect conditions required.)

If you're new to centering prayer, here are some tips to get you started:

1. **Pick a simple word or phrase.** Choose something short and easy to remember, such as *peace*, *beloved*, or *Here I am* to return to throughout your quiet time. This word is your reminder that God is with you and you want to be with God.
2. **Time it.** Set aside at least five minutes to pray. (You can always work your way to longer stretches! I find that it takes me a few minutes to just quiet the noise rattling inside me.)
3. **Get comfortable.** Sit with your eyes closed. Take a few deep breaths. And then just *be*. You're here to listen, not to list your prayer requests.
4. **Return.** When your thoughts wander (and they will) come back to your word or phrase. Think of it like touching home base.
5. **Stay and breathe.** At the end of the prayer period, stay in silence for a moment before returning to your day.[174]

JUNE 25

Yours, O LORD, is the greatness, the power, the glory, the victory, and the majesty. Everything in the heavens and on earth is yours, O LORD, and this is your kingdom. We adore you as the one who is over all things.

1 CHRONICLES 29:11 (NLT)

INHALE: Your breath
EXHALE: Is the center.

When my kids were younger, I sometimes had to pull them aside and ask, "Are you being a me-monster?" If you've ever been around a group of preschoolers, you've heard the chorus of "Mine!" But I'll be honest: I can slip into main-character mode pretty quickly too. If I'm not paying attention, everything becomes about *my* priorities, *my* preferences, *my* opinions. *Me. Me. Me.*

We live in a culture that rewards self-focus: "Do what's best for you" instead of "Do what's best for us." In all the noise about personal truths, it's easy to forget the truest thing of all: *God* is holding everything together. *God* is the power above all else. *God* is the victory over death. Everything in heaven and on earth belongs to our Maker, our Sustainer, our Redeemer.

King David's words here invite us into worship. Worship doesn't depend on fog machines or big stages. It begins in the heart—turning again and again toward God with humility and gratitude.

As people of God's Kingdom, all we do, all we say, and all we are should flow from God, not our egos. God doesn't leave us alone in this but, in Christ, gives us the Spirit to be with us and guide us in every breath. And that's something to be thankful for.

As you breathe and pray today, may you find the freedom that comes with not being the center. May your life become a living doxology of gratitude, humility, and worship.

PRACTICING THE WAY

Diaphragmatic (or belly) breathing supports the nervous system and can help calm stress, lower heart rate, and improve focus. Though it's a natural way of breathing, most of us need to retrain our bodies to do it intentionally until it becomes a habit.

Here's how to practice it:

1. **Lie down.** If you're able, lie on your back. Place one hand on the center of your chest and the other under your rib cage, where your abdomen begins.
2. **Inhale.** As you slowly inhale, pray, "Your breath." Feel the lower edge of your rib cage expand and your abdomen rise.
3. **Exhale.** As you exhale, pray, "Is the center." Feel your abs fall and your rib cage soften inward. Your upper chest should move very little.
4. **Repeat slowly.** Continue for several breaths, letting the prayer's words become a rhythm with your body.[175]

Over time, this practice can help you develop a more natural rhythm of deep breathing.

JUNE 26

God's Spirit touches our spirits and confirms who we really are. We know who he is, and we know who we are: Father and children. And we know we are going to get what's coming to us—an unbelievable inheritance!

ROMANS 8:16-17 (MSG)

INHALE: You know who I really am;
EXHALE: You've been with me all along.

Your truest self is a beloved child of God. Not the biggest mistake you've ever made. Not your career title. Not your personality type or your relationship status. Not your follower count on social media. Not your political affiliation or your church denomination. Not your popularity or where you live or what you wear. Your truest self is God's own. That's who you really are.

As a parent, I sometimes find myself flipping through family photo books and scrolling through digital albums of my children. I touch the memory, and I'm instantly transported to the sound of my child's voice before it deepened, the softness of their hand in mine. I see snapshots of baseball teams, first days of school, summer vacations, homemade crafts, and birthday parties and marvel at the mystery that I've loved them through every season of their lives, for exactly as they were then and exactly as they are now, always holding a hope for who they are becoming.

I wonder if God is like that—if, when God looks at us, our Father sees all the versions of ourselves, every one of our eras, and holds them with care alongside who we are now and who we might someday be.

When my kids say something cruel or do something that goes against their character, I often remind them, "This isn't who you really are." Romans 8 echoes this truth: "God's Spirit touches our spirits and confirms who we really are. We know who he is, and we know who we are: Father and children."

So much of faith is mystery. How can we fathom God's Spirit touching ours? And yet this is the promise: Today, right now, you don't have to earn God's love or prove your worth.

God already knows who you are. God already calls you child.

As you breathe and pray, reflect on where you tend to place your identity apart from God. What false names or labels might God be inviting you to release? How might you live differently if you trusted that you are already beloved?

BORROW THIS PRAYER

I've been chasing a finish line
That keeps moving,
A finish line
That doesn't exist.
I'll never run hard enough,
Fast enough.
I want to throw off my sneakers
And collapse into Your presence,
Where I don't have to be anything
Other than Yours.
Amen.

JUNE 27

Love from the center of who you are; don't fake it.
Run for dear life from evil; hold on for dear life to good.

ROMANS 12:9 (MSG)

INHALE: Help me love
EXHALE: From the center of who I am.

Body-language experts explain how to spot when someone isn't being honest. Do their eyes match their smile? Does the warmth reach their eyes or stay pasted across their mouths? Microexpressions give away whether someone's kindness is real . . . or a performance.

We've all been on the receiving end of false sincerity—words that sound sweet but are judgmental or bitter. Maybe someone told you, "Bless your heart," but it didn't feel quite so nice. Or maybe you've known a politician or two who say one thing and do another. Even in our churches, we're not immune to doublespeak.

Paul's words in Romans 12:9 cut through insincerity: "Love from the center of who you are; don't fake it. Run for dear life from evil; hold on for dear life to good."

Some translations of today's verse use the word *cling*. The Greek word for "cling" here—*kollaó*—literally means "to glue."[176] Paul was telling the church in Rome to glue themselves to God's character, even when their culture was pulling them in other directions.

Paul wrote these words to a diverse group of Christians living in the Roman Empire's swirl of spectacle. Social and political divisions bombarded them. (Perhaps not so different from the cultural climate we experience today.) Followers of Jesus were navigating a hot mess of competing allegiances and violent entertainment, trying to live out Jesus' teaching under the shadow of empire.[177]

Paul's words encouraged them to remember that sincere love isn't a nice idea but a countercultural force that can bring followers of Jesus together *and* set them apart.

Today's verse echoes Jesus' command in John 13:34-35 to "love one another . . . as I have loved you."* It aligns with the vision in 1 Corinthians 13:4 of a patient, kind love and the invitation in Philippians 4:8 to dwell on what is true and good.

We need all the reminders we can get to return to Christ as the center of who we are so our love might be an overflow of God's goodness.

Turn to today's breath prayer any time you need to give your brain and body a chance to reset and remember how to love from the center of who you are.

LET IT LINGER

Authentic love flows from the Holy Spirit at your center—cling to that love.

As you move through your day, notice where opportunities arise to enter a rhythm of genuine care and compassion. It may be as simple as listening well instead of nodding along while zoning out, offering a genuine compliment you actually mean, extending generosity when no one's watching, following through on what you said you'd do, or refraining from getting pulled into gossip.

---

* ESV.

JUNE 28

You've kept track of my every toss and turn through the sleepless nights, each tear entered in your ledger, each ache written in your book.

PSALM 56:8 (MSG)

INHALE: You hold
EXHALE: All my tears.

God knows.

God knows what you're carrying right now. God knows the pain you hold deep in your heart, the pain you dare not name aloud.

Every tear that's slipped down your cheek, every time you've stared at the ceiling in the dark, every ache you thought was invisible: God knows.

Maybe you want to pray, but you can't find the words. Maybe you're too tired to string a sentence together. You don't have to explain a thing. You don't have to collect your thoughts and hand them over in a neat and tidy prayer.

Just *be.*

When I was a new mom, I sometimes found myself awake at 2 a.m., my eyes fixed on my newborn, watching his chest rise and fall as he slept, noticing every shift, every sound. God's tender, watchful attention to us is the fullest picture of parental love.

God holds every toss and turn because God holds *you.*

Every night you couldn't sleep . . .

Every tear you wiped away before anyone noticed . . .

Every question, every doubt, every grief . . .

God was there.

God knows you and meets you in the unknown.

Tonight, borrow this breath prayer. As you turn off the lights and lie down, put one hand on your heart and one on your lower stomach. Breathe in as deeply as you can through your nose while praying, "You hold." Stay with your breath for a few counts before slowing your exhale, praying, "All my tears."

When you can't sleep, remember: Jesus sits beside you in the dark.

"Surely I am with you always, to the very end of the age."*

BORROW THIS PRAYER

When I cannot see
The path ahead,
When I don't know
Which way to turn,
When I pray
And I'm met with silence,
When all I can muster
Is *Why?*,
Meet me in the breeze,
Wipe away my tears,
Meet me in the meadow.
Breath of heaven,
Meet me in the unknowing
So that I might be known.

---

* Matthew 28:20, NIV.

JUNE 29

When life is heavy and hard to take,
go off by yourself. Enter the silence.

LAMENTATIONS 3:28 (MSG)

INHALE: God, meet me
EXHALE: In the silence.

I hide in the bathroom. The habit began when my kids were young, but I still do it—sneaking away to catch my breath. Sometimes I need a break from all the things I need to get done, all the ways I'm failing, all the news I can barely begin to metabolize.

We know that smoking is terrible for the lungs, but I understand the appeal of stepping outside for a few minutes of air. What if we replaced "smoke breaks" with "breath breaks," giving ourselves permission to slip outside for some fresh air as we reconnect with the One who gives each breath?

Jesus got away by Himself regularly. Luke 5:16 says, "As often as possible Jesus withdrew to out-of-the-way places for prayer."* If the Son of God could step away, so can you.

In his book *Into the Silent Land*, Martin Laird writes, "The grace of Christian wholeness . . . flowers in silence." He reminds us that when we take a moment to step out of the cacophony of our lives and let our minds be still, "a deeper truth presents itself: we are and have always been one with God and we all are one in God."[178]

Even just one minute of breath prayer can bring you back to this truth.

Sometimes the only thing we can do is to breathe. To bear witness to our own pain. To ask God to hold us when we can't hold ourselves up any longer. When we step away to catch our breath and suddenly life feels too quiet, that doesn't mean God is absent. Frederick Buechner writes, "I suspect that maybe God speaks to us most clearly through his silence, his absence, so that we know him best through our missing him."[179]

God will meet you in the silence.

PAUSE AND PONDER

Reflect on your plans for today. When and where could you take a one-minute "breath break" with God? (On your commute? When you're making dinner? Before a meeting?)

What's your relationship to silence? Do you seek it out—or does it feel a little scary? Do you tend to be more introverted or extroverted? How might you use your natural inclinations as a way to connect with God?

* MSG.

JUNE 30

In your generous love I am really living at last . . .
I bless you every time I take a breath.

PSALM 63:3-4 (MSG)

INHALE: My every breath
EXHALE: Is wrapped in Your love.

No matter who you are or what you're walking through, as long as you have breath in your lungs, you have reason to bless the One from whom all blessings flow.

God is with you right now, as your mind ticks through your to-do list. God is with you right now, as you navigate tricky relationships or try to seek clarity amid our noisy world.

Psalm 63 invites us to open ourselves to God's presence in our lives—to look up and breathe in goodness, even when papers pile up on the desk or we forget garbage day. Every breath can be an act of worship for the One who lavishes love upon us, right here in the midst of our ordinary lives.

"A breath prayer is a simple, intimate, and repetitive prayer that can be repeated during each inhalation and exhalation, drawing you nearer to the Spirit of God," writes Whitney Simpson. "This contemplative practice links prayer to the rhythm of your own breath."[180]

Every breath is a gift of grace. In light of that, we can give our breath as an offering of praise.

Today, let this poem by Tanner Olson speak into your heart:

And in the morning, sit with the waking, the waiting. Not lost, just becoming, as you learn to be still in a world that won't stop spinning. Before you move, slow down. Let time unfold: the sun rise, the dew lift, the birds sing. Breathe. And breathe. And breathe again. Let stillness find you, like waters stilled at the sound of Jesus' voice. You are not late to your own life. You are right here—right on time. Held by grace, not in pieces, but in place. And that's enough. That's enough for today.[181]

Let your breath become prayer.

As you breathe in, imagine the Holy Spirit filling you with love. If it's comfortable, hold your breath for a few counts before slowly releasing your breath, exhaling God's love back into the world. Repeat for several breaths until you feel your heart begin to beat a bit more slowly, until you feel a little steadier on your feet.

SACRED ECHOES

Every breath you take serves as a reminder of God's gift of life and the Spirit within.[182]

Whitney R. Simpson

JULY 1

I will put breath into you, and you will come to life.
Then you will know that I am the LORD.

EZEKIEL 37:6 (NLT)

INHALE: Breathe new life
EXHALE: Into my weary heart.

Every once in a while, my algorithm feeds me videos of cleaners power washing filthy, mud-caked rugs. In less than a minute, streams of water wash away each layer of dirt and grime, revealing stunning Turkish rugs underneath.

I'll be honest: If I had a rug that looked as terrible as the "before" images, I'd be tempted to toss it directly into the dumpster.

Gratefully, that's not what God is like with me. Sometimes I get myself into giant messes of my own making. I let my words get away from me, hurting the people I love. I say yes to too many things and then stagger under the weight of my commitments. I dig my heels into the sand and refuse to forgive until the only person I'm harming is myself.

God doesn't leave us alone in our mess.

Our Father renews hearts that are bruised and battered.

Jesus redeems what we fear has been ruined forever.

The Holy Spirit breathes hope into situations we think are too far gone.

In Ezekiel 37, the vision of dry bones represents Israel in exile. God's people were in poor shape. But God took the dry bones and breathed new life into them. This scene echoes Genesis 2:7, where God breathed life into dust, reminding us of God's power to restore and revive.

Just as God gathered Israel's scattered bones, God gathers the scattered parts of our lives and breathes new life into us.

Unlike the time-lapse cleaning videos, true restoration rarely happens in an instant. We don't get a magic wand to heal every wound overnight. Instead, we're invited into the slow, sacred work of repair, with God's grace filling in the gaps.

When I'm at my wit's end, when I have nothing left to give and need every ounce of God's help, I start fresh by taking a deep breath. Therapists call it a "cleansing breath" for a reason: Deep breathing activates the parasympathetic nervous system, which lowers heart rate and cortisol levels.[183]

A deep breath really does help restore us.

Match your inhales and exhales to today's breath prayer.

Where in your life do you long for God's renewal?

You are not too far gone. God is here with you. And wherever God's breath is, hope is there too.

SACRED ECHOES

The value of a deep breath is something we must continue to learn and relearn on the path to peace.[184]

Morgan Harper Nichols

JULY 2

Help me understand these things inside and out
so I can ponder your miracle-wonders.

PSALM 119:27 (MSG)

INHALE: Let me live
EXHALE: Whole and holy.

God's love and life-giving presence are a mystery we're invited to meditate on throughout Scripture.

Being a reflective person isn't exactly a cultural value in our fast-paced culture. But science reveals that when we meditate on God's Word, both sides of our brain become active. This balanced engagement of our left and right hemispheres helps us stay regulated and, as Dr. Timothy Jennings says, brings us "greater health and peace but also growth in Christlikeness."[185]

"God calls us to meditate *on his law of love*, which is an expression of his character of love," Jennings says. "This is no empty, mindless, thoughtless meditation, but a contemplative, deeply reflective meditation on the beauty of our infinite God and his methods of love."[186]

As you borrow today's breath prayer, linger on Psalm 119 and let your brain and body relax.

The chores and the inbox will still be there when you're done, but you may just return to them a little more rooted in who God is—and how deeply you're loved.

LET IT LINGER

Psalm 119 invites us to meditate on the truth and love that God breathes into us:[187]

- "I meditate on your precepts and consider your ways" (verse 15).
- "Cause me to understand the way of your precepts, that I may meditate on your wonderful deeds" (verse 27).
- "I reach out for your commands, which I love, that I may meditate on your decrees" (verse 48).*

* All list references are taken from the NIV.

JULY 3

He has sent me to comfort the brokenhearted and to proclaim that captives will be released and prisoners will be freed.

ISAIAH 61:1 (NLT)

INHALE: Comfort our broken hearts;
EXHALE: Free us with Your love.

My husband and I grew up with very different images of God. I believed God was *with* us, while my husband believed God was *watching* us.

Maybe you also picture a detached, disconnected version of God—a deity who observes our broken hearts and complicated realities from a safe, heavenly perch. But God doesn't keep a polite distance from our messy lives.

God enters in.

Throughout the Psalms, the books of the prophets, and the Gospels, God moves toward those who are hurting, binding up the brokenhearted and setting captives free.

If we want to understand the *with-ness* of God, we only have to look to Jesus, who said, referencing Isaiah 61, "The Spirit of the Lord is upon me, for he has anointed me to bring Good News to the poor. He has sent me to proclaim that captives will be released, that the blind will see, that the oppressed will be set free."*

The One who steps into human suffering with compassion is still pursuing us and liberating us today.

There are so many ways to enter into prayer and spend time with God. If you feel a bit distant from our powerful, personal God, one simple way to reconnect is through breath prayer. Wherever you are, whatever you're going through, you can offer a prayer alongside your breath and ask God to meet you there in every inhale and exhale.

Any prayer or practice, when offered with openness to the Spirit, can become a sacred space where we meet God.

Breath prayer is one of many ways we can draw closer to the Holy Spirit as the Holy Spirit draws closer to us. As Thomas Keating said, the Spirit is with us in every type of prayer, and following the Spirit's inspiration "is the sure path to perfect freedom."[188]

Place your hand over your heart. With each breath in, imagine God's comfort filling your lungs and mending your broken heart. With each breath out, release the burdens or fears that have held you captive.

What image of God are you holding? Is it bringing you closer to freedom or pushing you farther away?

SACRED ECHOES

We find compassion and salvation in Christ, who was intimately acquainted with human suffering because he became human. The divine nature of God brings us comfort because we know that as humans, we are made in his image, and the world and its sufferings are not what life is meant to be.[189]

Regina Chow Trammel and John Trent

* Luke 4:18, NLT.

JULY 4

INDEPENDENCE DAY (US)

Everything we know about God's Word is summed up in a single sentence: Love others as you love yourself. That's an act of true freedom.

GALATIANS 5:14 (MSG)

INHALE: Because of Your love
EXHALE: I will love freely.

A man, pamphlet in hand, recently knocked on my friend's front door. As soon as my friend opened it, the man launched into the exact steps to "get right with God." He even offered a scripted prayer to recite. His words were well-meaning, but they misinterpreted the liberating gospel of Christ's love as merely a formula for salvation.

Paul reminded the early church that reducing faith to legalistic rules and rituals was an exercise in missing the point. The whole of God's law, he said, is fulfilled in a single sentence: "Love others as you love yourself."

Jesus taught that love of God and love of neighbor are the heart of every command. Love isn't a sentimental afterthought—it's the center on which everything rests.

We don't have to be held back by religious rules that tell us we'll never be good enough *or* by the broken ways of our world that prompt us to disregard others and worship at the altar of self.

Our love for others reflects our relationship with Christ. Our love for God is the guiding force in all our interactions with our neighbors.

We are free from the pressure to perform, free from trying to pray the "perfect" prayer, free from needing to get everything exactly right. We don't have to make ourselves right with God—because in Christ, God has already made us whole. And when we trust in that truth, we live into a freedom that embodies love in real life. It is the overflow of God's love for us, which transforms into our love for others, moving beyond rote prayers into holy actions.

BORROW THIS PRAYER

Spirit of breath, Spirit of life,
You are the God who sets us free.
Part our lips, expand our lungs.
Help us drink deep
The cool promise of freedom,
The shattering of chains,
The fullness of You.

In You, we have
A new way,
A new breath,
A new hope.

We confess: Too often, we settle
For musty basement air
Over the liberating breath of heaven.
But now—fill us.
With peace.
With mercy.
With goodness.

In every inhale, we receive
What You restore.
Amen.

JULY 5

God's Spirit beckons. There are things to do and places to go!

ROMANS 8:14 (MSG)

INHALE: Help me do the good
EXHALE: That is mine to do.

There's nowhere you can go today where God is not. God's breath is in your lungs right here, right in this very moment.

When my husband and I were in the international adoption process for our son Joseph, we traveled to Nigeria several times to establish a connection and ensure that the process was done legally and ethically. On our first trip, I found myself on the biggest plane I'd ever been on, flying across the Atlantic Ocean for hours.

I stared at the little screen in the seat in front of me, the tiny airplane inching over the open sea showing our progress. There was no land in sight—just sea below and sky above.

Have you ever had that moment of realizing you're in a metal tube soaring over the ocean, suspended in the sky, and you're grateful for the marvel of engineering and pilot training that makes it possible . . . but also a little terrified?

As I turned this over in my mind, the plane hit some turbulence. My heart dropped along with the dipping plane, and I found myself praying. As the plane encountered air pockets, I began to feel a deep sense of peace. Not because I suddenly felt in control, but because I felt deep in my soul that there was nowhere I could go where God wasn't already.

God was with you the moment you took your first breath. God has been with you all along. Even when you wondered. Even when you were afraid. God was there.

And God is with you still.

There is so much more unfolding in your story. If you feel like life is a little mundane, like you're just going through the motions, take a breath and remember: The Spirit of God is with you. Yes, the future is full of unknowns. But nothing is unknown to God.

When you need to feel reenergized, borrow this Celtic prayer. Take your time reading, and let the words match the rhythm of your breath:

In the beginning O God
You shaped my soul and set its weave
You formed my body and gave it breath.
Renew me this day in the image of your love.
O great God, grant me your light
O great God, grant me your grace
O great God, grant me your joy this day
And let me be made pure in the well of
your health.[190]

As Romans 8:14 says, "All who are led by the Spirit of God are children of God."* No matter where your journey takes you, there are people you are called to love and places you are called to be, and no matter what—you do not go alone.

BREATHE THIS IN

Intentional breathwork (like mindfully praying alongside slow, deep breaths, inhaling through your nose and exhaling through your mouth) can lead to lower inflammation, more energy, and stronger immunity.[191]

* NLT.

JULY 6

Your ancient ruins shall be rebuilt; you shall raise up the foundations of many generations; you shall be called the repairer of the breach, the restorer of streets to live in.

ISAIAH 58:12 (NRSV)

INHALE: You repair,
EXHALE: You restore.

I'm a doodler, and I'm proud to say I've passed my penchant for grabbing whatever pen or pencil is at my disposal to my kids. Sometimes their doodles include watching drawing tutorials, but when the curve of a line doesn't turn out as they imagined or the proportions go awry, they wad the whole sheet up and toss it aside in frustration.

I try to show them that mistakes don't mean the end of the piece. That with a little imagination, sometimes the flaw becomes the most creative part. It can be reworked. Reimagined. It doesn't need to be thrown away.

We all know what it feels like when things don't go the way we hoped. We're bound to make mistakes. But God does not look at us as failures to be crumpled up and thrown away. God mends. God heals. God restores.

To the people of Jerusalem, Isaiah spoke of city walls in ruins, of streets that had become unsafe and deserted. When he said they'd be called "repairer of the breach" and "restorer of streets," his listeners would have understood that familiar, everyday language depicting the crumbling walls surrounding their city and the lively streets full of daily life.

God is a restorer, and God's people are called to participate in that restoration.

When people heard "repairer of the breach," they would have pictured someone who literally fixed the cracks in their city walls. Isaiah wasn't calling them to be construction workers but also to mend relationships and restore peace. Justice had been neglected. The vulnerable had been ignored. Restoring the streets where commerce took place and neighbors gathered involved making daily life whole again.

We're called into the sacred work of repair in our everyday lives too.

Because we follow the One who repairs and restores, our daily rhythms of love become acts of rebuilding, with God's help. Each small movement of loving-kindness is a brick in God's reconstruction, a flourishing touch on the canvas of our communities.

Through our daily choices, we choose peace and join with God in bringing those rhythms of restoration to the people in our messy, holy lives.

PAUSE AND PONDER

What is your typical reaction to making a mistake? Do you have a mender mentality, or do you easily fall into frustration? Where do you see breaches in your life or community that need to be mended?

JULY 7

He heals the heartbroken and bandages their wounds. He counts the stars and assigns each a name. Our Lord is great, with limitless strength; we'll never comprehend what he knows and does.

PSALM 147:3-5 (MSG)

INHALE: God, You heal
EXHALE: The brokenhearted.

Grief is part of being human.

When Lazarus died, Jesus knew that the story wasn't over. Jesus knew He was going to raise His friend back to life. Still, He didn't rush through His very real sorrow. Mary and Martha called to Jesus, and He came. He listened. He stood beside them. And He was deeply moved. Jesus didn't dismiss their pain or ignore their grief. He moved near the hurting and the pain, and He *stayed there*. He didn't just quickly wipe away a tear and move on.

No. He stood by the tomb. And He wept. Those tears revealed the depth of His love. To weep in your grief is a sacred act of love, modeled by God.

When your heart is breaking, your tears are not a betrayal of hope. As Jesus showed, tears are an overflow of love that can't be contained.

The same hands that shaped galaxies into being are the hands that tend to your pain. Psalm 147:3-5 reminds us that God heals our broken hearts and cares for our wounds. God is our Creator and knows His creation so intimately that He even names the stars. We cannot fully grasp the depths of God's infinite strength and knowledge. We cannot comprehend the vastness of everything God is doing right at this very moment.

God is vast and near, all at once. Our boundless God draws close enough to tend to a single broken heart. When your heart is heavy with sorrow, when you wonder if God cares, remember this truth: Our limitless God loves you with limitless love.

We live in the tension between heaven and earth, in the push and pull of joy and grief, hope and sorrow, resurrection and death. When the ache in your heart threatens to take your breath away, remember that God's limitless love is not afraid of your tears.

PAUSE AND PONDER

God both heals the brokenhearted and names the stars. Where do you most need God's nearness right now? Where do you need to remember God's vastness?

When you imagine Jesus weeping at the tomb of Lazarus, what does it stir in you to know that God does not bypass grief but enters into it?

JULY 8

Where the Spirit of the Lord is, there is freedom.

2 CORINTHIANS 3:17 (NIV)

INHALE: Where You are,

EXHALE: I am free.

God is not holding you back.

What dreams would you pursue if you really believed that God would go with you? What is the whisper in your heart that you try to ignore? What if those nudges aren't distractions but the Spirit breathing a new dream into you?

A dear friend of mine is taking a leap of faith she never imagined—she's running for office in a heated political climate. It's risky and vulnerable, but her hope is simple: to create change in her community, to listen well, to work for the good of all God's children. Her aim isn't partisan but rooted in love of her neighbors.

She knows that she can enter this because the Spirit of the Lord is with her, whether or not she's elected. And that makes her free. She's free from the judgment that will surely come. She's free from the praise that might flatter her. She's free from the cynicism that insists it will never work. She's free from the lie that she shouldn't even try.

Jesus promised us the Holy Spirit. That doesn't mean every dream we pursue will be easy or that stepping out will guarantee success. My friend doesn't know if she'll be elected. But she knows this: She's free to try, and she doesn't go alone.

Where is God breathing a new dream into you? Maybe God is freeing you to take a risk and gather neighbors for a monthly meal. Maybe the dream God is breathing into you is taking a pottery class or volunteering with a local nonprofit. Maybe it's starting a garden, mentoring a teenager, or finally signing up for that couch-to-5K race you've been putting off. Perhaps it's simply introducing yourself to someone new.

Freedom isn't the absence of fear but the presence of the Spirit.

In Christ, you are free to try. You are free to fail. You are free to begin again.

Our paths may split into countless possibilities, but no matter where we go, God's Spirit is with us. As you recite today's breath prayer, remember: The Spirit is here. And where the Spirit of the Lord is, there is freedom.

PAUSE AND PONDER

What would you try if you weren't afraid of failing? Where do you sense the Spirit nudging you toward freedom?

Who has encouraged you by stepping out in courage? Why? How might you encourage them by letting them know they encouraged you?

JULY 9

Blessed are the peacemakers, for they will be called children of God.

MATTHEW 5:9 (NIV)

INHALE: Help me

EXHALE: Be a peacemaker.

Jesus blessed those who make peace. Not those who appreciate it, not those who sit idly by, but those who roll up their sleeves, enter the tension, and cultivate peace right where they are.

In his book *Anatomy of the Soul*, Dr. Curt Thompson says we can use prayerful principles to help us live out the beatitude "Blessed are the peacemakers."[192]

Dr. Thompson, a psychiatrist and spiritual writer, reminds us that peacemaking is never passive. "Jesus leaves no doubt," he writes, "that war as a way of life, whether between family members, factions within a congregation, denominations, worldview representatives, nations, or humans and the earth, leads to mindless disintegration of the environment, individuals, families, and communities."[193]

What might Jesus' declaration "Blessed are the peacemakers" mean for us today? Maybe it looks something like this:

- *Blessed are you who discern the difference between peacekeeping and peacemaking, for your actions help build the Kingdom of God.*
- *Blessed are you who refuse to accept things as they are but hold hope for something brighter, for your hope illuminates the path for all of us.*
- *Blessed are you who pause before speaking, for your wisdom is needed in our warring world.*
- *Blessed are you who bravely enter complex conversations, for your courage makes us all braver.*

Every one of us is called to cultivate peace. Sometimes it looks like reconciling with a friend. Sometimes it looks like resisting cynicism or refusing to demonize someone who disagrees with you. Sometimes it's as simple (and as radical) as planting seeds of kindness in the unseen corners of our lives.

Christ is our peace.* And while the peaceful path may feel like it's overgrown with weeds, the Spirit will be with us as we follow God into this sacred, ongoing work.

When you feel overwhelmed and unsure of what making peace looks like in a given moment, return to your breath. Let your prayers rise and fall with each inhale and exhale, reminding you that the Spirit is as close as your next breath.

Where do you sense the Spirit nudging you toward peacemaking in your relationships or community? How might praying alongside your breath become a practice that grounds you in the holy work of peacemaking?

RHYTHM OF BREATH

Peace to the war inside,
Peace to the fight within,
Peace to the enemy lines
Drawn in my heart.

* See Ephesians 2:14.

JULY 10

Love your neighbor as yourself.

MARK 12:31 (NLT)

INHALE: Help me love others
EXHALE: Like You love me.

A few years ago, my husband and I moved our family from the suburbs to an older neighborhood on what some might call "the wrong side of the tracks." Every year, we pull out our lawn chairs for the annual block party. It's not fancy. The potluck is full of mystery dishes, and the band is usually a group of retirees playing the oldies—but it feels like a glimpse of God's Kingdom.

Kids run through the streets. Someone fires up a grill. Neighbors who don't vote the same, look the same, or earn the same sit side by side. It's messy and imperfect (and sometimes full of drama in the neighborhood group chat), but it's also the most "neighborly love" I've seen, more than in many churches. Someone gives up their chair for a retired man who lost his wife a few years ago. Another catches a toddler right before she falls and drops her ice cream. For one imperfect evening, people care for one another like family.

Jesus said we are to "love our neighbor as ourself." He was asked, "But who is my neighbor?"* Thousands of years later, it's a question humanity still wrestles with. But the answer is simple: We love whoever is right in front of us.

Once, neighbors lingered and lives intertwined. Now, it's easier to close the curtains than open the door. But as Ronald Rolheiser writes, "How we relate to each other is part of how we relate to God."[194] That means loving God isn't separate from loving the people on our block, in our workplaces, or at our tables. *It's the same thing.*

As long as you have breath in your lungs, there is someone in front of you to love. Your love doesn't have to be big or fancy—just pull up a chair.

How do you love your neighbor? As Shannan Martin says, "Start with hello."[195]

SACRED ECHOES

For Jesus, the two great commandments, to love God and love one's neighbor, can never be separated.[196]

Ronald Rolheiser

* See Mark 12:31; Luke 10:29.

JULY 11

Be good friends who love deeply.

ROMANS 12:10 (MSG)

INHALE: Help me remember
EXHALE: That we belong to each other.

After too many rounds of fatigue and migraines, my physician suggested an elimination diet to see if food might be part of the problem. In a tragic turn of events for someone who is married to a bread baker, I discovered that gluten was the culprit. I felt better without it, but suddenly meals became a whole new kind of challenge.

I usually just bring my own food to events. The day of my book club grill out, I figured I'd swing by the grocery store on the way to our meeting—until my afternoon completely unraveled. I faced an unexpected work deadline. My son got hurt in soccer. One of my dogs had an accident. My husband had a meeting at the same time, so my daughter needed to tag along. And of course, I still needed to cram three chapters for the book discussion.

By the time I pulled into the driveway, sweaty and frazzled, I wondered why I'd tried to come at all. *And* I was bunless.

But when I walked in, there was an entire spread waiting—including a package of (always overpriced) gluten-free buns. My friend, a single mom with her own full plate, had gone out of her way to make space for me at the table. I felt so known and cared for.

Every day, we have the chance to show up for our friends. Sometimes it's remembering a detail that matters. Even if it seems small to you, it might be really meaningful to them. Sometimes it's a text that simply says, "I'm thinking of you." Sometimes it's dropping off dinner when you know your friend is too tired to cook or helping a friend pack for a move, even when you hate the sound of packing tape. (Just me?)

Tending to friendships nourishes us—mind, body, and soul.

A Harvard study across eighty years found that the single greatest predictor of health and happiness isn't wealth or success but close relationships.[197]

Friendship is belonging built by small, intentional acts of love. When we realize that we belong to each other, we are all better for it. Maybe that's what Paul was getting at when he told early Christians to "be good friends who love deeply."

BREATHE THIS IN

"The surprising finding is that our relationships and how happy we are in our relationships has a powerful influence on our health," says Robert Waldinger, director of the happiness study and professor of psychiatry at Harvard Medical School. "Taking care of your body is important, but tending to your relationships is a form of self-care too. That, I think, is the revelation."[198]

JULY 12

Are you tired? Worn out? Burned out on religion? Come to me. Get away with me and you'll recover your life. I'll show you how to take a real rest.

MATTHEW 11:28 (MSG)

INHALE: I'm so tired;
EXHALE: Help me rest in You.

"I ordered us some new gum," my husband said, tearing open the cardboard package that had been left on our doorstep. "It has as much caffeine as a cup of coffee!"

It's no wonder products like that exist—around 80 percent of the world's population consumes caffeine daily.[199] While I adore a strong cup (or two) of freshly-brewed coffee, I know the boost is temporary. Even the best latte can't give me the mind and soul rest I actually need. The rest I was created for.

In Matthew 11, Jesus offers a simple, relational invitation: "Get away with me and you'll recover your life. I'll show you how to take a real rest." Notice what he doesn't say: He doesn't say that if you're tired, it's your fault. He doesn't tell you to pray harder or read your Bible more.

Instead, Jesus acknowledges what we *all* experience: weariness, exhaustion, burnout. And Jesus tells us we don't have to carry it alone. We can unload our baggage and bring it all to the One who offers an exhale for our souls.

The people who first heard these words were carrying heavy burdens of their own: oppressive taxes under Roman rule, strict religious demands, and the daily struggle to make a living. Jesus offered them the gift of rest—and He is still offering soul rest to us today.

If you're tired, worn out, or burned out, breathe through these promises: Jesus is peace for your heavy heart. Jesus is relief from the shame you've been holding. Jesus is freedom from the endless cycle of proving and performing. Jesus is rest for your racing mind and worn-out soul.

When you are at the end of what you can carry on your own, God welcomes you and restores you.

One way to "get away" with Jesus is through praying with your breath. Slow, intentional breathing calms your mind, balances stress in your body, and helps your body reset.[200]

Caffeine may carry us through the afternoon, but only Christ can meet us where our soul runs dry.

RHYTHM OF BREATH

When I don't have the energy,
When the words won't come—
I will lie down
And open my heart.
Do with it, Lord,
What You will.

I will listen for You
In the stillness of the night.
I will sit by the fire
And watch You dance in the flames.
I will loosen my grip
On the never-ending stream
Of news and needs.

In the quiet of the kitchen,
Before the world wakes,
I will do nothing—
Except breathe.

JULY 13

Come close and whisper your answer. I really need you.

PSALM 55:2 (MSG)

INHALE: I'm listening, God;
EXHALE: I really need You.

When we were in the adoption process with our eldest son, there was an endless barrage of paperwork and documentation. Hurry-up-and-wait became the rhythm of our days.

At the time, my husband and I were newly married and lived in a small house. The spare bedroom held only a queen bed dressed in steeply discounted purple sheets that no one else wanted, a minimum-thread-count jersey that looked like grape bubble gum. It was a makeshift guest room, but someday it would be our son's bedroom.

The purple bed became a holding spot for the small items we'd been collecting for the little boy we were preparing for: tiny socks, T-shirts with sharks and bulldozers, and a few toys. After a particularly exhausting day involving travel visas, when I didn't know if the paperwork would ever go through, I walked into that room and—for reasons I still can't explain—knelt beside the bed.

I don't know that I'd knelt beside a bed since I was five. But in that moment, surrounded by toddler-sized hope, I could do nothing except pray.

"Please, God," I whispered. "Why did You bring us here only to go silent? Would You give me just a sign that You are near—that in the end, things will be okay, whether this little boy is with us or not?"

And then a small windup giraffe, the kind with a music box tucked inside, began to play its song.

I wish I could tell you that was the end of the story. That I knew God was there and I trusted fully from then on. But if I'm being honest, I doubted. Maybe I'd bumped the toy when I knelt, triggering the tune. I wrestled with the push and pull: Was it God's whisper or just a coincidence?

I often want God's voice to be loud. I get discouraged when it isn't. *God must not care,* I think. Or worse: *Maybe God was never there in the first place.* But perhaps what I really want isn't just words in my ears. Maybe what I'm aching for is to know I'm not alone. To feel—deep down—that I am loved. Perhaps you've felt that way too.

God speaks to us in the sounds of our lives. It might not always come as a booming voice. Sometimes it's the quiet turn of a music box, the brush of wind against your cheek, or the silence that still somehow holds you.

Close your eyes and listen to the sound of your breath as you pray today's breath prayer. Maybe God is closer than you think.

SACRED ECHOES

Mightier than the crash of a thunderstorm,
mightier than the roar of the sea,
is God's voice silently speaking
in the depths of the listening heart.[201]

Stephen Mitchell

JULY 14

Let his banner over me be love.

SONG OF SOLOMON 2:4 (NIV)

INHALE: Speak love
EXHALE: Over me.

For forty-eight hours, I traded the symphony of children for the sound of crickets and cicadas to participate in a small writing retreat in the woods. When I couldn't string one more sentence together, I laced up my sneakers and, at the last minute, signed up for a guided forest hike.

The thick July humidity pressed down as the air buzzed with life. Our guide invited us to imagine ourselves as something that lived in the land we were walking through. At first, I balked. Imagining myself as a tree or a squirrel was . . . more than a few steps outside my comfort zone. But I tell my kids to try new things, so I decided to take my own advice and embrace the experience.

As I walked, my mind kept circling back to a giant tree near my cabin that locals call "Grandmother Oak." Her limbs stretched in every direction, strong and scarred, elegant and enduring. She had weathered blizzards and thunderstorms, swayed with spring breezes, blazed with autumn fire. And here she was in summer's fullness, shimmering green under the July sun.

Something in her steadiness spoke to my own longing to be rooted in God's love when the ground underneath me feels unsteady and my longing to be protected under the strong limbs of God's love.

With every inhale, we take in the oxygen trees release. With every exhale, we give back what was never ours to hold for long. Our very breathing is an exchange, a reminder that we are not separate from God's creation but part of it. Like trees, we move through seasons of storm and calm, growth and rest. Some days it feels like we're in full bloom; other days, it feels like all we can do is stand, roots deep in unseen soil.

And through it all, God's banner over us is love.

Love that shades us when the heat is too intense. Love that steadies us when winds howl. Love that makes space for bare branches, trusting that new leaves will one day come.

Just like with nature, our spiritual journeys follow rhythms established by our Creator. Life with Christ moves through cycles: inhaling life and exhaling loss, inhaling joy and exhaling sorrow, inhaling work and exhaling rest.

Whatever the season, the One who breathed the cosmos into being is breathing love over you still.

Take a breath. Feel the air in your lungs as you pray. The nurturing, protective God who gives you breath calls you beloved. And no matter the season you're in, that banner of love remains.

SACRED ECHOES

Life meanders like a path through the woods. We have seasons when we flourish and seasons when the leaves fall from us, revealing our bare bones. Given time, they grow again.[202]

Katherine May

JULY 15

Always be humble and gentle. Be patient with each other, making allowance for each other's faults because of your love.

EPHESIANS 4:2 (NLT)

INHALE: Because of Your love,
EXHALE: I can extend grace.

When I feel myself getting particularly self-righteous or judgmental, that's usually a cue I've gotten off track from the path God has for me. When I'm in step with the Spirit, I'm more aware of how much I need what only God can give—humility, gentleness, and patience.

Paul doesn't tell us to be humble and gentle only sometimes, but to *always* adopt this attitude of grace. Not just when you're rested. Not only when the other person deserves it. *Always.*

I don't know about you, but that's not something I can pull off on my own. God's love has a way of breaking open my indignation and my desire to dole out my own justice, reshaping my heart into a posture of loving others. God loves us so we love others. Because God is gentle with us, we can be gentle with others. Because God is patient with us, we can learn patience with others. Because God makes allowance for our failures, we can make allowance for theirs.

If these rhythms of grace feel countercultural, that's because they are. In Christ, we don't hop on the path of love only when we agree or when someone is kind in return, or only when every light is green and I get the best parking spot and feel like I have extra patience to give away.

Gentleness and patience are uncommon gifts in a reactive, me-first world. They don't always come naturally. But they're not out of reach. They're fruits of the Spirit, and they're not just for others' benefit but also for our own. The truth is, losing your cool rarely leaves you feeling better. Nitpicking someone's faults rarely brings peace.

In Christ, there's another way: to let love shape how we respond to others, even when it's hard.

When you feel your patience slipping, borrow today's breath prayer. You don't have to rely on your own reserves to extend grace to others. God is with you as you go.

PAUSE AND PONDER

How might remembering God's gentleness toward you soften the way you approach others today?

Think about a time when someone was patient with you. What happened? How did you feel?

JULY 16

May the words of my mouth and the meditation of my heart be pleasing to you, O LORD.

PSALM 19:14 (NLT)

INHALE: May my words
EXHALE: Reflect Your heart.

My husband asks me a simple question, and harsh words spill out before I even realize what I'm saying. *Where did that come from?*

The psalmist reminds us that what we speak begins in the soil of our hearts. The inner and outer life are intertwined. As Jesus says, "Out of the heart, the mouth speaks."* That's why tending our inner life with God matters. The quiet, unseen work we do with the Spirit shapes us so that our words carry traces of love instead of fragments of our unrest.

Spiritual formation may sound lofty, but at its core, it's simply opening ourselves to be shaped by God from the inside out. When our hearts rest in God, sharp retorts soften into gentleness. Defensiveness loosens its grip, and patience becomes possible.

Our words can wound or heal. They can reflect a heart that's running on empty or rooted in God's love.

We all get it wrong sometimes. But I've learned that when I find myself snapping or stewing, it's usually because my nervous system is already frayed. My inner life is spiraling. I'm stressed about that terrible headline I just read, my dog is barking at the mail carrier, and I'm running through a mental list of everything I need to accomplish by the end of the day.

Breath prayer is one of the simplest ways I know to return to God.

With each inhale and exhale, we create space for God's Spirit to settle us. And the more we practice breath prayer, the more we are shaped into Christ's likeness, over and over again, so that what flows from our lips isn't impatience or unrest but an overflow of the Spirit's good work within us.

How might breath prayer help the words of your mouth and the meditations of your heart align more closely with God's love this week?

BREATHE THIS IN

The breath prayer helps us to pray when we don't know how to pray.[203]

Ruth Haley Barton

---

* See Matthew 12:34.

JULY 17

I want some peace and quiet. I want a walk in the country, I want a cabin in the woods. I'm desperate for a change from rage and stormy weather.

PSALM 55:7-8 (MSG)

INHALE: You are peace
EXHALE: In the storm.

Nobody has a better pulse on the local weather than my mom. The National Weather Service sends me alerts, but somehow she still beats them to the punch with family group texts:

"Storm rolling in."

"Tornado sirens here."

"Hail coming—cars in garage?"

We tease her, but really, it's her way of showing love.

I honestly wish I had that same warning system for the storms of life—a heads-up before the next heartbreaking headline, a signal to brace myself before news of another shooting or legislation that harms the vulnerable. But the truth is, even ample warning wouldn't be able to prepare our hearts and minds for the weight of what's to come.

Living in the Midwest, I know what to do when the tornado sirens wail: Head to the basement, avoid windows, and wait it out. But when life's storms hit, I feel like the psalmist, longing to run away, to breathe freely under open skies and forget the chaos for a while.

We can make plans, we can board up windows, but we can't always escape the storm.

Still, Scripture promises that we aren't left alone when the winds pick up. Psalm 46:1 promises, "God is our refuge and strength, an ever-present help in trouble."* And Psalm 27:1 proclaims, "The LORD is my light and my salvation—whom shall I fear?"†

Our nervous systems can't stay in fight, flight, or freeze forever. We need places of safety to catch our breath, to let beauty remind us that storms don't have the last word. And when disaster strikes, I've seen the other side: people showing up for one another, bringing food, clearing debris, finding ways to repair and rebuild. The rainbow always comes.

Even in devastation, love finds a way. It always does.

PRACTICING THE WAY

Take a ten-minute (longer, if you're feeling up to it) prayer walk on a new-to-you path. Pause your podcasts and playlists. Notice the world both within you and around you. If walking isn't an option, consider pulling up a digital map (or using a paper one) and praying as you trace a path.

As you go, inhale for a count of four and exhale for a count of seven. (A longer exhalation helps you reset your nervous system.) Let each exhale remind you that God is your shelter.

* NIV.

† NIV.

JULY 18

May God himself, the God who makes everything holy and whole, make you holy and whole, put you together—spirit, soul, and body—and keep you fit for the coming of our Master, Jesus Christ.

1 THESSALONIANS 5:23 (MSG)

INHALE: Make me holy,
EXHALE: Make me whole.

God looks at us and sees the whole of who we are—and who we were created to be all along.

In the New Testament, the word "body" is often translated from the Greek *soma*, encompassing the entire self: body, emotions, mind, and will. Jesus came to redeem all of it—not just our spirits, not just our thoughts, but the fullness of our being.[204]

Because of the One who gives each inhale and exhale, you are being made new—becoming more of who our Creator has made you to be all along. With each breath, the Spirit gently loosens the protective layers that are no longer needed, restoring your truest self and moving you toward wholeness in Christ.

When everything else falls away, what remains is the life God breathes into us—the same breath that animated dust into life in Genesis, the same breath that gives us every inhale and exhale today.

Modern science underscores what Scripture has always known: Healing happens in the whole person. As Richard P. Brown and Patricia L. Gerbarg write in *The Healing Power of the Breath*:

> *Breathing practices have the power to restore a healthy balance in the stress-response system . . . . As this healing occurs, we rediscover our true selves and the capacity for love and bonding that are essential to our relationships.*[205]

Your very breath carries clues about how you're doing. Neuroscientist Antonio Damasio suggests that patterns of breathing can predict emotions—such as fear, anger, happiness, or sadness—with surprising accuracy. Before you even name what you're feeling, your body already knows.[206] And God knows too—with compassion.

Pause here. Take one slow inhale and one long exhale. Let your brain and body rest in the truth that God is with you.

Every breath is both a mirror of where you are and an invitation to return to God, who alone makes you whole. Whether you're catching yourself doomscrolling headlines, stuck in traffic, or lying awake with worries, you can borrow this prayer from the Psalms: "Let me live whole and holy, soul and body, so I can always walk with my head held high."*

LET IT LINGER

Your breath can reveal your exhaustion or your joy, your agitation or your sense of calm. But more than that, it can become prayer. With every inhale and exhale, you are drawn back to the God who makes all things whole, even you.

---

* Psalm 119:80, MSG.

JULY 19

True to your word, you let me catch my breath
and send me in the right direction.

PSALM 23:3 (MSG)

INHALE: You let me
EXHALE: Catch my breath.

We don't know what the future holds. Life often feels like we're just moving from one thing to the next, never slowing down enough to process any of it—let alone catch our breath.

Psalm 23 reminds us that God is a Shepherd who restores our souls. God doesn't demand that you push endlessly forward, doing all the things, being everything to everyone. God says, *Sit down. Catch your breath. And when you're ready, I'll show you the way.*

When your soul feels restless, when you don't know who you are or which way to turn, come back to who God is.

Try breathing in these promises, one by one:

On your inhale, pray: "When I'm . . ."
On your exhale, pray: "God is my . . ."

When I'm anxious, God is my Shepherd.
"The LORD is my shepherd, I lack nothing" (Psalm 23:1, NIV).

When I'm doubting, God is my Rock.
"Truly he is my rock and my salvation; he is my fortress, I will never be shaken." (Psalm 62:2, NIV).

When I'm afraid, God is my Light.
"The LORD is my light and my salvation—whom shall I fear?" (Psalm 27:1, NIV).

When I'm angry, God is my peace.
"He himself is our peace" (Ephesians 2:14, NIV).

When I'm disconnected, God is my comfort.
"The LORD is near to all who call on him" (Psalm 145:18, NIV).

When I'm weary, God is my rest.
"Come to me, all you who are weary and burdened, and I will give you rest" (Matthew 11:28, NIV).

You don't have to be anywhere else but here with your breath. Just for this moment, rest in the One who gives each inhale and exhale.

LET IT LINGER

Be here in this moment. Let yourself catch your breath. Notice how your heart slows as you breathe and pray. Let tomorrow be tomorrow. God will be there too, guiding you on the right path.

JULY 20

Be merciful, just as your Father is merciful.

LUKE 6:36 (NIV)

INHALE: Lord, have mercy;
EXHALE: Christ, have mercy.

Our world can feel like a hostile place. At any given moment, across platforms and perspectives, you'll find people making the case for why their enemies are not just wrong but should be punished—forever! End of story.

Mercy is a rare gift in this world.

I have three sons and sometimes feel like a referee. Sometimes they shift from their usual squabbles to being more aggressive, taking matters into their own hands. "He was mean! He deserved it!" one insists after righteously shoving his older brother into a wall. Even though the older brother was completely wrong to tease, retribution wasn't the solution. These moments become small but meaningful opportunities to discuss what it means to show mercy. In this case, that looked like extending a hand, lifting his brother off the floor, and handing him a soda.

In Christ, we're called to a different way of living that shows mercy when judgment seems easier, to be as gentle with others' hearts as we'd want someone to be with ours. I once heard that mercy is like a judge who could sentence you to prison for a crime you committed but instead offers rehabilitation. You're spared what could have rightly come to you.

Mercy is active compassion, not only withholding punishment but moving toward restoration.

I like to imagine I'm doing fine on my own, that mercy is just a nice extra for the moments when I really blow it. But the truth is, I need it every day.

God's mercy redeems and restores not just our big, dramatic failures but also the small moments that shape a life.

I wonder how our lives would change if we asked for mercy in the mundane moments of our lives:

God, have mercy on my short temper with my family.

God, have mercy on my sharp reply to a stranger on the internet.

God, have mercy on my quickness to judge instead of love.

God, have mercy on my mindless spending.

God, have mercy on my choice to ignore instead of help.

God remains fully present, empowering us to embody peace and extend mercy in a world at war with itself.

Where has compassion carried you recently? Where might God be inviting you to extend mercy to someone in your life?

Today, in your comings and goings, pause to whisper the words of another psalm: "Mark the milestones of your mercy and love, God."*

SACRED ECHOES

Maybe asking for God's mercy is like saying—we beg you, God, that our sin is not the final word. We beg you for your mercy to be with us, because ours is not enough.[207]

Nadia Bolz Weber

* Psalm 25:6, MSG.

JULY 21

Before you know it, a sense of God's wholeness
. . . will come and settle you down.

PHILIPPIANS 4:7 (MSG)

INHALE: Settle my spirit;
EXHALE: Make me whole.

The way we breathe when we sing resets our brains.

When we stretch out vowels or repeat phrases in worship, we're actually practicing what scientists call *resistance breathing*. I had no idea this was a thing. Musicians probably already know this, but when I started researching breath science, I thought, *Wait! God's people have been gathering to do this from the very beginning!*

There's a reason you feel different after singing certain songs in church or humming them on your own. The way your breath slows, extends, and vibrates signals to your nervous system that you're safe, leaving you feeling soothed and recharged.

Dr. Richard Brown and Dr. Patricia Gerbarg explain that this way of breathing provides "the optimal effect of feeling relaxed and at the same time energized."[208]

That's why after singing a favorite song, humming a hymn, or even chanting a psalm, you might feel not only calmer but also more awake to God's presence. Singing reshapes your breath and, in doing so, reshapes your body's posture toward peace.

My husband loves loud, rafter-shaking anthems that make me roll my eyes, while I prefer a more stripped-down, acoustic vibe. Either way, both of us are receiving the same gift: Our bodies are literally being regulated as we sing.

Worship isn't just something we offer God; it's also a gift God offers us, regulating our nervous systems and grounding us in peace.

Paul's words to the Philippians remind us that a sense of God's wholeness comes and settles us down. Sometimes the very act of lifting our voices is the Spirit's way of calming our hearts, minds, bodies, and souls so that peace has room to take hold.

PRACTICING THE WAY

Play a song you love. As you sing or hum along, try this simple exercise called *pursed-lip breathing*:[209]

- **Sit or lie down** in a comfortable position. Close your eyes if you wish.
- **Breathe in** slowly through your nose.
- **Purse your lips** as though you're about to whistle and exhale slowly through the small opening.
- **Repeat** for several minutes, letting your exhale last longer than your inhale.

This type of breathing helps calm your nervous system, creating space for the Spirit to settle you and awaken you to God's presence.

JULY 22

SAINT MARY MAGDALENE DAY

Mary Magdalene went to the disciples with the news: "I have seen the Lord!" And she told them that he had said these things to her.

JOHN 20:18 (NIV)

INHALE: Help me listen
EXHALE: To my life.

Dew drops on blades of grass. Bare feet on the lawn. The hand that finds yours at just the right time. Trees swaying in the breeze. A cold iced tea on a hot afternoon. These are some of the small gifts of a summer day.

If only we'd slow the beat of our hearts and the breath of our bodies, we might remember: God dwells in the details.

What would it look like to listen to your life?

"It is so easy to forget to listen, especially when we are harried, hurried, and worn out," write Regina Chow Trammel and John Trent. "So when we take a breath, when we take a moment, when we sit still and notice, the listening gift is refreshed."[210]

Mary Magdalene gives us a picture of what it looks like to stay open, to notice where the divine might be, even when life leaves us feeling overwhelmed and alone.

Mary Magdalene's role as the first witness to the resurrection highlights the surprising ways God works and the significant place women hold in the Gospel accounts. If you think your life is too chaotic or that you're too ordinary to experience God, remember that the first-ever proclamation of the resurrection came from a woman. This challenged cultural norms of her time, while affirming the value of all believers today.

When we slow down enough to see the sacred in the midst of our anxieties—in the noise and in the silence—we just might encounter Christ.

Where might you glimpse resurrection in the comings and goings of your day? Ask God to help you slow your breath and pay attention to where God is breathing life into your world.

BREATHE THIS IN

Even the act of simply noticing your breath slows and deepens it a bit, giving your mind and body a little nudge that you are safe and seen.[211]

JULY 23

God was pleased to have all his fullness dwell in him,
and through him to reconcile to himself all things . . .
making peace through his blood, shed on the cross.

COLOSSIANS 1:19-20 (NIV)

INHALE: You reconcile all things;
EXHALE: You are the fullness.

Too often, our world runs on division. We sort ourselves by politics, race, socioeconomic status, gender, and denomination. Sometimes it feels safer to huddle with people who look, think, or vote like us. But as long as our safety isn't literally at risk, Christ invites us into something far more expansive.

Paul's readers understood a culture of division: Jews and Gentiles were suspicious of one another, divided by culture, religious practices, and power dynamics.

But Paul insists that Jesus dismantles barriers and forms a new people.

In his letter to the Ephesians, Paul calls Jesus our peace, who "has broken down . . . the dividing wall of hostility."* Esau McCaulley writes that this means Christ takes down ethnic and cultural barriers and creates a new humanity in Himself.[212]

When we follow Jesus, we participate alongside Him in the work of reconciliation.

We let the Spirit dismantle the walls of prejudice or resentment inside our own hearts. We imagine a Kingdom where we honor the image of God in one another.

As you pray alongside your breath, reflect on where you're aching for God to reconcile and make peace in your heart, family, friendships, work, community, and country.

PAUSE AND PONDER

Where am I holding on to a "dividing wall" in my own heart?

What would it look like to see people not as "them" but as fellow image-bearers Christ has reconciled?

* Ephesians 2:14, ESV.

JULY 24

Hate evil and love what is good;
turn your courts into true halls of justice.

AMOS 5:15 (NLT)

INHALE: I will follow Your way
EXHALE: Of goodness and justice.

My church has a thriving group of older women who regularly meet to unite people, stitch by stitch. They gather to piece together quilts for newborns, prayer blankets for the ill, and lap quilts for those who are sick.

They call themselves "the Piecemakers."

Throughout history, women have done their part to "hate evil and love what is good" through something unexpected: quilting.

Some say enslaved Africans integrated quilts into the Underground Railroad, stitching hidden messages into the patterns of their quilts. A bow tie, for example, meant to wear a disguise. A bear paw pointed the way to animal trails that offered food and water.[213]

Quilts became maps of survival, signs of refuge, and acts of resistance.

The first time I visited the Smithsonian Museum in Washington, DC, I was surprised to see quilts displayed not as vintage keepsakes but as banners of peaceful protest—abolitionists proclaiming freedom, women demanding a vote, and grandmothers sewing against nuclear weapons.[214] Squares of fabric became testimonies.

And I recently attended a "quilt in," where women from different political backgrounds, inspired by their faith, gathered through the night to piece together squares stitched with prayers and messages for their representatives, reminding them—literally, with quilts hung in government buildings—to "love what is good" and to turn our halls into "halls of justice."

A quilt is a story told in scraps that shows the beauty that's possible when we don't go it alone.

Pieces of fabric might not seem like much on their own. But together, they tell a story.

When we're stitched together in love, we reflect the peaceable Kingdom of God.

PRACTICING THE WAY

Set aside a few minutes today to breathe and pray while coloring in this quilt square. Aim for a rhythm of breath that is about five or six breaths per minute. As you color, consider your place within God's story.

JULY 25

FEAST OF SAINT JAMES

"Come, follow me," Jesus said, "and I will send you out to fish for people."

MARK 1:17 (NIV)

INHALE: Nothing is ordinary
EXHALE: In Your Kingdom.

We live at a time when connection thrums at our fingertips. We have 24-7 access to one another, regardless of borders and time zones. A steady stream of world news, national news, and local news vies for our attention.

In five minutes, you might scroll past your college roommate's new cat, your great-aunt's political memes, and a plea from a local nonprofit. If you have kids in school, you know the chaos of juggling five different apps for grades, sports, and sign-ups.

Too often, it's just too much.

In the flood of big news and sweeping notifications, I begin to feel very small. Not the kind of smallness that rests in the tender palm of a Creator but the kind that feels like a drop swallowed by the sea. Does anything I say or do matter in this big world?

Maybe you've felt that way too.

James was no stranger to ordinary labor. He was a fisherman, calloused and sunburned, mending nets with his brother and father on the Sea of Galilee when Jesus saw him. With dirt under his fingernails and sweat on his brow, maybe he thought he was nothing remarkable. He lived in an area that was a hub of fishing activity—he didn't have a unique calling. His job was messy and dirty. He was used to hard work alongside his dad and brother.

And yet Jesus called him: "Come, follow me."

From that moment, James stepped into a bigger story than he could have imagined. James was among the first disciples Jesus brought into His closest circle. He was one of the "sons of thunder," and he witnessed moments of mystery and glory.*

Jesus chooses ordinary people for extraordinary purposes.

Your daily labor is not in vain. James reminds us that whether you're working on spreadsheets or waiting tables, caregiving or making sales calls, nothing is wasted in the Kingdom of God. How you show up matters. Your character matters.

There is so much more left in your story. Your work matters. What seems small may resound in eternity. When the flood of notifications leaves you dysregulated, Christ's call is there, reminding you of your truest purpose . . . to just *follow*.

In Christ's hands, the work of your ordinary life reverberates like thunder.

SACRED ECHOES

If You don't build it, we labor in vain . . .
O Lord, establish the work of our hands.

"Establish the Work of Our Hands" by The Porter's Gate

---

* Mark 3:17, NIV.

JULY 26

A gentle answer deflects anger, but harsh words make tempers flare.

PROVERBS 15:1 (NLT)

INHALE: Help me respond
EXHALE: With peace.

If our culture were a person, they'd likely look pretty dysregulated—constantly on alert, reacting instead of responding.

Dysregulation simply means our nervous system is overwhelmed and can't access its calm, rational self. Often, the harshest words come from hurting hearts. That doesn't excuse harm, but it does help us understand and makes us less likely to retaliate in the heat of the moment.

Internet culture rewards hot takes and instant reactions. It's easy to fire off words without thinking. But speed rarely equals wisdom. As soon as news hits, people jump to be the first to respond. But often these first responders hurt instead of heal.

In Christ, we're called to honor the belovedness of others.

Thankfully, with the Holy Spirit in us, we have a power beyond ourselves to uphold the dignity of everyone we encounter, even when we're triggered. Even when we feel like we're in the right and they are very, *very* wrong.

Our words are an overflow of the heart, revealing what's happening inside us.*

Before we speak, we can ask God to fill us with grace so that what we say will be life-giving and not something we wish we could take back. It's not that we don't speak truth to power or that we don't speak up when injustice occurs. But it *does* mean the language we use and the posture we speak from matter. We can often express the same sentiment in a healing way instead of a harmful one.

Today, take a few centering breaths before your next conversation or online comment.

Ask Christ to regulate your nervous system and guide your words so that even in a world running on outrage, your speech reflects a loving God.

PRACTICING THE WAY

Before you send that text or post a comment online, run your words through the filter of the fruit of the Spirit.† If what you're saying doesn't align with at least one attribute of a Spirit-filled life, pause. Waiting a moment often gives the Spirit space to redirect us toward compassion.

- Are your words full of love?
- Are you speaking from a place of joy?
- Is your posture one of peace?
- Are you being patient with your response?
- Are your words kind?
- Do your words promote goodness?
- Does your comment reflect your values?
- Are your words gentle?
- Is your response marked by self-control?

* See Matthew 12:34.

† See Galatians 5:22-23.

JULY 27

Give all your worries and cares to God, for he cares about you.

1 PETER 5:7 (NLT)

INHALE: God, You care for me;
EXHALE: I give my worries to You.

When I'm worried, I try to remember two things: I can control my breath, and the One who gives each breath is with me.

Breath prayer is one way I turn toward God and away from the swirl of worry in my mind. Since I'm a chronic worrier, I get *lots* of practice:

When I'm running late.
When my son is up to bat at the bottom of the ninth.
When I get a news alert that makes my chest tighten.
When my daughter spikes a fever.
When I realize I forgot a deadline.

As we enter into a slower rhythm of breathing, our nervous system begins to calm. Doctors Richard Brown and Patricia Gerbarg explain that this kind of breathing stimulates the vagus nerve—the body's natural "calm down" pathway—which quiets the overthinking loops in the brain.

This *coherent breathing* helps us turn off our brains' "worry centers."[215]

Here's a simple way to try it while you pray:[216]

Close your eyes and breathe slowly through your nose.
As you inhale, silently count: one, two. As you exhale, count: one, two.
Then lengthen it a beat: inhale, one, two, three . . . exhale, one, two, three.
Then add another: inhale, one, two, three, four . . . exhale, one, two, three, four.
Keep going until your breath is slow and steady, aiming for about five or six breaths per minute.

Every breath is a chance to return to God's care.

As you breathe, let each inhale remind you that God cares for you. With each exhale, release your worries to the One who holds your concerns with compassion.

Coherent Breathing

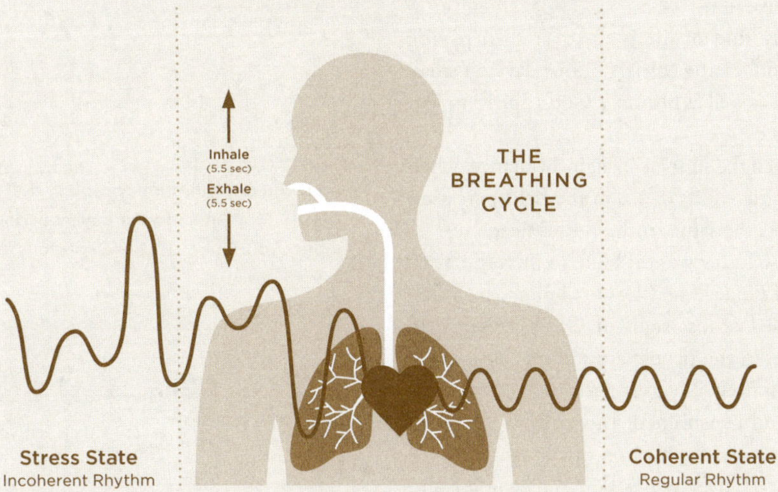

JULY 28

Attention to God leads us out into the open, into a spacious, free life.

ROMANS 8:6 (MSG)

INHALE: Help me
EXHALE: Pay attention.

The spacious life the Spirit leads us into isn't the absence of rules but the presence of God's love, alive in us.

This kind of life is discovered in paying attention. In the corners of our days, in small choices as well as big ones, God's Spirit nudges us awake.

When the sun sets in all its brilliance, when the prairie winds dance in the fields, creation whispers the same truth: God is near.

I also know what it's like to miss the nearness of God. When I am spiraling, it's often because I've lost sight of God's presence in my life, in the people around me, or even in creation itself. My gaze narrows, and life feels tight and constrained. But when I return to attentiveness, the horizon opens again.

Mary Oliver writes that the "wildest and wisest" thing she knows is that "the soul exists, and that it is built entirely out of attentiveness."[217]

Paying attention helps us to be present and awake to God's presence in the here and now.

What might God be inviting you to notice today?

PAUSE AND PONDER

What has been distracting you from paying attention to God today?

When you pay attention to God in the ordinary moments of your day, how does it affect your ability to live a spacious, free life?

JULY 29

Are any among you wise and understanding? Then show it in the way you live, doing good from a humble and wise heart.

JAMES 3:13 (FNV)

INHALE: Help me be humble;
EXHALE: Help me be wise.

Wisdom isn't something we prove with credentials or power. James reminds us: If we're wise, it shows up in the way we live—doing good with a humble heart.

That's a sharp contrast to much of what we see in the public square. Leaders who receive the most attention often rise through connections, wealth, and influence. But those values tend to be soaked in empire, not in God's Kingdom.

And if we're honest, we're not immune to the pull of power. We all slip into idolizing the wrong things. We justify our choices. We twist ourselves into knots to defend what we know deep down doesn't look much like Jesus, throwing our weight behind people, politicians, or platforms that contradict nearly everything Jesus taught.

James cuts through the noise with this message: If you're wise and understanding, show it in the way you live. Be humble. Live from a wise heart.

He doesn't mince words: "If your hearts are full of bitter envy and selfish desires, then stop boasting and speaking lies to cover up the truth about yourselves. This is not the kind of wisdom that comes down from the One Above Us All," he writes. "Instead, it is from this world. It is unspiritual and of the evil one. For where there is jealousy and selfish ways, you will also find confusion and all kinds of evil at work."*

The path of self leaves us empty and confused. The fruit on those trails is deceptive. It might look shiny and satisfying, but it's not the fruit of the Spirit.

James calls us back to humility and wisdom—reminding us to let *God* shape how we speak and how we live. One way to keep our eyes on what is true is to be mindful of our relationship with God, which naturally makes us mindful of our thoughts, words, and actions.

When jealousy or bitterness or confusion rises in us, it's an invitation to return to God. It's a sign to breathe and remember whose wisdom we really want shaping our lives.

As Regina Chow Trammel and John Trent write, "Mindfulness engages our minds, bodies, and souls. Christian mindfulness is holistic."[218]

Wisdom begins with surrender. With breath. With prayer. With choosing the way of Jesus—again and again—in the ordinary details of our days.

SACRED ECHOES

To enjoy each breath one at a time, to understand, to be able to go within: this is the true art of living.[219]

Prem Rawat

* James 3:14-16, FNV.

JULY 30

We will never turn our back on you; breathe life into our lungs so we can shout your name!

PSALM 80:18 (MSG)

INHALE: Breathe life
EXHALE: Into our lungs.

When I find myself wondering if God is still near, when I slip into worry about the future, I return to memories I have of when I glimpsed God's faithfulness in the midst of my ordinary days.

When we were adopting our son from West Africa, God breathed connections into being that we could never have orchestrated ourselves. We kept running into a young couple—first in Nigeria, then back in the US—at airports, in terminals, and finally at the Detroit airport, where our rerouted and then delayed flight had somehow landed all of us.

After about the seventh "coincidental" run-in at the airport Chili's, we finally introduced ourselves. Ugo, from Nigeria, and Amy, from Kansas, were newly married and about to move to Lagos for work. They were also Christians. Pam from *The Office* once wisely proclaimed, "I feel God in this Chili's." And let me tell you: We all did that day.

We exchanged information. Ugo wrote the visa invitation we needed. Our new friends generously opened their home in Lagos to us—just down the road from the US Consulate, where we made frequent visits—and even offered their driver to help us navigate the giant city.

We said our shaky yes to God. And thanks be to God, they said theirs to a bighearted, naive young couple. Joseph celebrated his first birthday in their apartment. He took his first steps there. He even shares a birthday with Amy. There is no way we could have arranged all that. But God could. And God did.

The Israelites had a name for this way of recalling God's faithfulness: *stones of remembrance.** After crossing the Jordan River, the people were instructed by God to set up stones so that generations to come would see these markers of God's faithfulness and ask, "What do these stones mean?"

This story about Joseph is one of my stones of remembrance, pointing me back to times when heaven brushed earth, when God breathed life into the world and whispered, *I am here. I am with you.*

As long as I have breath in my lungs, I will do my best to remember, to tell and retell the stories of God's goodness.

Here's your chance to make your own stones of remembrance.

* See Joshua 4:7.

PAUSE AND PONDER

Make your own stones of remembrance.

- Recall a situation that seemed like a coincidence at first but was actually a prayer God answered before you even prayed it.
- Think of a time someone showed up at just the right moment. How did that remind you of God's care?
- When did the Spirit lead you to reach out or be generous? Reflect on a time when you gave a hesitant *yes* to God and how God met you in it.

Write down a memory on each stone. Tell the story to someone you love. Consider placing a physical stone somewhere you'll see it as a marker of God's faithfulness you can return to when you find yourself battling with worry in the future.

These are your stones—your reminders that God is here and is still breathing life into you.

JULY 31

Put things in order . . . agree with one another, live in peace; and the God of love and peace will be with you.

2 CORINTHIANS 13:11 (NRSV)

INHALE: God of love and peace,
EXHALE: Be with us.

The pain of the world is so heavy that it can pull us under if we're not careful. Breath prayer is a gentle way to stay connected to God's peace and to one another as we navigate the whipping waves of life.

Paul concludes his letter to the Corinthians by summarizing his main points: "Put things in order . . . agree with one another, live in peace." (In today's shorthand, it's almost like a holy "TL;DR.")

The church in Corinth was chaotic. The Corinthians wanted to follow Jesus but needed guidance on how to do it well together. Paul didn't give them a long list of new rules but reminded them of what truly matters: restoration, joy, harmony, and peace. The Greek phrase for "put things in order" suggests mending what's torn—healing divisions rather than making them worse.

"Live in peace," Paul urged, because love is the bond that holds varied personalities together without erasing their differences.[220]

We don't do this work of making peace alone. Thankfully, we have God's help. One way we start this work is through our breath. When we allow the peace of Christ to dwell within us, each inhale and exhale becomes a small act of ordering a reminder that the God of love is with us. We don't have to breathe in the pollution of bitterness or exhale judgment into the world. Instead, we can breathe in the pure air of God's love.

That's one thing I love about breath prayer: I can lean into it while my hands are busy. As I'm driving to a meeting or pulling weeds in the front yard. As I'm slathering sunscreen on my kids, folding laundry, or walking the dog.

When we pray alongside our breath, even the most seemingly ordinary acts become whispered prayers, bringing peace to our hearts so we might exhale peace into the world around us.

Peace is a hallmark of a life transformed by God's love. Sometimes all we need to take the next step toward peace is the next breath.

SACRED ECHOES

Prayer has become a way of holding space for all that is broken in this world while my hands work toward creating a bit of cleanliness, a bit of order, a bit of beauty and life and healing around me.[221]

Sarah Bessey

AUGUST 1

The LORD, who created the heavens and stretched them out . . .
gives breath to the people upon it and spirit to those who walk in it.

ISAIAH 42:5 (NRSV)

INHALE: Creator of all,
EXHALE: Breathe life into me.

God is infinite. God is intimate.

The One who stretched the heavens wide also knit you together in your mother's womb.

Our human minds can't fathom the expansive power and tender care that linger in the breath of our Creator. "From the beginning, God gets as close to us as he can," Curt Thompson says.[222] And that has never changed. Our vast God comes close—and stays there—nearer than our next breath.

As we see in Isaiah 42, God gives us breath in our lungs *and* animates life within our souls. "How can anyone who is made to bear likeness to the maker of the cosmos be anything less than glory?" asks Cole Arthur Riley. "This is inherent dignity."[223]

Every breath is a gift. Each inhale, each exhale, is another reminder: Because God *is*, we *are*.

You can choose to rush past this miracle or to pause long enough to notice it. To receive it. To let gratitude rise with every inhale and awe flow with every exhale.

As you pray today's breath prayer, inhale through your nose, drawing air deep into your stomach. Imagine God breathing life into you, calling His creation *good*. Hold for a few counts before slowly releasing through your mouth.

Rest there, just for a moment, in the sweeping nearness of God's love for *you*.

SACRED ECHOES

To be a member of the human race is the proof that God loves you. It's his choice out of, not just a few billion choices, but out of an infinite number of persons who could be here—you're here![224]

Thomas Keating

AUGUST 2

Take my yoke upon you and learn from me, for I am gentle and humble in heart, and you will find rest for your souls.

MATTHEW 11:29 (NIV)

INHALE: Help me be
EXHALE: Humble in heart.

We live in a world that prizes self.

Say what you want, when you want. Protect your peace. Do what's best for you.

And while boundaries matter, if we're not careful, we can slip into a me-first way of being that leaves little room for humility. Or compassion for humanity.

Jesus goes first, saying, "I am gentle and humble in heart." His humility was strength anchored in love.

Thomas Keating writes, "Humility is an attitude of honesty with God, oneself, and all reality. It enables us to be at peace in the presence of our powerlessness and to rest in the forgetfulness of self."[225] Forgetting yourself doesn't mean ignoring your needs. It means remembering you are not the center of existence. It means loosening your grip on the need to be right.

Humility gives us a new lens for seeing others. It reframes how we respond when the woman in the checkout line snaps at us or when a stranger trolls us online. It interrupts our impulse to react with haughtiness or judgment.

Humility gives us space to remember: We are loved, and so is the person in front of us.

In a culture of quick comebacks and defensive edges, humility opens the door to peace.

Where do you feel the pull to be the center—always right, always heard, always in control? What would it look like to rest in the "gentle and humble" way of Jesus instead?

PRACTICING THE WAY

When you aren't sure what to pray, Harrison Scott Key breaks down four points of "ACTS" to breathe through:

Adoration: Let God know how awesome He is, setting your heart in humility.
Confession: Tell God the things you've done wrong, as only a humble heart can.
Thanksgiving: Thank God for all He has already done for you.
Supplication: Ask God to "do maybe a little more," if possible.[226]

AUGUST 3

Make every effort to keep the unity of the Spirit through the bond of peace.

EPHESIANS 4:3 (NIV)

INHALE: Bring us together
EXHALE: In Your peace.

Unity is not the same as false peacekeeping.

Sometimes unity gets twisted into silence: *Don't rock the boat. Don't speak up when someone is hurt or harmed. Don't push back on those in power.* But that's not the unity Paul speaks of in Ephesians.

Unity is a gift from God—a Spirit-breathed way of living that transforms us and the world.

Maybe that's why Paul says peace is the glue that holds the community together. Peace isn't passive. It's a gift and a calling, requiring us to actively seek reconciliation and repair with one another, to create a more flourishing world together.

Unity is honoring the image of God in one another.

Unity is working side by side to bring about goodness and justice.

Unity is using the unique ways God has formed each of us to reshape our communities.

Unity is calling one another in (as compared to calling someone out) with compassion and integrity when harm is done.

Unity is using our collective voices and resources to honor God by honoring others.

Jesus Himself prayed that "all of them may be one, Father, just as you are in me and I am in you."* Unity is spiritual and relational.

When we're living out our love in rhythms of peace, we're being the body of Christ.

This kind of unity begins when we remember that God loves every person—including those we'd rather disagree with or dismiss—as much as God loves us.

May we breathe in that truth. And may we breathe out that peace.

Together.

SACRED ECHOES

Peace, in the biblical sense, is more than the absence of conflict; it is the presence of harmony and wholeness.[227]

* John 17:21, NIV.

AUGUST 4

I'm staying on your trail; I'm putting one foot in front of the other. I'm not giving up.

PSALM 17:5 (MSG)

INHALE: On this journey,
EXHALE: I am seen.

The last time I hit the trails with my family, my youngest son was joking around with his brothers and swerved on his bike and almost careened down a ravine and into a lake. My heart stopped while his little life flashed before my eyes. (He landed in a soft thicket and was just fine.)

Staying on God's trail doesn't mean we won't wobble or swerve. But we're never abandoned. Even in the near misses, we're like children on a trail, free to explore—free to *be*—because our parent is right there with us.

As a child of God, you don't have to work for your belovedness.

When you're moving in step with the One who gives each breath, loving God and loving others, it doesn't matter if people misunderstand or judge you. It doesn't matter if you make mistakes, because you know that the only perfect human is Jesus, and our God is a God of restoration and renewal.

Wherever your path is taking you, God is already there—behind you, with you, and ahead of you, steadying your handlebars.

I know that sometimes, it's hard. You might feel like you've tumbled into the weeds, rolling down a hill and landing headfirst in the water. But guess what? There's still life to be had here. God is not done with you. There are lessons we can only learn by falling and rising, swerving and righting ourselves, again and again.

Where in your life do you feel like you're swerving off course? How might God be setting you free to keep going?

Don't give up. God is near, helping you back up and pointing you forward.

Take a deep breath of fresh air today. You're free.

RHYTHM OF BREATH

The sparrow cannot help but be free,
The lily cannot help but be untamed,
The star cannot help but light the way,
And I cannot help being called Yours.
I swim in wild rivers of belonging;
I climb the mountains of my soul;
And on the other side, I am known,
I am seen, I am loved.
My bare feet run in the open field
To One with arms stretched wide,
Calling me child, whispering,
You are Mine,
And I am yours.[228]

AUGUST 5

Gracious speech is like clover honey—good taste
to the soul, quick energy for the body.

PROVERBS 16:24 (MSG)

INHALE: Fill my words
EXHALE: With Your grace.

"Would you talk to a friend that way?" I text back to a friend.

We're often much harsher on ourselves than we would ever be toward someone we love. My friend Aundi Kolber reminds us that when we trust that God is gentle with us, we can also be gentle with ourselves.[229]

Whenever I catch a cold, I love adding honey to my tea. It's sweet and soothing, and it coats my throat, helping me feel better and bringing my voice back. Honey is known for its healing properties, and kind words work in the same gentle way. They have the power to heal what's hurting and restore what's strained.

Maybe you think you're not worth it—that you're just a vapor in this world, unworthy of the same care you'd give others. Maybe you feel insignificant in the grand scheme of things, unseen by God, so you stop seeing yourself with kindness.

But even the tiniest worker bee has meaning: "A worker bee weighs little more than a breath—around 100 milligrams—but she can carry half her body weight in nectar."[230]

The way we view God shapes how we see ourselves—and how we treat others. If we can't use gentle words with ourselves, it's nearly impossible to be gentle with others. If we see God as harsh or disappointed, our inner voice often echoes that tone. But if we view God as patient and kind, our words—both inward and outward—start to taste sweeter.

When your heart is sore, reach again for the sweetness of divine kindness. Let your words drip with the grace of God.

Further Reading for being gentle with yourself: Read *Try Softer: A Fresh Approach to Move Us Out of Anxiety, Stress, and Survival Mode—and Into a Life of Connection and Joy* by Aundi Kolber (specifically chapter 9, "Try Softer with Your Internal Critic").

Further Reading for being gentle with your family: Read *Words Like Honey: How to Avoid Unintentional Harm, Model Kindness, and Nurture Your Child's Faith Through What You Say* by Amy Hughes.

PRACTICING THE WAY

Fill out the honeycomb with positive attributes that describe who you *really* are.

AUGUST 6

You can't go wrong when you love others. When you add up everything in the law code, the sum total is love.

ROMANS 13:10 (MSG)

INHALE: Help me err
EXHALE: On the side of love.

We're very good at drawing lines. In. Out. Us. Them.

We draw lines in the sand until we're all alone, sinking in a circle of our own making.

We've baptized our boundaries and turned convictions into cages: You can't align with them because *they* believe *that*. You can't align with *them* because they *don't* believe that. Regardless of our politics or theology, we can all fall into this way of thinking if we aren't using love as our lens.

Being Christlike wins over being correct. Always. Paul writes to a divided community and reminds them (and us) that love is the whole point. "When you add it all up," he says, "the sum total is love."

It's like he's calling us all in and saying, "Take a breath. It's not that complicated."

Think of Jesus with the woman at the well—crossing cultural lines with compassion instead of contempt. His love wasn't theoretical. It looked like listening. Like offering living water to someone others ignored.

When I scroll through the news or overhear a conversation that makes me tense, my breath catches, and my mind starts to sort who's right and who's wrong. But when I pause long enough to exhale, I remember that God's love is the only thing that changes anything.

When in doubt, take a breath. Borrow today's breath prayer, and ask God how you might err on the side of love.

PAUSE AND PONDER

Where in your life have you been drawing lines? What pain or past experience might be underneath that division in your heart?

When have you experienced love as something that crosses dividing lines? How did that change you?

How do you know when you're operating from love rather than from judgment or fear? What does that feel like in your body?

AUGUST 7

The wisdom from above is first pure, then peaceable, gentle, willing to yield, full of mercy and good fruits.

JAMES 3:17 (NRSV)

INHALE: Guide me
EXHALE: In Your wisdom.

God's wisdom offers an exhale and a new perspective for making choices when we're overwhelmed.

I often find myself stuck in my own thoughts when making decisions. I get hung up on finding the *one* choice that God has for me. But this isn't how God works. God doesn't shout or push us into corners. Instead, the Spirit guides us to a gentler, freer way of making decisions—one based on peace, mercy, and the good fruit it yields.

Though it's easy to believe that having wisdom means finding the "right" answer, James shows us that wisdom from above isn't focused on *information* as much as it is on *formation.* Wisdom forms the center of who we are so we become more like Christ—"first pure, then peaceable."

Spiritual discernment isn't only for life-altering moments but also for everyday choices that shape who we are becoming.

When you're unsure of your next step, instead of rushing to figure it out, take a breath and ask: *Does this choice lead me deeper into God's peace and mercy? Does it bear good fruit in me and around me?*

These questions help us shed anxiety about the future and move toward trusting God, shifting our focus from what the outcome will be to aligning with the wisdom God breathes into the world. Julie Saad writes, "When discernment starts with going to God with our questions and desires, the answers will find us."[231]

Wisdom from above may not give you a map, but it heightens your awareness of God's presence and purpose in your life, helping you decide what's next with an open heart.

PRACTICING THE WAY

Henri Nouwen said that discernment is "learning to listen for and recognize over time the voice and character of God in our hearts and daily lives."[232]

1. **Recognize the need:** Notice when you feel pressure or confusion about a decision.
2. **Get quiet:** Take three slow breaths. Name the question honestly before God.
3. **Open your heart:** Pray to be openhanded and openhearted, letting go of your agenda. Ask God to help you hold your question with wisdom.
4. **Notice shifts:** Pay attention to where peace or tension settles within your body. Jot down what arises without judgment.
5. **Include others:** If you're stuck, it can be helpful to talk with a spiritual director, pastor, therapist, or trusted friend.
6. **Repeat:** Return to this process over time. Discernment continues beyond a onetime question.[233]

Contemplative discernment invites us to bring our decisions and desires to God, letting divine wisdom guide us in both big and small choices.

AUGUST 8

We know how much God loves us, and we have put our trust in his love. God is love.

1 JOHN 4:16 (NLT)

INHALE: I'm putting my trust
EXHALE: In Your love.

When I first started dating my boyfriend, everything became more fun. Suddenly, picking up some groceries for his mom was an opportunity to laugh. When he had to get gas in his truck, we had an adventure to go on, and maybe he'd even surprise me with a pack of my favorite gum.

The ordinary didn't seem so ordinary. The mundane wasn't quite so mundane.

God created us to love one another, whether we're sharing our lives with family, friends, or significant others. Love—real, shared love—transforms the everyday.

An extensive study recently found that people consistently rated every common daily activity (more than eighty different everyday tasks) as more significantly enjoyable when done with someone else, leading the researchers to conclude that "whether we are eating, reading, or even cleaning up around the house, happiness thrives in the company of others."[234]

God is love. To love and be loved is to participate in God's very nature.

Spoiler alert: I did marry that boyfriend, and he still makes everything more fun, twenty years later. But sharing our lives doesn't mean everyone needs to be married or wildly extroverted. We can share our lives in simple, sacred ways. God formed us to live in community alongside one another. We need people to help us practice being loved and known.

I was recently teaching our teenage son how to pump gas and caught myself saying, "Back in my day, we had to go inside to pay and actually talk to people." I get groceries delivered, work from home, and can go for days without seeing anyone outside my family. It's easy to drift into *house troll mode*—but it's rarely what my soul needs.

I've started working from coffee shops every once in a while and reading on the swing outside my front door. And somehow, in small slices of life, I've met neighbors I never knew and made connections I never would have made otherwise.

We really are better together. May God's love pull us out of isolation and into belonging.

PRACTICING THE WAY

We remember who we are through one another. If you feel lonely right now, that doesn't mean you're doing faith wrong—it means you're human. Where could you create space for intentional connection this week? Even small moments are better shared.

- **List the places you go**—school pickup, the grocery store, a walk around the block—and pray over them, asking God to help you connect with someone there.
- **Invite** someone to run errands with you.
- **Visit** your library or join a group at a church.
- **Call** a friend while driving.
- **Choose a lane** at the store that isn't a self-checkout lane and ask the cashier how their day is going.

AUGUST 9

The LORD will guide you continually, giving you water when you are dry and restoring your strength.

ISAIAH 58:11 (NLT)

INHALE: Guide me, O God;
EXHALE: Show me the way.

Gravel crunches under my feet as I make my way through the wooded path. Crickets chirp and cicadas sing as the late-afternoon sun filters through the canopy of oaks and maples.

A thought flutters through my mind: *It would be so special to see a deer.*

For a split second, I consider asking God to send one, but the thought instantly feels ridiculous. At any given second, children are crying with empty bellies. Our world groans under the weight of sorrow. *God doesn't work like that,* I think, shaking the silly prayer out of my mind. *Why am I so childish?*

I push aside my thoughts and keep walking the twisting trail. Mosquitoes flitter at my ankles as I climb a hill and make my way around the bend. I turn the corner, and what I see stops me in my tracks.

A deer stands across the trail, motionless, with eyes fixed on mine. It's close enough I could reach out and touch it. Neither of us moves. We just . . . look at each other. The sight takes my breath away.

God answered the prayer I hadn't even dared to pray.

We stay there for a few sacred seconds, and it feels like the whole forest is holding its breath. And deep within my heart, I know: I'm seen. I'm known. *Maybe our Creator meets us through creation, gazing at us with a wild, unexpected love—a love that doesn't just tolerate us but delights in us.*

We often complicate things, overthinking how we "should" pray or experience God. But perhaps God has been here all along, just waiting for us to notice.

Holding space to experience God isn't childish. And what's so wrong with being childlike, anyway? After all, Jesus told his followers to be like little children.*

If you're reading this and thinking, *I've never had a deer-in-the-woods moment*, take heart. God's gaze is upon you too. It might come in laughter shared with a friend, a child's hug, or sunlight spilling across your kitchen table. However it comes, may you feel seen. May you remember you are beloved.

Let your breath become prayer. As you inhale through your nose, imagine God gazing on you with love. Hold your breath for a few counts, reflecting on how God holds your prayers, even the ones you never say aloud. As you exhale, imagine looking back at Jesus in adoration.

SACRED ECHOES

The breath prayer is the prayer of the beggar and carries with it the intimacy of asking for what we need.[235]

Ruth Haley Barton

* See Matthew 18:3.

AUGUST 10

Each one of us needs to look after the good of the people around us, asking ourselves, "How can I help?"

ROMANS 15:2 (MSG)

INHALE: Help us
EXHALE: Help each other.

Mr. Rogers encouraged entire generations to "look for the helpers." In this weary world, there's no doubt that we need to tune our hearts to the ones who help in turbulent times. But if I were to expand on the idea, I'd add two things: (1) Be a helper, and (2) let yourself be helped.

Paul's words to a divided church in Rome hit close to home today. "Each one of us needs to look after the good of the people around us," he says. Not just when crisis strikes, but in the comings and goings of your ordinary days.

When our kids were little, we taught them to ask, "How can I help?" after their apology. Paul encouraged Christ followers to be people who asked that question too.

When the neighbor's dog slips through the fence? Chase after him. When someone whose hands are full needs a door opened? Easy win. I once watched two gruff New Yorkers wordlessly grab a stroller—one on each side—and carry it up the subway stairs for a mom who was struggling.

I'll admit, sometimes it's hard for me to ask for help. I get the idea that if people don't offer to help, then they don't want to. It leaves me resentful when I think, *People don't want to help*, but nine times out of ten, it's simply because I haven't asked. People aren't mind readers, and I'm learning that many *are* willing to help if we only give them the chance.

Here's the other piece: When we help, it's important to do so while honoring the other person's dignity. We don't always know what someone needs. Offer without assuming. Ask before acting. When we're helpers, our love honors consent and upholds the dignity of every person, even if they don't want our help the way we imagined.

I've started to think of helping the way I think of breath—we inhale, we exhale. We need help; we give help. Sometimes you make the meal; sometimes you receive it. Sometimes you're the one giving a ride, and sometimes you're the one who needs to be picked up. Sometimes you're the hands holding, and sometimes you're the one held.

If we all cared for those around us, what would the world look like? If we're paying attention, we get glimpses of it in carried strollers, open doors, a meal on a hard day, a gentle "How can I help?"

As you breathe in, imagine receiving help. As you breathe out, imagine extending it to someone else.

PAUSE AND PONDER

Where are you resisting the urge to ask for help? What story are you telling yourself about weakness?

AUGUST 11

How very good and pleasant it is when kindred live together in unity!

PSALM 133:1 (NRSV)

INHALE: Unify us
EXHALE: In Your love.

The Internet gives us instant access to share anything and everything that pops into our minds. It can be a tool for connection and community, but it can also bring out our worst tendencies. Algorithms are designed to keep us scrolling, rewarding spectacle because strong emotions keep us engaged. Content that elicits sorrow or anger drives reactions and revenue. Whether it's "ragebait" or "sadbait," the common factor is emotional manipulation.[236]

The more reactive we are, the more the system benefits. It's no surprise we often feel drained and discouraged after scrolling. We are a collection of individuals with dysregulated systems, using them to share our dysregulated thoughts. Unity feels almost impossible when we're constantly prompted to *react* instead of *reflect.*

Unity doesn't mean we all agree. That's not what the early church looked like, and it's not what the family of God looks like today.

The mystery—and the miracle—of following Christ is that our stories are bound up with people who are wildly different from us.

When we choose love and continue to choose it, we move toward a communal flourishing that reflects God's Kingdom. I'm always working on setting (and resetting) healthy boundaries around social media. When I see people lashing out online, I try to be curious and hold "every thought captive,"* especially when something triggers me.

As children of God, we have to see one another as siblings—as *kin.* We can't control algorithms, but we can resist their pull. We can pause before responding. We can choose compassion instead of contempt. (This doesn't mean tolerating hate, engaging with trolls, or staying in unsafe situations. It just means that we can take a breath and remember that every person, no matter how hurtful or even hateful, is more than what they post.)

The next time you feel the pull to respond in anger or judgment, return to today's breath prayer. A few minutes of controlled breathing can be enough of a reset to prevent you from saying something you'll regret. Remember your humanity—and the divine image in the one you're tempted to dismiss.

PAUSE AND PONDER

When you feel yourself getting drawn into online outrage, pause and take a breath before posting, commenting, or sharing. Consider these questions:

- What pain or perspective might this person be carrying?
- What reaction are they hoping to provoke—curiosity, conflict, validation?
- What am I feeling in my own body right now?
- What's the story behind the story?
- Am I feeding the outrage cycle—or breaking it?
- What would love look like in this moment?

* 2 Corinthians 10:5, NRSV.

AUGUST 12

Live creatively, friends. If someone falls into sin, forgivingly restore him, saving your critical comments for yourself. You might be needing forgiveness before the day's out.

GALATIANS 6:1 (MSG)

INHALE: Restorative God,
EXHALE: Help us live creatively.

When I was the editor of my school newspaper, I loved review days. It's hard to describe the thrill I'd get from poring over every page, red pen in hand, catching errors that made it to print. (I'm really fun at parties.)

It's one thing to point out mistakes as an editor, but we aren't meant to *live* like this, circling one another's every flaw and writing our critiques in the margins.

And yet I do this more often than I'd like to admit. I see where someone missed the mark and find myself quick to judge. It's easier to point out someone else's mistake than to face my own. I do this sometimes without even realizing it, and I need God's help to stop pointing out flaws.* Paul's call to "live creatively" is an invitation to an entirely new way of being.

He calls followers of Jesus to breathe new life into old, tired patterns of critique and comparison. To become people who live into forgiveness and restoration, letting mercy have the last word. Living these rhythms looks like pushing back against harmful patterns of shame and division, like asking God to help us imagine what love might look like in the midst of our busy, complicated lives. And that begins with humility—acknowledging our own humanity and our shared need for grace.

True restoration takes creativity.

As much as I love a red pen, we're not called to edit other people's lives into perfection. And thank goodness, because that work is *impossible*. All we're called to do is enter into the work God is already doing to heal what's broken in us and around us. When one of us hurts, we all hurt. And when one of us heals, we all start to heal. We're connected in ways we may not even realize.

Dr. Martin Luther King Jr. wrote from the Birmingham jail, "We are caught in an inescapable network of mutuality, tied in a single garment of destiny."[237] When we help restore another, we mend something within ourselves. When we offer compassion and work for the flourishing of all people, we become part of God's creative, healing work in the world.

PRACTICING THE WAY

Choose what part of today's verse resonates with you most, letting it become your prayer. God, I need help . . .

- *Living creatively* when I'm tempted to follow old, tired ways.
- *Forgiving others* when criticism feels easier than compassion.
- *Working for restoration* when repair feels too slow or too complicated.
- *Saving critical comments for myself* when I get judgmental.
- *Receiving forgiveness* when I can't stop circling my own mistakes.

* See Matthew 7:3-5.

AUGUST 13

Why is everyone hungry for more? . . . I have God's more-than-enough, more joy in one ordinary day than they get in all their shopping sprees.

PSALM 4:6-7 (MSG)

INHALE: No matter what,
EXHALE: You are enough.

When my husband and I got married, we were poor college students who were thrilled to rent a duplex from our university for about $550 a month. (It was a wild deal even back then.) We shared an old two-story house that was split into a duplex. We got the upstairs, and two frat boys had the downstairs.

It wasn't fancy, but it was *ours*. And it was more than enough.

We found furniture at the thrift store and repurposed it. We put wedding pictures in frames and bought a small bistro table that would fit in the kitchen. (We ate the top of our wedding cake there on our first anniversary.) Somehow we managed to fit a bed, a desk, and a small plastic dresser in the bedroom. (You could touch all three at once.) The entire home was about the size of our current living room, but I felt so *rich* in that little apartment.

Psalm 4 asks, "Why is everyone hungry for more?" It's a question as old as humanity. We think that one more purchase, one more promotion, one more *like*, or one more milestone will fill the ache inside us. But the math never adds up.

Billionaires want more money. Celebrities want more fame. Even neighbors who seem to have it all keep saying, "More, more." No amount of wealth or health can bring lasting peace. They can comfort us, but they'll never complete us.

We live in a culture that preaches a kind of prosperity gospel. We're told that if we just accumulate enough, we'll finally be content. But the gospel of Jesus completely flips that script: Peace comes from trusting that *God is already enough*.

"Fill us with goodness," the psalmist prays.* Maybe that's the antidote to "more." When we breathe in the goodness of God, we can stop reaching for what will never satisfy.

May the breath in your lungs and the belonging that holds you be enough for today.

BREATHE THIS IN

Have you ever sighed with contentment or breathed a sigh of relief? We've all felt that subtle settling in our bodies and souls when we realize—for this moment—that we have enough. We are safe.

Sighing is one of the ways our bodies keep us healthy. We sigh spontaneously many times an hour, taking deeper breaths that reinflate the millions of tiny air sacs in our lungs before releasing a long exhale. Scientists refer to sighing as a natural reset for our systems. That deep, audible breath has been shown to affect not just our bodies but our minds too.[238]

The next time you sigh as you sink into the couch after a long day, remember that God created your body with built-in pauses to help you feel calm and connected.

---

* See Psalm 107:9.

AUGUST 14

Friends, when life gets really difficult, don't jump to the conclusion that God isn't on the job.

1 PETER 4:12 (MSG)

INHALE: Even now, God,
EXHALE: You're still here.

I never set out to be a "medical mom." The hardest part of raising kids who have significant chronic illnesses isn't the endless appointments or medication schedules—it's knowing I can't take away their pain. I can't protect them from what might happen.

Sometimes love can leave us feeling so very powerless.

When I'm sitting in the emergency room or trying to soothe my son's pain, I often forget to breathe. My chest tightens. My mind spins with what-ifs. All the things I know about God seem to scatter, replaced with a sense of panic. *Prayer is great,* I think, *but right now my child needs medical help. Where are You, God?*

Sometimes it takes me a while to remember the truth tucked deep in my worried heart: *Even in the scariest moments of life, God is still here, with us in every single breath and every single heartbeat.*

What is it about our brains that makes us dive into panic mode? Why do we jump to the conclusion that God has left us?

Not long ago, after another late-night ER visit, my teenage son looked over at me in the car and said, "Thanks for always being by my side." I told him he didn't need to thank me—that's what parents are supposed to do. We show up.

Even in our darkest hours (even when everything feels like it's unraveling and we can barely breathe), God is always there.

God couldn't imagine *not* being by our side.

When life presses in and you find yourself slipping into worst-case scenarios, pause. Take a slow, deep breath through your nose, and then exhale gently.

The same God who has been with you through it all is breathing hope into you right now.

RHYTHM OF BREATH

I hoped,
But I did not see.
I asked,
But I did not receive.
And still I hope,
And I ask,
Not because of what will be
But because I don't want
To live in a world
Where hope doesn't exist.

AUGUST 15

This resurrection life you received from God is not a timid, grave-tending life. It's adventurously expectant, greeting God with a childlike "What's next, Papa?"

ROMANS 8:15 (MSG)

INHALE: Help me to be
EXHALE: Adventurously expectant.

When my husband and I were in our early twenties, our hopeful hearts were fertile ground for God to breathe new life into us in so many ways, including becoming parents to our son Joseph through adoption. But somewhere along the way, I let the responsibilities of real life take away my trust that God is with me wherever I go and wear down my expectancy that good and beautiful things are ahead.

Parenting Joseph offers glimmers that keep my heart open and hopeful for what God will do. Now a teenager, he has his moody moments but approaches life with a hopeful spirit, open and ready to tackle the next adventure. When he auditions for a play without prior experience, his courage and optimism remind me not to get stuck in my own head. When he's up to bat in baseball, when he embarks on a new class, when he tries a new-to-him food (he can't stop eating sushi now!), or even when he does something small like cracking open a new book, he does so with an open heart.

Joseph is far from naive. But he has something I want more of: courageous trust that there's more than what we see. That in this resurrection life, we can trust that God never stops breathing fresh life into us. He has faced more hardships than most kids his age—and many adults. He has known the loss of his birth family and his culture, and he lives with a serious chronic illness that has landed him in the emergency room more times than I can count. He understands what it's like to carry hard things. To quite literally have a hard time catching his breath.

I think that's why he is so stubborn in hope—because he knows how fragile life can be and how worthwhile it is to live with hopeful expectation that grace and glory can still be found, even when we feel lost or worn down. Hard-won hope is still hope.

We are resurrection people, filled with resurrection hope. It's the Holy Spirit who leads us into hope, not just our personality or determination. Life with God awakens expectancy, not escapism. Day by day, God renews us and reminds us that no matter where we go or what the future holds, we do not go alone.

Adventure awaits. (Even if it's simply being brave enough to get out of the house today.) And in Christ, the compass always points toward hope.

PAUSE AND PONDER

Who do you know who lives with hopeful expectancy? How can you let them know you appreciate them?

AUGUST 16

When you did it to one of the least of these
. . . you were doing it to me!

MATTHEW 25:40 (NLT)

INHALE: Help me love others
EXHALE: The way You love me.

When I was little, I was both terrified and fascinated by the opening scene of *Beauty and the Beast.*

A storm rages as an elderly woman, weary and dripping from the rain, knocks on a castle door, asking for shelter. The young prince (with an entire mansion to spare) refuses her entry. Spoiler alert for this 1991 animated classic: She turns him into a beast.

Even as a child, I sensed there was something sacred in that story—a warning about what happens when we shut the door on someone in need.

"Don't forget to show hospitality to strangers," Hebrews 13:2 says, "for some who have done this have entertained angels without realizing it!"* This verse is full of mystery. Our culture doesn't always know what to do with mystery, so we dismiss it, almost as if it were a fairy tale too. But a life of faith means a life of, well, *faith*: believing that there is more happening than what we can see or understand.

Jesus, knowing we'd have trouble living into the rhythms of grace that He calls us to, puts it even more plainly: "Whatever you did for the least of these, you did for me."

Jesus tells us that the way we treat those who need the most help is the way we treat Him. It makes sense in theory—but how do we actually live it in our real lives? Maybe it really is that simple: feeding the hungry, standing with the immigrant, inviting the stranger.

Jesus is here, if only we'd take a breath and notice.

In Anne Lamott's book *Somehow: Thoughts on Love*, she writes about experiencing God in an unexpected way in the face of a stranger: "It was Jesus in His distressing guise as a man in a tattered down jacket in 90-degree weather, smoking."[239]

From the castle door in a fairy tale to the door of our own hearts, the invitation remains: Open up. May we not get so caught up in our own lives that we fail to see Jesus right in front of us.

SACRED ECHOES

Look! I stand at the door and knock. If you hear my voice and open the door, I will come in, and we will share a meal together as friends.

Revelation 3:20 (NLT)

* NLT.

AUGUST 17

This is my prayer: that your love will flourish and that you will not only love much but well.

PHILIPPIANS 1:9 (MSG)

INHALE: Your goodness
EXHALE: Is all around me.

God is present all around us, but sometimes the to-dos and bad news wear us down, and we forget to notice God's presence in our everyday lives.

My family lives in a 120-year-old home with plenty of nooks and crannies, both inside and out. This summer, we've let a patch of yard grow wild with prairie grass, wildflowers, and, honestly, more weeds than I care to acknowledge. Calling it a pollinator garden might be a generous description for our little corner of wild earth, but the bees and butterflies don't seem to mind.

Taking out the garbage is a chore I detest and one I usually try to pass off on my husband or sons. But when it's my turn, I've started noticing what hovers in the yard—flashes of color and movement just beyond the bins. A moth drifts through the air, a butterfly balances on a purple coneflower, and for a brief second, I remember: *God is here too.*

Therapist Deb Dana uses the term *glimmers* to describe "micro-moments of safety and connection." She writes that a glimmer might come through a sound, a smell, a sight, or a feeling—and when we pause to notice it, our bodies begin to settle.[240]

When the world feels like it's on fire (or when life smells a little like garbage baking in the August sun), we have to become hope noticers. Staying awake to hope hidden in the weeds is how we make it through.[241]

The practice of being alive to God's goodness right here and now is holy work.

How might you savor glimpses of God today?

The glitter of sunlight on water. The clink of ice in your lemonade glass. The taste of sun-ripened tomato from your neighbor's garden. The sound of a car with its windows rolled down, playing your favorite song.

In his letter to the Philippians, Paul prays that love would flourish. Maybe flourishing begins in noticing God's little, luminous love notes scattered through our days. When we look for goodness in our weary world, we join God in cocreating a more flourishing one.

This is how we love well: awakening to the world around us. We can't love what we're asleep to. Noticing is an act of love.

Consider jotting down glimmers you experience today in a journal or even the notes app on your phone. If you're around others and spot one, point it out. Each time you catch one, pause, take a deep breath, and thank God for that little glimpse of goodness.

SACRED ECHOES

My deepest vocation is to be a witness to the glimpses of God I have been allowed to catch.[242]

Henri Nouwen

AUGUST 18

Let's not get tired of doing what is good. At just the right time we will reap a harvest of blessing.

GALATIANS 6:9 (NLT)

INHALE: I'm tired;

EXHALE: Help me keep going.

I know you're tired. You look around and sometimes quietly wonder why you even keep trying. No matter how much you attempt to cultivate goodness in your home, at work, or in your community, it feels like your efforts disappear into the dirt. You wonder if your words and actions ever mattered at all.

I get that. I really do.

I do my best to plant seeds of hope, but when it seems like nothing takes hold, I find myself asking, *What's the point?*

We don't always get to see the results. Our work today is preparing the soil for someone else's harvest tomorrow. We're so used to measuring success by what's visible, but in the Kingdom of God, rhythms of mercy and compassion echo into the future in ways we might never know.

When we visit national parks, we see signs that say, "Leave no trace," reminding us not to disturb the natural habitats. The love we breathe into the world *always* leaves a trace. It always disturbs the way things are and disrupts what is right now for the good that might someday be.

Not a single act of love is ever wasted.

I'm learning to accept that while the seeds we plant today might not bloom in our lifetime, we can still stubbornly hold on to the hope that the work we're doing is part of a sacred call to reshape the world in Christ's love. That the seeds we're planting will make life a little better for those who come after us.

We look at towering oaks and forget the hands that first planted the acorn. Maybe they never saw the sapling grow strong enough to shelter others. They never got to sit under its shade. Still, their small act of hope endures. I sometimes get so discouraged by the way things are that I forget all the peacemakers who planted seeds of goodness that have brought me to where I am.

We rest under the shade of trees that were planted long before we were born. Scripture uses the image of sitting "under their own vine and fig tree" as a picture of peace and safety.*

Flourishing outlasts the one who plants it. God breathes, and the fruits of our labor stretch beyond the work of our own hands.

As you breathe through today's prayer, rest in the promise that even when the ground feels hard and dry, the Spirit is breathing life. You might not see the harvest yet, but the seeds you've planted matter.

SACRED ECHOES

Legacy, what is a legacy?
It's planting seeds in a garden
you never get to see.

Lin Manuel-Miranda, "The World Was Wide Enough," in Hamilton

* See Micah 4:4.

AUGUST 19

Don't let evil conquer you, but conquer evil by doing good.

ROMANS 12:21 (NLT)

INHALE: Help us conquer evil
EXHALE: By doing good.

At my son's Little League game, one of the players on the other team—a powerful kid barreling down the third baseline—lowered his shoulder and *tackled* our catcher. On purpose. It was brutal to watch. The other team's coaches laughed it off: "Oops, he did it again!"

They were playing dirty.

After the dust settled, our coach gathered the team. "We play with integrity. No matter what the other team does, we keep playing the right way," he said. "At the end of the day, we want to walk off this field proud of who we are."

Romans 12:21 reminds us that we don't fight evil with evil. We don't mirror the world's meanness and call it strength. When we try to beat someone at their own game, we lose a piece of our truest selves in the process.

It's tempting to believe goodness is naive—that we have to fight fire with fire. But the gospel flips that script. Jesus shows us that love is the most subversive force in the universe.

The living water is more powerful than any dumpster fire that erupts this side of heaven.

In the US, our political landscape feels like a bit of a wasteland, with everyone slinging mud until we can't even recognize one another. I can't imagine the pressure of being a political figure—or being married to one. Michelle Obama made waves in 2016 when she encouraged Americans to respond to divisiveness with integrity, saying, "When they go low, we go high."[243]

Honestly, when I heard it, I rolled my eyes. *Yes, what she said aligns with the way of Jesus, but . . . it's not fair!*

Whether or not her statement was inspired by her faith, it's true: Sometimes "doing good" looks like refusing to take the bait. Like being strong enough *not* to get even. (Even when you have the *perfect* comeback.) Like forgiving someone who won't apologize or simply showing up with gentleness in a world addicted to outrage.

Every time we refuse to stoop to the lowest levels of dehumanization, we're part of a radical act of reordering the world in the way of Jesus. The evil around us propels us to partner with God to remake the world in righteousness.

God's love has the final say because *God* has the final say.

LET IT LINGER

When everything in you wants to fight back, when you're tempted to get even, take a breath. Retaliation is not the way. As followers of Christ, we can be people who live rooted in a love that transcends the mud-slinging ways of the world.

AUGUST 20

The LORD helps the fallen and lifts those bent beneath their loads.

PSALM 145:14 (NLT)

INHALE: When I crumble,
EXHALE: You catch me.

When I was in high school, a friend accidentally shot me with a paintball gun in his family room. The shot was close, and the pain was sharp. I clenched my jaw and worked hard not to cry as I drove myself home, my arm swelling to the size of a softball.

As soon as I walked in the front door and saw my mom walking toward me, I crumbled. I fell into her arms, knowing I was finally safe. *Felt safety* isn't really the absence of pain but the presence of love.

Years later, I saw the same thing in my son. He's an incredible soccer player, the kind of kid coaches can count on anywhere on the field. During his first game as a goalie, he took a powerful shot straight to the face. He shook it off, stayed tough, and sat out the rest of the game with a possible concussion. But when the final whistle blew and he found his dad and me, the tears came. It wasn't until he was safely in our arms that he let himself feel the pain.

We have to feel safe before we can let ourselves be seen.

The psalmist writes that God helps the fallen and lifts those bent beneath their burdens. Like a loving parent, God doesn't stand far off, waiting for us to toughen up, but bends low to lift what's too heavy for us to hold. God catches us when we crumble.

When I hear Sleeping at Last sing, "It's okay if you can't catch your breath, you can take the oxygen straight out of my own chest,"[244] I think of the God who nurtures like a mother: "As a mother comforts her child, so will I comfort you."*

You can crumble and still be caught. You don't have to hold it all in, you know. You can rest in the arms of Love.

BORROW THIS PRAYER

God of breath,
I've been holding mine
For way too long.
I want to exhale,
But I don't know how.
Be patient with me,
O Lord.
Help me be patient
With myself.
Help me let go
And move toward You.
I don't want to keep
Fighting for air.
I just want to fall
Into Your arms.
Pick up the pieces
Of my broken breath.
Make me whole.

* Isaiah 66:13, NIV.

AUGUST 21

Guard your heart above all else, for it determines the course of your life.

PROVERBS 4:23 (NLT)

INHALE: God, You hold
EXHALE: My heart with care.

Your heart is a living map, etched with the detours and destinations that have shaped who you are.

Proverbs 4 says our hearts determine the course of our lives. When we hear "guard," we imagine armor and shields, preventing feelings from getting inside or out. But I wonder how our perspective might change if we see guarding our hearts as caring for them with curiosity and compassion.

Cartography is the study and practice of making maps: "All maps are approximations; their clean lines and colours don't reflect the muddled nature of the reality they represent, and they can easily be used to support a point of view."[245] Cartographers understand that clean lines can't capture the chaos of real terrain. Just like our beautiful, complicated hearts.

Guarding our hearts means holding our feelings gently enough to name them. Dr. Brené Brown writes in *Atlas of the Heart* that naming our emotions helps us understand and manage them more effectively. She says, "Naming an experience doesn't give the experience more power, it gives us the power of understanding and meaning."[246]

Your heart shows you where you are. And when you pay attention to what it's telling you, you may just realize it's holy ground.

Your heart may feel like a messy, unfinished map—but it's still worth paying attention to.

PRACTICING THE WAY

The "Welcoming Prayer" is a way to consent to God's presence and action in your physical and emotional reactions to daily life.

1. **Pay attention** to what you're experiencing in your body at this moment. Do you have a headache? Are your shoulders relaxed?
2. **Name your emotion**—anger, excitement, anxiety, joy—and notice where you feel it.
3. **Welcome it**: "Welcome, fear." "Welcome, joy." (You're simply acknowledging what's already there.)
4. **Let go** by saying something like, "God, help me let go of my desire for security, affection, control. Help me embrace this moment as it is."[247]

AUGUST 22

May the Lord of peace himself give you his peace at all times and in every situation.

2 THESSALONIANS 3:16 (NLT)

INHALE: Breathe peace
EXHALE: Into all things.

If we want peace in our world, we have to cultivate it within ourselves.

Thankfully, we don't do this work alone. In Christ, we have access to a peace that passes all understanding, a peace that settles us deep within our souls so we can then extend it to others.

When Paul prayed this blessing over the Thessalonian church, he was writing to a community in the Roman Empire that was facing internal conflict and external pushback. His words remind them (and us) that peace isn't the absence of trouble but Christ's presence in the midst of whatever it is that we're going through.

Divine peace isn't bound by circumstance or time. Even in the most heart-wrenching parts of life, we can trust that God's presence holds the center through it all.

As Frederick Buechner writes, "The worst things will surely happen no matter what—that is to be understood—but beyond all our power to understand, . . . we will have peace both in heart and in mind."[248]

Peace grows as we tend our inner lives and act for the good of others. Sometimes peace looks like stillness and prayer. Other times, peace is doing the right thing, even when it disrupts the status quo.

If we long to heal the world but ignore the fractures within ourselves, we'll only spin our wheels. Peace in Christ is a continual replenishing that fills our open hearts and then overflows into the places and spaces we occupy.

Like Paul, we can pray for peace—for ourselves, for our neighbors, for our enemies, and for our weary world.

As you inhale, invite God's peace to surround you. Hold your breath for a few counts and then slowly exhale, imagining what it would look like to breathe peace into your day.

PAUSE AND PONDER

Recall a time when you had peace in the midst of a difficult circumstance. What happened? What did it look like to have peace in that situation?

Why is it important to have peace within our souls as we attempt to be peacemakers in our homes, workplaces, and communities?

AUGUST 23

At your command, O LORD, at the blast of your breath, the bottom of the sea could be seen, and the foundations of the earth were laid bare.

PSALM 18:15 (NLT)

INHALE: Your breath
EXHALE: Is power.

Our Creator's breath is love embodied. It's powerful and tender, gentle and strong. God breathes, and the sea splits into two. The same divine breath in the psalmist's song still holds everything in motion, including you.

We live and move in holy respiration. Though most days we hardly notice it, every divine inhale and exhale keeps the whole world spinning. We've never known an existence where God is not. Maybe that's why it's so easy to take God's presence for granted in our everyday lives.

More often than I care to admit, I forget to ask God to breathe into a situation when I've come up short every other way. It's easy to turn to prayer only when we need something.

But what if prayer were less a last resort and more a rhythm of breathing with God?

Breath prayer lets us "pray without ceasing"—carrying an ongoing conversation with God throughout our days.* Each inhale and exhale tunes our hearts to be more aware of just how marvelous it is that we get to live alongside our Maker.

PRACTICING THE WAY

We all need reminders to pay attention to how God is breathing in the world—and in our lives. Consider trying this prayerful meditation today.

- **Get into a comfortable position**, lying or sitting down. Close your eyes. Take a moment to notice your body as it is right now.
- **Gently massage** your hands, face, or neck. As you breathe, imagine the presence of Christ surrounding and sustaining you, maybe as a gentle light, a flowing stream, or a warm breeze.
- **Bring awareness** to any areas of discomfort or tension. Focus on one part of your body at a time—perhaps your jaw, shoulders, or chest—and picture that part gently breathing in and out.
- **Visualize God's breath** flowing through that space, bringing release and renewal.
- When it feels right, move to another part of your body until you sense the rhythm of divine peace filling you.
- Finally, **rest in stillness**. Let your whole body breathe slowly and gently, from the soles of your feet to the top of your head. Let any stressful or self-conscious thoughts float away. Let the breath of God sustain you.
- Close with today's breath prayer. Offer your thanks to the One who breathes into you and into our world over and over again.[249]

---

* 1 Thessalonians 5:17, ESV.

AUGUST 24

God has made everything beautiful for its own time.

ECCLESIASTES 3:11 (NLT)

INHALE: You are in
EXHALE: And out of time.

God works both within and beyond time.

The Greeks used two words for time: *chronos* and *kairos*. *Chronos* is the linear, steady drumbeat of chronological time—the hours and days, months and years that measure our lives. *Kairos* is God's time, measured in moments instead of minutes.[250] It's the sense that time is not just moving forward but folding in on itself, creating a thin space between heaven and earth.

God is not only the creator of time but also the keeper of time. He works within the constraints of our world as well as outside them.[251] We experience *kairos* when we lose track of time while laughing with a friend, when a song or sunset takes our breath away, when prayer feels like stillness instead of striving. *Kairos* time allows us to momentarily glimpse heaven, even as our feet remain firmly on the ground.[252]

As I write in *To Light Their Way*:

> *If chronos is a line, kairos is a circle. Chronos is our human way to measure time, but kairos is a mind-bending way to understand a God who is both in and out of time, in and out of our world, our galaxy, our universe.*[253]

We live in both: Our bodies live in *chronos*, while our souls stretch toward *kairos*. We pay bills, fold laundry, show up for work—and yet, in the midst of our ordinary movements of life, we catch extraordinary glimmers of eternity.

The mystery of *kairos* is that beauty unfolds in ways we can't measure or hurry or control. There's something freeing in time that can't be constrained because it means that everything—even this very second—holds the potential to be sacred.

God is making everything beautiful in its time, but I admit that when ugly headline after ugly headline fills the news, I find myself praying that God would hurry up and make everything beautiful *now*. It's in these moments I try to remember Psalm 90:4: "For you, a thousand years are as a passing day, as brief as a few night hours."*

Our time is not God's time.

When the world feels anything but beautiful, may God tune your heart to a truer sense of time that goes beyond understanding and holds eternity in a single breath.

RHYTHM OF BREATH

Everything beautiful,
Everything true,
Everything good
Bears the beauty,
The truth,
And the goodness
Of its Creator
In its own time.

---

* NLT.

AUGUST 25

You have been treated generously, so live generously.

MATTHEW 10:8 (MSG)

INHALE: Help me live
EXHALE: With open hands.

Generosity stretches far beyond our bank accounts. At any given moment, you can be generous in limitless ways. With your skills. Your kindness. Your forgiveness. Your creativity. Your resources. Your gentleness. Your time. Your knowledge. Your connections. Your patience. Your listening ear.

I'm not sure we can exist on the earth without generosity. Even in the hardest seasons, we survive because someone, somewhere, has been generous to us. (After all, none of us fed ourselves as babies.) Even the most independent among us live in rhythms touched by the unseen generosity of others.

Jesus told His followers, "Freely you have received; freely give."* It's all a gift—everything we have, everything we are. Our courage. Our callings. Our capacity to love. And gifts are meant to be shared. The grace we receive was never meant to end with us. It moves through us, breathing a little bit of fresh hope into our ordinary days.

Generosity is a way of *being* in the world. Christ's generosity invites us to live with the awareness that everything good is a gift.

Living in a posture of generosity means we stop trying to hold back the overflow of grace that was never ours to keep in the first place.

As you breathe through our breath prayer, place your hands in front of you, palms open. Notice the gifts you've received and consider how God might be inviting you to live into generosity today.

* Matthew 10:8, ESV.

RHYTHM OF BREATH

To the stranger,
The parent,
The child,
The neighbor,
The friend—

You were generous when
You held my hand,
Held my hair back,
Held my baby.
You took me to the airport
And welcomed me home.
You reheated lasagna,
Kept the light on,
Found my wallet.

You boxed up hand-me-downs
And carried the couch upstairs.

You offered your seat,
Asked me if I'd eaten,
Held me while I cried.
You waited with me,
Added sprinkles to my ice cream,
Loaned me your shoes.

You came to my party,
Threw me a party,
And made life a party.
You filled the tank,
Shared your blanket,
Ate my burned pancakes.
You split a stick of gum,
Left lilies on the porch,
Made space on the bench.
You saw me—
Really saw me.

AUGUST 26

Thank the miracle-working God, *His love never quits.*
The God whose skill formed the cosmos, *His love never quits.*
The God who laid out earth on ocean foundations, *His love never quits.*
The God who filled the skies with light, *His love never quits.*
The sun to watch over the day, *His love never quits.*
Moon and stars as guardians of the night, *His love never quits.*

PSALM 136:4-9 (MSG)

INHALE: Your love
EXHALE: Never quits.

God won't give up on you.

There's more to you than what so many people see. You are more than any label, more than any one thing.

God knows you fully and completely—more fully than you know yourself—and has reordered time and space just to be near *you.* Prayer doesn't have to be anything other than *being with.* As Thomas Keating wrote, prayer is "the offering *of ourselves,* of who we are just as we are."[254]

What if right now, just for this moment, you could let your anxieties float away with your exhale?

- Carve out a handful of minutes to put the phone away, go outside, and just be with God.
- Release your running list of thoughts, emotions, and requests, just for a moment.
- Center yourself in the One who gives each breath—who knows every particle of your humanity and lavishes love that never quits.

Prayer doesn't have to be complicated. You don't have to perform. You don't have to pretend. You don't have to prove anything. You don't have to have the perfect words or any words at all.

God looks at you in perfect love. There's no pretense needed. There's no plea to give or petition to offer. There's just space, today, to be near. Like when you're on a walk and suddenly the sun comes out from behind a cloud and you feel that warmth on your face. There's nothing you did to force that moment. You just had to be.

Inhale. Exhale. Trust that no matter how dark the night is, God's love never quits.

SACRED ECHOES

When we learn to enjoy and trust the presence of God, we will naturally turn to that presence in prayer.[255]

Richard Rohr

AUGUST 27

Don't let your hearts be troubled. Trust in God, and trust also in me.

JOHN 14:1 (NLT)

INHALE: Help me trust You,
EXHALE: Even when it's hard.

Jesus gathered his friends into the upper room. The air was charged. His friends' hearts were heavy as they breathed in the sorrow, sensing that something horrible was on the horizon. Into that ache, Jesus spoke: "Don't let your hearts be troubled."

Jesus wasn't being dismissive of pain. He knew every tear and bead of sweat and drop of blood that would someday touch the earth. He didn't explain it away or tell them they were wrong for the grief that was already rising in their hearts.

Jesus just said, "Trust me."

The pain of this world can take your breath away. Yet we can let Jesus' words remind us that the deepest part of us—the place where God's Spirit dwells—is what keeps us alive.

I imagine Jesus saying, "Friends, I love you and want you to know this: When you feel the aftershocks of sin and death—and you will—trust that the troubles of this world can never and will never take over the core of who you are. *You are* because *I am*. And no pain or storm or illness or injustice or act of violence or word of betrayal has the power to diminish who I am, because I am the God who is."*

None of us are immune to suffering. We've all felt the sting of loss. We've all witnessed injustice. We've all experienced betrayal. We've all known the exhaustion of trying to make it through while holding on to a wisp of hope that this isn't all there is.

The peace Jesus offers is not the absence of trouble but the presence of the One who was trustworthy then and is trustworthy now.

As Psalm 23:6 says, "Surely your goodness and unfailing love will pursue me all the days of my life, and I will live in the house of the LORD forever."†

Pause. Breathe deeply. Place a hand on your heart.

Why is your heart troubled? Where are you having a hard time trusting Christ?

Pull your breath deep into your core. As you inhale, picture Christ holding what troubles you. As you exhale, picture Jesus beside you, whispering, "Trust me."

RHYTHM OF BREATH

Every time I think
I am alone,
Every time I think
This is the end,
Every time I think
I am forgotten,
Help me remember
Your goodness
Has followed me
All my days.

* See Exodus 3:14; John 8:58.

† NLT.

AUGUST 28

The prayer of a person living right with God is something powerful to be reckoned with.

JAMES 5:16 (MSG)

INHALE: God of power,
EXHALE: Hear my prayer.

If you've spent time immersed in church culture, you've probably heard of prayer ministries. These groups are often filled with faithful older congregants who may not be able to serve in other ways but who commit to praying for people in their church and their community.

I admit that when I was younger, I wondered if prayer was simply something church leaders assigned to people so they would feel like they were contributing. I was completely missing the point. Flora Slosson Wuellner says that a vital foundation of prayer is "the realization that prayer does not merely inspire us to action but *is* action."[256]

I've lived enough now to believe that the faithful prayers of others have radically reordered my life. There have been times when I couldn't pray. When it seemed like all hope was lost, people kept praying. When my daughter was in intensive care, I posted a plea online asking others to pray. When red tape was preventing the US government from granting my son a visa, I did the same. The prayers held me together when I could barely catch my breath. The prayers of others are the fingerprints that have shaped who I am, and I can't begin to grasp the gravity of that or express my gratitude as much as I wish I could.

People remained faithful. They stood in the gap. I can't pretend to understand prayer. It's a mystery. Sometimes our prayers aren't answered the way we hope or imagine. But I do believe that prayer is far from passive.

When we pray, we participate in the ever-present work of God. Prayer connects us to God and to one another. Today's verse is found in the context of community—people praying for each other's healing. Our prayers don't change who God is, but they do change us. And that change can transform the world.

Who might you pray for today? A friend? An enemy? Bring the cry of your heart to the One who gives each breath.

PAUSE AND PONDER

Take a deep breath before you begin. Unclench your jaw. Let your shoulders drop. Let these words become your prayer.

God, I ask You to hold this prayer with gentleness.

I pray for ______________________.

I ask You to watch over __________ and to bring _________ where there is _________.

When I feel _________, remind me that You are ______________________. Amen.

AUGUST 29

Be still, and know that I am God.

PSALM 46:10 (NIV)

INHALE: Help me
EXHALE: Be still.

Maybe you feel like you're running in circles—a hamster spinning its wheel over and over again, wanting to get to the other side and just . . . stuck.

Take a breath.

If we're not careful, stress becomes our default setting. Dr. Michael Breus says that we're so used to operating in a constant cycle of stress that we don't even realize it. "But your body always knows, because your sympathetic nervous system is working overtime, locked in the 'on' position," he says. "In fight-flight-freeze, the adrenal glands dump cortisol into the system, which speeds up the heart, raises blood pressure, and inhibits digestion and other functions."[257]

Our bodies tell the truth before our minds do. When I'm stressed, migraines and backaches and fatigue begin to clue me in that little by little, I've begun to believe that there's a separation between myself and the One who made me.

I become less connected to the divine and more caught up in my own thoughts, the stories I'm spinning in my mind—pulled into an endless cycle of to-dos, frustrations, hurts, and overwhelm. I start to think, *God, don't You see all I'm dealing with? Why aren't You here?*

Contemplative author Martin Laird says that "our attention to the interior soap opera, the constant chatter of the cocktail party going on in our heads,"[258] leads to a sense of absence or distance from God. That, he says, is "the great illusion that we are caught up in; it is the human condition."[259]

He writes:

> *We run in tight, little circles, even while immersed in open fields of grace and freedom.*
>
> *The mind's obsessive running in tight circles generates and sustains the anguish that forms the mental cage in which we live much of our lives.*[260]

When we take a breath and dare to be still, we can let our brains and bodies rest in what is actually true: God is and always has been with us, and we are all welcomed into the life of God.*

Breath prayer is one way to bring a moment of stillness into your racing mind, reminding you that you were never separate from God to begin with. When we allow ourselves to get quiet and rest in who God is, the illusion of distance fades, and we discover that grace has been with us all along.

As you breathe in and out, release your shoulders. What would it be like to step off that hamster wheel and just be still?

PRACTICING THE WAY

God knows us better than we know ourselves. Christian mindfulness is a mind-body-soul practice that creates stillness, silence, time to pause, and a place to be ourselves in the presence of God.[261]

Regina Chow Trammel and John Trent

---

* See John 17:21.

AUGUST 30

At day's end I'm ready for sound sleep, for you,
God, have put my life back together.

PSALM 4:8 (MSG)

INHALE: After a long day,
EXHALE: You put me back together.

Some of my friends have beautifully detailed bedtime rituals. They sip tea or follow an extensive skincare routine or light candles or slip into their favorite pajamas.

I, on the other hand, usually just collapse into bed after a day of meeting deadlines, schlepping kids through the carpool line, feeding the dogs, and attending meetings.

Whether your evenings are peaceful or chaotic, choosing to rest and sleep peacefully is an act of faith we're all invited into.[262] Putting away our phones and simply returning to God at the end of the day feels like an act of resistance in a world intent on being connected, entertained, and wrapped in work every moment of every day.

David's words in Psalm 4 remind us to see sleep not merely as something our bodies need to recover, but as a *spiritual discipline*.[263]

Poet Wendell Berry reflects on this in his poem "The body in the invisible": "Sleep is the prayer the body prays."[264]

Tonight, as you get ready for bed, slow your breath. Let yourself rest in God's provision and protection. Return to today's Scripture, breath prayer, or this "prayer for bedtime." Reflect on your day as you read or pray. Notice what phrases stand out to you.

What do you connect with? What thoughts or longings rise to the surface?

BORROW THIS PRAYER

O God, we come to You
At the end of the day
And give all we're holding
Back to You.

As the moon and the stars
Illuminate the night
And we begin to rest,
We turn today's worries and fears
And today's joys and celebrations
Over to You, for You care for us. . . .

As we end this day together
And gather under the comfort
Of cozy blankets and warm beds,
We pray for those who work during the night
And those who are lonely
Or have nowhere safe
To lay their heads.

May this night bring peace
For all who need it.
Guard us from bad dreams
And untrue thoughts.
Guide us as we sleep
So we may rest
And be renewed
For another day.
Amen.[265]

From "A Prayer for Bedtime" in Every Season Sacred

AUGUST 31

If God gives such attention to the appearance of wildflowers–
most of which are never even seen—don't you think he'll
attend to you, take pride in you, do his best for you?

MATTHEW 6:30 (MSG)

INHALE: Help me believe
EXHALE: That You care for me.

It's easy for me to believe that God cares for those most vulnerable in our world today: the ones caught in the crossfires of war, hungry children, single parents doing their best, lonely widows, refugees trying to survive, and the innocent who have been harmed.

But sometimes I assume that because I'm "doing okay," God doesn't need to pay much attention to me. Maybe I imagine God focusing on people who *really* need divine intervention. Jesus interrupts that flawed ranking. Christ's love doesn't operate by triage.

Our Creator even tends the ditch flowers that no one ever notices.

So how much more does He care for us?

I'm a worrier. I slip into anxious thoughts because, deep down, I wonder if God actually cares about my worries, my fears, my doubts. Surely there are more urgent things on heaven's agenda. But thinking that way shrinks God to my size. God is God, and I am not.

Too often, I underestimate just how vast, how immeasurable, God's power and creativity and love are.

In 2022 the film *Everything Everywhere All at Once* broke open cinematic boundaries, crossing genres and themes. God is *everything, everywhere, all at once*—but I forget that in such immense power and glory, God is still tender enough to notice me. To care for my worries, even when I think they're not important. And the same is true for you.

As you breathe today, consider asking God to help you release the anxieties that keep looping through your mind so that you can receive the care God longs to give you.

RHYTHM OF BREATH

After worrying all day,
I walk through
The prairie
And dance among
The wildflowers.
The simple symphony
Of the sparrows
Keeps me company
In the golden light.
No one but One
Knows where I am,
And I breathe.
I can finally breathe.[266]

SEPTEMBER 1

Take a good look at God's wonders—they'll take your breath away.

PSALM 66:5 (MSG)

INHALE: God of wonder,
EXHALE: Open my eyes.

Holding a newborn in your arms, feeling their breath as their tiny hand wraps around your finger, and feeling like you have the whole world in your hands.

An elderly couple, paper-thin hands clasped as if what they hold is golden. A child squealing with delight as they catch a frog in the creek. The lift of the plane as it breaks through the clouds. The taste of your mom's rhubarb pie, fresh out of the oven, resting under a blanket of melting vanilla ice cream.

Crashing waves meeting the sandy shore.

A summer night freckled with stars.

The boom of thunder, the flash of lightning, and the stillness after a storm.

The turn in a trail that suddenly opens to a breathtaking view. The groom locking eyes with one he loves. The swell of a song when the band loses themselves in the moment. The hush when everyone you love most is gathered around the table. A tear that reminds you you're still alive.

Every once in a while, we catch a glimmer of heaven breaking into earth, right here in the midst of our ordinary lives, and it takes our breath away.

It's a vapor, a mist, something we breathe in but can't hold for long—a glimpse of God's glory that we must exhale back into the world.

These glimpses are small reflections of resurrection, refracting the Light and illuminating our lives, if only we pay attention—tiny twinkles of a divine eye that remind us that life is more than we can see. That in the moment in between breaths, God meets us.

Too often, we get caught in worlds of our own making. But wonder draws us out of our small stories and reminds us we are part of a more expansive, more eternal reality.

Nowhere is off limits to the One who is and is to come.

Borrow today's breath prayer as you go about your day. Consider setting a reminder on your phone to pause for a moment—to breathe and awaken to the wonder of Christ in the midst of your everyday life.

RHYTHM OF BREATH

My prayer is this:
That the wonders of God
Will take
Your breath away,
That one look
Will steal your breath
And hold it
Suspended in time,
And that you will catch
A glimpse of heaven
Before you catch your breath.

SEPTEMBER 2

Can worry add even one more step to the length of your life's journey?

MATTHEW 6:27 (FNV)

INHALE: I give my worry
EXHALE: To You, O God.

Sometimes I convince myself that worry helps—that it keeps my people safe and pushes me toward making the best possible choice. There's an ounce of truth in that: Concern can prompt wisdom. But mostly, my worry is an illusion of control. So much lies beyond my reach, yet anxiety tells me I can manage it all if I just imagine and plan for every future problem.

As much as I want to anticipate every twist and turn, I am human—finite and fallible. The whole lot of us are. When we worry, we pour brainpower into what we cannot change, and it drains attention from what we *can* do: create goodness, work for peace, show up for others, and return to God, again and again.

Jesus knows we're prone to worry, and He asks this gentle question: "Can worry add even one more step . . . to your life's journey?"

As much as I'd like to justify my worries about tomorrow, I know that ultimately, I'm not in control. And I never have been.

Christian mindfulness practices like breath prayer help us awaken to God's presence in the midst of our fears and equip us to notice intrusive, stressful thoughts and let them pass instead of chasing them.[267] Prayerful breath work can support our bodies' calming (parasympathetic) system, which is why slow, paced breathing often eases symptoms tied to everyday stress and anxiety.[268]

Try this for thirty seconds:

- Inhale through your nose for four counts.
- Exhale gently through pursed lips for six.
- On your inhale, pray, "I give my worry . . ."
- On your exhale, pray, "To You, O God."

As you breathe, may you remember that no concern is too big or too small to place into God's hands. The One who gives each breath is with you in every twist and turn of your journey. You do not go alone.

PAUSE AND PONDER

Create your own litany as an offering of your worries to the One who gives each breath.

When I think about the future, I'm worried that ____________________.

I give my worry to You, for no matter what happens, You are trustworthy.

When ____________________ happens, I feel ____________________.

I give my worry to You, for You are bigger than my fear.

When I start down the trail of worry, help me ____________________.

I give my worry to You, for You are with me wherever I go.

SEPTEMBER 3

For everything there is a season, and a time
for every matter under heaven.

ECCLESIASTES 3:1 (NRSV)

INHALE: In every season,
EXHALE: You are near.

This time of year often feels like standing on a precipice—between the *what was* of summer and the *what's next* of fall.

Just as nature follows a rhythm of changing seasons, so do we. Each stage of our lives can help us grow and guide us into a deeper relationship with God. Seasonal rhythms also shape the life of the church through the liturgical calendar.

Claude Atcho, author of *Rhythms of Faith*, says that the church year invites us to experience Christ in three cycles:[269]

- The Cycle of Light: Advent, Christmastide, Epiphany
- The Cycle of Life: Lent, Holy Week, Eastertide, Pentecost
- The Cycle of Love: Ordinary Time

Whether or not you grew up in a tradition that follows the church calendar—or whether or not you attend one now—keeping these sacred rhythms helps us stay rooted in God's unchanging goodness through every season.

Right now, we're in Ordinary Time, "the season in which all the cycles that have gone before form our daily lives," Atcho says.[270]

Transitions and transformations mark the passing of time. Even in uncertain seasons, we can find moments of exhale as we trust that God is still breathing life into us.

As you breathe and pray, reflect on what season your soul feels like it's in today.

PRACTICING THE WAY

The liturgical calendar is often visualized as a continuous circle.

It starts in Advent (the time of anticipation leading up to Christmas) and follows Christ's birth, life, death, and resurrection. (See the liturgical calendar in appendix A.)

SEPTEMBER 4

Make sure that you don't get so absorbed and exhausted in taking care of all your day-by-day obligations that you lose track of the time and doze off, oblivious to God.

ROMANS 13:11 (MSG)

INHALE: Awaken me
EXHALE: To Your presence.

Apparently, some church folk have a name for people who attend services mainly on Christmas and Easter—"Creaster" people.

As someone who grew up in a family that went through seasons of attending church and then not going at all, I've always found that term a bit demeaning. The cynical implication is that people are just performing their faith, that they don't really love Jesus.

But what if we viewed this through a lens of grace?

What if the story of Jesus' birth, life, death, and resurrection is so powerful that people can't help but show up? What if they're drawn to join others in remembering the God who became one of us: breath, body, bone, and blood?

The birth and resurrection of Jesus are so powerful that the reverberations of Christmas and Easter can't be contained within the church calendar. Jesus transforms everything, and when we stop focusing on the small details of our lives, the life-changing promise we have in Christ can spill into every ordinary moment.

In this space of Ordinary Time, we remember that God is with us in the endless to-do lists and the running commentary in our minds.

The Spirit is offering you an exhale, right here, right now, wherever you are and whatever you're doing. May our breath today help us let go of obsessing over life's details so we don't miss Christ's presence in the everyday.

Don't sleepwalk through the sacred ordinary. Stay awake to the God who is already here.

PAUSE AND PONDER

When do you most often feel "asleep" to what matters most? What helps you wake up again?

How might you build small moments of attentiveness into your daily routine—pausing before a meal, noticing your breath, whispering a prayer between tasks?

SEPTEMBER 5

Be brave. Be strong. Don't give up. Expect GOD to get here soon.

PSALM 31:24 (MSG)

INHALE: I'm not

EXHALE: Giving up.

I know you've been hurt.

Maybe someone dismissed your pain. Maybe no one was there to sit with you. Maybe someone told you that to have faith, you had to package up your pain and tuck it neatly away.

And for that, I'm so sorry.

I know you want to close shop. To board up your tender heart and replace your vulnerability with impenetrable walls.

Please don't.

We need your softness in this sharp-cornered world. We need *you*. God will never give up on you. So please don't give up on yourself.

Take one deep breath in through your nose.

Hold it for a moment.

Slowly let it go.

Let God breathe hope into the parts of your soul that are crying out in pain. Just for this moment, release what you've been holding. You don't have to rush toward the light. Just trust that it's still there, even when the night is dark.

Your breath is brave. Your breath is strong.

Don't give up. Hope is here.

If you find yourself in a season of discouragement or depression, or just feeling down, Justin McRoberts and Scott Erickson's book *In the Low: Honest Prayers for Dark Seasons* offers permission to name the ache in your heart without rushing to fix it.

SACRED ECHOES

In this Low,
give me the Light of Grace.[271]

Justin McRoberts and Scott Erickson

SEPTEMBER 6

As you learn more and more how God works,
you will learn how to do your work.

COLOSSIANS 1:10 (MSG)

INHALE: Be the beat of my heart
EXHALE: And the work of my hands.

My husband is painting our laundry room right now because, as he says, my painting is "too chaotic." He claims I paint walls like I "never graduated from preschool finger painting" and that I "don't think there's enough paint on the brush unless it's up to the metal."

He's not wrong.

He's showing our youngest son how to paint, teaching him how to blend wet brushstrokes with rolled-on paint, how to move slowly enough to create even layers. My son is learning by watching how his dad does it. I never really learned how to paint. But my husband was taught by his dad, who briefly ran a "Craig and Sons" painting side hustle.

Maybe that's what it means to be apprenticed to someone—to learn not just the task but the rhythm of the one who's teaching. In Matthew 11:29, Jesus says, "Walk with me and work with me—watch how I do it."* When we learn how God works—how Jesus moved through the world, how the Spirit breathes life into chaos—we begin to learn how to do our work too.

Vocation is when our work meets our calling.

Our verse today tells us that learning more about God and how God works shapes our own work. If we want to catch a glimpse of how God works, we can turn to the picture Paul paints in 1 Corinthians 13 and let it form our own posture toward work.

PRACTICING THE WAY

Whether you work from home, in a cubicle, or at a factory, whether your work is paid or unpaid, spend some time reflecting on how the rhythms of God might shape your posture toward work.

Love is patient, so I will ________________
________________________________.

Love is kind, so I will ________________
________________________________.

Love doesn't envy, so I will ______________
________________________________.

Love doesn't boast, so I will ______________
________________________________.

* MSG.

SEPTEMBER 7

The Spirit of God has made me; the breath of the Almighty gives me life.

JOB 33:4 (NIV)

INHALE: Your breath
EXHALE: Gives me life.

We're constantly rushed from one thing to the next.

The rhythm of our breath can bring us back to what's real.

When life moves fast, breath prayer can slow us down long enough to remember that each breath is a gift from the One who formed us and breathed us into being.

When we pray alongside our breath, we can rest, even if just for a moment, in the awareness that God is near.

Intentional breathing can lower stress and even renew our energy, depending on the breath work technique. But even more than that, each breath is a reminder that God's life-giving Spirit is working in us.

Eugene Peterson, the pastor and writer who created *The Message* paraphrase of the Bible, writes, "The majesty of the One who pulled a universe into order and beauty" is the "same God involved in the local troubles of a quite ordinary person."[272]

The God who spun stars into galaxies also meets us in the laundry room and in the traffic jam.

If we let it, breath prayer can reawaken our awe and remind us that the same Creator who spoke the world into being didn't just give us life *once* but, as today's verse says, *gives* us life—present tense. Over and over again.

God is not past tense or far away. God is here, breathing life into every ordinary moment.

As you pray today's breath prayer, let your breathing slow you down and bring you back not just to yourself but to the One who animates everything.

BREATHE THIS IN

The daily use of breath practices can reduce stress, improve quality of life, and, in some cases, even counteract disease progression.[273]

SEPTEMBER 8

Think straight. Awaken to the holiness of life.

1 CORINTHIANS 15:34 (MSG)

INHALE: Wake me up
EXHALE: With resurrection power.

Wherever you are, God is.

But it's so easy to sleepwalk through life, to close our eyes to the whispers of resurrection all around us. Paul's words to the Corinthians were a wake-up call. He told them to sober up, warning, "No more playing fast and loose with resurrection facts."*

The Greek word Paul used, *eknēphō*, means to "return to clear-mindedness and moral awareness"—to shake off distraction and remember what's real.[274] The early Christians in Corinth struggled with this, and we do too.

Poet Wendell Berry ends one of his most beloved poems with a two-word sentence: "Practice resurrection."[275]

The resurrection of Christ isn't a one-time thing but the very heartbeat of who we are. When we awaken to God's breath in our lives, we practice resurrection.

From the empty tomb to Pentecost, resurrection reverberates through God's story. As Laura Kelly Fanucci writes:

> *In the mysterious unity of the Trinity, God the Creator who breathed life into each of the disciples' lungs at birth is the same God who breathes new life on them now, sending the gift of the Holy Spirit upon them, just as the mighty wind swept over the face of the deep at the dawn of time. Resurrection is recreation.*[276]

The Spirit is here, breathing into your life so you might practice resurrection again and again—cultivating new life and rhythms of peace in the comings and goings of your days.

BREATHE THIS IN

Need an energy boost? A Stanford study found that participants who practiced a simple form of *cyclic breathing* for just five minutes a day over the course of a month reported lower anxiety, improved mood, and even greater feelings of joy and energy.[277]

Try it:

- Inhale gently through your nose.
- Take a second, smaller inhale to fully expand your lungs.
- Then exhale *all* the air out slowly through your mouth.
- Repeat for about five minutes.

* 1 Corinthians 15:34, MSG.

SEPTEMBER 9

As long as I'm alive in this body, there is good work for me to do.

PHILIPPIANS 1:22 (MSG)

INHALE: Help me do the good
EXHALE: That is mine to do.

It's easy to feel like the choices we make each day are just pebbles—too small to make a difference in an ocean of so much need and so much needless suffering. But even one small act of goodness can ripple across generations, reaching farther than we might fathom.

I'm living proof.

During World War II, my German great-grandparents were stuck in the crossfire of Hitler's horrific regime. They desperately wanted out of a country unraveling under (and ravaged by) its own cruelty. Resources were scarce, bomb sirens were frequent, and my great-grandmother visited a church coat drive to help her two little girls through another cold winter. She tried to leave the church quietly, but the volunteer insisted that she, too, should have a coat. She brought my grandmother back to the pile and helped her try one on. When she slipped her arms into a donated coat, her hand brushed a folded piece of paper tucked inside the pocket—a note from a woman in Iowa who had given the coat through her church.

The scribbled note said she was praying for whoever would wear the coat and, almost posthaste, included her name and address.

My great-grandmother wrote her a letter. Then another. The correspondence across the ocean grew, and eventually this woman's family in Iowa volunteered to sponsor my great-grandparents and their two young daughters. The four of them crossed the sea and immigrated to Iowa, briefly staying with that family, eating at their kitchen table, learning a brand-new culture, and eventually building a new life in the Midwest.

Without that woman's brave, small yes to God to donate a coat and hide a note inside, I might never have existed.

As long as we have breath in our lungs, God has inscribed goodness upon our hearts—a kind of goodness we're called to exhale into the world. We rarely see the full ripple of our yes.

You may never fully know what God will do with your small, faithful acts of love—but they matter more than you think.

What small, faithful acts of love have rippled through your life and shaped who you are? Where might God be inviting you to say a quiet yes that seems too small to matter but could reach far beyond what you can see?

PRACTICING THE WAY

Theologian Gustavo Gutiérrez said that to live a healthy Christian spirituality, we must nourish our souls in three ways: through prayer, through practicing justice, and through the good gifts that keep our hearts grateful.[278]

We can't transform the world through guilt or anger. True ripples of change flow from a grateful heart. If you aren't sure where to begin, let gratitude become your starting point. Pray. Do good. Enjoy something that makes your soul feel alive.

Even the smallest, shakiest yes can change the world.

SEPTEMBER 10

Even in darkness light dawns for the upright, for those who are gracious and compassionate and righteous.

PSALM 112:4 (NIV)

INHALE: Be with me
EXHALE: In the darkness.

When I was a kid, I was convinced that my bedroom ceiling rivaled our local planetarium. After holding every tiny plastic star by my lamp for five minutes to activate the glow, I carefully stuck them in constellations of my own making above my bed. That way, the light would be with me in the dark when bedtime came around.

As much as I wish it did, life doesn't come with glow-in-the-dark guarantees. Sometimes life just feels like one long night that will never end. Chaos can seem all-consuming. Compassion feels rare. Confusion abounds. Corruption hums beneath our public discourse. No matter who we are, at one point or another, we all find ourselves fumbling in the dark, longing for light.

Maybe you're wading through spiritual shadows.

Maybe you ache to shine a light on corruption.

Maybe you've been told that if your faith were stronger, you wouldn't be in the dark.

But faith doesn't erase the night. Faith teaches us how to live within it.

Darkness, like rain, falls on the just and the unjust alike.* No one escapes it. But in Christ, we're not left alone in it either. When the sun feels like it will never rise again, remember: Even here, hope glimmers. The Light still carries us.

In *Learning to Walk in the Dark*, Barbara Brown Taylor reminds us, "Even when light fades and darkness falls—as it does every single day, in every single life—God does not turn the world over to some other deity. Even when you cannot see where you are going and no one answers when you call, this is not sufficient proof that you are alone."[279]

We live in a world that often feels shrouded in ignorance, greed, and deceit. But even in the swirling shadows that tighten around us and threaten to take our breath away, the Light shines in the darkness, and the darkness has not overcome it.†

So we keep going, keep choosing goodness, keep moving in rhythms of grace.

"Here is the testimony of faith," Taylor says, "darkness is not dark to God; the night is as bright as the day."[280]

If the room is dark and you can't find the light, sit and rest awhile. Let your breath become prayer. God is nearer than your next inhale.

You are not—and never have been—alone.

PRACTICING THE WAY

Light a candle. As you sit with its glow, pray for those who are facing a dark time:

Light of the World, help ______________ *feel Your peace.*

* See Matthew 5:45.

† See John 1:5.

SEPTEMBER 11

Learn to do right; seek justice. Defend the oppressed.

ISAIAH 1:17 (NIV)

INHALE: Teach me, O God,
EXHALE: The way of justice.

I try to be wise about what I eat, but after a long day, nothing hits the spot like some salty, fresh-out-of-the-fryer french fries and a carbonated fountain soda. They're extras that are nice to add on every once in a while, but they're absolutely not necessary parts of a usual dinner.

Right rhythms and just ways aren't optional additions to a life with God. They're not little bonuses we tack on when we feel like it.

Justice and compassion aren't spiritual sides.

Isaiah's call to "seek justice" suggests active pursuit, not passive acceptance. Isaiah lived in a society whose leaders often exploited the vulnerable. His words cut through complacency then—and they still do now. He called the people of God to confront those who abuse their authority, "aligning with the prophetic tradition of speaking truth to power."[281]

It's not always easy to hold people in power accountable. It's not always convenient to stand on the side of the marginalized. It might cost you something. But it won't cost you your integrity, your Christlike character.

The call for God's people in Isaiah's time is the call on our lives today. God's character is unchanging, and in Christ, we have the Spirit to help us live courageously and compassionately. We are not left alone in this work.

Isaiah doesn't say, "Help the ones you think deserve your help."

He says, "Help the ones who need it."

He doesn't say, "Help the people who look like you and believe like you."

He says, "Defend the oppressed."

Partisan politics shouldn't decide who we care for—Jesus should.

Jesus cared for the hungry, the stranger, the sick, the forgotten, the outcast. That means we should too.

Justice begins in ordinary faithfulness, in the way you listen before reacting, in the way you show up for and alongside those who need help, in the way you keep caring even though it would be easier to ignore the plight of the suffering.

Don't underestimate small beginnings.

Keep going. Keep being faithful. God has breathed life into you so you can breathe hope into the world.

PRACTICING THE WAY

In the second part of today's verse, Isaiah says to care for the fatherless and the widows, groups that were particularly vulnerable in ancient times, often facing economic and social hardships.

What groups are most marginalized and experiencing inequality in your community?

Read through today's headlines. What stands out to you? In what ways might leaders be exploiting the vulnerable? How are the people of God stepping in? How are they not? How might you live with integrity and stand with those who are vulnerable?

SEPTEMBER 12

Let the light of this new day guide you onto a path of honor.

ROMANS 13:13 (FNV)

INHALE: Guide me, O God
EXHALE: Onto a path of honor.

We've all met people who say one thing but live another, like the comic book villain Two-Face, who smiles on one side and scowls on the other as he plots to take down Batman.

Jesus warned against this kind of double life.*

As followers of Jesus, we're invited to live in a way that lets the light of Christ shine as we move through the world.

Our conduct should match our convictions, reflecting integrity in all we do, in all we say, in all we are. We don't act one way in the night and another in the light. We let Christ shape our character, breathing love, joy, peace, patience, kindness, goodness, faithfulness, gentleness, and self-control into our world.†

What we think shapes who we are. What we do shapes who we are.

Who we are shapes what we think. Who we are shapes what we do.

We've all fallen short. But each sunrise is an invitation to begin again, to take a breath, and, with God's help, to move through our days with honesty and hope.

To walk in the light is to live awake—to notice where we've drifted from love and return to God's love, again and again.

What would it look like to move forward on a path of honor today?

PRACTICING THE WAY

Take a walk during the golden hour, just before twilight. Turn off your podcasts and playlists. Pray alongside your breath. As the sun breathes its last gasp for the day, notice what feels illuminated within you—and what might need to be brought into the light of God's love.

* See Matthew 23:27.
† See Galatians 5:22-23.

SEPTEMBER 13

Your word is a lamp to guide my feet and a light for my path.

PSALM 119:105 (NLT)

INHALE: Breath of God,
EXHALE: Light the way.

Some of the loudest voices in our culture claim to speak for Jesus, but their words don't sound like Christ's love, and their actions don't reflect Christ's compassion.

Life can be confusing. Where do you turn when you have more questions than answers—when you're wondering who God really is?

When we live openheartedly, we can meet God in many ways, such as through prayers and practices, silence, worship, and serving others.

What if, in the chaos of life, Scripture served as a light to help you see who God is and how God is breathing in the world right now?

If you grew up hearing the phrase "Read your Bible!" used as a weapon, you might hesitate to open Scripture again. As author Ruth Haley Barton says, "Many of us approach the Scriptures more like a textbook than like a love letter."[282] Encountering God doesn't mean memorizing verses for Bible drills—it means experiencing the heart of who God is and who you are in light of your true identity, within the greatest story of all.

What if you simply opened your heart to meet God in the poems, letters, and history that line the page?

As 2 Timothy 3:16 reminds us, "All Scripture is God-breathed."* Theologian Claude Atcho writes, "The statement that Scripture is God-breathed is another way of saying that Scripture is the breath of God."[283]

Through the written Word, we encounter the living Word—Christ Himself—who still breathes life into weary souls.

Scripture can be mysterious, baffling, and even frustrating. And that's okay. Atcho reminds us, "If Scripture is a divine encounter, it then makes sense why its words can at times be confusing. We should expect Scripture to be hard to grasp, for it speaks of God."[284]

When you're so overwhelmed by the noise of the world that you can't see straight, Scripture can light the way.

When you approach Scripture with an open heart, you remember that God's breath continues to move through these words—and through *you*, too.

SACRED ECHOES

Scripture is the result of God's desire to breathe life into a dead and dying world.[285]

Claude Atcho

* NIV.

SEPTEMBER 14

HOLY CROSS DAY

Through him God reconciled everything to himself. He made peace with everything in heaven and on earth by means of Christ's blood on the cross.

COLOSSIANS 1:20 (NLT)

INHALE: Reconciling God,
EXHALE: Help me be a peacemaker.

The first time I visited New York City, I was a college student from Iowa trying to decide if I should chase my dream of working in magazine publishing. I laid out my nicest clothes on my dorm bed. I made meticulous packing lists and checked them twice. I'd never traveled on a plane without my family before, and I wanted to be prepared. Hoping to seem effortlessly chic to the editors of *Glamour*, I packed a pair of sunglasses *and* a backup pair in case of emergency.

I was ready.

What I didn't realize was that in Manhattan, the skyscrapers block most of the sun. *Toto, I was not in Iowa anymore.*

After days surrounded by subways and streetlights, I finally visited Central Park. As soon as I stepped beneath the trees, I felt my body exhale. People of every race, age, and background filled the park. Kids ran. Artists sketched. Tourists snapped photos. Executives ate lunch on benches. For a moment, it felt like a glimpse of God's Kingdom: no hierarchy, no status, just a bunch of people breathing the same air.

When Jesus absorbed the pain of the world on the cross, "God reconciled everything." In other words, every person and every part of creation can be made new. The Kingdom of God doesn't operate on hierarchies.

Christ is the only mediator between the world and God. At the cross, Jesus laid the foundation for the peace of the whole world, for the reconciliation of all things.[286] At the cross, God and humanity exhale together—and creation begins to breathe again. When Jesus took His last breath, it opened the way for all of us to breathe the fresh air of grace.

The reality is that our world is full of beauty and life—and collapsing under the weight of death and destruction. Jesus has reconciled the divide between us and God and is restoring all things, inviting you to join in these rhythms of renewal. It's not on you to fix humanity's cries, but it's also not yours to ignore them.

Because of the cosmic reconciliation we have in Christ, we can live as people who exhale peace into our weary world.

What can you do today, led by God's Spirit, to help put the world right again?

PAUSE AND PONDER

What does it mean that through Jesus, "God reconciled everything"? Where do you long to see that reconciliation unfold in your own life or the world around you?

SEPTEMBER 15

FEAST OF OUR LADY OF SORROWS

You will grieve, but your grief will turn to joy.

JOHN 16:20 (NIV)

INHALE: You honor my grief
EXHALE: And hold all my sorrows.

Have you ever noticed that cartoon characters always seem to have the same outfits? They're unchanging, stuck not only in the same clothes but also the same places and scenarios, over and over again. They consistently repeat their catchphrases and respond in the same way.

It's easy to flatten historical figures into 2D characters, and that goes for people whose stories we see in the Bible too. But these were fully formed people—with personalities, hopes, dreams, struggles, and relationships. They experienced the fullness of life, just as we do.

Maybe that's why TV series like *The Chosen*, which follows Jesus and His disciples, resonate with so many—they offer a glimpse of these people living and breathing and interacting as they might have in real life.

When I think of Mary, Jesus' mother, I picture a young girl whose life radically changed and then imagine her as a mom raising Jesus. I don't often think of her as a woman who ached and hoped and endured profound loss. My Catholic brothers and sisters have a broader understanding of Mary's life beyond simply her role at Bethlehem.

Today is the Feast of Our Lady of Sorrows on the church calendar. It's a lesser known observance that may seem a bit gloom and doom, but I appreciate moments that act as touchstones and help normalize sorrow and grief as holy ground. The truth is, no one gets through this life without seasons of great sorrow. And God does not ask us to paper over our pain or pretend everything is okay.

Like every person who has lived and breathed on this earth, Mary experienced seasons of sorrow. Her grief didn't disappear, but in God's love, it was transformed. Her sorrow became a doorway to resurrection joy.

PRACTICING THE WAY

Rooted in Scripture and sacred tradition, these seven moments invite us to enter Mary's story. After you read through each movement, pause and pray today's breath prayer. Notice which sorrow stands out to you. What might God be whispering into your heart through this reflection?

1. **The prophecy of Simeon**: Mary hears that her child's life, and her own heart, will be pierced by pain (see Luke 2:35).
2. **The flight into Egypt**: Mary flees her home in the night to protect her son from danger (see Matthew 2:13).
3. **Losing the child Jesus in the Temple**: Mary searches for Jesus, who is lost in Jerusalem for three days (see Luke 2:48).
4. **Meeting Jesus carrying the cross**: Christian tradition imagines Mary meeting her son as He carries His cross (see John 19:17).
5. **Standing at the foot of the cross**: Mary remains beside Jesus as He dies, hearing His final words (see John 19:26).
6. **Receiving Jesus' body from the cross**: Mary witnesses Jesus' body being taken down from the cross (see John 19:38).
7. **The burial of Jesus**: Mary watches as Jesus is laid in the tomb and the stone is rolled into place (see Luke 23:55-56).[287]

SEPTEMBER 16

Dance with the ones who dance for joy, and shed tears with the ones whose hearts have fallen to the ground. Seek to live in harmony with all. Do not think you are better than others. Walk the road of life with the humble of heart, and do not be wise in your own eyes.

ROMANS 12:15-16 (FNV)

INHALE: Yes, life is complicated,
EXHALE: And You are with us.

When my husband and I were teenagers, we participated in an improv acting group together. One of the main rules of improv is to respond with "Yes, and . . ." When you're acting, you build. You learn to hold the tension of both this and that. Two things can be true at once.

Romans 12 invites us into the fullness of life together, calling us into the "Yes, and . . ." *Yes*, life can break your heart. When someone cries, cry with them. *And* life can also bring great joy. When someone celebrates, celebrate with them.

It has become popular for high school seniors to record themselves along with their families as they open letters from prospective colleges, finding out whether or not they're accepted. Many of these videos have gone viral, and for good reason—they offer a glimpse into the everyday sacredness of the "Yes, and . . ." As the mother of a high schooler, I would bounce and scream and hug and celebrate if my son was accepted to his dream school, and I would also feel a deep ache about letting him go. Both feelings can exist in the same moment.

We are called into life together—to walk alongside one another, holding hope in one hand and humility in the other. Paul reminds us that empathy and community are heartbeats of the people of God. When we rejoice with others, we reflect the heart of Christ; when we weep with others, we join Jesus in compassion.

Jesus shows us how to live this sacred "Yes, and . . ." He said *yes* to unfathomable love *and* indescribable pain, holding joy and sorrow at the same time.

In her book *Overwhelmed & Grateful*, Jillian Benfield explores this tension:

> *Jesus enjoyed friendships & ended up being betrayed by a friend. . . . Jesus knew darkness & He was the light.*[288]

What "Yes, and . . ." scenarios are you holding today? Breathe in through your nose, hold for a few counts, and then slowly release. As you breathe in, ask God to meet you in the tension. As you breathe out, ask God to help you meet others in the tension as well.

SACRED ECHOES

Let's learn to be the kind of people who have eyes to see, let's be the kind of people who create space to hold it all—the difficult & the beautiful.[289]

Jillian Benfield

SEPTEMBER 17

Trust in the LORD and do good;
dwell in the land and enjoy safe pasture.

PSALM 37:3 (NIV)

INHALE: Shape my days
EXHALE: With Your love.

Decision fatigue is real. Weekday mornings used to be stressful for one of my sons. Trying to find the "right" outfit could unravel the whole day. When his school introduced a simple dress code, peace returned. A few boundaries created space for freedom.

Creating a "rule of life" offers a similar kind of structure. Though the name may sound daunting, it's just a prayerful framework for helping you make big (and small) decisions rooted in a love of Christ.[290]

The ancient Benedictines used the word *rule* to describe a rhythm of grace—simple habits that helped them pray, work, and rest in God's presence. Our modern lives may look different, but we still need that rhythm.

A rule of life is less about creating strict rules and more about taking time to honestly reflect on your beliefs and values, giving you a chance to examine your life choices.

Returning to what matters most leads you to freedom when you're feeling stuck. A rule of life helps us make choices by encouraging us to ask, *What truly matters in this season?* Then it helps us shape our time and attention around those values.

As you pray through today's breath prayer, reflect:

- What truly matters in this season?
- How do your choices reflect—or distract from—your values?
- What rhythms help you live out what you believe?
- In what ways are your values cultural? In what ways are they of Christ?

Trust the Spirit to meet you in the everyday rhythms of your life so you can do the good that's yours to do. May your small, sacred choices help you stay where God has placed you.

PRACTICING THE WAY

You don't have to have it all figured out. God meets you where you are.

1. **Identify one to three core values** you want to live more deeply into in this season. What matters most to you, and why?
2. **Write a simple statement** that captures what these values look like in real life. For example, if you want to practice listening, you might write, *Because I value listening, I will listen to myself, to others, and to God with curiosity and compassion.*
3. **Name one small habit** that helps you live into each value. Maybe it's a five-minute morning pause before checking your phone, a walk without earbuds, or a regular moment of gratitude.
4. **Look at your calendar**. Where might these habits fit in your actual week? What would it look like to practice them regularly, with grace for the days you miss?

SEPTEMBER 18

He comforts us in all our troubles so that we can comfort others. When they are troubled, we will be able to give them the same comfort God has given us.

2 CORINTHIANS 1:4 (NLT)

INHALE: Help me comfort others
EXHALE: As You've comforted me.

A skinned knee. A hug. A bandage. A whisper of comfort as tears are wiped away.

In many ways, compassion is learned. When we're comforted and cared for by others in our pain, we begin to know how it's done—and we can then offer that Christlike love to others.

In his letter to the Corinthians, Paul says the comfort we receive is not just for ourselves but is meant to be shared. God's compassion flows through us like breath as it moves from one wounded heart to another.

What might it look like to use your experiences of receiving God's comfort to empathize with and minister to others in their afflictions?

In our individualized culture, we often lose sight of what it means to mutually care for one another. Paul urges the early church to create a community of shared comfort, where each person actively seeks to support those who are hurting.

Pain rarely has a quick explanation, and healing is rarely linear. The road is long and winding—not as simple as bandaging a skinned knee. While we don't cling to the hollow comfort of "Everything happens for a reason," we can still trust the God of comfort to meet us in the depths of our pain. In time, the same tenderness that once held us can become the balm we offer someone else.

Comfort is both received and practiced. As you breathe today, ask God to help you carry that compassion into your community.

PAUSE AND PONDER

Reflect on a time someone comforted you when you were in distress. What happened?

What can you see now that you couldn't see then? Name a few people who come to mind who are wading through their own experiences of pain or discouragement. How might you extend the comfort you've received?

SEPTEMBER 19

Make sure you don't take things for granted and go slack in working for the common good; share what you have with others. God takes particular pleasure in acts of worship—a different kind of "sacrifice"—that take place in kitchen and workplace and on the streets.

HEBREWS 13:16 (MSG)

INHALE: Help me work
EXHALE: For the common good.

We shuffle inside, leaving our own crammed schedules of work and family, kicking off shoes and greeting neighbors. Cookies and drinks make their way around the table. I look around at the intergenerational lot of us. We span backgrounds and perspectives, races and religions. Some are new to the neighborhood; others have watched decades pass and seasons change. There are grandmas and single adults, renters and homeowners, each of us bringing our own stories to the table as we take turns hosting in our homes.

As the neighborhood association president calls the meeting to order, I'm reminded that what brings us together is care for this place and for one another.

We move through our list of talking points—everything from planting trees to planning a Christmas gathering to replacing light bulbs in the square—and there's life scattered between each line of the agenda. It looks a lot like church to me as we pass the peace and the coffee around the table. (There are squabbles too, which is also a lot like church.)

It's hard to love your neighbor when you don't know their name. It's easy to get so caught up in the melodramas of our own lives that we overlook one another. But when we slow down, everything we do and everything we are can be an offering of love to others and an act of worship to the One who sees our work, even when we feel unseen.

The early church thrived on a culture of mutual support, and we're called to live into those same rhythms today, creating communities of compassion and generosity and hospitality right where we live, where everyone's gifts are valued and everyone's needs are met.

If you feel like your work for the common good is unseen, like the school lunches you pack, the texts you send to check in, or the leaves you rake in your neighbor's yard don't matter—they do. Everyday moments make up a life. When we care for one another, we are living our love for God out loud.

God delights in our ordinary acts of goodness. As you breathe through today's breath prayer, name one small offering of care for others that might become worship for you today.

SACRED ECHOES

How do we tame this status quo that lulls us into blindly accepting the things that divide us and keep us from our own holy longing for the mutuality of kinship—a sure and certain sense that we belong to each other?[291]

Gregory Boyle

SEPTEMBER 20

In quietness and trust is your strength.

ISAIAH 30:15 (NIV)

INHALE: Quiet my mind;
EXHALE: I trust You, O God.

Occam's razor is a philosophical principle often ascribed to William of Ockham, a Franciscan friar and logician who lived in the fourteenth century.[292] It means that the simplest explanation is usually the one closest to the truth.

I often think of this when my husband and I watch a thriller or mystery. When I'm trying to put the pieces together, I blurt out, "Occam's razor!" as if I've cracked the code.

Some scientists have used this idea to argue against the existence of a divine Creator, but I think Occam's razor actually leads us back to the simplicity of God.

We get tangled up in having the *right* answers and *right* theologies and *right* politics, forgetting what Jesus said summed up the law: "Love the Lord your God with all your heart" and "love your neighbor as yourself."*

Centuries before Jesus walked the earth, the prophet Isaiah tried to point God's people to the simplicity of a restorative God who longed for their return. They were doing everything but following God. They had gotten themselves tangled in trying to solve problems with their own strength and plans, trusting their unholy alliances instead of the One who gives each breath.[293] Isaiah's message was simple: *Come back. Let God restore you.*

When we turn from choices that hurt ourselves, others, and creation and move toward our Creator, we find peace. When we're quiet and trusting God, we find new strength. What was true for them is true for us too—we find true strength and God-breathed peace in stillness. Repent, rest, and regain your strength. Trust the One who loves you and wants to make you whole.

Take a deep breath. As you let it go, reflect on where you notice resistance to stillness. What might God be inviting you to release?

The next time you feel weak, remember: Strength comes in finally resting in the One who already holds it all.

BORROW THIS PRAYER

God of comfort,
Rest Your hand
On my heavy shoulder.
God of peace,
Draw me into
Your warm embrace.
In the darkness,
I'm reaching out to You,
Stumbling in the shadows.
It's easy to wonder
If what I saw in the light
Ever existed.
I want to find You
In the quiet.
I want to know You
In the dark.
God of comfort,
God of peace,
Teach me
To trust again.

* Matthew 22:37-39, NIV.

SEPTEMBER 21

FEAST OF SAINT MATTHEW

"I'm after mercy, not religion." I'm here to invite outsiders, not coddle insiders.

MATTHEW 9:13 (MSG)

INHALE: Embolden me
EXHALE: To love like You.

When Jesus called Matthew, a tax collector and one of the least likely disciples, He made it clear: God's mercy turns any pious ideas we have about religion upside down. This happened again when Jesus told the crowd to love their neighbor.

An immediate question arose (much like a "What about . . . ?" comment on social media): "But who is my neighbor?"*

I can just imagine the side-eye. Maybe it was a genuine question in good faith, or maybe it was an attempt at a *gotcha* moment. We weren't there, so we don't know the tone.

But we *do* know Jesus said that whatever we do for those most in need, we do for Him.† And we know that Jesus cared for the ones the world tends to forget or fear. The ones the world despises.

If we want our world to be a place of peace, we have to follow the One who is peace. If we want to follow Jesus, we have to love like Jesus.

In a world where everyone has what they think is the right take, we can take a breath.

Jesus has shown us the way. And the way is love.

LET IT LINGER

Here are some of the people Jesus loved that would have surprised people in his society:

- Those who were suffering (see Matthew 9:35).
- The children (see Mark 10:13-16).
- The outcast and the misunderstood (see Mark 5:1-20).
- The ones living in poverty (see Luke 4:18; 6:20).
- The hungry and thirsty (see Matthew 14:13-21; 25:35).
- The grieving (see John 11:33-35; Luke 7:13).
- The weary and burdened (see Matthew 11:28).
- The foreigner (see Luke 17:11-19) and a Roman centurion (see Matthew 8:5-13).
- The condemned criminal (see Luke 23:39-43).
- The ones who betrayed Him (see John 13:1-5; Luke 22:61-62).

---

* See Luke 10:29.
† See Matthew 25:40.

SEPTEMBER 22

Be still in the presence of the LORD, and wait patiently.

PSALM 37:7 (NLT)

INHALE: I will

EXHALE: Be still.

Today marks the first day of fall, a season that invites us to slow down and linger in the middle space of not-still-summer, not-quite-winter.*

We trade summer cookouts for soup simmering on the stove. We savor the steam rising from our favorite mug. We breathe in the crisp scent of autumn air. We inhale a little deeper. We exhale a little slower.

Psalm 37 reminds us to breathe in God's presence amid the chaos of our world. The Hebrew word for *be still* can be translated as *relax* or *let go*, "suggesting a release of anxiety and control."[294]

When was the last time you let your racing mind settle? What does it look like to, right here and right now, take a deep breath as you let yourself be present to God's presence?

God is with us in the middle spaces of our lives—in the waiting of what we hope for, in the worries that run laps around our minds.

The autumnal or fall equinox refers to the way the Earth is tilted, resulting in nearly equal amounts of daylight and darkness. I've always wanted to be in two places at once—to stand on a state line, one foot in one place and one in another. We get to do that today, standing in this balance of light and shadow.

Maybe the shifting seasons can invite us to draw near to the One who is closer than our every breath, getting us out of our worries and wonderings and woes just for a moment of stillness on our ever-tilting planet.

"If we could let go of our own obsession with what we think is the meaning of it all, we might be able to hear His call and follow Him in His mysterious, cosmic dance," monk and poet Thomas Merton writes. "We do not have to go very far to catch echoes. . . . When we are alone on a starlit night; when by chance we see the migrating birds in autumn descending on a grove of junipers to rest and eat; when we see children in a moment when they are really children; when we know love in our own hearts."[295]

Maybe that's what stillness really is: breathing in the balance, attentive to both heaven and earth. Maybe it means trusting that even now, in the very real realities where it seems like the bad guys win, the goodness of God is waiting to be found. Even now, we can be still. Even now, we can rest in the sacred presence of the One who gives each breath and is making everything beautiful in its time.

SACRED ECHOES

Fall invites us inward, beckoning us to notice God's peace and divine presence, not just around us but deep inside us too.[296]

Every Season Sacred†

* This is true if you live in the northern hemisphere. If you live in the southern hemisphere, lucky you! You're entering spring!

† For more seasonal readings and prayers, find the "Fall" section of my book *Every Season Sacred*.

SEPTEMBER 23

I'm absolutely convinced that nothing—nothing living or dead, angelic or demonic, today or tomorrow, high or low, thinkable or unthinkable—absolutely nothing can get between us and God's love because of the way that Jesus our Master has embraced us.

ROMANS 8:38-39 (MSG)

INHALE: Nothing can separate
EXHALE: Me from Your love.

God is closer than the breath in your lungs.

Every wall you've worked so hard to build around your heart can't distance you from the love of God. The guilt you hide, the shame you stuff down, the anger or doubt or sadness you try so hard to ignore—none of it can ever separate you from the One who loves you.

Even the hardest parts of your story, the words or choices you wish you could undo, can't remove you from the vast intimacy of God's love.

In Christ, the chasm between heaven and earth has been brought together. God's love binds and holds. What God has joined together, let no one separate.*

"We fail to believe that we are always with God and that He is part of every reality. The present moment, every object we see, our inmost nature are all rooted in Him," Thomas Keating writes. "But we hesitate to believe this until personal experience gives us the confidence to believe in it. This involves the gradual development of intimacy with God. God constantly speaks to us through each other as well as from within."[297]

One way to deepen your relationship with God is by borrowing breath prayer.

When we begin to believe that nothing can separate us from God's love, we can start living empowered by *pneuma*, a Greek word in the New Testament that means breath, wind, and spirit, used to describe the Holy Spirit.[298]

As you inhale, remember that not a single thing this world can throw at you, no protective fortress you might try to build around your heart, can separate you from the Giver of each breath. Hold your breath for a few counts before slowly letting it go.

BORROW THIS PRAYER

Holy Spirit
Closer than my breathing
Nearer than my heartbeat.[299]

Jack Levison

---

* See Mark 10:9.

SEPTEMBER 24

We're watching and waiting, holding our breath, awaiting your word of mercy.

PSALM 123:2 (MSG)

INHALE: God of mercy,
EXHALE: You are with us.

"Don't hold your breath." It's a common phrase we throw out to mean, "I wouldn't count on it."

How often do we move through life holding our breath—bracing for bad news, waiting for the other shoe to drop, keeping everything inside? How might your life look different if you lived with expectant hope instead of existential dread?

We weren't made to live with our lungs locked tight. Dr. Michael Breus writes that "holding your breath, which happens when you concentrate hard or are scared or surprised, instantly sends you into fight-or-flight mode and triggers a cortisol release."[300]

Cortisol is your body's natural stress hormone that kicks in when you sense danger. It's meant to protect you by making you more alert and ready to respond. But if you're constantly feeling stressed and under attack, that fight-or-flight mode can remain activated too long. This extended state of stress can wreak havoc on almost every part of your body. According to Mayo Clinic, it can raise your chances of experiencing anxiety, depression, digestive issues, headaches, heart disease, sleep troubles, muscle pain, and more.[301]

Holding our breath through life keeps us in a perpetual state of physical and spiritual stress. It feels almost radical to trust not only that we have a Maker but that our Maker loves us. Not only that, but our Creator extends compassion and forgiveness despite our shortcomings.

The psalmist wrote Psalm 123 using almost all plural pronouns, just as Jesus modeled praying for "*our* daily bread." What is causing our larger culture to hold its breath? In a world that is collectively and chronically stressed, followers of Jesus are called to extend an exhale, breathing mercy, not multiplying anxiety, into a weary world.

On your inhale, ask God to reveal areas of your life where you might be holding your breath. As you slowly release your breath, ask God how you might breathe peace into our overwhelmed world.

RHYTHM OF BREATH

God who is making us whole,
Help us release
The breath we've been holding.
Give us what we need for today.
Nourish us, care for us.
We come to You knowing full well
The ways we've fallen short
Of heaven's ways here on earth.
Help us hold tight to You,
The Breath of Life.
Free us from where lies hold us captive.
Protect us when the siren song
Of prosperity and power beckons.
All we are,
All of creation,
Every single breath—
Is Yours, ever and only,
All for Thee.

SEPTEMBER 25

Read it for yourself in Scripture: "As I live and breathe," God says, "every knee will bow before me; every tongue will tell the honest truth that I and only I am God."

ROMANS 14:11 (MSG)

INHALE: You and only You
EXHALE: Are the Giver of breath.

Our culture encourages worship at the altar of false gods that shimmer with the sheen of control, comfort, and certainty. We're encouraged to pursue whatever brings us the most happiness—to "follow our own truth," even if that leads to putting ourselves on a pedestal and potentially harming the collective whole.

Idolatry's allure is nothing new. Throughout Scripture, God's people were drawn to idols that promised what only the Creator can truly provide, things like comfort and safety. The golden calf glittered in the wilderness while God's presence burned on the mountain.[*] The prophets cried out as Israel bowed before gods of stone and wood, warning that lifeless idols can't save because they can't even *breathe.*[†]

Anything can become an idol. Work can become an altar if we're bowing to power, money, or status. Beauty or health can take on godlike weight when we confuse our inherent worth with our reflection in the mirror. Politics or national identity can be an object of worship when it replaces bowing at the foot of the cross. Even good desires—belonging, safety, influence—can be twisted into golden calves when we look to them to save us.

Every false god eventually demands more than it gives. We build idols out of what we think we can control because we fear what we cannot. When we do this, we're blinded from loving God and loving our neighbor. But when we loosen our grip on the illusion of control, we gain "a chance to feel the warmth of this gentle, wild, messy, holy world," according to Anne Lamott.[302]

Return to the One who gives each breath. Rest in the promise that you don't have to cover yourself in gold leaf and hold it all together as a god of your own making.

PRACTICING THE WAY

What has been occupying your mental space lately? Ask the Spirit to reveal anything that is taking up more room in your heart than it should. As you pray, let your breath follow this circle, imagining yourself being whole in the fullness of our true, triune God.

Breathe *in.*

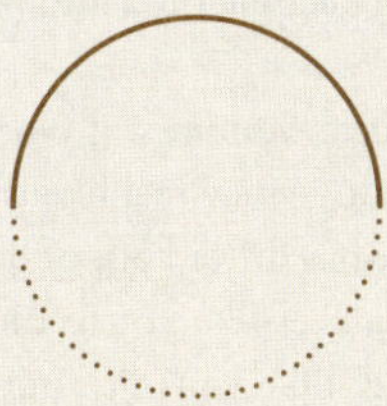

Breathe *out.*

[*] See Exodus 32.

[†] See Isaiah 44:9-20; Jeremiah 10:5.

SEPTEMBER 26

I have no doubts that the one who set your feet on this good path will keep walking it with you.

PHILIPPIANS 1:6 (FNV)

INHALE: Be with me, O God,
EXHALE: As I follow Your way.

"I'm running away!" my seven-year-old declares, his eyes brimming with tears. I'm not sure if it's a childhood rite of passage or something we've just picked up from pop culture, but he stomps up the stairs and slams his bedroom door. Then he begins filling his backpack with essentials: a teddy bear, a coloring book, and some extra socks. A few minutes later, his backpack is bursting at the seams as he clomps down the stairs with defiance before lingering at the back door. He lets it slam behind him as he heads out into the world, determined to make it on his own.

He doesn't make it past the corner of the backyard. I watch from the window, giving him space but never losing sight of him. Within ten minutes, he returns, and by the end of the evening, he's snuggling beside me on the couch, nestled under my arm.

Too often, I believe I can succeed on my own. I set out, full of intention and independence, only to become tired and unsure of the way forward.

Maybe you've wondered if God has moved on without you. It may feel like the One who was once close has drifted out of reach. Maybe right now you feel like you're on this winding path alone. Like you're trying to live into rhythms of goodness and generosity, hope and healing, yet you look around and wonder if God is with you.

The way is narrow. It's countercultural to choose peace over outrage, forgiveness over resentment, and generosity over fear. But the One who set your feet on this good path hasn't abandoned you. We don't have a distant, disconnected God. The same Spirit who breathed life into you still fills your lungs today. When you feel lonely and need to remember that you're not alone, pray with your breath, pausing to whisper, "Be with me, O God, as I follow Your way."

You are not forgotten. You are not forsaken. You do not go alone.

Keep going. The God who began this good work is with you wherever you go.

RHYTHM OF BREATH

When have you felt like running away from something uncomfortable? What stirred beneath that impulse—exhaustion, anger, disappointment, a longing for control? Offer that tender place to the One who keeps watch, even when you wander to the far edge of the yard.

SEPTEMBER 27

Everything of God gets expressed in him, so you can see and hear him clearly. You don't need a telescope, a microscope, or a horoscope to realize the fullness of Christ, and the emptiness of the universe without him.

COLOSSIANS 2:9 (MSG)

INHALE: Help me see
EXHALE: Your glory everywhere.

Curiosity is sacred. The more we learn about our world, the more we discover about the One who breathed it into being. The more glimpses of God we catch, the more we begin to grasp the fullness of God—and the fullness of who we are as people formed in divine likeness.

When Paul wrote today's letter to the Colossians, he reminded them that amid competing philosophies, Jesus is not just one voice among many. He is *the* voice—the full expression of the Creator. Completely human and fully divine, Jesus embodies the very core of God's being. As Paul writes earlier in his letter, "He existed before anything else, and he holds all creation together."*

Our modern world can tempt us to believe we've outgrown God. We have medicine, satellites, and quantum physics. Yet even our discoveries point us back to the Source of life. Francis Collins, a scientist who pioneered the Human Genome Project and founded BioLogos, has devoted his life's work to the belief that science complements rather than conflicts with the Bible.

Sacred curiosity about the world God so loves can strengthen our faith.

At a children's museum, my kids marveled at an exhibit showing how the bronchi in our lungs mirror the branches of trees. Creation bears the Creator's signature, sometimes hidden in plain sight. Every branch of science, when traced far enough, leads to the same mystery: Christ is behind it all.

While the fingerprints of God are on all creation, we don't have to search to understand what God is like. We only need to look at Jesus. When we see how Jesus moved through the world with compassion, truth, and healing, we see the fullness of God's glory breathing into every corner of the world and our very hearts. Our lungs, and indeed our very galaxy, would be empty without the breath of life expressed in Christ.

Step outside and pick up a leaf. Hold it in your hand and trace its lines. Notice how its veins branch out like the bronchi in your own lungs, carrying life. As you pray today's breath prayer, remember that the same Creator who shaped the stars and spun the galaxies also formed this leaf, this breath, and *you*.

SACRED ECHOES

Science can purify religion from error and superstition; religion can purify science from idolatry and false absolutes. Each can draw the other into a wider world, a world in which both can flourish.[303]

Pope John Paul II

* Colossians 1:17, NLT.

SEPTEMBER 28

The one who formed you says, "Do not be afraid, for I have ransomed you. I have called you by name; you are mine.

ISAIAH 43:1 (NLT)

INHALE: Form me
EXHALE: Into Your image.

When I lead workshops on spiritual formation, I sometimes pass around small containers of Play-Doh and invite people to shape their own little pots—to notice how their fingerprints press into the clay as it takes form.

Spiritual formation isn't something that's reserved for a transcendent few. It's happening to all of us, all the time. Maybe that's why Scripture so often describes us as clay in the hands of the Potter.* A life shaped by God's justice, mercy, and humility becomes a life that carries peace into the world.†

We're constantly being formed—every experience, every headline, every scroll leaves fingerprints on who we're becoming.

It's worth pausing to ask: *What's forming me? Where am I spending my time? Who am I listening to? What voices are shaping my heart?*

When we slow down to notice what's shaping us, we create space to breathe again, trusting our lives into the hands of our Creator. We remember that we are creations held in the loving hands of the One who, as Genesis 2:7 tells us, "breathed the breath of life" into humanity, forming us into being with perfect strength and perfect love.

The breath that formed life out of dust is the same breath moving through you now, forming you in love.

Pastor Rich Villodas writes, "Whether we know it or not, see it or not, or understand it or not, we are always at risk of being shallowly formed."[304] God's invitation isn't shame—it's shaping. It's a gentle call back to Love, who forms us from the inside out.

If every experience leaves fingerprints on who we are, how much more must God's own hands tenderly shape us with loving-kindness, breathing peace on our rough edges, forming us toward wholeness with every inhale and exhale?

As you breathe, rest in this truth: Even now, the breath of God is forming you.

BORROW THIS PRAYER

Creator God,
You breathed us into being out of dirt
and dust.
You are not done with the forming and
fashioning
Of who we are and who we are becoming.
When we have allowed our false selves
To become hardened in the fires of life,
Call us back so we may return
To being formed by love, joy, peace,
Patience, kindness, goodness,
Faithfulness, gentleness, and self-control.
Soften our harsh edges,
And form us into Your image,
Through Christ alone.
Amen.[305]

Adapted from Every Season Sacred

* See Isaiah 64:8.
† See Micah 6:8.

SEPTEMBER 29

We throw open our doors to God and discover at the same moment that he has already thrown open his door to us. We find ourselves standing where we always hoped we might stand—out in the wide open spaces of God's grace and glory, standing tall and shouting our praise.

ROMANS 5:2 (MSG)

INHALE: God of grace,
EXHALE: You open the door.

Graduating from college during an economic recession didn't come with many perks, but the crashing housing market dropped prices so low that it allowed my husband and me to afford our first little house. It was a small, postwar one-and-a-half-story with a pink tile bathroom that we cheerfully called "charming." We put up a fence, got a dog, and felt like real adults.

About a month in, we locked ourselves out. We panicked, searching for a spare key before remembering . . . we didn't have one. Calling a locksmith wasn't in the budget, so in a superhuman feat, my tall (and fearless) husband catapulted himself onto the roof and climbed through the half-story attic window to get us back inside.

We don't have to climb through windows—or jump through hoops—to reach God. Like the story Jesus told in Luke 15 about the wayward son who finally returned home, while we were still a long way off, God was already on the porch, running toward us with arms stretched wide, so focused on us that the door was left wide open.

"Faith is the key that opens the door to God's grace."[306] Paul writes that Christ is our access—our invitation into the very presence of God. The Greek word used here, *prosagōgē*, means to be "ushered into the presence of royalty."[307]

Paul reminds us that when we open our door to God, God is already opening the door to us. If you've ever stood between two doors in a Jack-and-Jill–style bathroom, you can picture both doors swinging wide, connecting what once felt separate.

As Jesus says, "Ask, and it will be given you; search, and you will find; knock, and the door will be opened for you."*

In God's Kingdom, grace is the air we breathe. Prayer, too, is a doorway. Every time you turn your heart toward God, even with a sigh or a whisper, you find the door already open, waiting. When you open your heart, grace rushes in. You don't have to climb through any windows. The door is already open.

Breathe it in. You already belong.

PRACTICING THE WAY

Find a doorway in your home. Pause there for a moment with your hand on the frame. Let it remind you that prayer is never about prying something open but about noticing the love that's already waiting to welcome you home. As you breathe in, whisper, "God of grace." As you breathe out, whisper, "You open the door."

* Matthew 7:7-8, NRSV.

SEPTEMBER 30

Deep calls to deep in the roar of your waterfalls; all your waves and breakers have swept over me.

PSALM 42:7 (NIV)

INHALE: Meet the depth of my pain
EXHALE: With the depth of Your love.

I love the stretched-out plains of the Midwest. Driving through the vast expanse of countryside always feels like an exhale as I take in the panoramic view of the unhurried horizon.

But since I'm usually landlocked, I take every chance I can to walk beside the ocean. Its immenseness undoes me a little. The tide rolls in and out like breath, reminding me how small I am and how near God is.

When I was a lifeguard, I had to pass a test by diving to the bottom of the pool to retrieve a brick. Even now, I can feel the weight of the water pressing against my body and can hear the muffled silence underneath the surface. When I stand along the Pacific and think of how deep the ocean truly goes—more than thirty-six thousand feet—I feel that same mixture of awe and ache.

It's beautiful. It's terrifying. It's holy.

The thought takes my breath away.

The psalmist knew something about that depth. "Deep calls to deep" is a cry of longing and faith in the middle of inner anguish. It's not a polished request or a casual prayer but a longing from deep within, the sound of a soul reaching for divine presence and the depth of God's fullness reaching back.

The psalmist paints a picture of what it feels like to stand in the surf of sorrow, withstanding the crashing waves of life . . . and still trust that Love will meet you there.

Each inhale draws life in, and each exhale releases it, echoing the rhythm of the ocean tide that surges and recedes.[308] When we're paying attention, each one of those breaths can act as a divine metronome, keeping time with our Creator's care.

When you feel pulled under, cling to the truth that the deep within you is met by God's deeper mercy. When the depths of your despair seem like too much to bear, reach out, and God will respond.

The One who walks on water is with you in the waves.

PRACTICING THE WAY

Let your breath mirror the tide with *oceanic breathing*.

- Find a quiet space to sit comfortably.
- Take a slow inhale through your nose.
- As you exhale, slightly constrict the back of your throat and let out a soft "Ahhh," like the sound of the sea inside a shell.
- Repeat several times, feeling the steady rhythm of *inhale, exhale, rise, fall.*[309]

As you breathe, remember that even in the roughest waters, even in the depths of your ache, you are held by the One who speaks peace into the deep.

OCTOBER 1

In his hand is the life of every living thing and the breath of every human being.

JOB 12:10 (NRSV)

INHALE: You hold my breath
EXHALE: In the palm of Your hand.

A photo of my eldest sits on a shelf in my office. He's five years old, holding two palms full of glitter with his cheeks puffed as he blows the confetti toward the camera. Tiny flecks of light scatter and swirl in the air, forever floating in a moment in time, a kaleidoscope of color dancing around him.

When I read today's verse, I imagine God cradling all of creation in a divine hand, breathing love into motion across time and space.

If you've ever done a glitter craft (or been the one to clean up afterward), you know how the sparkle lingers. You'll find shimmer weeks—sometimes months—later, on your hands, your clothes, maybe even the floorboards. The more we breathe in God's life-giving peace and the more we breathe it out, the more it lingers on everything we touch.

When you hold something precious, you cup your hands around it. Maybe that's what God does with every life-giving breath, protecting the glittering, ordinary beauty of us.

God breathes life into us so we can exhale peace into our anxious world.

Coregulation—the synchronizing of our breath and our heartbeats with another person's—reminds us we're not alone.[310] Our calm can help another person's nervous system settle. Our shared breaths reflects the image of a relational God. After the resurrection, Jesus breathed peace into his friends.* That same peace still moves through us now. God exhales, and we live.

We inhale, and—if we're not too caught up in the chaos—we can exhale peace, mercy, hope, and truth back into a weary world. Maybe for you, this looks like taking a slow breath before responding or turning to a borrowed prayer when you'd rather react immediately.

As you pray today's breath prayer, open your hands and lift them near your mouth. On your inhale, imagine receiving God's peace. On your exhale, gently blow across your palms, like you're scattering confetti into the air. This small gesture slows your breathing and signals safety to your body.

What would it look like today to live out of God's peace and scatter it like confetti?

BORROW THIS PRAYER

Out of an overflow
Of Your abundant love,
We speak life into
Our places and spaces.
Reorder our rhythms,
Reorient our hearts.
From our first breath
To our last,
You are the life
In our lungs,
Lavishing love
Upon us.
Amen.

* See John 20.

OCTOBER 2

Those who are peacemakers will plant seeds of peace and reap a harvest of righteousness.

JAMES 3:18 (NLT)

INHALE: Give me patience
EXHALE: As I cultivate peace.

By the time October rolls around, the fields near my house are heavy with corn and soybeans. Farmers who planted months earlier now reap what they've sown.

Peace, James reminds us, doesn't just appear out of thin air. Like a harvest, it's the result of intentional, patient planting: "Peacemakers who sow in peace reap a harvest of righteousness."*

Other versions say, "Those who make peace sow the seeds of justice by their peaceful acts,"† or, "You can develop a healthy, robust community . . . *only* if you do the hard work of getting along."‡

Cultivating peace in our lives takes work. It means choosing gentleness when responding harshly would be easier. It means refusing to keep score when resentment feels justified. It means doing the long, slow work of building trust and tending to relationships in our families and communities.

Sometimes the ground feels dry. People's hearts are hardened. We look at the small seeds of peace we're planting in the comings and goings of our days and wonder if they matter, if they'll actually take root and grow into something meaningful.

The wait for a more flourishing world stretches long.

Harvest never happens overnight. But the book of James promises that righteousness—living in right relationship with God through rhythms of mercy and justice—grows out of the seeds of peace we scatter along the way.

As Paul writes in Romans, "If it is possible, as far as it depends on you, live at peace with everyone."§

If you long for peace, start where you are.

Become an everyday peacemaker—one word, one action, one breath at a time. Trust that God is faithful to bring the harvest and is beginning that work deep within the soil of your soul.

PAUSE AND PONDER

When you feel impatient for peace, what emotions arise in you? Frustration? Anger? Cynicism? Defeat? What might it mean to let God nurture peace within you before you try to plant it around you?

James reminds us that peace and justice grow side by side. Ask God to open your heart to injustice in your community. What might it look like to plant even one seed of peace there this fall?

* James 3:18, NIV.
† CEB.
‡ MSG.
§ Romans 12:18, NIV.

OCTOBER 3

Accept one another, then, just as Christ accepted you.

ROMANS 15:7 (NIV)

INHALE: As You accept me,
EXHALE: Help me accept others.

"You don't really, ya know, *seem* like a pastor," a friend tells my husband. "And I mean that as a compliment."

When we meet new people, Jonny often hesitates before mentioning that he works in ministry. He loves what he does, but he also understands the reputation the church can carry. Too often, we have been known more for how we exclude than for how we love, more for how we accuse than for how we accept.

When Paul wrote to the early Christians in Rome, they were caught in their own struggle, stuck in a cycle of division and suspicion. They were a diverse group of believers trying to figure out how to belong to one another. Paul urged them to look to Jesus—the One who embraced people across backgrounds and loved them unconditionally. He didn't tell them to agree on everything but to accept each other the way Christ accepted them.

Two thousand years later, we're still learning.

I understand Jonny's hesitation. Recent surveys show that public trust in pastors is at an all-time low, especially among younger generations.[311] For many, church has become synonymous with hypocrisy or, heartbreakingly, even harm.

We've been on both sides of the story: Our hearts have been hurt by people who claimed Christ's name, and we've been healed by others whose quiet faithfulness looked like Jesus.

The way of Jesus isn't always reflected in the ways of Christians.

But with God's help, we can return to the path—refusing to take the "ragebait" and choosing compassion when contempt feels easier.

What if Christians were known by their humble hearts? By integrity and mercy? By kindness in ordinary moments, courage in the face of injustice, joy that creates beauty, and peace that disarms fear?

As you breathe through today's breath prayer, ask God how you might live in a way that leaves a legacy of love.

RHYTHM OF BREATH

Blessed are the ones
Who are known
By their love.
Blessed are the ones
Who dream of a better world,
Who refuse to dehumanize
And instead do the deep work
Of honoring the image of God
In the one who is difficult to love.

OCTOBER 4

FEAST OF SAINT FRANCIS

Look to the winged ones who soar on the wind. Do they plant seeds and gather the harvest into a storehouse? No! But your Father from above gives them plenty to eat.

MATTHEW 6:26 (FNV)

INHALE: My God,
EXHALE: My all.

"Look at the birds," Jesus told His followers. *Notice. See how they live under the care of their Creator.*

Saint Francis took that call to heart.

He understood that we experience God not by cloistering ourselves from the world but by prayerfully paying attention to it so we might truly experience how God holds everything together in love.

But Francis wasn't always that way.

In 1182, Francis of Assisi was born into a wealthy family. When he was young, he fell seriously ill and turned to God for comfort. In prayer, he realized how much of his life he'd spent chasing things that couldn't last. Convinced that he was wasting his life on frivolities instead of truly following Jesus, he didn't return to the lap of luxury when he recovered. Instead, he walked away from wealth and into wonder, trading status for simplicity and privilege for peace.

In a world obsessed with more, Saint Francis began to live as if the gospel *really* is enough—as if the very air can teach us how to trust God, if only we'd take a breath and slow down enough to pay attention.

As he observed nature, he felt himself awaken to God's presence in the ordinary, breathing through the flap of a bird's feathered wings or the hum of a bumblebee dancing in the breeze.

Francis's life reminds us that the way of Christ can be filled with joy and wonder as we marvel at the sacred simplicity of creation and dwell in the love of our Creator.

Today's breath prayer is inspired by a poetic song of praise Francis wrote called "The Canticle of the Sun." As writer Patti Normille puts it, "Everything that can be stated about prayer in the life of St. Francis of Assisi is expressed in . . . four little words"—"*My God and my all.*"[312]

As you pray today's breath prayer, consider what it would look like for you to live unrushed and unguarded today.

How might the Spirit be prompting you to turn from the trappings of our world and instead toward the One who gives each breath?

The same Spirit that stirred Francis's soul so many years ago is still moving through the trees and across the sky and into your lungs today.

BORROW THIS PRAYER

O Lord, all the animals and plants
And skies and seas
Reveal Your glory
Above us and below us and among us;
Show us Your handiwork.
Amen.[313]

Adapted from "A Prayer on the Feast Day of St. Francis of Assisi" in To Light Their Way

OCTOBER 5

God is a safe place to hide, ready to help when we need him.

PSALM 46:1 (MSG)

INHALE: I am safe
EXHALE: With You.

Your phone lights up, once again buzzing with breaking news.

The noise never really seems to stop.

It can feel like we're always holding our breath, bracing ourselves for the next bad thing. When we're facing constant chaos, our bodies slip into overdrive and cortisol (the stress hormone designed to help us survive) rushes in, keeping us on high alert and preparing us to fight, flee, or freeze.

But when life keeps making demands on us and rest never comes, we can end up living in an activated state for weeks (or even *years*) at a time. And that's not what we're made for.

"High levels of cortisol truly disrupt your system in every way," writes Carolyn Cowan. "This hormone creates a sense of agitation and endless checking for safety—for instance, looking at the news—perhaps overwhelming those around us with our need for them to make things right or do things to make us feel better."[314]

Environments that feel unpredictable or unsafe, like being in a difficult relationship or a tense workplace, can keep your stress response activated.[315] It's not your fault that your body feels tense—your body is trying to protect you. You're not broken for feeling on edge in a world that won't stop shouting. But you don't have to stay in this constant stress cycle. God invites us to learn gentler rhythms so we don't have to live in that high-alert state forever.

If you've ever noticed that prayer leaves you feeling a little calmer, there's a reason for that. Therapist Deborah Dana calls breath "a direct pathway to the nervous system."[316] The psalmist might not have used the word *cortisol*, but they knew what it meant to feel safe in God's presence.

Slow, intentional breathing whispers a sacred truth to your nervous system:

You are safe.
You are safe.
You are safe.

Each prayerful inhale and exhale can help establish new patterns of peace in your body. No matter who you are or what's happening around you, you can continue to learn new rhythms (slowly, over time) as you practice small moments of safety through breath prayer, again and again.[317]

Today, let your breath remind you of the One who is a safe harbor in every anxious hour.

BREATHE THIS IN

Researchers have found that diaphragmatic breathing (deep, slow breaths into your core rather than fast, quick breaths into your chest) can lower cortisol levels and increase the body's sense of calm. When we breathe in God's presence, we begin to remember what safety feels like.

OCTOBER 6

Feed the hungry, and help those in trouble. Then your light will shine out from the darkness.

ISAIAH 58:10 (NLT)

INHALE: Give us this day
EXHALE: Our daily bread.

Cake aglow with candles as the room sings. Nachos passed at the tailgate. Cups of coffee at brunch. Plates loaded with barbecue at your neighbor's house. Slices of pie that the church ladies make for the funeral lunch. Popcorn passed around on movie night. Reflect on some of your favorite memories that include food. Life happens around the table.

Every day, our church receives calls asking about our food pantry. The same God who meets us in the bread and the wine calls us to notice who's missing from the table. Food insecurity in the US is the highest it has been in over ten years—more than forty-seven million people are facing hunger, including fourteen million children.[318]

If you've ever felt hunger pangs or the fear of an empty pantry, know that God's heart beats with yours. Jesus told His followers to feed the hungry because, when we do, we are serving Him.

Hunger exists everywhere. Globally, nearly *350 million people* suffer from severe hunger. Behind these statistics are real stories—parents skipping meals so their children can eat, farmers unable to grow enough food, families forced to leave their homes in search of nourishment.[319]

Isaiah's imagery shows us that acts of compassion and justice illuminate a shadowy world. God's character shines through those who follow Him.[320] The light you shine can be part of fostering societal renewal. Feeding the hungry isn't just a onetime act of charity but an ongoing involvement in God's restorative work to bring the Kingdom to earth.

Where might God be nudging you to make room for someone else at the table?

PRACTICING THE WAY

If we want to practice peace, we can start by making sure everyone can eat. *Shalom*—the word in the Bible used to describe God's peace—is not just a sense of calmness but a kind of *wholeness* in which everyone has enough. Maybe that looks like

- praying before each meal with an awareness of those who hunger;
- donating to ministries that feed people in your community;
- delivering a meal to a neighbor;
- supporting small farmers and markets that make fresh food accessible;
- voting for policies that ensure children are fed;
- buying two when you shop—one for your pantry, one for the food bank;
- serving regularly (not just on holidays) at a community kitchen or food pantry;
- planting an extra row in your garden and sharing the harvest;
- inviting people into your home for meals that build belonging;
- keeping snacks or a grocery-store gift card in your wallet, ready to give away;
- eating a simple meal once a week and giving the savings to hunger relief.

OCTOBER 7

As for me, how good it is to be near God!

PSALM 73:28 (NLT)

INHALE: How good it is
EXHALE: To be near to You.

"Good guys finish last."

We've all heard that phrase (and maybe even believed it ourselves) when cruelty triumphs. When those who deceive or manipulate seem to climb higher while those who choose honesty and kindness are overlooked, it's easy to grow weary and wonder where God fits into the ache of our world.

Psalm 73 begins in frustration, asking God why the arrogant prosper while the faithful struggle. But as the prayer takes shape, the lament shifts into a sort of hopeful clarity: "As for me, how good it is to be near God!"

In Christ, nearness becomes enough.

Since the earliest moments of history, the world has followed its own set of rules, which Jesus came to turn upside down. Jesus didn't seek power—He emptied Himself of it.* He drew near the hurting, the outcast, and those the world forgets. The people in power hated Him for it.

Jesus ushered in a new reality. In the Kingdom of God, success looks like compassion, not cruelty. Greatness looks like gentleness, not gilded walls.

When life feels unjust and your hope feels fragile, draw near to the One who gives every breath. Remember what is real. Let God's presence reorient your heart, mind, body, and soul to what really matters.

Breath prayer offers a simple way to draw near to God.

April Yamasaki writes, "With every breath, we depend on God's Spirit who sustains the world. How fitting, then, to link our prayers to the rhythm of our breathing."[321]

Each breath we take offers a moment to rest in God's presence.

Pause here for a few beats. Take a slow breath. Let your shoulders drop. Feel your body soften into God's presence. On your inhale, pray, "How good it is." Then, as you slowly exhale, pray, "To be near You." The world will keep shouting, but for now, rest in the quiet promise that God is near and that nearness is enough.

As we draw close to God, God draws close to us.

This movement is a rhythm of grace we're invited into with every breath. When we pause to pray, we set our hearts to the sacred reminder that spiritual intimacy in Christ is more important than any success we chase or power we pursue.

While the world might see this as losing, in God's economy, those who are humble and overlooked and who continue to choose love are especially dear to His heart.

As Jesus said, "Many who are first will be last, and many who are last will be first."†

SACRED ECHOES

Breath prayers remind us that we depend on God as much as we depend on the air that we breathe.[322]

April Yamasaki

* See Philippians 2.

† Matthew 19:30, NIV.

OCTOBER 8

Let justice roll down like waters, and righteousness like an ever-flowing stream.

AMOS 5:24 (ESV)

INHALE: Let justice roll
EXHALE: Like a river.

The raft turns a corner, splashing a plume of water over the side. I glance at my sons and laugh as droplets cling to my eyelashes. Before I can catch my breath, we plunge down a drop, twisting through the current. Water seeps into my sneakers.

I am *soaked.*

If you've ever buckled into a river ride at an amusement park, you know there's no escaping getting drenched by that abnormally blue chlorinated water. You leave with every part of you dripping, your shoes squishing as you make your way to the next roller coaster.

In his prophetic words to God's people, Amos compares justice to a powerful, unstoppable river. In ancient Israel, rivers signified life. They were essential for farming and for survival in the arid environment.[323] But the people's life of faith had run dry. They sang songs and followed rituals while ignoring the cries of the poor, going through the motions while missing the point.

They ignored God's commands for justice and mercy.

Justice isn't optional for those who follow the way of Jesus. It's as essential to the Christian life as prayer or worship.

God wants us to actively chase justice—to treat others fairly, advocate for the oppressed, and live in ways that extend love to God and others in all aspects of our lives. Thankfully, we don't do this alone. Jesus promises to fill us with living water.* Because of this, we do the work of justice not out of obligation but from divine replenishment. We can draw from a well that never runs dry.

You don't have to rely on your own reserves.

You don't have to believe that everything that's wrong is yours to fix.

You don't have to be a savior, because you already have one.

You can breathe easily and, from that place of safety, overflow with love to share with a watching world.

That doesn't mean we always get it right, but God's mercy guides us as we show mercy to others. In the upside-down Kingdom of Christ, practicing rhythms of just living leaves us nourished, not depleted.

May the living water saturate your life in mercy until love overflows through you and into the world like a rushing river.

SACRED ECHOES

More than a few Christians might be surprised to learn that the call to be involved in creating justice for the poor is just as essential and nonnegotiable within the spiritual life as is Jesus' commandment to pray and keep our private lives in order.[324]

Ronald Rolheiser

* See John 4:10.

OCTOBER 9

You saw my pain.

PSALM 31:7 (MSG)

INHALE: My pain
EXHALE: Is not unseen.

God sees your pain.

Every tear you've cried, every moment it felt like your heart was as shattered as it could ever be, God was there.

God was with you then. And God is with you now.

There's a deep loneliness that comes from feeling unseen in your grief, like you've been forgotten and left alone in the rawness of your pain. Bearing witness to suffering, whether our own or someone else's, is a sacred act.

The psalmist writes that although religion can become performative, God remains trustworthy because God sees our pain and provides us room to breathe.

If you've ever spent a summer with kids, you've probably tended to a skinned knee. God sees your skinned knee and tenderly cleans it, not just covering your wound with a bandage but giving your pain space to heal, sitting beside you until you're ready to stand again.

We can hurt and heal at the same time, therapist Monica DiCristina writes in her book *Your Pain Has a Name*. "We are often taught . . . that healing is the absence of what hurts you," she writes, "You may hurt *and* feel presence and love."[325]

Psalm 31:6-9 in *The Message* says,

I hate all this silly religion,
but you, GOD, I trust.
I'm leaping and singing in the circle of your love;
you saw my pain,
you disarmed my tormentors,
You didn't leave me in their clutches
but gave me room to breathe.

The psalmist speaks plainly, naming the pain you may have carried in the past and may still carry now: heartbreak that threatens to take your breath away. Creation groans. Things are not as they should be. We endure diagnoses and death, disappointment and discouragement. Cruelty is all too common. Compassion is scarce.

And yet, even in the depths of your pain, our Healer sees *you.*

The One who witnessed the psalmist's anguish also holds yours, meeting you in the tender places of your deepest ache with compassion and care.

As you breathe through today's prayer, consider what it means to you that God doesn't turn away from your tears.

PAUSE AND PONDER

Think back to the last time you were in deep emotional or spiritual pain. What helped you feel less alone in your suffering? As time has passed, how has your perspective changed about whether God saw your pain?

OCTOBER 10

The path of the righteous is like the morning sun,
shining ever brighter till the full light of day.

PROVERBS 4:18 (NIV)

INHALE: Awaken me
EXHALE: To Your light.

I'm not a morning person.

To help me wake up less like a bear emerging from hibernation and more like a regular human, my husband bought us an alarm clock that mimics a sunrise. Its gentle light gradually brightens the room, easing us from darkness into daylight. (It's a small way to make those increasingly dark fall mornings slightly more bearable.)

It turns out, however, that I can sleep through *any* kind of light.

But even when I'm unaware of it, the light keeps rising. And that feels a lot like how the Spirit works within us.

Today's proverb paints a picture of a faith that unfolds like dawn breaking into day. When we walk in step with the Spirit, we are continually being formed—again and again—into people who reflect God's light. The work isn't instant; it's gradual and grounding.

Today's proverb says that when we walk in step with the Spirit, we're continually being formed into people who reflect the light of Christ.

We don't arrive at the spiritual life. We awaken to God's Spirit. Again and again and again.

In the animated film *Inside Out*, we meet characters who are embodied emotions, with names like Anger, Sadness, and Joy. The character Joy is the only one who doesn't cast a shadow. She is *luminous*. She glows from the inside out. When we live close to God's light on the path of righteousness, it changes what radiates from within us.

Eugene Peterson writes, "Joy is not a requirement of Christian discipleship, it is a consequence. It is not what we have to acquire in order to experience life in Christ; it is what comes to us when we are walking in the way of faith and obedience."[326]

Just as the sun climbs higher until it reaches its full brilliance, the Spirit shapes us little by little as we journey on, bringing clarity to our confusion and warmth to our weariness.

Over time, our lives begin to light the way for others too.

PRACTICING THE WAY

Choose a morning this week to pause and pray before your feet hit the floor.

Breathe deeply and whisper, "Awaken me to Your light." Feel the warmth behind your eyelids. Imagine the light of the Holy Spirit slowly filling you until your whole being glows with joy.

OCTOBER 11

He has shown you, O mortal, what is good. And what does the LORD require of you? To act justly and to love mercy and to walk humbly with your God.

MICAH 6:8 (NIV)

INHALE: Show me, O God,
EXHALE: What is good.

God breathes life into you so you can exhale that goodness into the world.

Why do you have breath in your lungs at this very moment? What does God ask of you?

The answer, spoken through the prophet Micah, is clear: *Act justly. Love mercy. Walk humbly.* Learning to live into these rhythms means asking God to shape our hearts as much as our habits.

Spiritual formation starts in the quiet places of our souls, where the Spirit teaches us, again and again, what God's love requires of us.

- **Acting justly** looks like choosing integrity, even when it's unpopular. It looks like living the way of Jesus at your workplace, in your home, and throughout your community. It's noticing who's missing from the table—and doing something about it. Justice requires the courage to do what's right, even when it's uncomfortable or inconvenient.
- **Loving mercy** means letting compassion crack open your heart. It's forgiving when holding a grudge seems easier, and choosing kindness and care for others—not because they've earned it, but because mercy is how God keeps loving the world.
- **Walking humbly** begins with moving through the day aware that you're not the center—yet you are still so very loved by God. It's aligning your steps with the One who walks beside you, listening before becoming defensive, and staying open to learning new perspectives while allowing the Spirit to transform you from the inside out. Humility creates space for God's presence in every step.

This path is not always easy. Thankfully, we only need to look to Jesus when we want our feet on the right path, because God has shown us "what is good" through Jesus Christ. And we don't go alone—we have the Holy Spirit to guide us when we lose our way. The Spirit is a patient teacher, guiding us back to justice, mercy, and humility. As you pray with your inhale and exhale, ask God how you might live into these rhythms today.

When you ask, God will always show you the path of goodness and lead you back to the way.

LET IT LINGER

When in doubt, borrow the prayer from Psalm 86:11: "Teach me your way, LORD, that I may rely on your faithfulness."*

* NIV.

OCTOBER 12

They worshiped worthless idols, so they became worthless themselves.

2 KINGS 17:15 (NLT)

INHALE: I worship
EXHALE: Only You.

False gods offer false peace.

Like a shiny apple that you realize is mealy the moment you bite into it, what once seemed sweet is actually spoiled. In a similar way, when we make an idol the center of our lives, we inevitably end up breathing the sour air of fear instead of the holy breath of God's peace.

It's tempting to bow before success, control, power, and image. But when we put anything that isn't God first in our lives, we end up sharing rotten fruit with the world.

When we "worship worthless idols," we lose our way, no longer living in the Spirit-led rhythms of love, joy, peace, patience, kindness, goodness, faithfulness, gentleness, and self-control.*

As the very first book of the Bible reminds us, the allure of rotten fruit—the temptation to worship at the altar of self—is timeless.

We still reach for what looks delicious and promises more, forgetting that it only separates us from God and never satisfies our souls.† Every idol promises freedom but feeds on fear, leaving us empty and hungry for more. But we don't have to stay stuck in false worship.

Idolatry may isolate, but Jesus liberates.

When we turn away from idols that will never satisfy, we experience the profound peace of Christ—a peace that passes understanding.‡ A peace that renews our minds, bodies, and souls. A peace that bears good fruit and nourishes the flourishing of our communities.

PRACTICING THE WAY

If you can, consider visiting an apple orchard (or pause in the produce aisle at your grocery store). Take a moment to hold an apple in your hand. Feel its weight in your palm. Notice the curve of its skin, the way light gleams across its surface. Bring it close and breathe in its faint sweetness.

As you hold it, whisper today's breath prayer. Ask God to reveal what you might be elevating above Christ. Status? Money? Relationships? Control? Health? Image? Let the question linger for a few breaths.

As you turn the apple in your hand, take a moment or two to examine your life. Where do you sense fruit that is ripe and nourishing? Where might something be starting to spoil?

When you're ready, set down the apple and open your hands. Take a final breath in and out as you offer yourself back to the One who cultivates peace in your heart.

* See Galatians 5:22-23.
† See Genesis 3:6-8.
‡ See Philippians 4:7.

OCTOBER 13

The fundamental fact of existence is that this trust in God, this faith, is the firm foundation under everything that makes life worth living. It's our handle on what we can't see.

HEBREWS 11:1 (MSG)

INHALE: Ground me
EXHALE: In Your presence.

After a particularly turbulent plane ride and bumpy landing, I must have looked pretty woozy, because as I waited to deplane, an airline attendant asked me if I was okay.

"I'm fine," I said as I walked (albeit shakily) toward the jet bridge. "I'll feel better when my feet are on solid ground."

God is the solid ground beneath our feet—the firm foundation when everything else feels like shifting sand.

I grew up feeling oddly terrified about quicksand. I'm not sure why a ten-year-old from Iowa would need to mentally prepare for what to do in case of a quicksand emergency, but enough Saturday morning cartoons and evening sitcoms taught me that you have to be still—you can't panic—or the sinking sand will swallow you whole.

Scripture tells us that God is not only our foundation but also the One who breathed into the dust of the ground and formed us from it. Genesis 2:7 tells us, "God formed the man from the dust of the ground. He breathed the breath of life into the man's nostrils, and the man became a living person."*

We're made *by* God and *from* God. We're formed from dust and filled with divine breath. When life feels like a turbulent plane ride or shifting sand, prayerful mindfulness grounded in Christ can hold us and point us back to that truth.

Faith is trust that puts our feet on solid ground. When life leaves you feeling dizzy, you can trust God to be the foundation that, as today's verse says, "makes life worth living."

What are the shifting sands in your life right now? What does it mean that God is both the ground you stand on and the breath in your lungs?

* NLT.

PRACTICING THE WAY

When you feel turbulence inside you, a grounding mindfulness exercise can help you return to what's true and stay planted in the present moment, rather than sinking into the quicksand of anxiety or overwhelm.[327]

You can use this prayerful grounding practice anytime, anywhere:

- Close your eyes.
- Plant your feet flat on the floor.
- Feel yourself supported by the ground beneath you.
- Reflect on the foundation in Christ that holds you.
- Straighten your spine.
- Notice your breathing.
- Thank God for being the ground that holds you and the breath that fills you.
- Take a few deep breaths.
- When you're ready, open your eyes.
- Ask God to help you stay present to God's presence.

OCTOBER 14

He has created us anew in Christ Jesus, so we can do the good things he planned for us long ago.

EPHESIANS 2:10 (NLT)

INHALE: You're making
EXHALE: Me new.

When you pray alongside your breath, every inhale offers a moment of renewal.

God is continually working to renew, restore, and redeem. But so often, we forget this reality. It's so easy to get caught up in the whirlwind of life. We focus on errands, meetings, social media posts, and our endless to-do lists, forgetting that each breath is an opportunity to reset. We overlook the fact that no matter what's happening in our world, no pressing deadline or breaking headline can separate us from the presence of the One who is remaking us—and the world—in love.

Maybe you're tired with that kind of exhaustion you feel deep in your bones.

Maybe your mind is racing, and you can't seem to slow it down.

Maybe you're overwhelmed. Or frustrated. Or angry. Or sad.

Maybe you've been holding your breath way too long.

What if, just for a moment, you took a deep breath and drew close to the One who is making you new?

In the bridge of their song "Beautiful Things," the band Gungor sings, "You make me new, You are making me new."

Every breath you take is part of a living system that's constantly being repaired and renewed. Our Creator has designed your lungs to have the capacity for repair. The tiny air sacs in your lungs (alveoli) exchange oxygen and carbon dioxide each time you breathe. Scientists have found that even though these cells work nonstop, they can regrow and replace damaged ones when needed.[328]

With every breath, God is renewing you—body and soul. One way to remember this is to simply turn to breath prayer throughout the day. As you inhale and exhale during today's prayer, reflect on how you sense God breathing renewal into your life today.

The renewal God breathes into us is never just for us—it's so we can breathe renewal into our own communities, so "we can do the good things" God has prepared for us since before we took our first breath.

How might your day change with the reminder that you are being renewed, breath by breath?

BORROW THIS PRAYER

I need a breath,
I need a moment,
When I am not doing.
Help me be
In this moment,
In this breath.
Amen.

OCTOBER 15

I bless you every time I take a breath.

PSALM 63:4 (MSG)

INHALE: I bless You
EXHALE: With every breath.

It's one thing to say you'll bless God with every breath.

But the average person takes about twenty thousand breaths per day.

That's a *lot* of blessings.

I don't know about you, but I'm not sure even a fraction of my breaths bless God.

Many theologians agree that David was likely the author of this psalm. We know that David wasn't a perfect man. Not even close. He used his privilege to pursue a woman who wasn't his wife. He used his power to take what was not his—including Bathsheba, whose consent Scripture never makes clear—and then arranged her husband's death.

And yet David's story reminds us that even in our failures, God meets us with mercy. David didn't get everything right, but he kept returning to God, again and again.

He was fully human.

Just like me.

Just like you.

Just like all of us.

David vowed to bless God with his every breath because he was grateful to the One who gives each breath. He had inhaled God's goodness and wanted to exhale gratitude. He didn't promise to be perfect, but he used poetry to express the longings of his heart. His hope was to live awake to God's presence.

It's never too late to take a new breath and begin again. To get honest with God and name the ways we've gotten it wrong—not to fixate on it or dwell in shame, but to bless God with our honesty.

No matter who you are or where you've been, you can let every breath bring you closer to the One who gives it.

How might you order your days so that breath becomes a blessing? How might your choices, your words, your use of time, your media habits, your relationships, and your acts of service all help you breathe blessing into the world? And how might blessing God also include showing grace to yourself?

God breathes life. We return it in praise.

Pause for a moment. Feel your breath moving in and out. Offer gratitude to the One who gives it.

BORROW THIS PRAYER

May every breath
That passes my lips
Be an offering of Your love,
So that I might be present
To the people
And places
Set before me.
Amen.

OCTOBER 16

The mystery in a nutshell is just this: Christ is in you, so therefore you can look forward to sharing in God's glory. It's that simple.

COLOSSIANS 1:27 (MSG)

INHALE: I am held
EXHALE: In the mystery.

I sit on the plastic chair across from my son's teacher. She's a recent college graduate brimming with enthusiasm for her students. After we go over my son's grades, the conversation turns to the writing she does when she's not on the clock. I tell her I'm a writer and ask what she's working on.

"I'm writing a historical fiction novel," she says, leaning in. "It takes place in 2006." I cough. *Since when is 2006 historical fiction?* I think. I feel like I could close my eyes and be transported back to that time in an instant. What feels like yesterday to me is ancient history to someone else. Time is a mystery.

In the New Testament, two Greek words describe time: *chronos* time, the kind we count with clocks and calendars, and *kairos* time, the sacred fullness of time that can be felt but never measured.[329] The mystery of God isn't confined by time or space. God holds galaxies and grocery lists, black holes and backpacks. The same divine breath that shaped the stars also fills your lungs.

Paul fills his letter to the early church with *kairos* wisdom. He talks about a mystery once hidden but now revealed in such a wondrous way that it still ripples through time: Jesus doesn't just walk *beside* us—the Spirit lives *within* us. What once felt distant is now as close as our own breath. The "glorious riches" Paul describes is God's boundless presence that crosses generations, cultures, and time itself.*

We live within the mystery, and it dwells within us.

What was now is and what is now was.

Richard Rohr writes, "We bear the mystery of God."[330] Mystery makes us, and we reflect that mystery. Through the passing of time and beyond it, Christ within us holds us in a love that holds every era and every ordinary hour.

Feel your own breath marking this moment. Inhale. Let yourself feel the mystery and movement of time. Exhale. You are in the embrace of the One who spans it all.

RHYTHM OF BREATH

We live in before,
We live in after,
We live in time.
Beyond our understanding,
In the passing,
You are near.
Keeper of time,
Holder of hearts,
Giver of breath,
All exists
In You
And through You.
You were with me then,
You are with me now,
Beyond my understanding.
Your grace laces through hours,
Slips through our fingers.
With You
Time stops and marches forward,
And all that is left to do
Is be.

* Colossians 1:27, NIV.

OCTOBER 17

God, make a fresh start in me, shape a Genesis week from the chaos of my life.

PSALM 51:10 (MSG)

INHALE: Bring beauty
EXHALE: Out of chaos.

My home is a swirl of activity on Monday mornings. On a good day, we're working together, moving in sync as coffee is made and poured and sipped, as we fill backpacks and find missing belts and feed dogs.

But sometimes it feels as though I'm captured in a tornado of chaos, unable to catch my breath in the winds of the day's demands.

But eventually, everyone gets where they need to be in the morning. Our historic home exhales, and so do I. I make my office at the dining room table, stacks of books scattered around me like long-lost friends gathered near as I open my laptop and ask God to help me find the right words to put on the page.

I glance outside through the wavy glass of the hundred-year-old windows and see that the mighty maples are now tipped with gold. Sunlight peeks through the trees as the autumn wind dances through the leaves, sending them floating down one by one in a sacred dance.

I exhale.

I exhale.

I exhale.

I can breathe again.

And I thank God for shaping the newness of life from the chaos of my days.

In this transitional season, where might God be breathing new life and shaping new beginnings from the swirl of chaos in your days?

RHYTHM OF BREATH

In that time, beneath the changing tree,
I rested in a keeping not my own.[331]

Wendell Berry

OCTOBER 18

FEAST OF SAINT LUKE

The Spirit of the Lord is on me, because he has anointed me to proclaim good news to the poor.

LUKE 4:18 (NIV)

INHALE: Help me tell
EXHALE: The story of Your love.

Headline after headline brings news of another tragedy. Another ache. Each one threatens to take my breath away. When the bad news keeps compounding, when I feel powerless and on the edge of hopelessness, I return to breath prayer.

It doesn't fix the world. But it gives God a chance to tend to the fractures of my own heart. It gives me a breath to just *be*. To remember that God is still whispering. To catch a glimmer of hope held in the stories of my own life.

Today, we remember Luke, a physician, an artist, and a storyteller, who saw the world through a lens of compassion. He used his curiosity and gift for paying attention to listen and to hold others' stories with care. Then he wrote down what he heard, giving us one of the four Gospels. Luke's keen observations, empathetic spirit, and unique perspective shaped his account of Jesus' life, helping us see God's presence in even the most complicated stories.

Luke tells stories the other Gospel writers don't include—of an angel whispering to a woman, of shepherds startled by light, of lost sons finding their way home. His account is told through a lens of mercy, filled with the kind of healing that mends both body and soul. Every name he records and every detail he includes offers us a new glimpse of the One who steps fully into our humanity.

Each of us is called, like Luke, to listen. To notice. And to tell of God's nearness in our own way. Even if you don't realize it, *you* are a storyteller. The roles you have, the paths you've journeyed, the history you carry, the work you do . . . *you* have been given ways of seeing the world that only you have to offer. And because of that, *you* can illuminate new angles of who our brilliant God is and help others see who they are in light of that glorious love.

I look around and see so much suffering, so much pain in the stories the world tells. But I wonder how I might be like Luke, writing down the beautiful glimpses of God I've been given, using my own perspective to tell the best story of all, in a way only I can.

How might you listen like Luke? How might you tell of God's presence in the stories you share?

LET IT LINGER

Today, choose a few verses to linger over that are unique to Luke's account. Consider praying today's breath prayer before and after you read:

- Zechariah and Elizabeth (1:5-25)
- The angel's announcement to Mary (1:26-38)
- Mary's visit to Elizabeth (1:39-56)
- Angels appearing to the shepherds (2:8-20)
- Simeon and Anna meeting Jesus (2:25-38)
- The parable of the good Samaritan (10:25-37)
- The parable of the prodigal son (15:11-32)

OCTOBER 19

Forgive as the Lord forgave you.

COLOSSIANS 3:13 (NIV)

INHALE: God of grace,
EXHALE: Help me forgive.

Sometimes the words Christians use can feel jargony, like a stew of Christianese bubbling up in a cauldron.

Grace. Mercy. Forgiveness. These words can blur together in our minds. We hear them so much that they can start to lose their meaning and maybe even feel a little bland, like a fall soup simmering on the stove that needs salt and seasoning to bring out the flavors. But if we pay attention, each of these words can reveal something unique about the heart of God and our own tender, broken hearts.

- *Grace* gives us what we don't deserve.
- *Mercy* spares us from what we deserve.
- *Forgiveness* restores the relationship by releasing what has come between two parties.

Sometimes forgiveness feels impossible. Wounds run deep. Some people might never take responsibility for or repent of the harm they've caused. All of this is so true and real and valid. When we forgive, we don't excuse harm or pretend something didn't hurt when it did. When we forgive, we access a strength beyond our own, refusing to carry the weight of resentment.

"As much as we may desire to follow Jesus's example and live with hearts open to love, as human beings we carry the baggage of the past in unresolved hurt, shame, conflict, anger, resentment, and woundedness, which often causes us to continue to suffer," contemplative teacher Julie Saad writes.[332] But God doesn't intend for us to stay in the suffering.

Jesus teaches us to forgive because forgiveness sets us free to breathe again.

Neuroscience reflects this truth: Forgiveness reduces stress responses in the body, lowering cortisol and calming our hearts. In other words, forgiveness *literally heals us*.[333]

Grace lifts us. Mercy shields us. Forgiveness frees us.

You don't do this work of forgiveness alone. As Jesus reminds us, "In prayer there is a connection between what God does and what you do."* When we're deeply aware that God forgives us, we can access a power beyond ourselves to forgive others.

Be gentle with yourself. Just as forgiveness is a practice and a prayer, it's a process too. As you inhale and exhale through today's breath prayer, invite the Spirit into the places you're hurting. Ask God where forgiveness might be found in this season. Receive the grace and mercy God is breathing into you, right here, right now.

PAUSE AND PONDER

In what ways are you resisting forgiving someone? In what ways are you resisting forgiving yourself?

____

____

____

* Matthew 6:14, MSG.

OCTOBER 20

You must love the Lord your God with all your heart, all your soul, all your mind, and all your strength.

MARK 12:30 (NLT)

INHALE: Help me love You

EXHALE: With every part of me.

Sometimes we get lost in thinking that the way we love God is by how much we *know* about God. Other times we get trapped in the cycle of proving our love by what we *do*. Or maybe we think of faith as simply something we *feel*.

But Jesus calls us to love God with every part of who we are—heart, soul, mind, and strength.

What does it look like to love God with the four corners of your very being?[334]

Heart: Your heart refers to your emotions, your desires, your tenderness, your affection, and your commitments. What are you treasuring? What emotions are stirring in your heart that you can offer up in love?

Soul: This is the part of us that endures, that goes beyond what we can see or hold or touch, that connects us to God's eternal love. Your very existence can be a prayer. How might you spend intentional time with God today?

Mind: Loving God with your mind means feeding your thoughts what is true, lovely, and good.* What are you filling your mind with? What does it look like to have a thoughtful and informed faith?

Strength: Your strength is how you show up in the world. No matter your abilities or limits, the way you show up in the world can be an offering of love. How well do your hands align with your heart?

PRACTICING THE WAY

Box breathing is a simple way to connect with God in prayer. Let your breath remind you that all you feel, all you think, all you do, and all you are can be an offering of love to the One who gives each breath.

- *Inhale:* I love You with all my heart.
- *Hold:* I love You with all my soul.
- *Exhale:* I love You with all my mind.
- *Hold:* I love You with all my strength.

BOX BREATHING

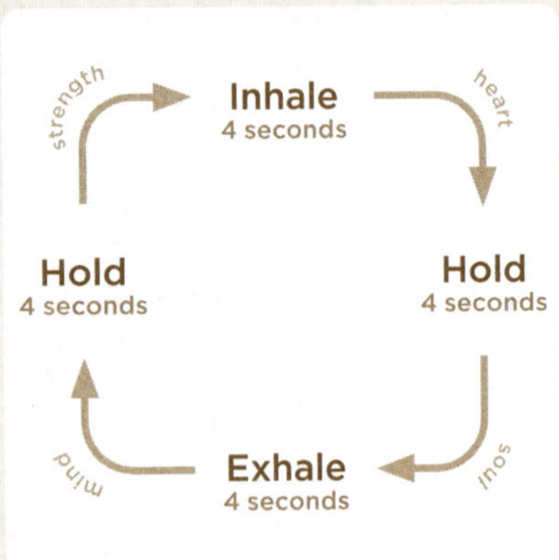

* See Philippians 4:8.

OCTOBER 21

God blesses those who hunger and thirst for justice, for they will be satisfied.

MATTHEW 5:6 (NLT)

INHALE: Make us whole
EXHALE: In You, O Lord.

My husband is a Protestant pastor. Two of my kids attend a Catholic school. At times, this fact earns me the side-eye from both Protestants and Catholics. But I'm unbothered.

Honestly, I'm forever grateful to have experienced the body of Christ in many expressions of faith.

From wooden church pews to stadium-style seating, from folding chairs to park benches, from centuries-old liturgies to spontaneous prayer in multiple languages, every tradition holds beauty—and its fair share of brokenness too.

To hunger and thirst for justice is to long for the world—and the church—to be made *whole*. James Bryan Smith writes that each of the most common faith movements, or "streams," is rooted in Jesus, and each of them has goodness to teach us:

- **Contemplative**: Seeing Christ at prayer; learning intimacy with God
- **Holiness**: Seeing Christ resisting evil; learning the virtues of the heart
- **Charismatic**: Seeing Christ ministering; learning the power of the Spirit
- **Social justice**: Seeing Christ caring for the poor; learning love for neighbor
- **Evangelical**: Seeing Christ opening Scripture; learning the Word[335]

We need the healthy parts of all five movements of faith, Smith says, because "one without the others—or one that dominates the others—will naturally lead to dangerous extremes."[336]

I wonder if, just as we're called to love God with all our heart, soul, mind, and strength, we also need to work together as one body with many parts* while we pray, "Your will be done, on earth as it is in heaven."†

As you breathe through today's breath prayer, ask the Spirit to reveal which part of Christ's body you're being invited to nurture right now.

PAUSE AND PONDER

Sometimes faith movements overemphasize their strength and drift to extremes. For example:

- The contemplative who prays but neglects the needs of the world
- The moralist who strives for purity but forgets to show compassion
- The charismatic who seeks spiritual gifts but neglects the One who gives them
- The social activist who works for justice but doesn't listen to God's voice
- The Bible student who downplays the need for the Spirit[337]

Which of these extremes have you seen abused in your own experiences? How has that shaped your view of the church and of your place in the body of Christ? How might God heal the hurt you carry? What have you been missing in your own faith experience?

* See 1 Corinthians 12:12-27; Ephesians 4:3-6.
† Matthew 6:10, NRSV.

OCTOBER 22

Be brave. Be strong. Don't give up. Expect GOD to get here soon.

PSALM 31:24 (MSG)

INHALE: I'm not giving up;
EXHALE: Help me be strong.

You are doing your best.

And I know sometimes it feels like it's not enough.

Keep going.

Not because you have anything to prove. But because you are *beloved*. And there's a reason that right here, right now, there's breath in your lungs. As Frederick Buechner writes:

> *Be alive this first and holy day because order has been created out of chaos, light out of dark, so you can see, touch, taste, and smell and tell this day that you have never seen before because it has never been before.*[338]

Today is a new day. The story isn't over. It's not by accident that God is breathing life into your lungs at this very moment.

Life is loud. Peace too often feels out of reach. But no matter how awful your situation is, how irredeemable everything feels, or how long you've been waiting for something to change, this will not last forever. This too shall pass.

Be brave. Be strong. Don't give up. Expect God to get here soon.

When the psalmist wrote those words, it was before believers were given God's own Spirit through Christ. Now that same Spirit breathes in you. Nothing—no circumstance, not all the pain and suffering and injustice of the whole world—can separate you from the love of God.*

We're often so much harder on ourselves than we need to be. The voices telling us that we should be on high alert, that we never do anything right, that we can't let our guard down—those voices are not of God. When lies swirl in your soul, remember what God says: "My grace is all you need. My power works best in weakness."†

When the voices in your head whisper that you're getting it wrong and you always will, listen for the still small voice of God that says: "There is no condemnation for those who belong to Christ Jesus."‡

You are safe in God's love. Even in the waiting, God is here.

As you rest in this truth, let your breath become prayer. On your inhale, take a deep breath through your nose. On your exhale, slowly let it go through your mouth.

God is the One breathing bravery and strength into you, even now.

So don't give up.

BORROW THIS PRAYER

Walk me into
The sacred act
Of remembering.
Whisper the ways
You've been with
Me all along.

* See Romans 8:38-39.

† 2 Corinthians 12:9, NLT.

‡ Romans 8:1, NLT.

OCTOBER 23

I'm finding my way down the road of right living, but how long before you show up? I'm doing the very best I can, and I'm doing it at home, where it counts.

PSALM 101:2 (MSG)

INHALE: Guide my steps
EXHALE: Toward what is right.

Golden light filters through the autumn air as we climb the stairs into Boston's Granary Burying Ground. The rays dance across the weathered gravestones of Paul Revere, Samuel Adams, and countless others whose names time has nearly worn away.

We've been walking the Freedom Trail, a path that traces both liberty and lament. "I'm finding my way down the road of right living," I think, echoing Psalm 101 as I marvel at how these same streets that once reverberated with revolution now hum with tourists and school groups.

I pause at a stone: *Samuel Sewall.* A judge during the horrific Salem witch trials, he condemned innocent lives to execution. Five years later, weighed with remorse, he stood before his church congregation and publicly confessed. A few years later, in 1700, Sewall wrote the first antislavery tract published in New England. In it, he refuted justifications of enslavement and cited Scripture to decry it as a crime against God and humanity.

I linger, the contrast of his life choices stirring within me. A man who once used his power to harm later used it to heal. Conviction gave way to repentance, which grew into redemption.

I long for more hearts to turn and leaders to confess, for more everyday people to redirect their lives toward the path of love and justice as they follow the way of Christ.

We all have places where fear or pride once ruled. The Spirit still whispers, *It's not too late to turn around.* Maybe the "road of right living" begins right where we are—doing the very best we can, letting our footsteps lead us to rhythms of truth in our homes, our churches, and our communities—"where it counts."

As you breathe, open your heart. Ask God to illuminate your path.

PAUSE AND PONDER

Where in your life do you sense God inviting you to turn around—to repent and realign? When have you been silent when you could have spoken? Complicit when you could have been courageous?

OCTOBER 24

Just as you do not know how the breath comes to the bones in the mother's womb, so you do not know the work of God, who makes everything.

ECCLESIASTES 11:5 (NRSV)

INHALE: I release my need to know;
EXHALE: I trust You to hold it all.

I don't understand the work of God. I sure wish I did, though.

My husband grew up with a timeline of the "end times." Though Jesus said, "No one knows the day or hour," we still want answers.* We want tidy timelines and proof that things will one day be set right.

We still fall for the age-old trap of thinking that if we just gain enough knowledge, we can be like God. The temptation to trade wonder for control goes all the way back to Eden. But Solomon reminds us, "You do not know the work of God." In Hebrew, the word *ruach* means both *breath* and *wind*, a reminder that the Spirit moves in ways beyond our grasp. If the wind and the womb baffle us, surely the wider workings of God will too.[339]

We don't always want to linger in the mystery. Yet mystery is often the place where faith and trust and awe in our Maker meet.

I always think of Solomon as a little bit emo. And I mean that as a compliment. He wrestled honestly with God about the meaning of life. He didn't pretend to have all the answers. In his wisdom, he knew all that he *didn't know*.

When I travel, I like to settle in as a "passenger princess." When someone else takes the responsibility to navigate us and get us where we're going, I don't need to micromanage. I don't insist on knowing which roads we'll take. I trust that the driver will get us there. I don't understand the intricacies of how the engine works or how the brakes hold. I trust that we'll arrive where we're meant to go.

Faith accepts the mystery of God's work. It relinquishes the desire to always be in control and in the know. It isn't intellectually lazy but inherently curious and rooted in wonder.

The last part of Solomon's verse names God as "the Maker of all things," concluding in awe, grounding every mystery in divine creativity and care.†

Where are you aching to know the *how* when God invites you to rest in the *who*—our Maker, the One who holds it all together?‡

* Matthew 24:36, NLT.

BREATHE THIS IN

You don't have to think about breathing to make it happen. Like the wind, God's unseen work moves through you. Your body already knows what to do. You don't have to control every inhale and exhale—the Maker has shaped you with an automatic rhythm that keeps you alive, breath by breath.

Yet our ever-active, relational God gives you the choice to join in. You can slow your breath or hold it. You can change its cadence with a song or a sigh. When you need to take a break, you can let go, trusting the Giver of each sustaining breath.

Today, how might you notice the quiet miracle of being sustained by God's unseen work?

† NIV.

‡ See Colossians 1:16-17.

OCTOBER 25

There is no room in love for fear. Well-formed love banishes fear. Since fear is crippling, a fearful life—fear of death, fear of judgment—is one not yet fully formed in love. We, though, are going to love—love and be loved. First we were loved, now we love. He loved us first.

1 JOHN 4:18-19 (MSG)

INHALE: Your perfect love
EXHALE: Casts out fear.

Fear knocks on the door constantly. It's polite at first, just a ring or two of a doorbell. But soon it's pounding with its fists, begging to be let in.

Sometimes fear is a needed visitor that keeps us alert and safe from harm. But if fear overstays its welcome, it moves in and takes over—leaving dirty dishes in the sink and socks in the couch cushions, never sharing the remote and demanding attention at all hours of the day and night.

Your heart is a house with limited room. When it's filled with love, there's no space for fear to move in, unpack its suitcase, and get comfy on the couch. Yet fear always tries to make our hearts its home. If we're not careful, fear will drag its baggage inside and invite its friends—control, judgment, and apathy—to stay awhile too.

So much suffering in our world begins when fear displaces peace in the human heart. Fear of being wrong. Fear of being left out. Fear of losing power. Fear that keeps us from seeing our neighbor as fully human.

With God's love, we can kick fear to the curb. As Paul writes, "God gave us a spirit not of fear but of power and love and self-control."* When fear tries to settle in, love is the eviction notice. Fear loses its power when we crack the windows and open the door to God's fresh air of perfect love.

When we're afraid, when we sense danger, our breath quickens. Our muscles tense and our hearts race. But we can remind our bodies that we're safe by taking slow, deep belly breaths rather than quick, shallow breaths in our chests. Belly breathing activates our bodies' relaxation response, reducing our blood pressure, heart rate, and overall stress levels.[340]

Where has fear been knocking on the door of your heart? What might it look like to let God's love answer the door instead?

As you pray today's breath prayer, inhale deep within your core. Slowly let it go, asking God to evict fear from the corners of your heart.

PRACTICING THE WAY

When fear tries to break in, try a simple posture of peace.

1. Sit in a chair.
2. Lean forward.
3. Put your elbows on your knees.
4. Notice your natural breath.

When you feel fear begin to take over, take three slow, controlled belly breaths to interrupt the fight-or-flight response.[341]

* 2 Timothy 1:7, ESV.

OCTOBER 26

Don't panic. I'm with you. There's no need to fear for I'm your God.

ISAIAH 41:10 (MSG)

INHALE: You are here;
EXHALE: I am held.

I sit on the couch next to the fireplace, wrapped in a blanket with a mug of coffee in one hand and my phone in the other. The house is finally quiet. I scroll through the latest headlines: food pantries lacking funds, Christians fighting about Halloween, ten new ways to look younger, a hot holiday decor trend I apparently need to follow.

Panic rises within me. I read the words of Isaiah and Amos and Micah, all prophets speaking words of warning and words of promise to the people of God in shaky times. Still, I find no comfort. Panic bubbles up like a cauldron of toxic stew, threatening to boil over.

I fear a lot. I fear for children's stomachs that ache with hunger. I fear for what's at stake when the church turns inward and forgets its calling. I fear what we say to one another about worth when we spend thousands trying to erase the signs of living. I fear the whisper of scarcity that hums beneath our consumption.

I sit on my couch, and the panic spills over into tears. Where is God in all this? How do we move through a world that's so frayed, so fragile . . . without losing hope?

"Don't panic. I'm with you."

The words Isaiah wrote so long ago meet me like a gentle hand on my heavy shoulders. The promise of God's presence doesn't take away the weight of the world, but when my heart begins to crack under the weight of it, the reminder of God's nearness helps me feel less alone. Less hopeless. God's proximity to our panic doesn't dismiss our fears or deny our worries but points us back to the promise that God knows. God sees. God cares. God *loves.*

I let the tears fall.

When the panic turns to a boil, pause. Set down your phone. Place a hand on your heart. Breathe in slowly and whisper, "You are here." Breathe out and whisper, "I am held." Let your tears spill over. Let your breath become prayer. Let the promise of God's presence settle deep into your soul until peace feels possible again.

BORROW THIS PRAYER

Help me see
That hope exists
Within me
And beyond me.
Help me know
That You are working
Beyond what I can fathom.
Whisper within me
That I get to cocreate
Rhythms of reconciliation
Alongside You,
Beyond what I can imagine.
When I need to catch my breath,
Help me remember
That my humanity
Does not hinder
Your divinity.

OCTOBER 27

Take your everyday, ordinary life—your sleeping, eating, going-to-work, and walking-around life—and place it before God as an offering.

ROMANS 12:1 (MSG)

INHALE: This, too,
EXHALE: Is worship.

If I could pull you aside and tell you anything, I'd put my hands on your shoulders and look you straight in the eye and speak two words:

It matters.

The work you do. The patience you show. The peace you cultivate.

The time you spend listening. The crust you cut off sandwiches. The leaves you rake for a neighbor. The door you hold for the person behind you.

The time you spend praying on your way to work. The conversations you have deep into the night. The homework you help with.

The dishes you scrub. The laundry you fold. The meals you share. How you treat your server. How you treat the person in front of you.

The way you speak to (and about) your coworkers. The bedtime stories you read. The books you tuck into the Little Free Library. The committee meetings you keep showing up to. The emails you send. The door you open. The hug you give.

This, too, is peace.

As Dorothy Day wrote:

> *Paperwork, cleaning the house, dealing with the innumerable visitors who come all through the day, answering the phone, keeping patience and acting intelligently, which is to find some meaning in all these encounters—these things too are the work of peace, and often seem like a very little way.*[342]

As you move through your ordinary day, notice the holiness hiding in plain sight.

Nothing is wasted in God's Kingdom. Everything matters, even the pieces that seem small or even meaningless.

The work of peace is wide and vast.

Don't give up.

It matters. *You* matter.

SACRED ECHOES

Follow your feet. Put on the coffee. Start the orange juice, the bacon, the toast. Then go wake up your children and your wife. Think about the work of your hands. . . . Live in the needs of the day.[343]

Frederick Buechner

OCTOBER 28

FEAST OF SAINT SIMON AND SAINT JUDE

Beloved, build yourselves up on your most holy faith; pray in the Holy Spirit.

JUDE 1:20 (NRSV)

INHALE: There are no lost causes
EXHALE: In Your Kingdom.

When my grandma died, I helped my mom go through some of her belongings. In one box, we found a small autograph book from when she was a girl. I laughed at the silly poems and limericks her friends—and a few boyfriends—had scribbled on the pages.

On the very last page, in thin, elegant script, was a note from her mother: a plea to hold on to faith and stay the course, and a promise that when she took her last breath, she would meet Peter at the gates of heaven.

Reading those unexpected words, just days after my grandma took her last breath, took my own breath away.

The God my grandma was introduced to wasn't always loving or kind. She grew up in a tradition that focused more on sin than mercy, more on fear than grace. And yet she held on to faith. Imperfectly (like all of us) but genuinely.

In Scripture, Jude—Jesus' half brother and a leader in the early church—wrote to believers who were facing confusion and corruption in their community. Much like today, false teachers were twisting the truth and sowing division. Jude wrote to them to stay faithful, to keep praying, and to remain steadfast in the Spirit.

When I was a child, my grandma sent me letters written in blue ink, always signed, "Love, Nana." Jude wrote his letter to the early church with this same kind of affection, calling his readers "beloved" and urging them to build one another up in faith and prayer.

My grandma's heart was sustained by both faith and medicine. As a child, she battled rheumatic fever that damaged her heart. Later, she received two heart valves in surgery made possible through research from St. Jude Hospital—a place that carries on Jude's mission of mercy. As a result, my grandma's heart beat much longer than doctors would have predicted.

The same Spirit who inspired Jude—and who strengthened Judy—dwells in our hearts today.

As you breathe through today's breath prayer, ask the Spirit to help you build your life on faith. Reflect on how you might let love flow into your everyday life.

PAUSE AND PONDER

Who is someone whose faith—imperfect but real—has been breathed into you? What might it mean to honor that inheritance and keep that legacy of love beating in your own heart today?

OCTOBER 29

I will sing to the LORD as long as I live.
I will praise my God to my last breath!

PSALM 104:33 (NLT)

INHALE: Let my breath
EXHALE: Be an offering of praise.

Your life is a song.

Your life is a prayer.

Your life is a breath.

You have the freedom to craft the melody—to create entire symphonies with what you breathe into the world.

Every situation in your day offers a chance to play a note in your song:

Your patience with the coworker who tests you.

Your kindness toward a neighbor who just received hard news.

Your courage when someone tells a racist "joke."

The way you spend your money, your time, your resources, your energy—all of it can become a song of praise with the rhythms of your heart.

The question is: Who does your song point to? Yourself? The culture that's shaping you? Or the One who gives you every single breath?

As you pray today's breath prayer, inhale slowly through your nose, pulling the air deep from your diaphragm. Hold for a few beats, then gently release your breath through your nose.

BREATHE THIS IN

Prayer, like poetry—like breath, like our own names—has a fundamental rhythm in our bodies.[344]

Pádraig Ó Tuama

OCTOBER 30

You, beloved, are worth so much more than a whole flock of sparrows. God knows everything about you, even the number of hairs on your head. So do not fear.

MATTHEW 10:30-31 (THE VOICE)

INHALE: I'm worth more
EXHALE: Than many sparrows.

"Mom!" he bellows from upstairs. I've just sunk into the couch cushions after a particularly long day. My head throbs. My muscles ache. I sigh and stand, knees creaking, to climb upstairs.

I pad into his room and find my youngest son wide-eyed in his bunk bed, which doubles as a stuffed-animal rescue.

"What happened?" I whisper, brushing the hair from his forehead.

"I can't sleep."

"Why?"

"It's . . . *spooky season.*"

He says he thought he heard something—maybe a monster, maybe a ghost. I pray with him, turn on some soft music, and hand him a book to quiet his mind.

I tiptoe back down the hall and hear the steps creak underneath me. Fear shows up for all of us. I'm afraid of a lot of things in this world too. Sometimes I slip into believing I'm too small for God to really care about. God is so big, and I'm just . . . me.

But Jesus said that when we find ourselves swallowed by worry or stretched thin by fear, we can remember the birds—the ordinary sparrows. The ones so common they often go unnoticed.

The same God who fills our lungs with breath knows every single feather, every single flight path. If God cares for creation like that, how much more does God care for us—the ones God became human to dwell among, the ones Christ suffered for, the ones who carry the very breath of God?

When sleep won't come, maybe we don't need to count sheep—we can count sparrows. We can remember we're not alone in our fears. And just as my son calls out to his parents in the night, we can cry out to the One who knows every hair on our heads and calls us beloved.

PAUSE AND PONDER

When I am afraid of ____________, help me remember that You notice even the sparrows. When I feel ______________, remind me that You call me beloved. When I have trouble sleeping, speak __________ into my soul. Help me, O God, remember that You are __________ and __________. When I feel unseen, remind me of Your ____________. Thank You, God, for caring for me when I'm worried about __________ and ___________, and for loving me more than I can understand. Amen.

OCTOBER 31

REFORMATION DAY; ALL HALLOWS' EVE

Teach us to number our days, that we may gain a heart of wisdom.

PSALM 90:12 (NIV)

INHALE: Teach us
EXHALE: To number our days.

Crisp golden leaves crunch underfoot as the late-afternoon sun turns to dusk. Porch lights flicker on. A ballerina, with her glittery tutu swaying in the breeze, skips down the sidewalk. Behind her, a farmer and an inflatable cow companion shuffle down the street. A football player, scooping fallen candy into his jack-o'-lantern pail, shouts for them to wait up.

For many families on this side of town, our historic neighborhood is the closest, safest place to trick-or-treat. Hundreds of kids weave through the streets, and neighbors stay bundled in blankets on their front steps, tallying visitors and giving out candy by the handful.

In 835, the church formally established All Saints' Day on November 1, intentionally reframing a Celtic festival called Samhain, during which people wore costumes and imitated sorcery practices to ward off evil spirits and appease the dead. Instead of fearing the dead, Christians turned their gaze toward hope—the communion of saints, the great cloud of witnesses, and the holy ones whose stories testify that in Christ, death is not the end.

All Hallows' Eve (what we now call Halloween) is the night before All Saints' Day, when Christians have long honored those who lived faithfully before us.

Over the centuries and across cultures, the tradition has shifted in form, but one theme has endured: the ancient Christian practice of *memento mori* ("remember your death"). This isn't meant to be morbid but rather is a spiritual practice of perspective. We remember our mortality when we pray along with Psalm 90:12, "Teach us to number our days, that we may gain a heart of wisdom."

Understandably, some Christians feel uneasy about Halloween—the stories about it have gotten tangled over time. While any celebration can be twisted into practices that stray from God's ways, ideas about Halloween being evil come from misinformation—rumors that took hold centuries ago, notes Danielle Hitchen, author of *Sacred Seasons*.[345]

During the Reformation, some Protestants spread stories to discredit Catholic practices surrounding All Saints' and All Souls' Days.

Although false claims about Halloween still echo through pop culture and from pulpits, the real heart of All Hallows' Eve has always been about remembering that life is fleeting and that, in Christ, death doesn't get the final word.

The cute costumes and neighborly care are pretty sweet too.

BORROW THIS PRAYER

O Light of the World, illuminate the darkness that haunts us. As we follow You, we know we are not immune to fear, but fear cannot hold us captive.[346]

Read more in the "Our Hauntings" chapter of Every Season Sacred.

NOVEMBER 1

ALL SAINTS' DAY

Those who trust God's action in them find that God's Spirit is in them—living and breathing God!

ROMANS 8:5 (MSG)

INHALE: May our lives
EXHALE: Tell Your story.

Sometimes I get stuck in a time warp, forgetting that my here and now isn't the only reality. Right now, more than eight billion people worldwide are experiencing the beauty and heartbreak of being human.

When I get so wrapped up in the pressing demands of the day—and the endless stream of headlines—I lose my sense of perspective. I forget all the stories being lived right now. I forget the ones who came before me, who shaped my story in ways I may never know this side of heaven.

I start to think, *Things are so bad. Things have never been worse.* And in those moments, I lose sight of the generations who held on to faith through their own dark nights—people who never saw all that they were promised but trusted anyway.

The writer of Hebrews tells of Abel, Enoch, Noah, and Abraham, saying, "All these people were still living by faith when they died. They did not receive the things promised; they only saw them and welcomed them from a distance, admitting that they were foreigners and strangers on earth."* The author goes on to list a whole multitude of women and men who lived by faith, even when they were misunderstood and mistreated.

Today is All Saints' Day. This day invites all of us to remember that we're part of a much larger story—the communion of saints, the living and the dead, bound together in Christ. Today, we honor those whose faith shaped us, even if we never knew their names.

Artist Kreg Yingst creates sacred portraits of people of faith across centuries and cultures, depicting saints, mystics, reformers, and activists through woodcuts and linocuts. "Their commonality," he says, "is their love for God and their enduring awareness of God's love for them."[347] His collection *Everything Could Be a Prayer* offers glimpses into their lives, reminding us that faithfulness takes many shapes.

When I reflect on the lives of faithful ones, like Francis of Assisi and Ignatius of Loyola, Dietrich Bonhoeffer and Maximilian Kolbe, Ida B. Wells and Óscar Romero, Martin Luther King Jr. and Josephine Bakhita, I am reminded that while our stories may look completely different, the same Spirit who breathed in them then is still breathing in us today.

Whose faith has shaped you? How might your life of faith light the way for someone else?

BORROW THIS PRAYER

O God who holds all time and trials,
All saints and all souls
In the palm of Your hand,
We thank You for the great cloud of
  witnesses
That goes before us.[348]

Adapted from "A Prayer for All Saints' Day" in To Light Their Way

* Hebrews 11:13, NIV.

NOVEMBER 2

ALL SOULS' DAY

God blesses those who mourn, for they will be comforted.

MATTHEW 5:4 (NLT)

INHALE: We hold their memory;
EXHALE: You hold our tears.

"She's gone."

In a sacred irony, I sat down to write this reflection for All Souls' Day just as my cousin called, her voice trembling as she told me a beloved family member, always a dear presence in our lives, had taken her last breath.

I've been blessed to love and be loved by so many wonderful people. My dad's side of the family has always been tight-knit—cousins and second cousins, boisterous great-aunts and great-uncles gathered at every graduation, wedding, barbecue, and family reunion. It has always felt special.

And now, in grief, it feels holy too.

It's a gift to bear the ache of having someone in your life worth missing.

There's never enough time with the people we love. There are words we wish we'd said, apologies we wish we'd made, hugs we wish we could tuck ourselves into, stories we wish we could hear one more time. But while we have to let them go, whether we're ready or not, we are not left alone. We hold the memories, tucking them deep into our hearts.

When we grieve, we don't just mourn the person we've lost. We also mourn the version of ourselves that existed when they were still on this side of heaven. Our tears are sacred. And as Scripture tells us, our tears are held.*

On All Souls' Day, we reflect on the ones who have gone before us—the flawed, complicated, beautiful souls who shaped who we are and continue to shape who we're becoming.

My friend Alissa, who is Catholic and Mexican American, invited a group of friends to share the names of loved ones we were remembering for her family's *ofrenda*—a small altar to honor those we miss. She texted a photo of a table layered with flowers, candles, and framed pictures. Each name told a story of love and loss and legacy. Though my grandpa died when I was a child, there was something sacred about a friend inviting me into her tradition and making space for me to remember him.

Today, we remember.

We remember because love doesn't end when a heartbeat stops. We remember because memory lingers long after the last breath.

Who are you missing today? Let the breath you've been holding go. As you breathe through today's prayer, let the memory hold you. Inhale. Exhale. Take your time. Be gentle with yourself. There is no one way to grieve. You don't have to rush your breath—or your remembering.

God holds and comforts those who mourn. God holds and comforts *you*.

BORROW THIS PRAYER

For all the souls who have left this world,
For all those of great faith who sacrificed much,
We thank You for their examples
That show us which paths to take
And which to leave covered in brambles.[349]

Adapted from "A Prayer for All Saints' Day" in To Light Their Way

* See Psalm 56:8.

NOVEMBER 3

The LORD is my strength and shield. I trust him with all my heart. He helps me, and my heart is filled with joy.

PSALM 28:7 (NLT)

INHALE: Fill my lungs with life;
EXHALE: Fill my heart with joy.

Joy is for *you*. Right here, right now.

Of course, there's a difference between happiness and joy.

"Happiness turns up more or less where you'd expect it to—a good marriage, a rewarding job, a pleasant vacation," Frederick Buechner once wrote. "Joy, on the other hand, is as notoriously unpredictable as the one who bequeaths it."[350]

In college, I fell in love with a haunting minor-chord version of a childhood song. "I've got the joy, joy, joy, joy down in my heart," the singer-songwriter croons as he strums his guitar. My husband teases me, saying I like happy songs that sound sad. It's true. I do. I'm drawn to the word *melancholy* because it holds space for more than one truth at the same time. We can laugh through our tears. We can grieve and give thanks in the same breath.

We are wonderfully, heartbreakingly human.

Joy, unlike happiness, isn't dependent on circumstance. It can't be manufactured or purchased. It's only given and received. It's a gift that fills our lungs and sustains us, a deep wellspring flowing in even the most hopeless seasons.

Jesus, who was no stranger to melancholy Himself, told His friends as they gathered at their final meal together, "I have told you this so that my joy may be in you and that your joy may be complete."*

Joy is the unguarded smile you have when you catch a glimmer of heaven on earth, the one your friend captures in a candid snap where you're radiant and don't even realize it. Happy is the posed photo. It's not bad; it's just not *joy*.

It's easy to feel weighed down by the world's grief. By the headlines, by the noise, by the ache of it all. But it's not nothing to keep showing up. To stay awake not only to the pain but also to the small glimmers of complete joy—the ones no person or principality or power can take away.

Joy is the blessed assurance that even in the hard parts of life, we can exhale.

Because God is near.

RHYTHM OF BREATH

Leaves dance in the wind,
Swaying in the breeze,
As Joy breathes over them—
Dipping and twirling,
Delighting in the letting-go.
Breathe over me.
I am ready to dance.

* John 15:11, NLT.

NOVEMBER 4

Keep loving each other as brothers and sisters of the sacred family. Do not forget to be kind and welcoming to strangers.

HEBREWS 13:1-2 (FNV)

INHALE: Help us
EXHALE: Keep loving each other.

A sibling relationship is a special bond. You don't have to talk every day to share a deep knowing. There are stories from childhood that no one else could tell quite the same way—moments only the ones who lived them alongside you will ever truly understand.

We're called to love one another in the family of God as brothers and sisters. And if you've ever had a sibling, you know that squabbles are part of it. There's rivalry and misunderstanding, tenderness and forgiveness. There's the ache of being the responsible oldest or the overlooked middle or the left-out youngest. There's laughter and the absolute anger that culminates in shouting, "Mooooom!" There are jealousies and inside jokes.

As followers of Christ, we carry a memory far deeper than childhood—we share the story of redemption, of who we really are. We hold the photo albums of faith: the holidays, the remembrances, the prayers, the promises. We belong to a sacred family that stretches beyond bloodline and background, beyond race and language and nation.

Siblings don't always share the same perspective. We can look back at the same story and remember it in a different way. We can disagree on so much and still share a name. Even across time and distance, we're linked by love.

This love doesn't stay confined to the family circle. The writer of Hebrews reminds us that hospitality is part of holiness: "Do not forget to be kind and welcoming to strangers." Our faith is not a gated community but a table that keeps expanding.

I wish the church were known by that kind of love—by the grace we lavish on each other, the mercy we extend, the way we speak truth with tenderness. I wish our churches were known for flinging the doors wide open, for scooting down the pews, and for making room for more at the table, even as opinions and politics threaten to pull us apart.

In God's family, love is our language. And welcome is our way.

PAUSE AND PONDER

Who do you consider "family" in your faith journey? How has that circle shifted or expanded over time?

____

____

____

When have you experienced the beauty (and challenges) of belonging to a spiritual family in which people have different perspectives and opinions?

____

____

____

NOVEMBER 5

If your first concern is to look after yourself,
you'll never find yourself.

MATTHEW 10:39 (MSG)

INHALE: Reveal what's true;
EXHALE: Teach me to notice.

Maybe you don't usually think of self-awareness as a spiritual practice. But learning to see what's truly happening inside us—our patterns, reactions, and attachments—is part of how we're formed into who God created us to be.

When Jesus says, "If your first concern is to look after yourself, you'll never find yourself," He isn't telling us to neglect our needs. He's inviting us to release the false self—the ego that clings to control, self-protection, and self-importance—so we can awaken to our truest identity in Christ.

One simple way to do this is through a reflective, prayerful practice known as logging. Julie Saad, in *Contemplative Life*, describes *logging* as a form of reflection that helps us notice what's beneath the surface of our days.[351]

Logging isn't the same as journaling or keeping a diary. It's not so much about recounting every detail or dramatizing your stories as it is about noticing and recording moments when strong emotions, reactions, or stories we tell ourselves surface. When you take a minute or two to log something that happened, you write in a simple "captain's log" style, trusting that, over time, God will help you notice patterns underneath.

As we practice logging, we realize something freeing: We're not the only characters in the story. Logging provides perspective. It's a simple exercise that helps us see that our emotions (even the powerful ones) aren't permanent. When I review old entries, I often notice that what once felt unbearably heavy or intense has softened over time. What seemed urgent in the moment loses its grip once it's named and brought before God.

When we honestly bring our inner lives into God's light (without judgment), we start to see how hidden motivations and unexamined emotions influence our choices. Awareness becomes an act of surrender, a way of releasing the false self so the true self can breathe again. And as we awaken, we make more room to love and care for the people God has placed along our path.

PRACTICING THE WAY

Here are some ways to begin a spiritual logging practice (adapted from Julie Saad's *Contemplative Life*).

1. Begin with a short prayer.
2. Recall any moment from the day that stands out.
3. Grab a journal or piece of paper.
4. In one to three sentences, describe the event and your emotional reaction.
5. Write honestly, but don't analyze or judge.
6. Refrain from using "I" statements as much as possible.
7. Don't worry about grammar, spelling, or structure.
8. At the end of the week or month, prayerfully reread what you've written.[352]

NOVEMBER 6

When you give them your breath, life is created,
and you renew the face of the earth.

PSALM 104:30 (NLT)

INHALE: Breath of heaven,
EXHALE: Settle my soul.

I could have avoided a lot of heartache in my life if I'd simply taken a breath before saying—or posting—something I'd later regret. One of the quiet gifts of breath prayer is that it gives us sacred space between what happens and how we respond.

Sometimes practicing that pause saves entire afternoons.

When my son was in second grade, he struggled with big emotions whenever he didn't get a perfect score on an assignment. His frustration often spilled into tears and slammed doors. After talking with the school counselor, my son came home excited to tell me about his "belly breaths."

"We all get frustrated sometimes, and that's okay. But when I get frustrated, I can put my hand on my belly and take a big, deep breath," he told me.

I shared that while he was breathing, he could say a silent prayer, too, asking God for help while taking those big, deep breaths. When he remembers to do this, he feels settled. Science backs up his claim: Slow, intentional diaphragmatic breathing calms the nervous system and reminds our body that we're safe.

Take a deep breath right now—not a shallow breath from your chest, but one from your core. Inhale through your nose for five seconds, hold, and then exhale for eight seconds.

You feel a little better than you did before, don't you?

The simple act of breathing with awareness of God's presence invites the Spirit who first breathed life into creation to breathe renewal into us.

As Psalm 104 reminds us, when God gives breath, new life springs forth, and the earth is made new. That same Spirit moves in our lungs, whispering peace when the world feels loud.

"Christian mindfulness . . . allows us to invite God into all aspects of how we were created," write Regina Chow Trammel and John Trent. "What we consider to be the thinking aspect of mindfulness is grounded in the wisdom that comes from our relationship with Christ."[353]

As you slow down to breathe with intention through today's breath prayer, you are joining the rhythm of divine renewal—the same rhythm that keeps creation alive.

SACRED ECHOES

The presence of the Holy Spirit is made palpable through Christ's breath. If you have ever marveled at the breeze on your face or the wind through the trees, you have already understood invisible power and presence. God, too, can be as real as wind and close as breath.[354]

Laura Kelly Fanucci

NOVEMBER 7

Don't forget to do good and to share with those in need.

HEBREWS 13:16 (NLT)

INHALE: Help me extend
EXHALE: An exhale of love.

He barrels down the hallway, barely able to see over the cardboard boxes towering in his arms. A faithful volunteer in his retirement, he's carrying the stacked pallets to our church's food pantry—each box brimming with cans of green beans, boxes of pasta, and bunches of bananas.

"Here, let me grab that door for you," I say, swinging it open and clearing space for him to get through. I hear him audibly exhale.

It's easy to forget that our breath is shared. It cost me nothing to pause and extend an exhale of help.

This is what we do: We share our breath with those who need it. We exhale God's love into a world that's gasping for air. When we participate in God's sustaining Spirit, our generosity leaves us not depleted but renewed. There's a holy paradox in this: The more we give, the more the Spirit replenishes. We don't run out of breath by giving it away.

Something sacred happens in those everyday exchanges, doesn't it? In that moment at church, when I held the door, both of us caught our breath. I had been rushing, but the Spirit helped me notice someone who needed a hand—and in extending that small kindness, I found my own breath again.

Generosity softens our edges and breathes new life into our hearts.

Research shows that acts of generosity—such as volunteering and even doing simple gestures of kindness—benefit us physically, emotionally, and spiritually. Consistent acts of kindness can lower blood pressure, decrease anxiety and depression, and even strengthen the immune system. A study found that older adults who volunteered for altruistic reasons had a lower risk of mortality over four years than those who didn't.[355]

Goodness and generosity aren't one-time acts of charity but rhythms that, with God's help, can become as natural as breathing. We do good not to earn a gold star on some cosmic chore chart but because when we're filled with the breath of God, we can't help but breathe that goodness back into the world.

How might you offer an exhale to someone today? Where might you pause long enough to offer the simple gift of your attention, presence, or care?

PRACTICING THE WAY

When you're stressed, your sympathetic nervous system is on high alert. Box breathing, according to Cleveland Clinic, helps move your body out of fight-or-flight mode by activating the parasympathetic nervous system—the body's natural way to rest and reset.[356]

- Inhale through your nose for four counts.
- Hold your breath for four counts. Notice how the air fills your lungs and belly.
- Exhale slowly through your mouth for a count of four.
- Hold the emptiness for four counts.
- Repeat several times, inviting the Spirit to fill you with renewal and release.

NOVEMBER 8

Where do you think all these appalling wars and quarrels come from? Do you think they just happen? Think again. They come about because you want your own way, and fight for it deep inside yourselves.

JAMES 4:1 (MSG)

INHALE: Heal our wounds

EXHALE: So they won't turn into wars.

Everything comes from *something*.

Wars don't just appear on the horizon. Fights don't erupt out of nowhere. They begin deep within us—in desires that twist toward control, fear, or pride.

If you go back far enough in that galaxy far, far away, even Darth Vader had a wound that became a war.

The battles we see "out there" often echo the unrest "in here." When anger or defensiveness spills over, it's usually because those feelings have been simmering in our souls for a while. The conflicts we unleash into the world often start small, like the first small bubbles rising to the surface in a cauldron of resentment or insecurity, until they spill over and burn everything they touch.

"Are not our wars, our riots, our plots, suspicions, arms races, all signals and symptoms that our community bodies are still suffering and bleeding from unhealed agony, unhealed hostility, and mutual assaulting over many centuries?" asks Flora Slosson Wuellner. She says that just as our physical bodies send us signs through pain or fever, so do our communal bodies.

"What if we began to listen?" she asks. "What if we began to pray, not just for the surface symptoms, but for the depths of pain and disease?"[357]

The contemplative path turns inward, not in self-absorption, but in holy awareness. Praying alongside our breath is a simple way to ask God to tend the places within us where conflict begins. When we slow down long enough to notice what's happening beneath the surface, we realize that the external chaos often mirrors our internal unease. Everything comes from something—and in God's grace, healing does too.

Peace on earth is planted in the soil of our souls.

As contemplative writer Caroline Oakes writes in her book *Practice the Pause*, God is both within us and beyond us, "a universal and yet intimate inner presence and power that can *transform humanity*."[358] Through prayer and practice, she writes, we open our hearts to that transforming Spirit.

What if transformation begins not just in nations or systems but in souls that learn to breathe goodness instead of stewing in greed?

LET IT LINGER

When James speaks of conflict arising from disordered desires, he points us toward *formation* rather than *condemnation*. The battles of ego, fear, and scarcity begin within—but so does the peace of Christ.

NOVEMBER 9

We know how dearly God loves us, because he has given us the Holy Spirit.

ROMANS 5:5 (NLT)

INHALE: God of love,
EXHALE: Fill me with Your Spirit.

"Make yourself at home," my friend Lauren says, smiling as she hands me a mug of coffee and swivels my suitcase toward the hallway.

Road-weary, I kick off my sneakers and exhale.

I take in every lampshade and piece of art on the walls. Intentionality shines through every nook and cranny, each bedroom representing a continent in the world God so loves. Lauren and her husband have poured themselves into every detail of their home—windows that welcome the morning light, shelves filled with stories and wisdom, corners softened by blankets and pillows that invite lingering. They want anyone who walks through their doors to breathe a sigh of relief.

They call their home *Pneuma Creek*.

Nestled beside a bubbling brook in Middle Tennessee, their home is named after the Greek word *pneuma*, which means "breath," "wind," or "spirit." It's the same word the New Testament uses for the Holy Spirit, the very breath of God that animates and renews all things. In Hebrew, the word is *ruach*—the breath that hovered over the waters at creation and filled the prophets with courage. *Pneuma* and *ruach* both tell us that God's love moves us, fills us, and gives us hope.[359]

When Paul writes in his letter to the Romans that "we know how dearly God loves us, because he has given us the Holy Spirit," he isn't offering an empty reassurance. He's naming the reason we can keep hoping when the world feels off its axis.

Hope is listening to the quiet whisper that God's Spirit breathes within us, even when we can't yet see what's ahead.

At Pneuma Creek, my friends created a space where hope is found and where weary souls can come and breathe again. But you don't need to travel to Tennessee to find that kind of rest. Wherever you are, the Spirit is already near, pouring love into the cracks of your tired heart, reminding you that disappointment doesn't have the final word.

Take a breath. Feel it move through you. That's *pneuma*. That's *ruach*. That's God's love. And as long as that love is near, so is hope.

PRACTICING THE WAY

If you're able, take a short walk outside. Feel the autumn air entering and leaving your lungs—God's Spirit breathing life into you. Notice the world around you. Do you see the sway of the trees? Smell the leaves? Feel the early November chill?

As you walk, whisper today's breath prayer. Let the cadence of your steps and the rhythm of your breath keep you company. Let each inhale remind you that hope isn't far away. Let each exhale remind you that hope is here, right here, right now.

When your walk ends, pause and pray: *Spirit of love, thank You for breathing hope into me again.*

NOVEMBER 10

The one who formed you says, "Do not be afraid, for I have ransomed you. I have called you by name; you are mine."

ISAIAH 43:1 (NLT)

INHALE: You call me by name;
EXHALE: I will not be afraid.

"We're going downstairs!" I shout as the sky turns an unsettling shade of green. Once everyone is safe and settled, I glance out the window and watch as the wind bends trees as if they're rubber. The force tears through neighborhood after neighborhood, ripping century-old roots from the ground and splitting our city open.

Sometimes the worst storms don't come with warning sirens and weather alerts—they're the whirlwinds of our own making—tornadoes of striving and control, in which we twist ourselves up to hold everything together. We rush and spin, hoping motion will save us, afraid of what will happen if we just . . . stop.

In all the noise and chaos and striving, Isaiah tells us that we don't have to be afraid. God still whispers, *Do not be afraid. I have called you by name. You are Mine.*

When my children spin in their own small tempests of frustration or fatigue, I sometimes place a hand on their shoulder and say their name. That little reminder of being known calls them back to the moment, reminding them of who they are and that they belong here, at home, not in the land of Oz.

Calling someone by name is intimate. Isaiah describes God's care and attention for His people, offering a preview of what's to come in John 10:3, when Jesus, the Good Shepherd, calls His sheep by name. At the resurrection, Jesus finally says, "Mary," to get her attention. He calls her by her name, and in that moment, her heart, battered and bruised after witnessing His death on the cross, awakens. She knows His voice.* And she knows deep within her soul that the One who calls her name can truly quell any storm.

When you forget who you are, God whispers your name back into the storm. Even when the chaos is of your own making, the One who calls you beloved is the One who stills the winds within too.

The breath that formed you is stronger than any wind that tries to pull you apart.

As you breathe through today's breath prayer, reflect on the storms stirring within you. What inner or outer winds are threatening to steal your balance?

PRACTICING THE WAY

Sit down in a chair with your feet flat on the ground. Imagine standing in a storm, the swirl of the wind wrapping around you, threatening to pull you off your feet and carry you into the unknown.

Whisper today's breath prayer.

Imagine Jesus placing His hand on your shoulder, whispering your name. Feel your feet on the ground beneath you, and let your breathing slow.

As you close, offer a word of thanks for the One who is in every storm.

---

* See John 20:16.

NOVEMBER 11

VETERANS DAY

God blesses those who work for peace,
for they will be called the children of God.

MATTHEW 5:9 (NLT)

INHALE: May the work of peace
EXHALE: Begin in me, O God.

With a few quick clicks, groceries appear on my doorstep. I can video-call a friend in seconds. Clean water flows from the tap. A machine washes my clothes while I write these words. The hum of the heater kicks on as I pop open a can of ice-cold sparkling water from the fridge.

The privilege of not having to labor over what my ancestors toiled for—and what many still do today—is not lost on me. But no matter how much ease we hold at our fingertips, peace isn't delivered with a click or secured by a post. Peace takes work. Real, everyday work.

Jesus didn't bless those who avoided conflict to keep things comfortable. He blessed the ones willing to roll up their sleeves and do the long, slow, sometimes messy work of peacemaking—the ones who plant and tend peace in their ordinary lives.

When we're disconnected from that kind of work, we become like the people Jeremiah warned of: "They dress the wound of my people as though it were not serious. 'Peace, peace,' they say, when there is no peace."*

Talking about peace and *doing the work* of peace are two very different things. Jeremiah exposed the surface-level solutions of leaders who half-heartedly covered gaping wounds with tiny Band-Aids, using words instead of action. Their carelessness revealed a lack of genuine concern, a refusal to engage in the sacred work of *shalom*—the wholeness and harmony of life with God, others, and oneself.

But working for peace—true peace—goes beyond our personal preferences. It means having compassion for the people in our homes, workplaces, and communities. Being a peacemaker isn't just saying the right thing but doing it—and doing it *again* and *again* and *again*. Even when it's hard. Peacemaking becomes a rhythm of lived faith.

We can't cultivate peace in our families, neighborhoods, or churches if we neglect the work of peace within our own hearts. True peace requires humility, forgiveness, and sometimes sacrifice. It invites us to put others' needs before our own and to seek God's wisdom in the midst of the tension. Peacemaking unsettles the powerful and unnerves the complacent.

Thankfully, we don't do this work alone.

Pause for a breath right now. On your inhale, breathe in *shalom*. On your exhale, ask God what keeps you separated from this kind of peace. Ask God to strengthen your heart so you might be an everyday peacemaker, today and in the days to come.

SACRED ECHOES

[Peace] does not mean we must avoid conflict. Rather, peace is a reflection of what is to come in heaven in our relationships with God.[360]

Regina Chow Trammel and John Trent

* Jeremiah 6:14, NIV.

NOVEMBER 12

Your beauty and love chase after me every day of my life.

PSALM 23:6 (MSG)

INHALE: Your beauty and love
EXHALE: Chase after me.

God's love chases us through both the beautiful and the terrible.

It's not some Holy Spirit version of capture the flag—God's love chases you to be with you, to surround you with light, to guide you, to laugh with you, to hold your tears.

To *stay*.

So much of this life isn't beautiful, we know that. As Frederick Buechner writes,

> *The grace of God means something like: Here is your life. You might never have been, but you are because the party wouldn't have been complete without you. Here is the world. Beautiful and terrible things will happen. Don't be afraid. I am with you. Nothing can ever separate us. It's for you I created the universe. I love you.*
>
> *There's only one catch. Like any other gift, the gift of grace can be yours only if you'll reach out and take it.*
>
> *Maybe being able to reach out and take it is a gift too."*[361]

God's beauty and love have chased after you all the days of your life.

That time you climbed the tree and fell.

Your first smile, your first wobbly steps.

The tooth you tucked beneath your pillow.

The night you cried into that same pillow after your first heartbreak.

The first slow dance. The packed boxes. The hush of the first snow.

The waiting room at the hospital, when time stood still.

The weddings. The funerals. The long, quiet walks.

The babies you've held and the children you've chased.

Every blown-out candle and every blown-out tire.

You've never been alone. All those tears you've cried, those questions you've carried—grace has been there all along, and it's running toward you still.

Take a deep breath. Feel it fill your lungs. That's grace—you didn't earn it, and still it comes.

Even in the terrible parts, even when you can't feel it, Love hasn't stopped chasing you.

LET IT LINGER

Pause for a moment. Breathe in the gift of being loved. Exhale the fear that you've been forgotten. You are here—because Love wanted you here.

NOVEMBER 13

God's Sunrise will break in upon us, shining on those in the darkness . . . then showing us the way, one foot at a time, down the path of peace.

LUKE 1:78-79 (MSG)

INHALE: Light the way
EXHALE: To the path of peace.

As days grow shorter and autumn skies turn gray, darkness can feel like a mist settling over everything. We long for the sun-drenched hope of summer, yet the seasons shift whether we're ready or not.

Even in the darkest season, dawn keeps coming.

The promise of Luke's Gospel is that light has already broken in through Christ, even when we can't yet see it clearly.

Zechariah, the father of John the Baptist, finally spoke after months of silence. He had doubted, yet when his voice returned, he sang of God's sunrise breaking through the shadows, of a steady beam of sacred light guiding our steps, one at a time, down the path of peace.*

Peace is a path that leads us toward wholeness, illuminated from within by the Light of the World.

When everything feels dim, pause.

What if your breath could remind you that the Light is still showing you the way?

"The value of a deep breath is something we must continue to learn and relearn on the path to peace," artist and poet Morgan Harper Nichols writes. We exchange "quick, shallow breaths for a cycle of breath that represents the fullness of how we were meant to breathe—mindfully, wholly."[362]

As you pray, take a slow, deep breath for a count of seven. Feel your lungs fill with air. Exhale just as slowly, imagining your breath illuminating the darkness.

Let this rhythm—the rise and fall of your breath, the sound of your feet stepping one in front of another on the path of peace—be a prayer, a reminder that even in darkness, the Light is closer than your next breath.

RHYTHM OF BREATH

Peace to the one who wonders,
Peace to the one who feels alone,
Peace to the hurting, the tired, the weary,
Peace to the one who can't let go.
Peace go before you, beside you,
  behind you,
Peace in the places no one knows.
Peace to the hallowed halls of your heart,
Peace in the morning light,
Peace in the evening whispers of dusk,
Peace, peace, peace.

* See Luke 1:78-79.

NOVEMBER 14

As we have opportunity, let us do good to all people.

GALATIANS 6:10 (NIV)

INHALE: As long as I have breath,
EXHALE: Help me speak peace.

You have a story worth telling.

And as long as you have breath in your lungs, other people need to hear it. Your story matters—and it's yours to tell. You may feel like your life has been small, tucked into ordinary routines that no one really notices. But in a world where the loudest voices often receive the most attention, we need stories of quiet faithfulness, of everyday acts of peace, goodness, and hope in our weary world.

Even the faintest whispers of peace do more for the Kingdom of God than the loudest shouts of greed and power. In God's economy, the smallest acts of love can outpower the biggest acts of hate.

The widow's two coins, offered without fanfare, carried more weight than the lavish gifts of the wealthy but hard-hearted.*

The smallest act of love can upend the most profound hatred. The Kingdom Jesus talks about turns our ideas about worth and what matters upside down.

The world says, "Be big." The Kingdom says, "Be faithful."

The world says, "Be loud." The Kingdom says, "Listen well."

The world says, "Fight for power." The Kingdom says, "Serve in love."

The One who could have ridden in on a warhorse chose a donkey.

The One who could have feasted with kings broke bread with friends.

The One who could have commanded the world to bow knelt to wash feet.†

In this upside-down kingdom, the humble path is the way.

As long as there's breath in your lungs, there is good for you to do—good that you are uniquely situated to breathe into the world.

PAUSE AND PONDER

Reflect on a time when you felt that your quiet faithfulness went unnoticed. How might God be reminding you that small doesn't mean insignificant?

When you reflect on Jesus—the humble King who rode a donkey, broke bread, and washed feet—what do you notice stirring in your heart? How do you sense the Spirit inviting you to trade big for small or power for service?

* See Luke 21:1-4.

† See Luke 16:10; James 1:19; Mark 10:45; Matthew 21:7; Luke 7:34; and John 13:4-5.

NOVEMBER 15

The Spirit of God has made me, and the breath of the Almighty gives me life.

JOB 33:4 (NLT)

INHALE: As I breathe,
EXHALE: I hope, O God.

Every inhale, every exhale, is a gift. But if we're honest, that declaration feels a bit cliché. How can something so constant, so seemingly ordinary, be . . . *sacred*? Really?

We don't earn or deserve the breath in our lungs. We can't achieve it or pass it along. Breath is an act of divine generosity that only the Creator can give.

In a whirlwind of unimaginable loss, Job doesn't say, "God *gave* me life." He says, "God *gives* me life." The Hebrew word *ruach*—meaning breath, wind, spirit—reminds us that God's life-giving presence is not a past event but an ongoing act of creation and sustenance.[363]

Each time air fills our lungs, God holds us together, moment by moment, breath by breath. Every healthy cell in your body is oxygenated by divine generosity. Every heartbeat is proof that God is making you whole as God holds you together.

"Just as God breathed the breath of life into the first living being, so our deep, instinctive taking of breath is receiving again the gift of life from God for each moment," writes Flora Slosson Wuellner.[364] As long as we have breath, we have hope. Hope that's so near we forget to see it, fail to feel it coursing through our veins and beating in the chambers of our hearts. Hope that God is near and this is not the end.

All the wars and shouting and infighting, all the needless suffering and unfathomable sorrows, all the talking points and lines in the sand—none of it, not one breath of it, gets the final word.

The One who formed you is breathing into you. Right here. Right now.

"*Dum spiro spero*," the Roman philosopher Cicero said.

As I breathe, I hope.[365]

SACRED ECHOES

When we observe our loved ones sleeping, old or young, human or pet, we are instinctively drawn to their breath. There is something essential in it we are all attuned to, something we both automatically and unconsciously equate with life. Each time we check on each other, we are validating the words of the Roman philosopher Cicero, *dum spiro, spero*, "As I breathe, I hope."[366]

Michael J. Stephen

NOVEMBER 16

The LORD is close to the brokenhearted.

PSALM 34:18 (NLT)

INHALE: Take this broken heart
EXHALE: And make me whole.

He leads me into a room, where a giant rectangle covered in wrapping paper waits patiently on an easel. "Go ahead, open it," my husband says with a smile. "Just . . . be careful."

I peel back the layers of wrapping to reveal a large stained glass window—an intricate design inspired by the cover of my book *Every Season Sacred*. It takes my breath away. The detailed glass shapes, each with its own color and texture, have been pieced together to make something beautiful. Light filters through, and I can almost see the water move, the fields sway, the snow fall, the sun glisten.

My generous, creative, and ever-supportive husband commissioned our friend Scott to create it—a window mirroring my book's cover, itself inspired by the sanctuary-style windows on the third floor of our 115-year-old home.

"Do you recognize those pieces?" he asks, pointing to the thick, wavy panes in the center. "They're from a window that used to be in the sunroom. I gave Scott a pane I found in the basement."

Scott is a friend, a neighbor, a member of our church family. A father and a grandfather. A retiree from John Deere who once worked with heavy machinery and now works with light. He often says he meets God in the quiet of his basement workshop. He takes shards others might overlook and calls them beautiful, bringing them into a new story filled with light.

I can't imagine a clearer picture of the gospel.

Artists are the ones among us who pay attention. The ones who feel the brokenness alongside us and can't help but offer something beautiful in the midst of it. "Art is an invitation to empathy. Empathy is the space where we are reminded that there is abundant room for what we are feeling," artist Morgan Harper Nichols writes. "And when we sense we have permission to truly feel our emotions, we are free to put our guard down and breathe."[367]

When the sun hits that stained glass window, my whole office glows. What was once fractured now tells a new story—one that couldn't exist without breaking.

There have been seasons when sorrow wrapped around my chest like a vice, when every breath was a battle, when I could only whisper *why*. But the same God who shaped the stars gathers the shards of your heart, holding them with the care of an artist. In divine hands, even the smallest, sharpest fragments hold meaning.

The story isn't over. The light will find its way through the cracks.

Your broken heart doesn't scare away the One who breathes life into you.

PRACTICING THE WAY

Visio divina invites us to ask what God might be revealing to us through art. Just as lectio divina helps us listen for God through Scripture, visio divina helps us look for the sacred through sight.

As you look at this window, imagine God as Artist, gathering the pieces of your heart and fitting them together with gentleness, care, and purpose to tell a story of love. What might it look like as light filters through?

NOVEMBER 17

One's life does not consist in the abundance of possessions.

LUKE 12:15 (NRSV)

INHALE: Help me resist
EXHALE: The siren song of more.

"Run, don't walk!" she shouts, shopping bags hanging from her arms. "You *have* to have these shoes, but *hurry*! The sale won't last long!"

I sigh and swipe out of the app. If I wanted to run, I'd take the pile of clothes off my treadmill.

As a kid of the nineties, I grew up on a steady stream of infomercials not dissimilar to the influencer culture infiltrating social media today. Enraptured by the commercials that punctuated my cartoons, I was fascinated by why every price ended in .97 or .99 and why everything from rotisserie cookers to exercise contraptions was offered for a "low, low price." I hadn't yet learned the intricacies of marketing psychology.

Today, our shopping channels fit in the palm of our hands. Algorithms track not just our clicks but the content we linger on and what we search for, quietly tailoring sponsored content to our insecurities and desires. The average American now sees four thousand to ten thousand ads *per day*.[368]

Jesus' warning in Luke 12:15 came as he addressed a man demanding his share of his inheritance. He saw through the surface argument to the deeper problem of *pleonexia*—the Greek word for "greed," meaning an insatiable desire for *more*.[369]

My friend Tara, who runs an organizing business called House Peace, often sees this. She helps people declutter not only their homes but also their hearts. Sometimes she works with those in hoarding situations, quietly donating her own time and resources to help them find freedom. Where others might see a punchline, Tara sees a person—someone who is hurting and also beloved, worthy of peace.

No matter how much we accumulate, we can't take it with us.

It's a simple truth but a hard one to grasp: Only God can satisfy our souls.

When do you feel the strongest desire to buy your way to a better life? What might that moment be revealing about what you truly long for?

BORROW THIS PRAYER

For those chasing more,
Lord, in Your mercy, hear our prayer.
For those burdened by debt,
Lord, in Your mercy, hear our prayer.
For those who accumulate instead of share,
Lord, in Your mercy, hear our prayer.
For those who don't have enough,
Lord, in Your mercy, hear our prayer.
For those whose insecurities are preyed upon,
Lord, in Your mercy, hear our prayer.
For those who equate status with worth,
Lord, in Your mercy, hear our prayer.
For those who believe they must buy to be seen,
Lord, in Your mercy, hear our prayer.

NOVEMBER 18

Pray diligently. Stay alert, with your eyes wide open in gratitude.

COLOSSIANS 4:2 (MSG)

INHALE: Here You are, God;
EXHALE: I'm paying attention.

When I worked in journalism, every editor on the magazine masthead had a specific role, falling into macro- and micro-editing.

Editors tasked with macro-editing helped shape the overall direction of the features and articles, capturing the essence of each piece and refining the writer's tone and voice. The copy editors, who focused on micro-editing, ensured that every comma was correctly placed and each word was spelled perfectly.

Both types of editors were needed to make a cohesive publication.

I think of our deep and wide conversations with God as macro prayers: long stretches of simply listening with our hearts or cathartic listings of everything on our minds.

When I think of breath prayers, I see them as micro moments of prayer with God, tucked into the pockets of everyday life.

Breath prayer is one way to, as Colossians reminds us, "pray diligently."

You can inhale and exhale as you walk the dog, rake the leaves, shop for groceries, or wait for an oil change. It's a way to pray without ceasing—to open your eyes and recognize God's presence in the middle of your real life.

Contemplatives refer to breath prayer as a form of *active prayer*—a way of praying that accompanies us, helping us remain present with God as we go about our days. It's a way to, as Psalm 119 says, ponder "the miracle-wonders" of God in our everyday lives.*

When we intentionally connect with God through prayer during our daily routines, noticing God's beauty in our actual lives, we are shaped more into Christ's image.

"The contemplative tradition suggests that to be so acutely aware of God's beauty in anything leads to awareness of God's beauty in everything, save that which is evil," Dr. Curt Thompson writes. "Thus, we see God's beauty and presence even in those people whom we consider to be our enemies, as well as in the brokenness and chaos of this world. And we are compelled to become agents of mercy and justice where they are so desperately needed."[370]

Going through the motions is easy. But with God's help, we can recognize what's already right in front of us—the beautiful, glorious wonder of the One who was, is, and is to come.

And that changes *everything*.

PRACTICING THE WAY

What small, ordinary moment could become your breath prayer cue today?

Choose something like waiting at a stoplight, the ping of a text notification, or a fresh cup of coffee to serve as a tiny reminder to pray in the midst of your everyday life.

* Psalm 119:17-24, MSG.

NOVEMBER 19

Everything God created is good, and to be received with thanks.

1 TIMOTHY 4:4 (MSG)

INHALE: I receive Your goodness
EXHALE: With thanks, O God.

My husband tucks the hospital blanket around our son. We count his fingers, then his toes. He's less than a day old. He's impossibly small, and at the same time, he's also the whole world, swaddled inside that bundle. Rosy cheeks. Big, alert eyes.

My husband turns and places the baby into my younger brother's arms. He's in college, and he has never held a baby before. His arms stiffen; his shoulders tense. For a moment, he holds the baby like a football player gripping a freshly won trophy, unsure what to do next.

Because I'm an older sister, I laugh. But I know he's got this. And he does. His arms relax. His body softens. I look at him, seeing the little boy who is now an uncle, holding my little boy, and I see glistening in him what I've seen in the eyes of every other visitor—from our pastor to my grandparents—*awe*. That quiet reverence that sneaks in when you come face-to-face with something undeniably good.

The earth seems to hold its breath in that sacred pause when someone welcomes a newborn. Creation waits just for a moment as strong arms become gentle and every sense sharpens with wonder. Then, like an exhale, when the baby is placed in outstretched arms, we can almost hear our Creator whisper, *This is good.*

That's the heartbeat of Paul's reminder to Timothy: "Everything God created is good."

The inherent goodness of creation is a gift—and the only fitting response to a gift so good is gratitude.

How we receive the world shapes how we live in it. Do we open our hands and say, "Thank You," or do we clench our fists tight, afraid of losing what we have?

How might the way you treat others change if you reflected on the fact that they, too, were once a vulnerable baby—and for them, as for you, creation once held its breath as they were placed in someone's arms?

As we stand at the precipice of Advent, anticipating the arrival of the baby who took His first breath and changed the course of history forever, we pause here, in the posture of thanksgiving. In the sacred rhythm of noticing the goodness of God, receiving the gifts of creation, and whispering, "Thank You."

Everything God made is good because God is good.

And every piece of God-breathed creation—including *you*—was meant to be received with love.

As you pray through today's breath prayer, receive each inhale with thanks.

BREATHE THIS IN

From their very first days of life, babies' breathing and heartbeats work together. Healthy newborns exhibit a natural rhythm between their respiratory rate and heart rate. Even before a baby learns to smile, their body is already practicing harmony.[371]

This built-in rhythm reminds us that our Maker created us with intention and connection, ordering us in love, down to the tiniest pulse within us.

What a good gift.

NOVEMBER 20

My dear friends, don't let public opinion influence how you live out our glorious, Christ-originated faith.

JAMES 2:1 (MSG)

INHALE: I live for You
EXHALE: And no one else.

We live in times when anyone can share their opinion about anything at any time.

And sadly, when we veer from Christ, our thoughts and judgments become a lot more critical and a lot less compassionate. The court of public opinion is swift—and often cruel.

God didn't create us to constantly calculate what other people think of us. As a mom of tweens and teens, I see it every day: the pressure to perform, to curate, to be seen a certain way. I remember those middle school years, when I felt utterly undone by the thought of what people might think of me. Some days, I still feel that tug.

But what Jesus said matters most. He said everything can be summed up in this greatest commandment: "Love the Lord your God with all your heart, soul, mind, and strength—and love your neighbor as yourself."*

James reminds the early church that their actions should mirror Christ, who treats everyone with dignity and respect—without care for social status, without favoritism or pretense. Life in Christ doesn't play favorites—it scoots over and says, "You can sit with us."

Faith lived out looks like joy in justice lived out.† It sounds simple, but sometimes the way of love is misunderstood or even mocked.

People might not understand why you keep showing up at the food pantry, quietly stocking shelves instead of posting about it. They might not get why you don't join the chaos of the comment section or why you speak up against injustice when silence would be easier. Or they might not be able to wrap their minds around how, in a world with so much pain, you keep an eye open for goodness and beauty and humor and hope. Why you spend time resting or creating when there's just so much that needs to be done.

Sometimes, even those closest to us—our families, our churches, our communities—don't quite know what to do with us. I've felt that tension too. When you care deeply about Jesus *and* justice *and* joy, it's hard to fit neatly into anyone's box. But maybe that's the point.

Because of Jesus, we can enter into the hardest places and still find beauty. Because of Jesus, we can work for a more flourishing world *and* delight in the laughter that surprises us along the way. We can weep with those who weep and rejoice with those who rejoice.‡

Christ holds the center. And because we're held together by peace that passes understanding—the peace only Christ can give—we can hold justice in one hand and joy in the other.

---

* See Mark 12:28-34.
† See Psalm 97:1-2.
‡ See Romans 12:15.

PAUSE AND PONDER

On this chart, write *Jesus* in the bottom circle, *justice* on the left, and *joy* on the right. In each circle, write a prayer, a word, or a phrase that describes how these show up in your life right now. Where do they overlap?

Notice what rises in you as you reflect. Where might Jesus be inviting you to hold justice and joy together?

NOVEMBER 21

He rescues those whose spirits are crushed.

PSALM 34:18 (NLT)

INHALE: When I am crushed,
EXHALE: You are near.

In the heartache you try to hide. In the questions you're afraid to ask. In every tear you fight so valiantly to hold back. In every moment you've felt so deeply, utterly alone . . . God is near.

That ache you feel—the heaviness in your bones, the cotton-wool haze in your mind, the heart that feels like bits of sea glass adrift in the abyss—none of it frightens the One who made you.*

When sorrow wraps around your heart like a vice, when every breath feels like a battle to survive, when each inhale stings and each exhale reminds you how empty the room sounds without the one you love, the dream you held, the hope you lost—the Holy One comes close.†

When all you can manage is *why* or *what now*, when the tears run dry and you're left treading water in an ocean of grief, the One who walks on water, the One who speaks and calms the roaring sea moves toward *you*.‡

You don't have to keep fighting to stay afloat. You don't have to grip the raft so hard. You are safe. You are *held*.

There's not a single breath you take that isn't held by the One who holds you.§

It was never supposed to be this way—all this sorrow, all this pain. And yet even here, rescue begins.¶

This will not last forever. The tide will turn. Somehow, someway, you will catch your breath.

And when you do, may you feel the calm presence of the One who never left your side.

BORROW THIS PRAYER

Comfort the hurting,
Heal the brokenhearted,
Remind me that
This is not the end.
Amen.

* See Psalm 139:13-14; Isaiah 46:4.
† See 2 Corinthians 1:3-4.
‡ See Psalm 107:28-30.
§ See Isaiah 46:4.
¶ See Romans 8:22; John 16:33.

NOVEMBER 22

Let all that I am praise the LORD; may I never forget the good things he does for me.

PSALM 103:2 (NLT)

INHALE: Help me remember;
EXHALE: I don't want to forget.

"Stand over here," my father-in-law calls to me. "And I'll show you what it's like."

He places a handful of "flowers" (forks) in my hands and uses me as an object lesson for our family. One by one, he removes a fork to show what it can feel like for someone living with dementia—how memories begin to slip from reach.

My husband's grandfather had just moved in with Jonny's parents and needed more daily care. Though it was uncomfortable and awkward to stand there in the living room holding forks, Jonny's dad was trying to show us what was happening. (To his credit, that was twenty-five years ago, and I haven't forgotten it.)

We are a people of memory, of telling and retelling who we are and who God is, reminding one another not to forget God's goodness.*

In the Old Testament, God's people set up "stones of remembrance"† so future generations would ask, "What do these stones mean?" and be told of God's faithfulness.‡

Jesus tells His followers that the Holy Spirit "will remind you of everything I have said to you."§

As Dr. Curt Thompson writes:

> *Even now, as modern science learns more about memory, Scripture reminds us that over three thousand years ago our ancestors were sure of what neuroscience is now confirming. For when we remember all the benefits of the Lord—his forgiveness, healing, redeeming, crowning, satisfying, and renewing—in the fullness of our regenerated memories, our future, and the future of our children and of others with whom we are in relationship, will be changed.*[372]

My father-in-law is now in the early stages of his own memory loss. But his identity in Christ is not fragile. And neither is ours.

Jesus knows we're prone to spiritual forgetfulness too. That's why He tore the bread and poured the wine and gave us a practice to carry this memory—"Do this in remembrance of me."¶

PRACTICING THE WAY

In a world where so much fades, God's love does not. Place a small stone on your desk or in your coat pocket. Each time you notice it, pray today's breath prayer.

When remembering the goodness of God doesn't come easy, try to remember one good thing, however small, that God has done. As Lamentations 3:21 says, "This I call to mind and therefore I have hope."**

* See Psalm 103:2-5.
† Exodus 28:12, ESV.
‡ See Deuteronomy 6:12; Joshua 4:4-7.
§ John 14:26, NIV.
¶ Luke 22:19, NLT.
** NIV.

NOVEMBER 23

God is sheer beauty, all-generous in love, loyal always and ever.

PSALM 100:5 (MSG)

INHALE: Awaken me, God,
EXHALE: To Your beauty in the ordinary.

The kitchen garbage can has gone from full to bursting. Hands full of trash, I sigh, realizing I can't shove the bin's contents down any farther. My phone pings with a reminder that I have a meeting in five minutes. Panic rises as I realize I still haven't run a hairbrush through my bedhead. A dog barks, a light bulb fizzles out, and as I shimmy the garbage bag out of the bin, an unidentified slime oozes onto the floor.

Life doesn't always feel beautiful.

Awakening to God's beauty in our lives doesn't mean everything is always serene and peaceful and full of flourishing touches. Real life is messy and weird. And sometimes it stinks.

I get the leaking bag outside, toss it into the receptacle, and return to my knees with cleaner and paper towels, sopping up whatever vegetable has gone very, very wrong. When the smell dissipates and the faint aroma of fall-scented all-purpose cleaner fills the air, I pause.

I let myself draw a long, deep breath in through my nose. I stay there for a moment with my breath held and wonder when I last went onto my increasingly cracking knees to pray. I ask God to help me see the beauty in the ordinary, in the parts of life that feel so unpretty. I slowly exhale, feeling my breath deep in my core, as I begin a tornado of getting ready for my work call in the three minutes I have remaining.

When we notice God's beauty in the broken pieces of our lives, we're not glossing over real life. We're paying attention to the One who is as present with us in the mundane—sitting beside us as we scrub the floor and haul trash to the curb—as He is when we're spending intentional time in prayer or reading Scripture.

When life feels messy and complicated, when beautiful feels impossible to spot in the chaos of your life, take a breath.

God's love is, as Psalm 100 reminds us, "loyal always and ever."

As you breathe through today's breath prayer, reflect on how it feels to trust that God's love does not leave, even when life feels anything but beautiful.

PAUSE AND PONDER

How might you practice noticing rather than numbing in moments of everyday frustration or overwhelm?

Think of a recent moment that felt messy or frustrating. Revisit that memory. How was God with you all along?

NOVEMBER 24

It's obvious, isn't it? The place where your treasure is, is the place you will most want to be, and end up being.

MATTHEW 6:21 (MSG)

INHALE: Help me treasure
EXHALE: The right things.

It sounded like something out of a movie.

In 2025, a group of thieves pulled off a daring heist at the Louvre Museum in Paris, stealing rare jewels and crowns worth more than $100 million. The suspects were clever. The detectives relentless. Glittering with international intrigue, the caper captured imaginations across continents.

In a world wary of never-ending headlines about war, famine, and division, there was something about the spectacle that felt almost light against the barrage of bad news.

When Jesus told His followers, "Where your treasure is, there your heart will be also,"* He was speaking to people who stored their wealth in precious metals and gemstones—things that could be tarnished, lost, or, yes, even stolen. Jesus contrasted those treasures with what truly matters, reminding us not to become so caught up in accumulating wealth that we lose sight of what is actually valuable—our relationships with God and one another.†

We're quick to marvel at treasures that shimmer, to get caught up in glittering stories that promise to satisfy but never do. The treasure we store up in our hearts isn't just literal stuff but anything we chase for worth or meaning: success, security, reputation, approval . . . the list goes on.

What are you guarding? What are you measuring your life against? What do you fear losing most?

No matter how mesmerizing it is, the allure of all that dazzles will never satisfy the ache in our hearts.‡

Moths eat. Rust corrodes. Thieves break in.§

The kind of treasure Jesus speaks of isn't stored in vaults or displayed in glass cases. It's acts of mercy no one notices, forgiveness offered without fanfare.

Where your treasure is, your heart will follow. And your heart shapes the story of your life.

LET IT LINGER

In Hebrew understanding, the heart wasn't just a wellspring of emotion; it was also the center of thought, will, and moral direction.[373] What we treasure shapes who we become. "Above all else, guard your heart, for everything you do flows from it."¶

May your heart learn to treasure what cannot be stolen—only given and received: grace, compassion, peace, and love.

* Matthew 6:21, NIV.
† See Matthew 22:37-39.
‡ See Ecclesiastes 5:10.
§ See Matthew 6:19.
¶ Proverbs 4:23, NIV.

NOVEMBER 25

I will give thanks to the LORD with my whole heart;
I will tell of all your wonderful deeds.

PSALM 9:1 (NRSV)

INHALE: I remember with thanks
EXHALE: The stories of Your love.

Some might say we're breaking the rules by decorating the tree on Thanksgiving weekend, but I can't think of a better way to practice gratitude.

On the day after Thanksgiving, we gather in my parents' living room to decorate their Christmas tree. What used to feel like a chore when I was a teen has become a beloved tradition I share with my kids. My mom has a box of ornaments for each of us—every child, grandchild, and spouse. Wrapped in tissue paper and twine, the boxes are time capsules, an array of stories we unwrap year after year as we hold the memories of the people we've been and the places we've gone.

We hang a hodgepodge of handmade and store-bought ornaments: elementary school crafts, toothless grins pasted inside glittery wreaths, beloved cartoon characters, a glass bulb I splurged on at the college bookstore with money I didn't really have, a tiny stocking my mom bought when we were waiting on our son's adoption paperwork and our hope was as fragile as tissue paper. And some ornaments with my grandma's handwriting on the back, which I rub with my finger, recognizing she's no longer here to hang it herself.

The memories are often funny and sometimes tender. We hold some of the stories in our hearts as the room comes alive with story after story, as we find open spots on the ever-filling branches.

When we share our stories, we practice remembering God's faithfulness—how grace and goodness have carried us through the seasons of our lives. The psalmist writes, "I will give thanks . . . with my whole heart." When we tell and retell our stories, it points us back to gratitude. The passing of seasons, the days set apart to remind us to be thankful, help us take a collective breath and pay attention to the sacred thread that runs through our stories—the hilarious ones, the heartwarming ones, and the hard ones too.

We cultivate gratitude when we take time to remember and share stories of goodness and grace in our weary world. We are far too prone to forget. Story by story, memory by memory, we just may notice how Love was there all along, through all the eras of our lives.

PAUSE AND PONDER

Why might telling stories help us grow in gratitude? What tradition do you have of telling stories with loved ones (or what tradition could you start)?

NOVEMBER 26

Thanksgiving is our dialect.

EPHESIANS 5:4 (MSG)

INHALE: My gratitude
EXHALE: Makes room.

We all breathe the same air.

It drifts over oceans and across borders. It fills the lungs of the young and the old, the joyful and the grieving, the neighbor and the stranger. No matter what walls we build—political, cultural, or physical—the same air moves through us all.*

If we pay attention, each breath can serve as a reminder of our shared humanity. But too often, we forget, building barriers of status, politics, culture, race, and religion to divide *us* from *them*.†

Decades ago, as the Berlin Wall crumbled, people around the world exhaled a collective sigh of relief—a breath of hope that what divides us can, indeed, come down. God's Spirit is a mighty wind strong enough to tear down every wall we erect.‡

God breathes and bricks crumble. God breathes and nothing is ever, ever the same.

In 2017, artist Jen Bloomer created a print showing a beautifully diverse group gathered around a table loaded with food. It echoes Jesus' feeding of the five thousand and the last supper at once, featuring this quote: "When you have more than you need / build a longer table not a higher wall."

Jesus showed us the way. He shared meals with tax collectors and day laborers, crossed social boundaries, and invited the overlooked into places of belonging.

He set the table and said, "This is for you."§

Every meal can be an invitation to God's outstretched love, a reminder that gratitude makes space for others to exhale too. When we live with thankful hearts, our very breath is a reminder that the air sustaining us is the same air sustaining our neighbor—and our enemy too.¶

What if we took that seriously? What if, instead of guarding our tables, we widened our circles? What if we made space for the ones who have been turned away, the ones who hunger to be seen, known, and loved?

Every breath is an invitation to gratitude. Every exhale is a chance to make room.

Thanksgiving is the language of heaven. And when we speak it, walls come down.

BORROW THIS PRAYER

We give thanks, O God,
For laughter around the table
And for arms around each other.
We give thanks, O God,
For shoulders to cry on
And hands to hold.
We give thanks, O God,
For memories made
And for hope in what is to come.[374]

Adapted from "A Prayer for a Grateful Spirit" in To Light Their Way

* See Acts 17:25-26.
† See Ephesians 2:14-16.
‡ See Acts 2:2.

§ See Luke 22:19.
¶ See Matthew 5:43-45.

NOVEMBER 27

You will be enriched in every way so that you can be generous on every occasion, and through us your generosity will result in thanksgiving to God.

2 CORINTHIANS 9:11 (NIV)

INHALE: Generous God, help me
EXHALE: Breathe out Your generosity.

Good news doesn't sound so good when you're hungry.

Or when you're lonely, overlooked, or bone-tired.

When the medical bills keep stacking higher.

When you aren't sure how you're going to keep the heat on.

When your screen is full of suffering and your soul feels numb.

When you're parenting by yourself and working two jobs to stay afloat.

When you grew up in multiple foster homes but never felt love.

When none of the loudest Christians seemed to notice . . . or care.

The gospel was never meant to ring hollow in the hearts of those who are hurting.

The gospel is good news for the poor.* The poor in spirit, the poor in wealth, the poor in relationship, the poor in health. In Christ, generosity is a rhythm of breath—a way of breathing in God's love and breathing out compassion to a world left worn and weary.

God is generous to us, lavishing grace upon grace, and because of that, we can extend that same grace to others.† We can say as much as we want to about Jesus, but if we aren't following in the way—if our lives don't speak peace, if we don't actually love our local and global neighbors—we're nothing but "a resounding gong or a clanging cymbal."‡

When we see every good thing in our lives as a gift (not something we've earned or are entitled to), we begin to live out of an overflow of generosity. With God's help, gratitude can become action, and love can become not just what we feel or think or even what we do but *who we are* as people of God.

Generosity becomes both an act of worship and the work of our hands.

As you borrow today's prayer, ask the Giver to show you where your generosity might create room for someone else to breathe a little easier—where your open heart might become someone else's answered prayer.

We give not because we feel obligated or guilty but because we have an overflow of goodness, thanks to God's generosity to us.

SACRED ECHOES

To give thanks even when we cannot see the goodness of the Giver, to learn this is to find the path to peace of heart. For happiness is not what makes us grateful. It is gratefulness that makes us happy.[375]

David Steindl-Rast

* See Luke 4:18-19.
† See Ephesians 1:7-8.
‡ 1 Corinthians 13:1, NIV.

NOVEMBER 28

Don't be obsessed with getting more material things. Be relaxed with what you have. Since God assured us, "I'll never let you down, never walk off and leave you," we can boldly quote, God is there, ready to help; I'm fearless no matter what. Who or what can get to me?

HEBREWS 13:5-6 (MSG)

INHALE: You are enough;
EXHALE: You never let me down.

One of my sons performed Rick Astley's 1987 hit "Never Gonna Give You Up" at his fifth-grade talent show. Never mind that the song is as old as I am—it'll probably live forever in pop-culture infamy thanks to the internet prank known as "rickrolling."

After the performance, my son decided to write a letter to Mr. Astley. We found a fan mail address in the UK, affixed the appropriate postage, and sent it off. Months passed, and I forgot all about it . . . until an envelope arrived with Royal Mail stamps.

Inside was a signed photograph from the aging pop star.

My own mailbox rickrolled me.

The writer of Hebrews concludes a warning about the accumulation of more stuff with a kind of divine Rick Astley moment: *God is never gonna give you up, never gonna let you down, never gonna run around and desert you.*

God's care and provision and reliability and goodness are obviously so much more than an eighties pop song. The reason the author of Hebrews underscores God's care and provision is because as humans, we've always been tempted to chase *more.* To believe that one more purchase, one more raise, one more upgrade will finally fill the hollow ache inside. But what we're really chasing after to fill the void will never satisfy, because the One who holds us with care is already with us.

As God reminds us time and time again: "*I will never leave you nor forsake you.*"*

In 2024, shoppers spent a record $10.8 billion online on Black Friday. Between 10 a.m. and 2 p.m., people shopping online spent $11.3 million *per minute.*[376] In a culture that thrives on a scarcity mindset, God invites us to breathe in the abundance of the soul and remember that the One who provides breath will not fail.

What would it look like to let contentment be your quiet rebellion this Advent season?

The God who never gives you up has already given you what you need.

BORROW THIS PRAYER

We thank You, O Lord,
For what You have given us.
And while we lament our inclinations to excess,
We also ask for Your guidance
To live in gospel generosity
And lavish love.
Amen.[377]

Adapted from "A Prayer for Consumerism" in To Light Their Way

---

* See Deuteronomy 31:6; Hebrews 13:5.

NOVEMBER 29

He'll judge the needy by what is right, render decisions on earth's poor with justice.

ISAIAH 11:4 (MSG)

INHALE: You breathe
EXHALE: And set the world right.

This isn't all there is.

All this suffering. All this injustice. All this cruelty that goes unchecked.

It won't have the final say.

Isaiah looked around at the corruption, violence, wars, and suffering of his time and saw a picture beyond what others could see—a vision breaking through the darkness, a glimpse of what will be when God's justice fully reigns. He saw a future where not one ounce of inequity will remain because Christ, the righteous Judge, will reign instead.

When I see the powerful exploiting the powerless today, when I read headlines that make me weep and my heart sink, I cling with stubborn hope to Isaiah's vision that someday Jesus *will* overturn every system that harms and every vile lie that upholds it.

Isaiah speaks of a day when we will finally breathe a sigh of relief, knowing the justice of Jesus is righteous and restorative, never cruel or capricious. On that day, Isaiah writes, "a mere breath from his lips will topple the wicked."

A mere breath.

Isaiah doesn't say Jesus will charge in with a violent army to topple the wicked. He says a single breath from the lips of God will bring down every monument that mocked the marginalized, every scaffolding that took advantage of the poor, every structure that was entrenched in evil.

God breathes, and everything changes. The same breath that animates all creation will one day set the world right again.

As we enter the Advent season and anticipate the birth of Christ, we remember that the manger is only the beginning of a much larger story of redemption. A baby's cry broke into our world, and with it came a promise: *This is not the end.*

Maybe as you look around, you feel discouraged. You doubt. You wonder. When evil leaves you overwhelmed and despair threatens to steal your hope, take a deep, slow breath in. The same Spirit-breath that brought life to dust and spoke light into darkness is not finished yet.

As you breathe, may you remember the might and power of Christ, the coming King. And may your own breath be a prayer for peace on earth, not just in the future but in the here and now.

BORROW THIS PRAYER

If we have abundance,
Let it be an abundance of peace.
If we have wealth,
Let it be the wealth of memories together.[378]

Adapted from "A Prayer for Consumerism" in To Light Their Way

NOVEMBER 30

Let my soul be at rest again, for the LORD has been good to me.

PSALM 116:7 (NLT)

INHALE: Let my soul
EXHALE: Be at rest.

The fireplace pops and crackles. Embers glow as daylight grows ever dimmer. The day is done, and for one glorious evening, there are no school concerts to get to or basketball practices to shuttle to. The cold night has brought us together under thick sweaters and cozy blankets.

I grab a book, light a few candles, and feel myself finally exhale.

Don't get me wrong—all is not calm. Two of my sons wrestle as my daughter chucks a pillow across the room. (She has taken the name *throw pillow* quite literally.) A dog barks. A video game chimes. There's laundry to be folded and dishes to be washed—the never-ending rhythms of a busy household.

But in this moment, I feel the psalmist's words deep in my soul: *The Lord has been good to me.*

I struggle with not knowing what the future holds. I want everyone to be okay. I want to do everything in my power to protect my kids from pain, from the ache that comes for all of us in this human experience. I can get so caught up in anticipating what might be that I lose track of the goodness that *is*.

I set aside my novel. I might not read another page tonight. Tomorrow will have new things to worry about. But just for now, just for this beautifully ordinary moment, my soul is at rest.

I can breathe.

When was the last time you let yourself fully exhale?

Rest is an act of faith in the One who provides, regardless of our striving. When we're used to rushing from one thing to the next, rest feels unsettling. Still, we can practice returning to rest with our breath.

According to Harvard Health, one of the simplest ways to calm a worried mind is to focus attention on your breathing. This simple mindfulness practice offers an immediate sense of relaxation and, over time, can help lower chronic stress and enhance your overall well-being.

Start by silently counting your inhalations and exhalations: Inhale (one beat), exhale (two beats), inhale (three beats), exhale (four beats), and so on. This gives you something to focus on besides anxious thoughts.[379]

As you breathe this prayer today, rest in the goodness of the One who holds your soul with utmost care, even on the most ordinary evening at home.

SACRED ECHOES

None can touch the ground of the soul but God.[380]

Meister Eckhart

DECEMBER 1

The LORD God formed the man from the dust of the ground. He breathed the breath of life into the man's nostrils, and the man became a living person.

GENESIS 2:7 (NLT)

INHALE: You breathe life
EXHALE: Into me.

My breath lingers in the winter air. I exhale and watch the cloud hang in the thin space between what is visible and what is unseen. For just a heartbeat, I see it—the essence of us. I reach out, but it's already gone.

In the beginning, God breathed.

The Word—Christ—set the cosmos into motion with a single exhale. "Through him all things were made," we read in John 1:3-4. "Without him nothing was made that has been made. In him was life, and that life was the light of all humankind."*

Our Creator has never been afraid of getting close. Genesis tells us that God stooped low, shaping dust and breathing "the breath of life" into our nostrils.

God has always been moving toward humanity. Advent marks the beginning of the liturgical year, a sacred turn in the circle of time that invites us to journey from the shadows that cling to this earth toward the light that awaits us in the arrival of the Word made flesh.

We can participate in all the countdowns we want, but Advent's truest invitation is to marvel at the mystery. Before time began, Christ was. Through Christ, all things came to be—every heartbeat, every breath, every new beginning. And in tender mercy, our God entered our world, willingly carrying the full weight and wonder of being human.

It wasn't enough for the Word to be an ethereal mystery, like a puff of air on a cold December morning. God longed for intimacy, attachment, and connection.

Did the One who holds us desire to be held? Did the One who breathes the breath of life want to experience what it's like to begin, like the rest of us, with an inhale? "We have seen his glory, the glory of the one and only Son, who came from the Father, full of grace and truth."†

Pause for a moment to borrow today's breath prayer. In the beginning, God breathed. And through the mystery of time—as Advent reminds us—it is still the beginning.

Where, in this season of beginnings, do you sense God breathing new life into you?

To find out more about Advent, see the liturgical calendar in appendix A.

SACRED ECHOES

All we know is that once upon a time or, rather, once before time, Christ called everything into being in a great breath of creativity.[381]

Madeleine L'Engle

* NIV.

† John 1:14, NIV.

DECEMBER 2

The people who walk in darkness will see a great light.
For those who live in a land of deep darkness, a light will shine.

ISAIAH 9:2 (NLT)

INHALE: Light of the World,
EXHALE: Every story is Yours.

Sometimes I stand on the hardwood floors of our house and think about all the people—all the stories—these worn planks have held. Construction began on this house in 1908. I hang a garland along the curved staircase and try to imagine all the little ones who have run the halls, all the tears that have been shed, all the laughter, all the longings.

It's humbling to realize how many stories these walls have witnessed—and comforting to know that light has always found its way in.

I can see it: the house shifting and changing through the eras, through world wars and ever-evolving fashions, through quiet family moments and Christmas mornings and everything in between. I can see it: all the celebrations and sorrows, all the Iowa pine trees lugged in and the same giant windowpanes breathed on by children and drawn on with their fingers. I can see it: the passing of time all at once. And I'm somehow part of it and outside of it.

Advent invites us to see our own lives this way—to notice God's presence not only in the past or the future but right here, in our ordinary living rooms.

There's something about the rhythms and rituals of setting up a home for Christmas that makes you reflect on what was, on the passing of time—on who you were and who you are still becoming.

"You will never see this day again once it has passed, and never again will you be this self," Frederick Buechner writes.[382] This, too, is the invitation of Advent—to remember that time is somehow but a breath and also *is* breadth.

I think of the patch of land Isaiah sat on as he wrote these wild words: "The people who walk in darkness will see a great light. For those who live in a land of deep darkness, a light will shine." Did Isaiah know the gravity of his own words? Prophets rarely do. Their words echo beyond their knowing. Could he fathom that so many years later, Jesus would walk this same wild earth? Could he imagine that we would hold his words so many years later?

That same light Isaiah spoke of took on flesh, stepping over the threshold and illuminating every corner of our ordinary lives.

As you breathe through today's prayer, open your heart to what God might be whispering to you across time and place this Advent season.

BORROW THIS PRAYER

Help us to reflect Jesus this Advent, caring for those who feel unseen and cast into the shadows. May we cultivate peace for all people in this season and in the days to come. Amen.[383]

Adapted from Every Season Sacred

DECEMBER 3

I pray that God, the source of hope, will fill you completely with joy and peace because you trust in him.

ROMANS 15:13 (NLT)

INHALE: God of peace and joy,
EXHALE: I place my trust in You.

Wander the aisles of any big-box store this time of year, and you're bound to see Christmas decor emblazoned with words like *peace, joy,* and *hope.* We throw the feel-good sentiments on pillows, blankets, mugs—even tiny sweaters for tiny dogs. We see the words so often that they start to feel like empty clichés, void of much meaning.

Yet they draw us in this time of year. It's like we collectively take a breath, look around at the state of our world, and think, *It's not supposed to be this way.* All the fighting, all the war, all the hate . . . We were made for something more.

It's true, you know. *You* were made to have peace. *You* were made to have joy. *You* were made to have hope. *You* were made to trust the One who gives each breath.

Advent points us back to that reality—the truths that make up who we are—because it points us back to the truest thing about who *God* is: the One who keeps promises. Across time and tradition, God has kept His word, fulfilling every claim in ways both quiet and miraculous.

Christ is the culmination of every promise.

And Advent is the story of a God who breaks into life as we know it and changes the course of history forever. Still, things are not as they should be. All is not calm. All is not bright. Creation groans. We are painfully aware of our need for God to set things right. We've lost our way, looking for goodness in all the wrong places—our bank accounts, our social status, our relationships, our illusion of control, our ability to string the perfect holiday lights or wrap the perfect gifts under the perfect tree.

Joy and peace aren't seasonal decorations but what overflows when we trust in God's promise and presence—even in the chaos of life. Joy in your soul isn't dependent on circumstances, and peace in your soul isn't contingent on mood. (Good news for those moments when we're feeling a bit Grinch-like.)

Maybe this season feels anything but peaceful for you. But it's here, in the ordinary overwhelm of life, where Paul's benediction meets us: "I pray that God, the source of hope, will fill you completely with joy and peace because you trust in him."

Let hope rise in the space between your inhale and exhale today.

BORROW THIS PRAYER

O come, Emmanuel.
We enter this time of Advent
With holy anticipation.
O come, Emmanuel.
We anticipate great news
That we so desperately need.
Break into this world
Again and again and again,
Like You did so many years ago.[384]

Adapted from "A Prayer for Advent" in To Light Their Way

DECEMBER 4

You are blessed because you believed that the Lord would do what he said.

LUKE 1:45 (NLT)

INHALE: I wonder
EXHALE: As I wander.

I lie in bed. The wind batters the tree outside the window. I listen to the *tick-tap* of the branches as I bring the comforter up to my face.

My husband snores. And I, once again, can't sleep. I lie on my back, unable to see much of anything now that I've taken off my glasses. As I listen to the sounds of the night and see nothing but vague shapes and shadows, a ticker-tape parade of *what-ifs* starts marching around in my mind.

I rest my hand on my stomach and take a deep, slow breath. "I don't trust You, God," I whisper. "But I trust You."

Sometimes faith sounds less like a sermon and more like a sigh in the dark.

"Why did you name me Abram and not Abraham?" my youngest son asks me in the morning. I tell him that I felt drawn to *Abram* because "Abram believed the LORD, and the LORD credited it as righteousness to him."*

As we dig out our Advent wreath—the one with melted pools of purple and pink wax all over it—I think of how, like Abram, Mary believed God when the angel spoke to her. According to her cousin Elizabeth, the belief was the blessing. Mary believed that God's impossible promise was possible—and that belief became her blessing.

Belief is holding on to the promise even in the dark, even in the wondering. It's not knowing how things will work out and trusting God anyway. Advent invites us to believe even when we haven't seen.

And there lies the blessing.

The first line of a 1934 Christmas hymn says, "I wonder as I wander, out under the sky." It was written during the thick of the Great Depression, in impoverished Appalachia, where millions of people were hungry, tired, and adrift. I imagine the songwriter lying in bed at night, wanting to believe that God was good, yet unable to trust that there would be food on the table come morning.

Sometimes we wonder. Sometimes we wander. It's okay to lie awake, unsure, and still whisper the words that tether you to hope. That doesn't make you less connected to God . . . it just means you're human.

The wind keeps tapping at the window, but somehow I breathe a little easier. Though I don't know the how or the why, I trust that what was true then is true now: *The star will lead us home.*

PAUSE AND PONDER

How might your posture toward prayer, God's presence, and God's promises change if you let yourself name the ribbons of distrust or unbelief woven into your heart?

---

* Genesis 15:6, NET.

DECEMBER 5

My soul magnifies the Lord, and my spirit rejoices in God my Savior.

LUKE 1:46-47 (NRSV)

INHALE: May Your good news
EXHALE: Turn us upside down.

Our culture casts a vision of Mary as serene and sacred, a silent figure set apart in stained glass. But in this characterization, we lose sight of the girl who prayed a fiery prayer of fierce hope.

Mary, pregnant with Jesus in a wild, wonderful miracle, visited her cousin Elizabeth, who was also expecting a baby in a God-breathed mystery. Elizabeth could tell, on a deep soul level, that there was more happening than either of them could fathom. As the baby within her kicked and flipped, she blurted out the blessing she felt in her bones, because *Mary was carrying the very presence of God.*

Elizabeth blessed Mary, and Mary responded not with quiet piety or a solemn nod but with a bold song that shook the foundations of power.

In her day, *euangelion*—"good news"—was part of the language of the Roman Empire, used to announce Caesar's victories.[385] Mary reclaimed this idea, declaring that God's reign, not Rome's, would bring justice to the poor and mercy to the forgotten. True peace and power, Mary sang, ride in on God's very breath.

The gospel isn't a box on a religious checklist or a private, purely personal comfort—it's good news that fills the hungry and lifts the humble. It's good news that subverts both the political empire and the religious establishment. It's good news that turns the world upside down through the womb of a young girl.

Mary's impassioned psalm of praise proclaims a God who topples the powerful, raises the lowly, remembers the forgotten, and radically reorders the world in love.

Mary proclaimed that the baby growing in her womb was, quite literally, good news for the weary world and good news for the welfare of its people. Our communal Christ reorders religion and breathes revolution into real lives. Jesus is truly good news worth sharing.

As you breathe through today's prayer, consider what it might mean for your soul to magnify the Lord in this Advent season.

SACRED ECHOES

Mary's prayer of praise after Elizabeth calls her blessed is often referred to as "The Magnificat." Here's the beginning of the song that changed the world.

And Mary said:

"My soul glorifies the Lord
and my spirit rejoices in God my Savior,
for he has been mindful
of the humble state of his servant.
From now on all generations will call me blessed."

Luke 1:46-48, NIV

DECEMBER 6

SAINT NICHOLAS DAY

When you give to the needy, do not let your left hand know what your right hand is doing, so that your giving may be in secret.

MATTHEW 6:3-4 (NIV)

INHALE: Help me notice
EXHALE: So that I may give.

We know plenty about Santa Claus. But who was Saint Nicholas, really?

Saint Nicholas of Myra lived a life marked by Christlike mercy, compassion, and generosity. Centuries after his life, stories began to circulate about this fourth-century bishop known for his selfless giving. As artist and writer Kreg Yingst explains, few records survive about Nicholas himself, but a ninth-century monk gathered what tradition remembered into the story we now tell.[386]

Legend has it that Nicholas lost both of his parents as a young man and, moved by his faith in Jesus, used his inheritance to help those living on the margins. He's remembered, all these years later, for his mercy and kindness. One story tells of a poor father in what is now Turkey who had no money for marriage dowries for his three daughters. Without help, the girls faced a future of exploitation—an all-too-common fate for unmarried women of that era.

When Nicholas heard of their plight, he longed to help in a way that would preserve the family's dignity. Under the cover of night, he tossed small bags of gold through the family's window—three times in all—ensuring each daughter's future. On the third night, the father stayed awake to catch him, but Nicholas asked him to keep it secret.

Ned Bustard, author of *Saint Nicholas the Giftgiver*, says, "Saint Nicholas was a real person who loved Jesus, served the church, and was generous. We can have fun with the magic and legends about Saint Nick without sacrificing the truths of his life and the centrality of Christ."[387]

Saint Nicholas gave generously and discreetly throughout his life—the opposite of the performative giving so prevalent in our culture today.

This Advent season, may God open your heart to notice those on the margins and open your hands to those who could use some help. In every tradition and celebration to come this month, may you remember who Christ is—a friend to those in need, a protector of weary hearts, and a helper to all who need it—and who you're called to be in light of that glorious love.

BORROW THIS PRAYER

We thank You for St. Nicholas of Myra,
Whom we celebrate on this day.
We rejoice over a life lived so long ago
Out of great love for You.
We pray that we will be like St. Nicholas,
Whose devotion to You
Is seen in the stories of his quiet love for those
Society often deemed unworthy of being seen—
The children and the laborers
And those struggling to make ends meet.[388]

Adapted from "A Prayer for the Feast Day of St. Nicholas" in To Light Their Way

DECEMBER 7

The wolf will live with the lamb . . . and a little child will lead them.

ISAIAH 11:6 (NIV)

INHALE: Make room, O God,
EXHALE: For peace in our hearts.

Children, of course, are wild things.

They stomp and shout and laugh so hard it startles the room. They imagine whole worlds into being. Their creativity, their wonder, their spectrum of emotion, their very essence jostles us from the way we've so carefully ordered our lives.

The prophet Isaiah says it's a child who will lead the wildest things of all—the fiercest, fearsome wolves—into *peace.*

In Isaiah's time, children had no power, no place at the table. There were no preschools, no social-emotional learning initiatives, no sticker charts or emotion wheels. The expectation was for them to be unseen and unheard.

Yet the prophet casts the vision for a world reordered by the smallest among us—a world where predator and prey lie side by side and where creation itself exhales in relief as a little child leads us into peace.*

Isaiah's words had to seem, well, weird. (It's a recurring theme with prophets.)

But centuries later, Isaiah's wild vision finally began to take shape. God entered the world not with force or fanfare but in vulnerability—through a mother's labor, a child's first breath. The expanse of all that is became small, wrapped in swaddling clothes, lying in the hay, crying among the animals. God loves to subvert our notions of what is orderly and what is holy and flip our expectations upside down. And thank goodness for that.

Even now, Christ makes room for those who are misunderstood or marginalized. But we still wait for the grand finale. The fullness of Isaiah's dream waits to be realized. The wolf and the lamb are still learning how to live together. We are too.

We wait for Christ to set things right, to restore all the ways creation has turned in on itself and each other.

We wait, but we don't wait idly. We live in anticipation of peace, actively joining God's reconciling work in our everyday lives—making room for those who are often shooed away, listening before speaking, extending mercy when we'd rather not, creating beauty, choosing tenderness, breathing hope into the comings and goings of our days.

Take a deep breath in. Hold it for a few seconds before slowly releasing. As you pray through today's breath prayer, consider how peace might begin in small, unexpected places in your carefully ordered world today.

BORROW THIS PRAYER

O come, Emmanuel.
Ignite in us the awe of a child,
Looking into a manger scene
As we wait on the promise
Of the coming infant King
In a humble stable.[389]

Adapted from "A Prayer for Advent" in To Light Their Way

---

* See Isaiah 9:6.

DECEMBER 8

The light shines in the darkness,
and the darkness can never extinguish it.

JOHN 1:5 (NLT)

INHALE: Even now
EXHALE: The light still shines.

The beauty of Advent is that it's for all of us.

Whether you're part of a church community that feels like home or you're not sure what you believe anymore, this sacred season will meet you where you are.

Advent doesn't rush us out of the dark—it sits with us here, keeping us company as we wait for light to break through.

This liturgical season is a time of "now and not yet" in the church calendar—a cosmic invitation to wait with bated breath for the birth of Jesus, of Love embodied, of Light overcoming all the darkness this world has to throw at us.

I hold my daughter on my hip as I stand in our sanctuary, singing "O Come, O Come, Emmanuel." She's getting bigger, heavier. I won't always be able to hold her like this. Her disabilities are many, and I'm not sure what the future holds for her. For me. For us. I'm not sure what the future holds for *any* of us these days. As I reflect on what feels like a never-ending cycle of heartbreaking headlines, the hymn hits me: *Disperse the gloomy clouds of night / And death's dark shadows put to flight.*

We sing, and sunlight pours through the stained glass, surrounding the cross in a kaleidoscope of gold and blue and orange and white. The light dances across the faces around me—strangers and friends, each of us holding some mix of grief and hope as we bring our cracked voices into the chorus.

The mystery of the body of Christ is that your prayer can become mine and mine can become yours, and somehow we keep muddling through, grasping for glimmers of light and breathing in what peace we can *together*.

It doesn't make any sense, really. Yet now we find ourselves squarely in what Madeleine L'Engle describes as "the irrational season." If we're filled with reason, how will there be room for the child?[390]

During Advent, we marvel at a love so unreasonable, so unfathomable that we return year after year. We keep living here in darkness and keep showing up, lighting candles, and singing about a Light so radiant and a Love so everlasting that no darkness could ever extinguish it. It doesn't make any sense, but here we are, ever and always, holding the light.

As you breathe through today's prayer, feel your breath. Feel it rise and fall. Inhale slowly through your nose; exhale softly through your mouth. Let each breath remind you that no matter how dark or long the night, the light still shines. For you. For me. For all of us.

It always has, and as Advent reminds us, it always will.

BORROW THIS PRAYER

We pray for those who hold the weight of grief and ask that You would move us to be agents of comfort in this Advent season. Amen.[391]

Adapted from "Bearing Witness" in Every Season Sacred

DECEMBER 9

He's solid rock under my feet, breathing room for my soul.

PSALM 62:2 (MSG)

INHALE: I will not fear;
EXHALE: I walk with You.

One of the most sacred aspects of my husband's vocation as a pastor is visiting those who can no longer leave their homes—people who remain integral parts of our church family, even if they can't gather with us in person.

One of these dear ones, Sue, took her last breath recently.

Jonny visited her regularly over the years. "You might not have known her," he said, "but she knew you. She prayed for us, and for each of our children by name, faithfully, day after day, for years."

After her death, Jonny shared with her family how grateful he was for her steadfast commitment to prayer. He wanted them to know that it mattered. That she made a difference.

Then they told him something he didn't know: She passed peacefully in her chair, our church prayer list resting on her lap.

Every morning and evening, Sue sat in that chair and walked with God.

With one breath, Sue was in prayer, and in the next, she was with God in a completely new reality. Could it be that a pause between breaths during prayer carried her into eternity, like Enoch, who was faithful and "walked with God; then he was no more, because God took him"?*

We hear it at every Christmas pageant, the angels saying, "Do not be afraid." But how do we actually *live* unafraid? After all, there are so many fears in our weary world, not the least of these being the fear of death! But perhaps prayer strengthens us more than we know, nurturing a peace deep within our souls.

I don't know if Sue knew the power she held in her recliner, but I have a feeling she did. Prayer is an active, transformative connection with God and the ongoing work of God in the world.

Prayer is a form of mindfulness, and studies have shown that mindfulness changes us from the inside out. It changes brain activity, moving us toward calm yet focused states of attention. Research even suggests that those who practice mindfulness frequently—like Sue did in prayer—may experience noticeable changes in their brains.[392] When we slow our breath in prayer, our bodies begin to truly believe they're safe. From the inside out, we become less afraid and more rooted in the deep peace of God's presence.

Maybe peace begins to grow in the spaces where we pause long enough to notice the One who is breathing room for our souls. Maybe living unafraid starts with something as simple as one slow exhale.

PAUSE AND PONDER

How might you practice "walking with God" in the ordinary spaces of your own life—in your favorite chair, on your commute, or at your kitchen sink?

---

* Genesis 5:24, NRSV.

DECEMBER 10

Listen! It's the voice of someone shouting, "Clear the way through the wilderness for the LORD!"

ISAIAH 40:3 (NLT)

INHALE: Help me listen;
EXHALE: I want to hear You.

Listen.

Can you hear it?

If you get really quiet, if you let your heart grow still, if you turn down the noise of your mind and hush the shouting of the day, even for just this breath, maybe you'll hear it—that sound of the sacred in the ordinary soundtrack of your life.

It might not sound like a shout. It might come as a whisper, a promise that the Christ we await is still coming, clearing a way through the wilderness, again and again.

The hush after the first fall of snow.

The hiss of a teapot.

The crackle and pop of logs on the fire.

The clink of coins in the collection kettle.

The church bells in the distance.

The laughter.

The gentle "Let me take your coat."

The ding of the kitchen timer.

The voice on the radio crooning, "I'll Be Home for Christmas."

When we cultivate listening hearts, we practice *holy attention*, meeting each moment as it comes without rushing past it.

Isaiah's call to the people of God was to listen and make space for the holy, even in the wilderness of their lives. The invitation stands for us today too. No matter how chaotic our lives are, no matter how barren our souls feel, there's still space for our hearts to, as the old carol goes, prepare Him room.

In the New Testament, John the Baptist echoes Isaiah's cry, calling people to ready their hearts for the One who will change everything. The wilderness, it turns out, isn't merely a place of punishment but a place of preparation, a sacred space where new life is breathed into what once seemed hopeless.

When the world is a constant din of voices screaming and never hearing, cultivating a listening heart is a subversive act of peace. A quiet rebellion of hope. A way of breathing in the world and believing that somehow, in some way, God is already speaking in the soundtrack of our ordinary lives.

Take a breath. Listen. Do you hear what I hear?

RHYTHM OF BREATH

In a world at war,
Listen.
Listen for the sound of your breath,
For the drumbeat of your heart.
Hope is all around you,
If you listen.

DECEMBER 11

He shows mercy from generation to generation to all who fear him.

LUKE 1:50 (NLT)

INHALE: God of mercy,
EXHALE: Help me be merciful.

Like Mary did so many years ago, with a hand on her bump and an eye toward heaven, we marvel at the mystery of mercy.

Time turns over, year after year, and we so desperately need the Advent reminder that just as God is merciful to us, God's breath within us empowers us to show mercy to others too.*

Jesus, the One who was born in a barn because no one could be bothered to make room for His pregnant and laboring mother, told His followers there would come a time when mercy would be the measure. He said that one day He would call people blessed, for they had fed Him when He was hungry and clothed Him when He was cold. Confused, they piped up: "What are You talking about? When did we ever see You hungry?"

I imagine Jesus looking at them the way you look at someone you've explained something to a thousand times and they're still. Just. Not. Getting. It. "What you did for the least of these," He said, "you did for Me."†

Dietrich Bonhoeffer, a Lutheran pastor who knew what it meant to breathe mercy under the suffocating thumb of a merciless empire, was at the center of German Protestant resistance to the Nazi regime. He said:

> *Jesus stands at the door and knocks, in complete reality. He asks you for help in the form of a beggar, in the form of a ruined human being in torn clothing. He confronts you in every person that you meet. . . . That is the greatest seriousness and the greatest blessedness of the Advent message.*[393]

Jesus stands in line at the food pantry and on the sidewalk with a cardboard sign. Jesus is the child without a coat, the unwanted immigrant, the man with Down syndrome practicing grocery shopping, the siblings trying to survive an abusive home, the aging widow who eats alone and barely eats at all.‡

Because of God's great mercy, your heart can be tuned to the blessed audacity of Advent, a season that insists that when the world flicks on the "No Vacancy" sign, we demonstrate the sacred power of welcome.§

We pray for peace on earth and now enter into those prayers, trusting that the way of peace is the way of mercy.¶

SACRED ECHOES

Christ stands at the door. He lives in the form of the person in our midst. Will you keep the door locked or open it to him?[394]

Dietrich Bonhoeffer

---

* See Titus 3:5.

† See Matthew 25:31-40.

‡ See Proverbs 19:17; Hebrews 13:2.

§ See Romans 15:7.

¶ See Luke 1:78-79.

DECEMBER 12

We will never turn our back on you; breathe life into our lungs so we can shout your name!

PSALM 80:18 (MSG)

INHALE: Breathe life into me

EXHALE: So I can shout Your name.

During Advent, we wait in anticipation for the coming Christ—journeying from darkness toward the Light of the World.[*] But we must journey through the darkest days to reach redemption's dawn.[†]

Psalm 80 proclaims a bold pledge to God: "We will never turn our back on you." Yet history tells the truth—we did. We do. Again and again. Humanity turned its back when there was no room for Mary to give birth.[‡] Again, we turned our backs when palms that waved in welcome became shouts of betrayal.[§]

The story of God and God's people has always been one of turning away and being turned back by mercy.[¶]

Asaph wrote his psalm from the perspective of people who knew what it was like to stray and suffer. If we're honest, not much has changed for us today. We promise to love God and our neighbor, then we scroll past suffering. We use words to wound instead of heal. We hoard instead of share. We judge instead of welcome. On and on it goes.

We turn away, time after time . . . yet God, full of mercy, still turns toward us.[**]

Advent reminds us that the story doesn't end with our failure but with God's faithfulness. The God we betrayed still breathes life into us. The breath we pray for in Psalm 80 is the same breath that filled a baby's lungs in Bethlehem and resurrected Christ from the tomb.[††] The same Spirit who hovered over creation fills our lungs right now so we can shout God's name once more.

When we go astray, we can pray alongside our inhales and exhales until we've turned back to God: "Breathe life into our lungs so we can shout your name."

No one gets it right all the time. But God never asks for perfection. That's why we have Jesus.[‡‡] And as long as we have breath in our lungs, we can trust that even when we turn our backs, Christ keeps turning toward us.[§§]

BREATHE THIS IN

Slow, intentional breathing (around five to six breaths per minute) may help regulate the nervous system and strengthen the body's natural stress-response pathways. A 2023 analysis of twenty-six studies of twelve randomized trials found that breathwork practices were linked to reductions in stress, anxiety, and depression.[395]

* See John 1:5.
† See Romans 13:12.
‡ See Luke 2:7.
§ See Matthew 21:9; 27:22-23.
¶ See Psalm 103:8.
** See 2 Timothy 2:13.
†† See John 20:22.
‡‡ See Romans 8:1.
§§ See Revelation 3:20.

DECEMBER 13

SAINT LUCIA'S DAY

The true light that gives light to everyone was coming into the world.

JOHN 1:9 (NIV)

INHALE: Light of the World,
EXHALE: Illuminate my path.

December 13 is Saint Lucia's Day, a feast honoring Saint Lucy, the patron saint of light. Saint Lucy lived in the fourth century and was martyred at a young age for refusing to renounce Christ. She's remembered for her courage, her generosity toward the poor, and her faith in a Light that could not be extinguished, even in death.

Legend tells us that Lucy carried food to persecuted Christians who were hiding in the catacombs of Rome. As she made her rounds, she wore a crown of candles to light her way through the darkness. Her name, *Lucia*—from the Latin *lux*, meaning "light"—seems fitting. Her life reminds us that faith, even when it flickers, can still cast out the shadows.

Growing up, I was enchanted by the Kirsten American Girl doll and books. Her story follows a Swedish immigrant family in the mid-1800s. Saint Lucia Day (*Luciadagen*) has been celebrated in Scandinavia since the eighteenth century. The white gown symbolizes purity, the red sash represents martyrdom, and the candle crown signifies bringing light through darkness. Kirsten had a Saint Lucia costume set, complete with a white gown, a red sash, and a candle crown. (I'll be honest—I was an anxious child who worried endlessly about this fictional Swedish girl setting her hair on fire.)

I'd twirl around, imagining myself as Kirsten, gracefully and courageously lighting the way for her family through a cold, dark winter's night. (I was imaginative as well as anxious.) Even as a child, something in me longed for that kind of courage—the kind Saint Lucia had, the kind Kirsten had, the kind that makes young girls brave enough to carry light into dark places.

I'm no longer a young girl, but I do share a birthday with Saint Lucy. Even now, long after my American Girl days (mostly), I think of her candle crown when I blow out the candles on my cake and reflect on this Advent season of waiting for light to break into the darkness. As Isaiah foretold so long ago: "The people walking in darkness have seen a great light."[*]

We're called to bring light into the shadows in both small and significant ways. To be, as Jesus said, "the light of the world"—not only during Advent, but in the ordinary days that follow.[†] To light the way in our workplaces, our neighborhoods, our relationships, and even our online presence with hands full of mercy and generosity and love. We are light-bearers, not just during Advent but also in the days after all the Christmas cheer has been packed up and stored away.

This is what we do: We find ways to light the way for ourselves and for each other.

[*] Isaiah 9:2, NIV.
[†] Matthew 5:14, NLT.

PRACTICING THE WAY

Saint Lucia's crown traditionally holds seven candles—symbols of light pushing back darkness. Label each candle with a quality of light you hope to embody this Advent season: hope, courage, generosity, gentleness, clarity, peace, love. Pause and breathe after naming each one. Let the light of Christ rise in you again.

DECEMBER 14

The Life-Light blazed out of the darkness;
the darkness couldn't put it out.

JOHN 1:5 (MSG)

INHALE: Light of the World,
EXHALE: Darkness will never win.

"Let's move near that window," I say, ushering the group of holiday partygoers from the dimly lit corner toward the soft natural light. The first photo would have been covered in shadows, but now I can see the glint in their eyes, and I can capture a moment in time when joy bubbles up, like the fizz in their cups. They throw their arms around one another, leaning in and doubling over in laughter.

"There," I say. "Now I can see you."

"I love that whenever you're taking a picture, you look for the light," someone says.

I'm no professional photographer, but I know enough to understand that light matters. It reveals the truth about what's there—and helps us see the beauty we might have overlooked.

I've been looking for the light a lot these days. Shadows of despair, exhaustion, confusion, and loneliness linger around every corner of modern life. Darkness touches every heartbreaking headline, every disappointing piece of news.

In those moments, I have to remember that *darkness cannot overcome the light*—because all the evils of this world can't even *comprehend* it. The Greek word for *overcome* can also mean "to comprehend" or "to understand,"* reminding us that darkness can neither *extinguish* nor *fully fathom* the light of Christ.[396] In other words, evil is not as powerful or even as smart as I tend to give it credit for.

If we're seeking it, light has a way of finding us—resting on our faces, even if just for a breath, reminding us to cling to the truth that all the lies, corruption, and heartache will not get the final word. Not now, not ever.

Even when the world is at its weariest, the Light wins. Every single time.

It's not always obvious, though. Sometimes we have to stubbornly search for it, fighting our way through the thick shadows that surround us to make our way toward it.

We do our best to share the light we have with one another as we fumble our way home.

As The Brilliance sings in their song "May You Find a Light":

Lost and weary traveler . . .
May you find a light

When you can't find your way, when you're unsure where to go, when you're lost, worn, and weary—look for the light. And trust that it's chasing after you too.

BORROW THIS PRAYER

In all the expectations
And clanging cymbals
Of the holiday season,
Help our hearts get quiet.
May every Nativity scene
Help us remember
The Love that lies
In the manger.[397]

From "A Prayer for Winter" in Every Season Sacred

* See John 1:5, NIV.

DECEMBER 15

He himself gives everyone life and breath and everything else.

ACTS 17:25 (NIV)

INHALE: You give life, O God;
EXHALE: You give everything.

As we journey toward Christmas, we remember that the One who needs nothing gives everything.

From the first breath in Eden to the breath of the newborn Christ in Bethlehem, life has always been a gift. Because of that, we can stop giving all we have to try to satisfy the glittering idols in our lives. Instead, we can just . . . breathe again. Every idol we set on a proverbial pedestal always takes and never gives.

Worship at the altar of more?

It demands full carts, maxed-out cards, and a calendar packed to the brim.

Worship at the altar of perfection?

It requires glossy family photos and a spotless home that no one has the freedom to enjoy.

Worship at the altar of appearance?

It takes time, treatments, and your sense of worth.

Worship at the altar of productivity?

It devours rest and relationships, all in the name of achievement.

It's not inherently wrong to care for our bodies, work, or connections—but when they demand everything, they stop giving life. Many of us come to these altars out of fear of not being enough. When we lose our way, God meets us there with compassion, not condemnation.

The false gods of our lives are mirages that vanish the moment we think we finally achieve them. Paul knew something about this. In Acts 17, he addresses the Athenians and contrasts their lifeless idols with the living God. Unlike the gods made by human hands—the ones that take and take—Paul points out that our Creator isn't served by human effort.

God doesn't take, he says. God doesn't need to. In fact, "he himself gives everyone life and breath and everything else." This Advent, we can open our hearts to receiving life, not getting it sucked out of us.

What might it look like to breathe with gratitude today, rather than grasping for what exhausts you?

Start by taking a deep inhale. As you breathe in, reflect on the One who gives every breath, who gives life everlasting. Exhale slowly, releasing all that false gods demand.

LET IT LINGER

This Advent, may you exhale what the false gods demand and inhale the gift of God's own breath. The One who gives life and breath and everything else still whispers, *Breathe.*

DECEMBER 16

She will give birth to a son and will call him Immanuel.

ISAIAH 7:14 (NLT)

INHALE: God incarnate,
EXHALE: We wait for You.

Over the years, I've collected nativity scenes from around the world. We have some made in Kenya, Mexico, Brazil, and Japan, and even one hand-carved by Indigenous artists. Across materials and textures and shapes and sizes, across different cultures and ethnicities, each sets the same scene: *the moment all creation held its breath.*

A laboring mother, breathing through contractions. *Inhale.*

Her fiancé by her side, overwhelmed and trusting God. *Exhale.*

The sights, sounds, and smells of a barn. *Inhale.*

She pushes. He prays. *Exhale.*

All creation holds its breath.

And then a cry. A look. A promise.

An exhale.

Immanuel. God with us.

Life will never be the same.

Time stood still. The One who was promised and was long waited for was here among us, breathing the same air, feeling the same pull of gravity, wrapped in the warmth of a mother.

"She will give birth to a son and will call him Immanuel," Isaiah wrote.* Centuries later, Matthew echoed these same words, naming Jesus as the fulfillment of that ancient promise: *Immanuel, God with us.*†

It takes a little sacred imagination and holy wonder to ponder what it was like in the space between *before* and *after*, in the hush before that first cry.

What was it like when creation collectively held its breath?

Take a few slow breaths. Imagine yourself in the stable, watching this holy moment unfold. What stirs in you as you breathe with creation? What do you feel when you see that baby take His first breath? How can it be that God became one of us, vulnerable and humble, reordering the world with a single inhale?

We still live in the tension between now and not yet, waiting for Jesus to come again, to make all things new. But each Advent, we remember that God has already come close—and still comes close, again and again.

BORROW THIS PRAYER

O Christ who dwells in us and among us,
Help us to be people of courage and vulnerability.
Jesus, You went first, breaking through
To our world as an infant,
Swaddled and held by a mother.
May we feel safe, known, and loved, never forgetting
That You're always pursuing us and
Making a way where there is no way.
You know what it's like to be carried
And to be the One who carries.
May we take time to reflect on
This beautiful mystery.
Amen.[398]

Adapted from "Vulnerable God" in Every Season Sacred

* Isaiah 7:14, NLT.
† See Matthew 1:23.

DECEMBER 17

The Word gave life to everything that was created,
and his life brought light to everyone.

JOHN 1:4 (NLT)

INHALE: Your life
EXHALE: Brings light.

The "most wonderful time of the year" often doesn't feel quite so wonderful.

We rise under cover of darkness and return home under the dim light of the moon. There are gifts to buy, plans to make, and never enough time or money or energy to do it all. The joy we're told to feel sometimes feels out of reach. We get picture-perfect cards in the mail—the highlight reels of other people's lives—while we're intimately acquainted with our messy, chaotic behind-the-scenes.

Comparison leads us into dark places.

I love reading the end-of-year updates from friends and family, but I'll be honest: I feel the sting when I know that my disabled daughter might never meet the milestones of the peers I read about. I love seeing captures of family vacations while also holding the tension that travel looks different when you have a child who uses a wheelchair and needs a G-tube to eat.

I wonder how Joseph and Mary might have felt, peering into windows of warm homes, seeing soft places to land, looking longingly at those who had what they didn't have.

The One whose life brings light to everyone meets our feelings of comparison with compassion.

The light that shines on everyone doesn't erase our differences; it reminds us that we are all fully seen and known by God. The next time you begin to fall into those all-too-real rhythms of feeling like you're not enough or not doing enough this holiday season, take a breath.

Take a breath when you get another Christmas card and feel like everyone has it together but you.

When you catch yourself comparing, pause and breathe. Instead of letting your mind spiral into dark shadows, turn toward the light with a breath prayer. Let each inhale remind you that Christ—the Light of the World—is already within you.

Breathing not only sustains life but helps calm our bodies and clear our minds. Research shows that breath plays a key role in offering mental clarity and emotional regulation.[399] This is one reason breath prayer creates a powerful connection between us and our life-giving God, helping us experience peace that passes understanding in our minds, bodies, and souls.*

Where has comparison been trying to steal your light this week? As you pray alongside your breath, invite the light of God's compassion to fill that space.

BREATHE THIS IN

Exhale comparison. Inhale compassion. The act of breathing helps balance oxygen and carbon-dioxide levels, influencing brain networks that regulate emotion.[400] When you feel comparison creeping in or find yourself living under the shadows of envy, let your slow, deep breaths become a prayer.

* See Philippians 4:7.

DECEMBER 18

Do not be afraid; for see—I am bringing you good news of great joy for all the people: to you is born this day . . . a Savior.

LUKE 2:10-11 (NRSV)

INHALE: Open my heart
EXHALE: To all of Your love.

I turn the snow globe over in my hands, watching white dust swirl around a small golden bird in the middle. It's heavy in my palms as I wind the little metal key. A soft, tinny whisper of "Silent Night" begins to play. I place it gently on a shelf, high enough to be safe from the curious hands of our young children.

I bought the globe on clearance. It's not fancy, but in this stage of burp rags and sticky fingers, it feels good to hold something delicate and beautiful.

If you've ever been around young children, you might know where this story is going.

The snow globe is . . . no longer with us. In fact, it didn't have a long life.

"I'm sorry, Mommy," he sniffles, eyes rimmed with tears. "We were scared you'd be mad."

I pull him close. "It's okay," I say, smoothing his hair as I wrap him in a hug. *It's for you that I set out the decorations. It's all for you.*

I think of that night so many years ago, when a blaze of light filled the sky and said, "Do not be afraid. I bring you good news of great joy for all people."

The shepherds trembled before the brightness of heaven, but God's message was clear. This new reality wasn't to sit on a shelf. *It's all for you.*

Maybe that's why, later, the One whose birth made stars shine and angels sing gathered His friends around a table, breaking bread, and, with His very life, said, *It's all for you.*

All this peace. All this joy. All this light in the darkness.

It's not for show. It's out of love.

And it's all for you.

PRACTICING THE WAY

Lectio divina is a way to prayerfully read Scripture. Take a few minutes to sit with today's passage:

The angel said to them, "Do not be afraid, for see, I am bringing you good news of great joy for all the people: to you is born this day in the city of David a Savior, who is the Messiah, the Lord."

- **Read.** As you read and slowly reread this passage, notice the words or phrases that stand out.
- **Reflect.** What might God be saying to you through this word or phrase?
- **Respond.** Speak honestly to God about what arises in you.
- **Rest.** Sit in silence for a few breaths, receiving the good news that is *for you.*

DECEMBER 19

By the tender mercy of our God, the dawn from on high will break upon us, to give light to those who sit in darkness and in the shadow of death, to guide our feet into the way of peace.

LUKE 1:78-79 (NRSV)

INHALE: Your mercy
EXHALE: Guides me to peace.

I've gotten into the bad habit of scrolling social media feeds before the sun comes up. (Highly *not* recommended.) I sip my morning coffee and read headline after headline of darkness and division and despair.

We so desperately ache for peace on earth, I think as I read about another act of violence, another reason to wonder if light will ever break through.

Some mornings, the world feels like one long night.

But if I'm standing in my kitchen at just the right time—there with my pajamas and bedhead, hands wrapped around a steaming mug of coffee—I begin to see the dawn break through. Soft ribbons of pink swirl across the sky, bold against our frosted lawn. Beams of light filter through our old windows, warming my face as they whisper, *The night, no matter how dark, won't last forever.*

Day after day, God's mercy can't help but rise.

God breathes, and life begins again—in relationships, churches, neighborhoods, even the corners of our own hearts we thought were too far gone.

Inhale, exhale.
Night, day.
Darkness, light.

Turn after turn, time after time, God's compassion keeps circling back. Yes, you bear witness to the dark . . . but will you stay awake to the light too?

Luke calls the light of God's mercy "the dawn from on high." At any given moment, it's easy for my mind to get away from me, fixating on what has gone wrong or what *could* go wrong.

But what might change if we let God's love spill across the landscape of our darkest nights, illuminating hope and guiding our feet onto the way of peace?

The world may insist on night, but Christ's mercy, like the winter sun climbing the horizon on a cold December morning, keeps rising.

On the darkest nights (and dark mornings too), borrow today's breath prayer. Yes, the world is weary. But even so, you can find reason to rejoice: The One who painted the first sunrise is still, in tender mercy, guiding you on the path of peace.

PRACTICING THE WAY

Set aside five quiet minutes this week to watch the sunrise.

Inhale God's mercy. Exhale what feels heavy.

As we draw closer to Christmas, let each breath remind you that, because of God's tender mercy, the Light of the World still rises to guide your path toward peace.

DECEMBER 20

You're sons of Light, daughters of Day. We live under wide open skies and know where we stand. So let's not sleepwalk through life like those others. Let's keep our eyes open and be smart.

1 THESSALONIANS 5:5-6 (MSG)

INHALE: Spirit of God,
EXHALE: Help me breathe with You.

Advent interrupts us.

While the holiday season vies for our attention with crammed calendars and countdowns warning how many shopping days are left, this season offers a sacred invitation to just . . . *breathe*. To slow down instead of rushing ahead.

To awaken to the eternal in our everyday lives instead of breathlessly or mindlessly moving full speed ahead, wrapped up in to-do lists, with arms full of boxes stacked so high that we can barely see.

Advent isn't merely a countdown to Christmas (no matter how fun those cardboard calendars with the tiny chocolates may be). At its essence, Advent is a time set aside to remember that God's rhythm of breath interrupts our hurried, harried ways. In fact, right now is the perfect time to draw near to the One who breathes—and is our breath itself.

When our world shouts *more*, this season of waiting draws us into a sacred pause, a place of anticipation. Douglas Scott Dent, in his thesis *Breathing with God: Inhaling God's Spirit, Exhaling God's Reign*, reimagines Saint Augustine's famous line, "Our hearts are restless until they find rest in Thee," to be "Our spirits are breathless until they breathe with God."[401]

What might it look like to breathe with God?

- **Inspire:** Let every inhale serve as a reminder of Genesis 2:7, when God breathed life into humanity.
- **Aspire:** Align with the way of Jesus by walking in rhythms of mercy, peace, justice, and compassion.
- **Conspire:** Breathe together with God for the sake of the world. (From the Latin *con spirare*—"to breathe together," as Jesus breathed on the disciples, filling them with the Spirit, in John 20:22.)[402]

Take a deep breath. Lift your eyes. Inhale through your nose. Ask God to awaken you to the presence of Christ. When you're ready, let your breath go.

PAUSE AND PONDER

What might it look like to awaken to God's presence so you might breathe with the Spirit as we move through these last days leading up to Christmas? What do you need to let go of? What do you need to move toward?

DECEMBER 21

WINTER SOLSTICE/BEGINNING OF WINTER

I am counting on the LORD; yes, I am counting on him. I have put my hope in his word.

PSALM 130:5 (NLT)

INHALE: This darkness won't last forever;
EXHALE: I put my hope in You, O Lord.

Flashing red and blue lights spill through our bedroom window from all directions, waking me up. I reach for my glasses, climb out of bed, and pull back the curtain to see fire trucks and ambulances parked in front of our neighbors' house. Their harsh lights mix with the soft glow of Christmas decorations.

I notice what appears to be a stretcher and immediately look away.

My heart drops. For a minute, I can't find my breath. I don't know what's happening, but I know something is very, very wrong. I grab my phone to send a message to our neighbor, but something deep inside gives me pause. I sense, even then, that he won't respond.

I find out a few hours later that he's gone.

I sit on the edge of my bed, stunned. The air feels frozen with what I don't know how to say. I want to hide under the covers, to pretend it's not happening—not our street, not our neighbor. There are moments when words fail, when all we can do is sit in silence and let the tears come.

Horrible things happen all the time, but tragedy feels particularly cruel near Christmas. A faith that doesn't make space for the hard things is no faith worth holding. We have hope, even in the worst parts of life, because we have a God who weeps with us. A God who draws near to our deepest sorrows and aching hearts. A God who sits with us in the dark when we feel so very alone.*

The beginning of winter marks the shortest days and longest nights of the year. But afterward, little by little, the world will grow lighter again. Hope doesn't deny the depths of our despair; it waits there, trusting that dawn will come.† We hold hope because, however wobbly our trust may be, we believe the One who said, *This is not the end*—the One who takes away the sting of death, who strips evil of its power.‡ Whatever depths you're praying out of today—your sorrow, your anger, your doubt—it doesn't scare God. You're not alone in your loss. You're not alone in your ache. You're not alone in your tears or your middle-of-the-night wonderings.

Tonight, as the longest night falls, we pray. The beauty of shared liturgies is that we pray them together—on the same day, with the same heart, to the same God.

BORROW THIS PRAYER

Spark in us a holy hope,
For You are Immanuel—
You are with us.
Light our way toward You.
Amen.[403]

Adapted from "A Light Still Shines" in Every Season Sacred

* See John 11:35; Psalm 34:18; Psalm 139:11-12.

† See Lamentations 3:25-26.
‡ See 1 Corinthians 15:55-57.

DECEMBER 22

The Word became human and made his home among us.

JOHN 1:14 (NLT)

INHALE: You make Your
EXHALE: Home among us.

God desires to be near you.

So much so that God took on flesh and became one of us, walking our roads, breathing our air, sharing our tears.

"The central mystery within all of Christianity, undergirding everything else, is the mystery of the incarnation," writes theologian Ronald Rolheiser.[404]

The incarnation, simply put, means Jesus "moved into the neighborhood." He came to live with us as one of us. As John 1:14 in *The Message* says:

The Word became flesh and blood,
and moved into the neighborhood.
We saw the glory with our own eyes,
the one-of-a-kind glory,
like Father, like Son,
Generous inside and out,
true from start to finish.

Because God delights to dwell among us, there's not a single moment when we cannot draw near in return.

Take a deep breath, right here in this moment. Inhale through your nose. Feel the air expand within you. Hold it for a few beats before slowly releasing it through your mouth. Repeat this a few times, letting your breath become a prayer of its own as you sit in the marvelous mystery that the God who breathed life into humanity once breathed this same air.

"The God-with-us is a close God, a God whom we call our refuge, our stronghold, our wisdom, and even, more intimately, our helper, our shepherd, our love," writes Henri Nouwen. "We will never really know God as a compassionate God if we do not understand with our heart and mind that 'he lived among us.'"[405]

God moves toward us so we can move toward others. God shows compassion to us so we can show compassion to others. We inhale God's goodness, and with God's help, we exhale back into the world.

Christmas reminds us that we don't have a distant, disconnected God. We have a God who moved into the neighborhood out of deep, abiding love.

BORROW THIS PRAYER

O Word that became flesh,
Thank You for making
Your home among us
And within us.
We can hardly fathom
The mystery and grace
Of Your presence.
In this Advent season,
Invite us into rhythms
Of soulful reflection.
Amen.[406]

Adapted from "The Word" in Every Season Sacred

DECEMBER 23

While he was still a long way off, his father saw him and was filled with compassion for him; he ran to his son, threw his arms around him and kissed him.

LUKE 15:20 (NIV)

INHALE: Compassionate God,
EXHALE: You welcome me home.

Airports are chaotic—especially this time of year. But when I find myself waiting for a suitcase at baggage claim, I don't mind. I love sitting near arrivals. It restores my faith in humanity every single time. Grown men sprinting toward their mothers. Laughter and tears mingling as arms wrap around one another.

There's something special about watching someone be welcomed home.

Jesus tells a story about a son who loses his way, hurts his family terribly, and squanders his inheritance, ending up broke and all alone. Desperate, he decides to make his way home, ready to beg for forgiveness, rehearsing his apology with each weary step.

His father could be angry. Could make him grovel. Could be stubborn or demanding. But instead, Jesus says, while the son is "still a long way off," the father is "filled with compassion." He doesn't just wait on the front porch or slam the door in disappointment—he *runs*. And when he gets to his beloved son, he wraps him in his arms and kisses him.

The story is true for us too. "The Father's love and acceptance are absolutely free," writes Tim Keller in *The Prodigal God*.[407]

The heartbeat of Christmas is that God, seeing humanity still a long way off, ran toward us in the person of Jesus.

One of my favorite movies is *Planes, Trains, and Automobiles*. Every year, I laugh as hijinks ensue. Amid all the chaos and comedy, what gets me is the heart. Yes, it's about two strangers trying to get home for the holidays, but it's really about realizing that we find home in those we love.

There's a line I think about every year: "Love . . . is not a big enough word."

That's the Father's heart too. There are no words big enough to capture the love our Father has for you. No matter where you've been, no matter where you're going, take a breath. Close your eyes. Picture the Father running toward you. Feel the rush of welcome. Feel the warmth of an embrace that whispers, *You're home. You're home. You're home.*

RHYTHM OF BREATH

My favorite place
To people-watch
Is the airport escalator:
Arms open,
Eyes sparkling.
There you are—
Let me get a good look,
Let me take your bag.
I missed you,
I love you.
You are *home*.
You are home.

DECEMBER 24

CHRISTMAS EVE

That night there were shepherds staying in the fields nearby, guarding their flocks of sheep. Suddenly, an angel of the Lord appeared among them, and the radiance of the Lord's glory surrounded them.

LUKE 2:8-9 (NLT)

INHALE: Breath of heaven,
EXHALE: Here You are.

Tonight is for you. Tonight is for all of us.

The worn, the weary. The wonderer, the wanderer. *The whole world.*

We find ourselves at the precipice. All of creation has held its breath, and now we stand at the edge of a long-awaited exhale—where heaven and earth meet in the cry of an infant, and nothing will ever be the same.

In the blink of an eye, in the beat of a heart, in the gasp of a breath, the soul feels its worth.

Tonight reminds us that hope breaks through in unexpected ways. Hope doesn't come through earthly empires but through a baby. The earth-shattering love of God rarely takes the shape we expect, but it always meets us where we are, turning our notions of glory and power upside down.

When the angels announced the good news, they didn't appear to the powerful or the popular. They didn't visit palaces or parties. They appeared to shepherds—the ones laboring in the fields, keeping watch by night. God showed up there, in the dark, among the ordinary, announcing that divine glory does not stay distant but draws near to the rest of us.

God shows up in the most unexpected places, illuminating our ordinary lives and inviting us to both know our Savior and be known by Him.

You are not alone in all that you hold, in the ways you've long felt unseen or forgotten. Your Creator understands.

God sees our pain and doesn't leave us to muddle through alone. The long-awaited Messiah came not with military might but with the fragile cry of a newborn.

"God entered into our world not with the crushing impact of unbearable glory," writes Brennan Manning, "but in the way of weakness, vulnerability and need."[408]

Let go of that breath you've been holding. Right here, right now, God has drawn near—not just to the world, but to *you.* He's swaddled in strips of cloth, waiting to be held.

Tonight, we light our candles. Tonight, we are known. Tonight, we exhale.

BORROW THIS PRAYER

Help us to get quiet, to get small
So we can make space in our souls
For the Newborn
Who will illuminate the darkness
And change everything.

O come,
O come,
Emmanuel.[409]

From "A Prayer for Advent"
in To Light Their Way

DECEMBER 25

CHRISTMAS DAY

Glory to God in the highest heaven, and on earth peace among those whom he favors!

LUKE 2:14 (NRSV)

INHALE: Every breath I take
EXHALE: Will sing Your praise.

As a child, I saw *The Muppet Christmas Carol* in the theater and became immediately transfixed. I think I've watched it every year since.

Legendary actor Michael Caine plays Ebenezer Scrooge in the whimsical adaptation of Charles Dickens's masterpiece. He takes the role seriously, even when surrounded by singing costars Kermit the Frog and Miss Piggy, and somehow—*it works*. I don't think it's an exaggeration to say this children's movie has shaped my theology. God has used it, year after year, as a reminder that redemption is always within reach.

It's a story of a man who has forgotten what it means to love, so hardened by greed, bitterness, and loneliness that he can no longer see the image of God in his neighbor—or in himself.

Hardened hearts are far from fictional. Every day, the news is full of indifference toward the sick and the suffering, lack of care for the poor, refusal to protect workers, and apathy toward those who are most vulnerable.

When I start to believe people are too far gone, I remember Ebenezer Scrooge. Christ can transform even the cruelest, most closed-off hearts. That's the gospel. The good news of Christmas morning is that peace is possible even for the most calloused among us. If it's true for Scrooge, then by God's cosmic grace, it's true for you. It's true for me. It's true for the richest, meanest old miser you know.

My take on the tale is that Scrooge meets the Holy Spirit in a dream and is changed forever. After his long night of reckoning, Scrooge throws open the window of his London apartment, light spilling in.

He repents, giving away his wealth to those he has wronged. He reconciles, showing up at his nephew's home to share a meal. He repairs, raising the salary of his employee and caring for the poor he once ignored. It's a deeply Christian story of compassion, generosity of spirit, and action, of following the call to love our neighbors and lift the lowly. It's a song of a man reborn into the greatest story of all.

On Christmas, we remember the miracle that Jesus is born in unlikely places and in unlikely people. No one—not even the most hard-hearted—has drifted beyond the reach of God's grace.

Take a deep breath. Throw open the windows of your heart. Let the light spill in. For today, in Bethlehem, the Savior—the Messiah, the Lord—has been born.*

BORROW THIS PRAYER

O God of mercy,
We rejoice, for on this morning
We celebrate the day of Christ's arrival—
The day that changed everything.
And we give all the glory to You
Forevermore.[410]

From "A Prayer for Christmas Morning" in To Light Their Way

---

* See Luke 2:11.

DECEMBER 26

BOXING DAY/FEAST OF SAINT STEPHEN

To us a child is born, to us a son is given, and the government will be on his shoulders. And he will be called Wonderful Counselor, Mighty God, Everlasting Father, Prince of Peace.

ISAIAH 9:6 (NIV)

INHALE: Help me breathe Your peace
EXHALE: Into the world, O God.

I used to think Boxing Day meant it was time to lug the storage totes upstairs and box up the Christmas decorations. But really, it's the start of the twelve days of Christmas.

Today calls us to let the celebration of Christ's birth spill into acts of compassion, carrying a light long after the last Advent candle flickers out.

Boxing Day gets its name from the historical practice of churches opening their alms boxes—donation boxes used to collect gifts for those in need—on the day after Christmas. It was common for employers to give their servants and workers boxes filled with food or gifts, reflecting the spirit of generosity associated with Saint Stephen.

December 26 honors Stephen, the first Christian martyr, a man who lived with compassion and gave his life for the gospel of peace.* Stephen's story reminds us that the peace of Christ is not passive but an active expression of compassion-fueled courage. His empathy for the poor and his forgiveness for his killers reflects the light of the Christ he followed.†

Yesterday, we celebrated the birth of Christ. Today, we continue that celebration by carrying His peace into the world.

Christmas doesn't stop at the manger. The Prince of Peace we welcomed invites us to bring peace on earth throughout the year through everyday rhythms of generosity, forgiveness, sacrifice, and service.‡

Maybe you're tired from all the work of Christmas . . . wrapping gifts, making meals, filling calendars. Maybe you have a stomachache from going too hard on all the sugar cookies and eggnog. Take a breath. Carrying the peace of Christ into your everyday life doesn't have to be a giant gesture. Being a peacemaker flows out of the love you breathe into the world as a follower of Jesus.§

Before you pack away the stockings and tear down the garland, take a moment to breathe. The light of Christmas still lingers, and the work of peace continues—in you, through you, for the healing of the world.¶

RHYTHM OF BREATH

When the song of the angels is stilled . . .
The work of Christmas begins:
To find the lost,
To heal the broken,
To feed the hungry,
To release the prisoner,
To rebuild the nations,
To bring peace among brothers,
To make music in the heart.[411]

Howard Thurman

---

* See Acts 6–7.
† See Acts 7:60.
‡ See Romans 12:18; Colossians 3:14-15.
§ See Matthew 5:9.
¶ See John 20:21-22.

DECEMBER 27

FEAST OF SAINT JOHN

Beloved, let us love one another, because love is from God; everyone who loves is born of God and knows God.

1 JOHN 4:7 (NRSV)

INHALE: God incarnate,
EXHALE: Help me love like You.

Today, we honor Saint John the Evangelist, the disciple who was a dear friend of Jesus—the one who leaned close enough to hear the heartbeat of God.*

John's Gospel skips the manger scene, but it gives us something else: a sweeping vision of what it means for the Light of the World to dwell among us.

John shows that the story of Jesus is the ongoing story of God taking on flesh and breaking through the darkness again and again.† John doesn't just tell us about Jesus but invites us to know the living Christ and be known by Him.

How might you let that love transform how you see (and serve) the world God so loves?‡

The God John reveals isn't detached from suffering but humbly enters into it.

The One who could have come in glory, born into palaces and power, chose to enter poverty under the power of an unfriendly empire. The Light that John describes is the presence of God showing up to the lonely and the lowly. God's glory broke in among ordinary people who were longing for liberation. The way God decided to come into the world tells us something about how we're called to live in it: with humility, compassion, and solidarity.

If the Christ-child was born among the poor, then how might we notice God's Light in the places the empires of our day overlook?

If we're looking for Jesus, maybe we'll find Him in prisons and shelters, in hospital rooms and at border crossings.

The incarnation is God's declaration that no place of suffering is godforsaken.

If "God is light, pure light,"§ then every time we extend God's love to others through compassion and mercy and kindness and goodness and peace, we light the way for others to meet the Prince of Peace. We live out the spirit of Christmas by living as Jesus did—cultivating peace even when it's unpopular, extending love where fear looms, and trusting that the light of God's love is stronger than the darkness.

What would it look like to love someone today in a way that lets God's light shine through you?

When the world feels loud and fractured, when it feels like the peace of Christmas is but a moment in time, breathe through today's breath prayer. Let your inhale and exhale remind you that just as Christ breathed peace on His disciples, He breathes through you still.¶

SACRED ECHOES

God is revealed in Jesus Christ and, through him, in human history and in the least important and poorest sector of those who make it up.[412]

Gustavo Gutiérrez

---

* See John 13:23.
† See John 1:14; 8:12.
‡ See 1 John 4:12.

§ 1 John 1:5, MSG.
¶ See John 14:17.

DECEMBER 28

FEAST OF THE HOLY INNOCENTS

A cry was heard in Ramah—weeping and great mourning.

MATTHEW 2:18 (NLT)

INHALE: God of justice,
EXHALE: You hear my cries.

Ever since His birth, Jesus has unsettled the powerful who cling to control.

Thousands of years ago, a baby was born, and the ruthless, cowardly king felt so threatened by this little one's power, so terrified of losing control over those he ruled, that he ordered the killing of all baby boys in and around Bethlehem. But Herod's empire of fear was not—and never will be—a match for Christ's Kingdom of love.

Today is the Feast of the Holy Innocents, a day to honor the memory of infants killed under Herod's order after Jesus' birth.

When the Magi saw the stunning star that led them to Jerusalem, they made their way to Herod's palace to learn more about the newborn king. Herod told them to report back after they found the child. But after meeting Jesus, the Magi realized the King's spiteful intentions and refused to return.

Enraged, Herod unleashed violence against the most vulnerable.

As we read in Matthew 2:16-17, "Herod was furious when he realized that the wise men had outwitted him. He sent soldiers to kill all the boys in and around Bethlehem who were two years old and under, based on the wise men's report of the star's first appearance."*

We still see Herods—those who cling to power at any cost—in our world today. But even when it seems like evil reigns victorious, it will never have the final word. What others intend for harm, God works toward redemption.† The world may rule through fear and control, but the way of Jesus restores and redeems.‡

As you pray, ask God to help you trust that even amid the world's horrors, even when you can't see how God is working amid the pain and suffering, Christ's love will always win and God's justice will always prevail.

PAUSE AND PONDER

Prayers of lament are part of our faith. As followers of Jesus, we don't turn away from suffering—we bear witness and invite God into our pain. Set aside a few moments today to write your own prayer of lament:

Christ our King, I cry out for ______________ ______________. I grieve ______________ ______________ and lament ______________ ______________. Draw near to the pain of ______________________________.

When I am ______________________________, remind me that You are ______________ ______________. Bring ______________ ______________ to the suffering. Give ______________________________ to those who cry out for Your ______________.

And when I am discouraged by ______________ ______________, breathe hope in me that ______________________________.

* NLT.

† See Genesis 50:20; Acts 4:27-28.

‡ See John 10:10.

DECEMBER 29

Your love, LORD, reaches to the heavens,
your faithfulness to the skies.

PSALM 36:5 (NIV)

INHALE: Through it all, O God,
EXHALE: You have been faithful.

The rush has slowed. The gifts have been unwrapped. The holiday to-do lists have lost their urgency. But if we're honest, in the stillness, we feel a bit restless.

What if we received today as a sacred pause—a moment to reflect before moving forward?

These quiet days between Christmas and the New Year act as an in-between space to finally catch our breath. The Examen, a centuries-old prayer practice rooted in the wisdom of Saint Ignatius, invites us to notice where God has been present throughout the day (or year). It helps us pay attention—not to evaluate or judge—but to see our lives through the loving gaze of God.

The Examen is a simple prayer that helps us examine where, how, and when we've experienced God's faithful presence in our lives. (It's not a time to rank our wins and losses or fall into self-criticism.)

In our loud world, praying the Examen helps us quiet our souls and listen for grace where we may have missed it. I think of it as a guide to help me stay awake to God's peace, God's presence, and God's promptings.

May the Examen help you see your year immersed in God's faithfulness—in every joy and every sorrow. May the Examen offer you another way to encounter God, who is always with you. May you reflect on and be transformed by God's grace, resulting in a peaceful heart so you can cultivate peace in your community and the world.

PRACTICING THE WAY

1. **Become aware of God's presence.** It may be helpful to light a candle or pray something simple like "God, be with me."
2. **Begin with gratitude.** Reflect on your year through a lens of thankfulness. Let God begin to repair your weary heart as you give thanks.
3. **Review the year.** Get curious about how God has spoken to you through the places you've gone, the people in your midst, and the events that have happened. Notice where God was with you. Who showed you love? Who did you extend love to? How did you experience God? Where might God have been inviting you into something? Pay attention to your emotions as you reflect.
4. **Get honest.** In light of Christ's mercy, you don't have to hide the times you may have hurt or dishonored yourself, God, or someone else with your words or thoughts, your action or inaction. Make space to repent. Ask God to help you grow in humility.
5. **Look toward the New Year in grace.** As you turn toward another year, name what you're anticipating and ask God to guide you in love.[413]

To learn more about the Examen, visit ignatianspirituality.com or read Father James Martin's book *Learning to Pray*.

DECEMBER 30

By the breath of God ice is given, and the broad waters are frozen fast.

JOB 37:10 (ESV)

INHALE: God, You breathe,
EXHALE: And it takes my breath away.

We live in a world that can explain away almost anything. A quick search yields pages of facts and figures that break down the wonder of our world into tidy little data points.

If we're not careful, we can lose our sense of awe—forgetting that behind every heartbeat, every snowflake, every frozen pond, every breath is the One who gives life itself.*

As this year draws its final breath, how might you pause—step away from the noise and simply be with the One who holds every season with tenderness and care?

You don't have to chase new resolutions or set lofty goals. Jesus invites us into rhythms of rest, not resolutions of striving.†

In every inhale, every exhale, God has been with you. When you were scared and when you felt safe, when you were lonely and when you felt deeply loved—God was there. And God will be with you still. The same Spirit who hovered over creation and breathed life into all of it breathes in *you*.‡

If you're able to, get outside today. Let the fresh air fill your lungs. Watch the ice-coated branches shimmer in the daylight. Watch your breath hang in clouds like a prayer in the winter night sky.

Every breath you take is an offering of love from the One who has been with you all along. You don't have to explain it. You don't even have to understand it.

What a wonder. What a gift.

Further Reading: Read the "Gathering the Stones" chapter in *Every Season Sacred.*

RHYTHM OF BREATH

I set aside my shiny maps
And shimmering plans
And wait for You, O God.
I stay here
With open hands,
Free from the weight
Of another thing to do,
Another person to be,
Another place to go.
I stay here
Just as I am—
Hearing You
Over countdowns and noisemakers.
There's nothing I have to do
But be.
There's nowhere I have to go
But here.
There's no one I have to be
But me.[414]

---

* See Genesis 2:7; John 1:3-4.
† See Matthew 11:28-29.
‡ See John 20:21-22.

DECEMBER 31

Give your entire attention to what God is doing right now, and don't get worked up about what may or may not happen tomorrow. God will help you deal with whatever hard things come up when the time comes.

MATTHEW 6:34 (MSG)

INHALE: God of all time,
EXHALE: Help me be present.

Your mind races ahead, tracking every possibility, bracing for what might come next.

What if things don't go as planned? What if it's too much? What if you drop the ball?

But right here, right now, the Spirit of God is with you.

How might your day change if you thought of Jesus' words in Matthew as a hand on your shoulder, steady and sure?

God knows how quickly your mind skips to the future, how the weight of *what-ifs* can steal the gift of *what is*.

"Tomorrow will come," Jesus told his disciples, "but you don't have to figure it out today." He wasn't telling them to ignore tomorrow but to trust that they didn't have to live there yet.

Breathe.

Let your inhale remind you that you're held.

Let your exhale be a blessed assurance that God is here.

Today, let your breath act as an anchor to the holy ground of *now*.

As you pray through today's breath prayer, open your hands. Ask God to help you release your grip on what has not yet come. When anxiety pulls you forward into the unknown, let your breath bring you back to the present.

Further Reading: Read "A Prayer for a New Year" in *To Light Their Way*.

BORROW THIS PRAYER

As we look at fresh calendars
And hold planners full of promise,
Help us to be intentional in
How we spend our days
And where we invest our time.
We thank You for the magic
Of capturing snowflakes on our tongues
And tasting the promise
Of a fresh start to a New Year.[415]

Adapted from "A Prayer for Winter" in Every Season Sacred

APPENDIX A

LITURGICAL CALENDAR*

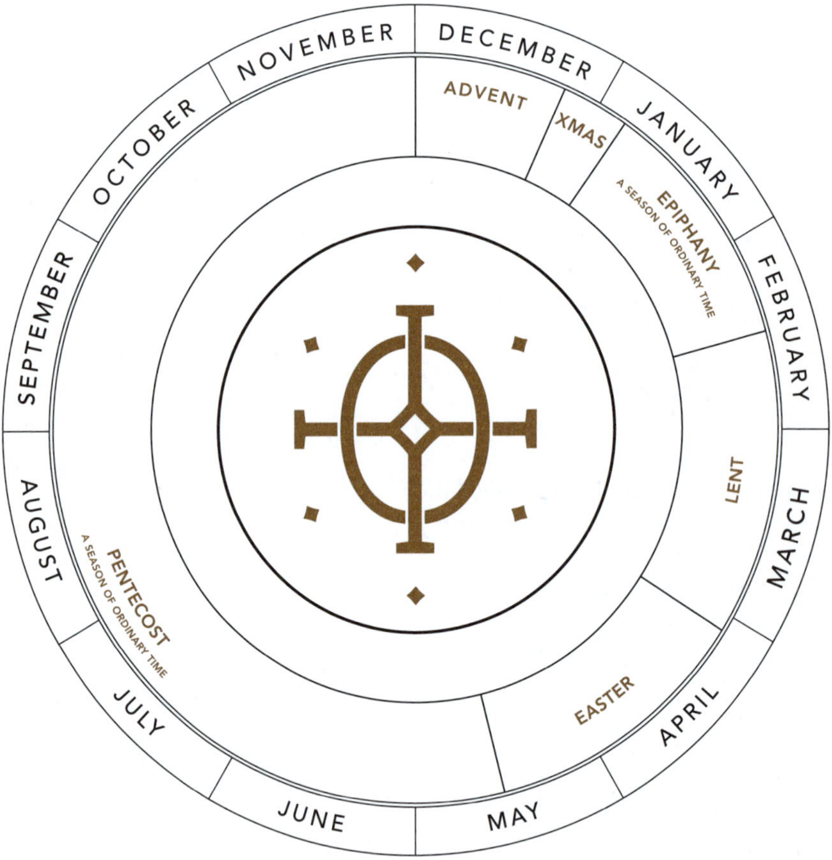

*Used with permission from Sacred Ordinary Days

NOTES

1. Monica DiCristina, "A Therapist's Toolkit for Emotionally Stressful Times," *The In-Between*, January 22, 2025, https://monicadicristina.substack.com/p/a-therapists-toolkit?utm_source=post-email-title&publication_id=789516&post_id=155432880&utm_campaign=email-post-title&isFreemail=true&r=1tbhj&triedRedirect=true&utm_medium=email.
2. Frederick Buechner, *Beyond Words: Daily Readings in the ABC's of Faith* (HarperCollins, 2009), 139.
3. Shivani Zoting, "Personal Development Market Empowering Growth Through Wellness, Coaching, and Digital Learning," Precedence Research, June 25, 2025, https://www.precedenceresearch.com/personal-development-market.
4. Richard Rohr, *Everything Belongs: The Gift of Contemplative Prayer* (The Crossroad Publishing Company, 2003), 154.
5. Regina Chow Trammel and John Trent, *A Counselor's Guide to Christian Mindfulness: Engaging the Mind, Body, and Soul in Biblical Practices and Therapies* (Zondervan Reflective, 2021), 41.
6. Jan Richardson, *Circle of Grace: A Book of Blessings for the Seasons* (Wanton Gospeller Press, 2015), 47–48.
7. "Romans 14:19," Bible Hub, accessed December 15, 2025, https://biblehub.com/romans/14-19.htm#study.
8. Aundi Kolber, *Try Softer: A Fresh Approach to Move Us Out of Anxiety, Stress, and Survival Mode—and into a Life of Connection and Joy* (Tyndale, 2020), 25.
9. Kolber, *Try Softer*, 25.
10. Henri J. M. Nouwen, *Discernment: Reading the Signs of Daily Life* (HarperOne, 2013), 8.
11. Julie Saad, *Contemplative Life: Discovering Our Path into the Heart of God* (Balboa Press, 2021), 147–149.
12. Adapted from Saad, *Contemplative Life*, 153.
13. Thomas Keating, "The Most Excellent Path, Part 2, with Thomas Keating" excerpted from *The Spiritual Journey Part 5, Divine Love*, virtual lecture, posted May 6, 2022, by Contemplative Outreach, YouTube, https://www.youtube.com/watch?v=me9v836X8vE.
14. Thomas Keating, "The Four Yous," *Contemplative Outreach News* 23, no. 2 (June 2008): 2, https://www.contemplativeoutreach.org/wp-content/uploads/2018/02/conewsletterjune2008.pdf.
15. Adapted from "Notes for: Contemplative Prayer," Center for Action and Contemplation, accessed December 3, 2025, https://cac.org/wp-content/uploads/2016/01/CACFoundationSet_digital-insert.pdf.
16. Hadley Leggett, "'Cyclic Sighing' Can Help Breathe Away Anxiety," Stanford Medicine, February 9, 2023, https://med.stanford.edu/news/insights/2023/02/cyclic-sighing-can-help-breathe-away-anxiety.html.
17. James Nestor, *Breath: The New Science of a Lost Art* (Riverhead Books, 2020), 82.
18. Nestor, *Breath*, 83.
19. Madison N. Pierce, "Letter to the Hebrews," in *The New Testament in Color: A Multiethnic Bible Commentary*, ed. Esau D. McCaulley et. al. (IVP Academic, 2024), 589–590.
20. Erlisa Demneri, "Bridging the Gap: Self-Help Books as Accessible Introductions to Other Genres and Cultures," *Harvard Crimson*, November 7, 2024, https://www.thecrimson.com/article/2024/11/7/self-help-books-accessible-introductions-cultures-genres/.
21. Alison Cook, *I Shouldn't Feel This Way: Name What's Hard, Tame Your Guilt, and Transform Self-Sabotage into Brave Action* (Thomas Nelson, 2024), 21.
22. Michael Merschel, "It's Not Just Inspiration: Careful Breathing Can Help Your Health," American Heart Association, July 7, 2023, https://www.heart.org/en/news/2023/07/07/its-not-just-inspiration-careful-breathing-can-help-your-health.
23. Anis Mojgani, "Anis Mojgani Performs Shake the Dust at HEAVY AND LIGHT," video, January 9, 2010, posted January 14, 2010, by To Write Love on Her Arms, YouTube, 2 mins. 57 sec., https://www.youtube.com/watch?v=0qDtHdloK44.
24. Howard Thurman, *The Luminous Darkness: A Personal Interpretation of the Anatomy of Segregation and the Ground of Hope* (Harper and Row, 1963), 64.
25. Thurman, *Luminous Darkness*, 65.
26. Adapted from "A Prayer for Martin Luther King Jr. Day" in Kayla Craig, *To Light Their Way: A Collection of Prayers and Liturgies for Parents* (Tyndale, 2021), 141.
27. "Ruach," Bible Hub, accessed December 18, 2025, https://biblehub.com/hebrew/7307.htm; "Pneuma," Bible Hub, accessed December 18, 2025, https://biblehub.com/greek/4151.htm.
28. Walter Brueggemann, *Awed to Heaven, Rooted in Earth: Prayers of Walter Brueggemann* (Fortress Press, 2002), 93.
29. Ronald Rolheiser, *The Holy Longing: The Search for a Christian Spirituality* (Doubleday, 1999), 83.
30. Rolheiser, *Holy Longing*, 83.
31. Kate Bowler, *Have a Beautiful, Terrible Day! Daily Meditations for the Ups, Downs, & In-Betweens* (Convergent Books, 2024), 97.
32. Michael Breus, *Sleep Drink Breathe: Simple Daily Habits for Profound Long-Term Health* (Little, Brown Spark, 2024), 190.

33. Breus, *Sleep Drink Breathe*, 190.
34. Whitney R. Simpson, *Holy Listening with Breath, Body, and the Spirit* (Upper Room Books, 2016), 27.
35. Thomas Keating, *Open Mind, Open Heart: The Contemplative Dimension of the Gospel*, 20th anniversary ed. (Bloomsbury Continuum, 2019), 66.
36. Eugene H. Peterson, *A Long Obedience in the Same Direction: Discipleship in an Instant Society* (InterVarsity Press, 2000), 78.
37. Peterson, *Long Obedience*, 79.
38. Richard P. Brown and Patricia L. Gerbarg, *The Healing Power of the Breath: Simple Techniques to Reduce Stress and Anxiety, Enhance Concentration, and Balance Your Emotions* (Shambhala Publications, 2012), 132.
39. Breus, *Sleep Drink Breathe*, 201.
40. Frederick Buechner, *The Sacred Journey: A Memoir of Early Days* (HarperOne, 1991), 46.
41. Breus, *Sleep Drink Breathe*, 202.
42. Buechner, *Sacred Journey*, 46.
43. Douglas Scott Dent, "Breathing with God: Inhaling God's Spirit, Exhaling God's Reign" (DMin thesis, Luther Seminary, 2019), 2, https://digitalcommons.luthersem.edu/cgi/viewcontent.cgi?article=1047&context=dmin_theses.
44. Flora Slosson Wuellner, *Prayer and Our Bodies* (The Upper Room, 1987), 53.
45. Karl Barth, *Evangelical Theology: An Introduction*, trans. Grover Foley (Eerdmans, 1979), 184.
46. Madeleine L'Engle, *A Wrinkle in Time* (Square Fish, 2007), 53, 199–200.
47. Wuellner, *Prayer and Our Bodies*, 10.
48. James Finley, *The Contemplative Heart* (Sorin Books, 2000), 42.
49. Breus, *Sleep Drink Breathe*, Kindle, chapter 9.
50. "Romans 12:12," Bible Hub, accessed December 19, 2025, https://biblehub.com/romans/12-12.htm#study.
51. Keating, *Open Mind, Open Heart*, 164.
52. Julia Cameron, *The Artist's Way: A Spiritual Path to Higher Creativity* (Tarcher, 2016), 9–10.
53. "John 13:34," Bible Hub, accessed December 19, 2025, https://biblehub.com/interlinear/john/13-34.htm.
54. "Romans 8:29," Bible Hub, accessed December 19, 2025, https://biblehub.com/romans/8-29.htm#study.
55. Adapted from Jasmine Marie's advice for breathwork beginners in *Black Girls Breathing: Heal from Trauma, Combat Chronic Stress, and Find Your Freedom* (Balance, 2024), 35–36.
56. Ayesh Perera, "The Pygmalion Effect: Definition and Examples," Simply Psychology, February 13, 2024, https://www.simplypsychology.org/pygmalion-effect.html.
57. Adapted from Kayla Craig, *Every Season Sacred: Reflections, Prayers, and Invitations to Nourish Your Soul and Nurture Your Family Throughout the Year* (Tyndale, 2023), 296–298.
58. "Psalm 34:18," Bible Hub, accessed December 15, 2025, https://biblehub.com/psalms/34-18.htm#study.
59. Julian of Norwich, quoted in Joyce Rupp, *Prayer Seeds: A Gathering of Blessings, Reflections, and Poems for Spiritual Growth* (Ave Maria Press, 2017), 61.
60. Adapted from Pamela C. Hawkins, *The Awkward Season: Prayers for Lent* (Upper Room Books, 2009), 111–112. Find more at upperroom.org/resources/praying-with-a-finger-labyrinth.
61. Timothy R. Jennings, *The God-Shaped Brain: How Changing Your View of God Transforms Your Life* (InterVarsity Press, 2013), 63–65.
62. Jennings, *God-Shaped Brain*, 27.
63. Keating, *Open Mind, Open Heart*, 160.
64. Jennings, *God-Shaped Brain*, 27.
65. Michael J. Stephen, *Breath Taking: The Power, Fragility, and Future of Our Extraordinary Lungs* (Grove Atlantic, 2023), prologue, Kindle.
66. Stephen, *Breath Taking*, prologue.
67. Keating, *Open Mind, Open Heart*, 129.
68. Howard Thurman, *Howard Thurman: Essential Writings*, selected with an introduction by Luther E. Smith Jr. (Orbis Books, 2006), 60.
69. Susan McNamara et al., "Chronic Insomnia," National Library of Medicine, March 28, 2025, https://www.ncbi.nlm.nih.gov/books/NBK526136/.
70. "Psalm 4:8," Bible Hub, accessed December 15, 2025, https://biblehub.com/psalms/4-8.htm#study.
71. Stephen W. Porges, "Polyvagal Theory: A Science of Safety," Frontiers in Integrative Neuroscience 16 (May 2022): 871227, https://doi:10.3389/fnint.2022.871227.
72. Sharon McMahon (@sharonsaysso), "If you're standing up for what's right and it feels like no one is standing with you—keep going," Instagram, July 22, 2025, https://www.instagram.com/p/DMbjI2yqNDD/.
73. Buechner, *Beyond Words*, 160.
74. Nestor, *Breath*, 84.
75. MeiLan K. Han, *Breathing Lessons: A Doctor's Guide to Lung Health* (W. W. Norton, 2022), 23.
76. Ruth Haley Barton, *Sacred Rhythms: Arranging Our Lives for Spiritual Transformation* (InterVarsity Press, 2006), 12.
77. Tarlach O'Raifeartaigh and René Ostberg, "St. Patrick: Bishop and Patron Saint of Ireland," *Encyclopedia Britannica*, October 11, 2025, https://www.britannica.com/biography/Saint-Patrick.
78. Adapted from "A Prayer for St. Patrick's Day," in Craig, *To Light Their Way*, 160.
79. Thomas Keating, *Invitation to Love: The Way of Christian Contemplation* (Bloomsbury Continuum, 2012), 105.
80. Bob Stahl and Wendy Millstine, *Calming the Rush of Panic: A Mindfulness-Based Stress Reduction Guide to Freeing Yourself from Panic Attacks and Living a Vital Life* (New Harbinger Publications, 2013), 14, 30.
81. Stahl and Millstine, *Calming the Rush of Panic*, 30.
82. This book is intended for parents, but it's a helpful resource for anyone who wants to learn about God's character as revealed through Scripture.
83. Madeleine L'Engle, "A Sky Full of Children," in *Watch for the Light: Readings for Advent and Christmas* (Orbis Books, 2004), 80.
84. Geyze Diniz et al., "The Effects of Gratitude Interventions: A Systematic Review and

Meta-Analysis," *Einstein* 21 (August 2023): eRW0371, http://doi:10.31744/einstein_journal/2023RW0371.
85. "Genesis 2:7," Bible Hub, accessed December 19, 2025, https://biblehub.com/genesis/2-7.htm#study.
86. Drew Jackson (@d.jacksonpoetics), "Contemplation," Instagram, March 1, 2024, https://www.instagram.com/p/C3- QDAXLHUA/.
87. Rohr, *Everything Belongs*, 29.
88. Han, *Breathing Lessons*, 4.
89. Robin Wall Kimmerer, *Braiding Sweetgrass: Indigenous Wisdom, Scientific Knowledge and the Teachings of Plants* (Milkweed Editions, 2013), 1.
90. "Isaiah 26:3," Bible Hub, accessed December 19, 2025, https://biblehub.com/isaiah/26-3.htm#study.
91. Nestor, *Breath*, 61.
92. Bessel A. van der Kolk, *The Body Keeps the Score: Brain, Mind, and Body in the Healing of Trauma* (Penguin Books, 2015), 269.
93. "Ephesians 2:14," Bible Hub, accessed December 19, 2025, https://biblehub.com/ephesians/2-14.htm#study.
94. Frederick Buechner, *Wishful Thinking: A Seeker's ABC*, rev. ed. (Mowbray, 1994), 83.
95. "Ruach," Bible Hub; "Pneuma," Bible Hub.
96. Nestor, *Breath*, 143.
97. Nestor, *Breath*, 144.
98. Whitney R. Simpson, *With God in Every Breath: A Guide to Drawing Closer to Jesus Through Your Senses* (NavPress, 2025), 66.
99. Kolber, *Try Softer*, 206–207; quote formatted for space.
100. Mary Oliver, "Don't Hesitate," in *Devotions: The Selected Poems of Mary Oliver* (Penguin Books, 2020), 61.
101. Oliver, "Don't Hesitate," in *Devotions*, 61.
102. "Psalm 85:10," Bible Hub, accessed December 19, 2025, https://biblehub.com/psalms/85-10.htm#study.
103. Jill Dale, "New Report: Nearly Half of People in U.S. Exposed to Dangerous Air Pollution Levels," American Lung Association, April 23, 2025, https://www.lung.org/media/press-releases/state-of-the-air-2025.
104. Rose Davidson, "History of Earth Day," National Geographic Kids, accessed December 9, 2025, https://kids.nationalgeographic.com/celebrations/article/earth-day.
105. Diniz, "The Effects of Gratitude;" Stahl and Millstine, *Calming the Rush of Panic*, 14, 30.
106. Han, *Breathing Lessons*, 25.
107. Susan Forshey, "31 Days of Contemplative Living: {Day 15} Color Your Prayer," The Contemplative Cottage, https://contemplativecottage.com/2011/10/15/day-15-color-your-prayer/.
108. Forshey, "31 Days of Contemplative Living."
109. Keating, *Open Mind, Open Heart*, 55.
110. Curt Thompson, *Anatomy of the Soul: Surprising Connections Between Neuroscience and Spiritual Practices That Can Transform Your Life and Relationships* (Tyndale, 2010), 84.
111. Van der Kolk, *The Body Keeps the Score*, 136.
112. Trammel and Trent, *Counselor's Guide to Christian Mindfulness*, 17.
113. Oliver, "Sometimes," in *Devotions*, 105.
114. Wuellner, *Prayer and Our Bodies*, 75.
115. Wuellner, *Prayer and Our Bodies*, 74.
116. Adapted from Wuellner, *Prayer and Our Bodies*, 75.
117. Debie Thomas, "I Have Longed," Journey with Jesus, March 6, 2022, https://www.journeywithjesus.net/essays/3341-i-have-longed.
118. Louise Bartlett, "What Is Ocean Breathing and How Can It Help Me?" *Louise Bartlett* (blog), accessed December 16, 2025, https://www.louisebartlett.com/new-blog/2019/5/31/what-is-ocean-breathing-and-how-can-it-help-me.
119. "Isaiah 66:13," Bible Hub, accessed December 19, 2025, https://biblehub.com/isaiah/66-13.htm#study.
120. "Psalm 19:1," Bible Hub, accessed December 19, 2025, https://biblehub.com/psalms/19-1.htm#study.
121. Anthony de Mello, "The Benediction," in *Wellsprings: A Book of Spiritual Exercises* (Doubleday, 1984), 171.
122. "Proverbs 17:17," Bible Hub, accessed December 19, 2025, https://www.biblehub.com/proverbs/17-17.htm#study.
123. M. Basil Pennington, *Centering Prayer: Renewing an Ancient Christian Prayer Form* (Doubleday, 1980), 89.
124. Wuellner, *Prayer and Our Bodies*, 53.
125. Stahl and Millstine, *Calming the Rush of Panic*, 30.
126. Stahl and Millstine, *Calming the Rush of Panic*, 30.
127. Barton, *Sacred Rhythms*, 70–71.
128. Caroline Oakes, *Practice the Pause: Jesus' Contemplative Practice, New Brain Science, and What It Means to Be Fully Human* (Broadleaf Books, 2023), 227.
129. Oakes, *Practice the Pause*, 227.
130. "Ruach," Bible Hub; "Pneuma," Bible Hub.
131. Saad, *Contemplative Life*, 148.
132. Anthony de Mello, *Sadhana: A Way to God; Christian Exercises in Eastern Form* (Image, 1984), 120.
133. De Mello, *Sadhana*, 120.
134. Rich Villodas, *The Deeply Formed Life: Five Transformative Values to Root Us in the Way of Jesus* (WaterBrook, 2020), xv.
135. Adapted from the "Formed" chapter of my book *Every Season Sacred*.
136. Adapted from the "Formed" chapter of my book *Every Season Sacred*.
137. Nancy S. Wiens, "Breath Prayer: An Ancient Spiritual Practice Connected with Science," BioLogos, July 1, 2019, https://biologos.org/articles/breath-prayer-an-ancient-spiritual-practice-connected-with-science.
138. Mark Fischetti and Jen Christiansen, "Our Bodies Replace Billions of Cells Every Day," *Scientific American*, April 1, 2021, https://www.scientificamerican.com/article/our-bodies-replace-billions-of-cells-every-day/.
139. Amrisha Vaish et al., "Not All Emotions Are Created Equal: The Negativity Bias in Social-Emotional Development," *Psychological Bulletin* 134, no. 3 (2008): 383–403, https://pmc.ncbi.nlm.nih.gov/articles/PMC3652533/.
140. Carolyn Cowan, *Breathwork for Pregnancy: How to Find Calm Throughout the Four Trimesters* (Zeitgeist, 2024), 39.
141. Cowan, *Breathwork for Pregnancy*, 39.

142. Kreg Yingst, *Everything Could Be a Prayer: 100 Portraits of Saints and Mystics* (Broadleaf Books, 2024), 90.
143. Yingst, *Everything Could Be a Prayer*, 90.
144. Yingst, *Everything Could Be a Prayer*, 90.
145. Yingst, *Everything Could Be a Prayer*, 90.
146. "Back to the Basics: Engaging Scripture," June 22, 2025, Westminster Presbyterian Church, YouTube, 1 hour, 11 min., 29 sec., https://www.youtube.com/watch?v=40xVX4mYbzo. See the sermon about the book of James and grace, beginning at 33:21.
147. Morgan Harper Nichols, *How Far You Have Come: Musings on Beauty and Courage* (Zondervan, 2021), 164–165.
148. Brown and Gerbarg, *Healing Power of the Breath*, 134.
149. Shawn A. Ginwright, *The Four Pivots: Reimagining Justice, Reimagining Ourselves* (North Atlantic Books, 2022), 121.
150. "James 1:27," Bible Hub, accessed December 19, 2025, https://biblehub.com/james/1-27.htm#study.
151. Ginwright, *The Four Pivots*, 121.
152. Denice Williams, "How to Fix a Flat Bike Tire," REI Co-op, accessed December 17, 2025, https://www.rei.com/learn/expert-advice/flat-tire.html.
153. Mary Oliver, "The Summer Day," *in Devotions*, 316.
154. Scot McKnight, *The Jesus Creed: Loving God, Loving Others* (Paraclete Press, 2004), 12.
155. "A Prayer for Morning," in Craig, *Every Season Sacred*, 302.
156. Emily E. Scott et al., "The Autonomic Nervous System in Its Natural Environment: Immersion in Nature Is Associated with Changes in Heart Rate and Heart Rate Variability," *Psychophysiology* 58, no. 4 (2021): e13698, https://doi.org/10.1111/psyp.13698.
157. L'Engle, "A Sky Full of Children,"in *Watch for the Light*, 81.
158. "Ruach," Bible Hub; "Pneuma," Bible Hub.
159. Dent, "Breathing with God," 8.
160. Frederick Buechner, *Listening to Your Life: Daily Meditations with Frederick Buechner* (HarperCollins, 2009), 127.
161. The Cambridge dictionary describes this phrase as "to speak angrily to someone about something they have done and warn that person that they will be punished if it happens again." *Cambridge Dictionary*, "read (someone) the riot act," accessed December 11, 2025, https://dictionary.cambridge.org/dictionary/english/read-the-riot-act.https://dictionary.cambridge.org/dictionary/english/read-the-riot-act.
162. Anne Lamott, *Bird by Bird: Some Instructions on Writing and Life* (Knopf Doubleday, 2007), 22.
163. John Gramlich, "What the Data Says About Gun Deaths in the U.S.," Pew Research Center, March 5, 2025, https://pewrsr.ch/448q4hU.
164. Wuellner, *Prayer and Our Bodies*, 53.
165. Andrea Zaccaro, et al., "How Breath-Control Can Change Your Life: A Systematic Review on Psycho-Physiological Correlates of Slow Breathing," *Frontiers in Human Neuroscience* 12 (September 2018): 353, https:// doi:10.3389/fnhum.2018.00353.
166. "Amos 5:24," Bible Hub, accessed December 15, 2025, https://biblehub.com/amos/5-24.htm#study.
167. Marie, *Black Girls Breathing*, 10.
168. Marie, *Black Girls Breathing*, 136.
169. Dorena Williamson, "A Prayer for Juneteenth," quoted on Kayla Craig (@liturgies for parents), "Juneteenth marks the day in 1865 when enslaved people in Galveston, Texas, were told they were freed," June 19, 2024, Instagram, https://www.instagram.com/p/C8ZuTl7R5Tq/?hl=en.
170. Cole Arthur Riley, *This Here Flesh: Spirituality, Liberation, and the Stories That Make Us* (Convergent, 2022), 32.
171. To read more about this method of prayer, see "The Ignatian Method of Prayer," The Upper Room, accessed December 17, 2025, https://www.upperroom.org/resources/the-ignatian-method-of-prayer.
172. Cowan, *Breathwork for Pregnancy*, 67.
173. Makoto Fujimura, *Art and Faith: A Theology of Making* (Yale University Press, 2020), 63.
174. Dive into centering prayer more at contemplativeoutreach.org or in Julie Saad's book *Contemplative Life: Discovering Our Path into the Heart of God*.
175. Adapted from Swami Rama et al., *Science of Breath: A Practical Guide* (Himalayan Institute Press, 1998), 87.
176. "Romans 12:9," Bible Hub, accessed December 19, 2025, https://biblehub.com/romans/12-9.htm#study.
177. "Romans 12:9," Bible Hub.
178. Martin Laird, *Into the Silent Land: A Guide to the Christian Practice of Contemplation* (Oxford University Press, 2006), 16.
179. Buechner, *Listening to Your Life*, 128.
180. Simpson, *Holy Listening*, 27.
181. Tanner Olson (@writtentospeak), "And in the morning, sit with the walking, the waiting," Instagram, April 16, 2025, https://www.instagram.com/p/DIghF8izK9d/.
182. Simpson, *Holy Listening*, 27.
183. Lata Patel, "Top 5 Stress-Relief Breathing Techniques for Healthcare Professionals," *Healing Breaths* (blog), March 21, 2025, https://healingbreaths.org/blog/stress-relief-breathing-techniques/.
184. Morgan Harper Nichols, *Peace Is a Practice: An Invitation to Breathe Deep and Find a New Rhythm for Life* (Zondervan, 2022), 15.
185. Jennings, *God-Shaped Brain*, 226.
186. Jennings, *God-Shaped Brain*, 226.
187. Jennings, *God-Shaped Brain*, 226.
188. Keating, *Open Mind, Open Heart*, 165.
189. Trammel and Trent, *Counselor's Guide to Christian Mindfulness*, 16.
190. J. Philip Newell, *Celtic Prayers from Iona* (Paulist Press, 1997), 25.
191. Breus, *Sleep Drink Breathe*, 207–208.
192. Thompson, *Anatomy of the Soul*, 264.
193. Thompson, *Anatomy of the Soul*, 264.
194. Rolheiser, *Holy Longing*, 68.
195. Shannan Martin, *Start with Hello (And Other Simple Ways to Live as Neighbors)* (Revell, 2022).
196. Rolheiser, *Holy Longing*, 68.

197. Liz Mineo, "Good Genes Are Nice, but Joy Is Better," *The Harvard Gazette*, April 11, 2017, https://news.harvard.edu/gazette/story/2017/04/over-nearly-80-years-harvard-study-has-been-showing-how-to-live-a-healthy-and-happy-life/.
198. Mineo, "Good Genes Are Nice."
199. Antonella Samoggia and Tommaso Rezzaghi, "The Consumption of Caffeine-Containing Products to Enhance Sports Performance: An Application of an Extended Model of the Theory of Planned Behavior," *Nutrients* 13, no. 2 (2021): 344, https:// doi:10.3390/nu13020344.
200. Brown and Gerbarg, *Healing Power of the Breath*, 2.
201. Stephen Mitchell, "Psalm 93," in *A Book of Psalms: Selected and Adapted from the Hebrew* (HarperCollins, 1993), 42.
202. Katherine May, *Wintering: The Power of Rest and Retreat in Difficult Times* (Riverhead Books, 2020), 68.
203. Barton, *Sacred Rhythms*, 70–71.
204. Wuellner, *Prayer and Our Bodies*, 9–10.
205. Brown and Gerbarg, *Healing Power of the Breath*, 121.
206. Susan L. Smalley and Diana Winston, *Fully Present: The Science, Art, and Practice of Mindfulness* (Da Capo Lifelong Books, 2010), 37.
207. Nadia Bolz Weber, "Sermon on the Kyrie, Peter's Own Smell of Shame and the God of Easter," *Patheos* (blog), April 16, 2013, https://www.patheos.com/blogs/nadiabolzweber/2013/04/sermon-on-the-kyrie-peters-own-smell-of-shame-and-the-god-of-easter/.
208. Brown and Gerbarg, *Healing Power of the Breath*, 36.
209. Adapted from Brown and Gerbarg, *Healing Power of the Breath*, 37.
210. Trammel and Trent, *Counselor's Guide to Christian Mindfulness*, 42.
211. Deb Dana, *Anchored: How to Befriend Your Nervous System Using Polyvagal Theory* (Sounds True, 2021), 115.
212. Esau D. McCaulley, "Letter to the Ephesians," in McCaulley, *New Testament in Color*, 419.
213. Kaila Philo, "From the Antebellum South to the Civil Rights Movement, Black American Women Have Long Told Their Stories Through Quilts," *Smithsonian*, February 24, 2025, https://www.smithsonianmag.com/smithsonian-institution/from-the-antebellum-south-to-the-civil-rights-movement-black-american-women-have-long-told-their-stories-through-quilts-180986106/.
214. "Quilting for the Constitution Peace by Piece," Women Building Peace, accessed December 17, 2025, https://www.womenbuildingpeace.us/peace-by-piece.
215. Brown and Gerbarg, *Healing Power of the Breath*, 63.
216. Adapted from Brown and Gerbarg, *Healing Power of the Breath*, 15.
217. Mary Oliver, "Low Tide: What the Sea Gives to the Human Soul," *Amicus Journal* 18, no. 4 (Winter 1997): 34.
218. Trammel and Trent, *Counselor's Guide to Christian Mindfulness*, 9–10.
219. Prem Rawat, *Breath: Wake Up to Life* (St. Martin's Essentials, 2025), 83.
220. "2 Corinthians 13:11," Bible Hub, accessed December 18, 2025, https://biblehub.com/2_corinthians/13-11.htm#study.
221. Sarah Bessey, *Miracles and Other Reasonable Things: A Story of Unlearning and Relearning God* (Howard Books, 2020), 147.
222. Thompson, *Anatomy of the Soul*, 206.
223. Cole Arthur Riley, *This Here Flesh*, 7.
224. Thomas Keating, "Dismantling the Emotional Programs, Part 1," excerpted from *The Spiritual Journey Part 2, The Human Condition*, virtual lecture, posted May 6, 2022, by Contemplative Outreach, YouTube, https://www.youtube.com/watch?v=fCbIWW_IdOY&t=2s.
225. Keating, *Open Mind, Open Heart*, 164.
226. Adapted from Harrison Scott Key, *How to Stay Married: The Most Insane Love Story Ever Told* (Avid Reader Press, 2024), 120.
227. "Ephesians 4:3," Bible Hub, accessed December 17, 2025, https://biblehub.com/ephesians/4-3.htm#study.
228. This poem was inspired by a poetry prompt in Joseph Fasano, *The Magic Words: Simple Poetry Prompts That Unlock the Creativity in Everyone* (Tarcher, 2024), 53.
229. Kolber, *Try Softer*, 190–192.
230. Jodi Picoult and Jennifer Finney Boylan, *Mad Honey* (Random House, 2022), 179–180.
231. Saad, *Contemplative Life*, 148.
232. Nouwen, *Discernment*, 18.
233. Inspired by guidelines in Saad, *Contemplative Life*, 149–150, and Nouwen, *Discernment*, 18.
234. Dunigan Folk and Elizabeth Dunn, "Everything Is Better Together: Analyzing the Relationship Between Socializing and Happiness in the American Time Use Survey," *Social Psychological and Personality Science*, August 16, 2025, https://doi.org/10.1177/19485506251364333.
235. Barton, *Sacred Rhythms*, 49.
236. Aidan Walker, "'Sadbait': Why Algorithms, Audiences and Creators Love to Cry Online," *BBC*, January 18, 2025, https://www.bbc.com/future/article/20250117-sadbait-why-algorithms-and-audiences-cant-get-enough-of-depressing-content.
237. Martin Luther King Jr., "Letter from a Birmingham Jail," April 16, 1963, African Studies Center, University of Pennsylvania, https://www.africa.upenn.edu/Articles_Gen/Letter_Birmingham.html.
238. Dana, *Anchored*, 117.
239. Anne Lamott, *Somehow: Thoughts on Love* (Riverhead Books, 2024), 14.
240. Dana, *Anchored*, 91.
241. Dana, *Anchored*, 101.
242. Henri J. M. Nouwen, *Beyond the Mirror: Reflections on Death and Life* (Crossroad, 1990), 12.
243. "Remarks by the First Lady at the Democratic National Convention," The White House, July 25, 2016, https://obamawhitehouse.archives.gov/the-press-office/2016/07/25/remarks-first-lady-democratic-national-convention.
244. "Two," by Sleeping at Last, on *Atlas: Year Two*, released November 1, 2019, https://www.sleepingatlast.com/blog/2017/11/17/two.
245. "Maps and Cartographic Resources," UCLA Library, updated August 15, 2025, https://guides.library.ucla.edu/maps/cartography.

246. Brené Brown, *Atlas of the Heart: Mapping Meaningful Connection and the Language of Human Experience* (Random House Publishing Group, 2021), xxi.
247. Adapted from "Welcoming Prayer," Contemplative Outreach, accessed December 17, 2025, https://contemplativeoutreach.org/welcoming-prayer-method/.
248. Buechner, *Listening to Your Life*, 222.
249. Adapted from Wuellner, *Prayer and Our Bodies*, 61.
250. "What Defines a Kairos Moment?," Bible Hub, accessed December 18, 2025, https://biblehub.com/q/what_defines_a_kairos_moment.htm.
251. Craig, *To Light Their Way*, 137.
252. Craig, *Every Season Sacred*, 107.
253. Craig, *To Light Their Way*, 138.
254. Keating, *Open Mind, Open Heart*, 13.
255. Rohr, *Everything Belongs*, 147.
256. Wuellner, *Prayer and Our Bodies*, 40.
257. Breus, *Sleep Drink Breathe*, 190.
258. Laird, *Into the Silent Land*, 15.
259. Laird, *Into the Silent Land*, 15.
260. Laird, *Into the Silent Land*, 20.
261. Trammel and Trent, *Counselor's Guide to Christian Mindfulness*, 37.
262. "Psalm 4:8," Bible Hub, accessed December 18, 2025, https://biblehub.com/psalms/4-8.htm#study.
263. "Psalm 4:8," Bible Hub.
264. Wendell Berry, "The body in the invisible," in *This Day: Sabbath Poems Collected and New, 1979–2012* (Counterpoint, 2013), 103.
265. "A Prayer for Bedtime," in Craig, *Every Season Sacred*, 305.
266. This poem was inspired by a poetry prompt in Fasano, *The Magic Words*, 45.
267. Trammel and Trent, *Counselor's Guide to Christian Mindfulness*, 23.
268. Brown and Gerbarg, *Healing Power of the Breath*, 122.
269. Claude Atcho, *Rhythms of Faith: A Devotional Pilgrimage Through the Church Year* (WaterBrook, 2025), xvii.
270. Atcho, *Rhythms of Faith*, xviii.
271. Justin McRoberts and Scott Erickson, *In the Low: Honest Prayers for Dark Seasons* (Baker Books, 2025), 26.
272. Peterson, *Long Obedience*, 78.
273. Brown and Gerbarg, *Healing Power of the Breath*, 3.
274. "1 Corinthians 15:34," Bible Hub, accessed December 18, 2025, https://biblehub.com/1_corinthians/15-34.htm#study.
275. Wendell Berry, "Manifesto: The Mad Farmer Liberation Front," in *The Country of Marriage* (Harcourt Brace Jovanovich, 1973), 17. See the poem online at the University of Arizona website https://cales.arizona.edu/~steidl/Liberation.html.
276. Laura Kelly Fanucci, *Living Easter: 50 Days to Practice Resurrection* (Ave Maria Press, 2026), 146.
277. Hadley Leggett, "Breathing Anxiety Away," *Stanford Medicine*, June 2, 2023, https://stanmed.stanford.edu/cyclic-sighing-stress-relief/.
278. Rolheiser, *Holy Longing*, 66–67.
279. Barbara Brown Taylor, *Learning to Walk in the Dark* (HarperOne, 2014), 15–16.
280. Taylor, *Learning to Walk in the Dark*, 16.
281. "Isaiah 1:17," Bible Hub, accessed December 18, 2025, https://biblehub.com/isaiah/1-17.htm#study.
282. Barton, *Sacred Rhythms*, 49.
283. Atcho, *Rhythms of Faith*, 308.
284. Atcho, *Rhythms of Faith*, 310.
285. Atcho, *Rhythms of Faith*, 311.
286. "Colossians 1:20, Study Bible," Bible Hub, accessed December 18, 2025, https://biblehub.com/colossians/1-20.htm#study.
287. Adapted from Jeanette Martino Land, "The Seven Sorrows of Mary," *St. Anthony Messenger*, September 2017, https://www.franciscanmedia.org/st-anthony-messenger/september-2017/the-seven-sorrows-of-mary/.
288. Jillian Benfield, *Overwhelmed & Grateful: The Key to Finding God's Goodness in All Life's Ups & Downs* (Baker Publishing Group, 2025), 27.
289. Benfield, *Overwhelmed & Grateful*, 27.
290. Adapted from Craig, *Every Season Sacred*, 293–295.
291. Gregory Boyle, *Barking to the Choir: The Power of Radical Kinship* (Simon & Schuster, 2017), 9.
292. Phil Gibbs, "What Is Occam's Razor?" UC Riverside Department of Mathematics, 1996, https://math.ucr.edu/home/baez/physics/General/occam.html.
293. "Isaiah 30:15," Bible Hub, accessed December 18, 2025, https://biblehub.com/study/isaiah/30-15.htm.
294. "Psalm 37:7," Bible Hub, accessed December 18, 2025, https://biblehub.com/psalms/37-7.htm#study.
295. Thomas Merton, *New Seeds of Contemplation* (Shambhala, 2003), 302–303.
296. Craig, *Every Season Sacred*, 11.
297. S. Stephanie Iachetta, compiler, *The Daily Reader for Contemplative Living: Excerpts from the Works of Father Thomas Keating, O.C.S.O., Sacred Scripture, and Other Spiritual Writings* (Continuum International Publishing Group, 2009), 7.
298. "Pneuma," Bible Hub.
299. Jack Levison, *40 Days with the Holy Spirit: Fresh Air for Every Day* (Paraclete Press, 2015), 23.
300. Breus, *Sleep Drink Breathe*, 203.
301. "Stress Management: Chronic Stress Puts Your Health at Risk," Mayo Clinic, August 1, 2023, https://www.mayoclinic.org/healthy-lifestyle/stress-management/in-depth/stress/art-20046037.
302. Lamott, *Somehow*, 10.
303. Pope John Paul II to the Reverend George V. Coyne, June 1, 1988, in *Papal Addresses* (Pontifical Academy of Sciences, 2003), 300.
304. Rich Villodas, *The Deeply Formed Life: Five Transformative Values to Root Us in the Way of Jesus* (WaterBrook, 2020), xv.
305. Adapted from Craig, *Every Season Sacred*, 140.
306. "Romans 5:2," Bible Hub, accessed December 18, 2025, https://biblehub.com/romans/5-2.htm#study.
307. "Meaning of 'Access by Faith' Today?" Bible Hub, accessed December 18, 2025, https://biblehub.com/q/Meaning_of_access_by_faith_today.htm.
308. Nestor, *Breath*, 61.
309. Brown and Gerbarg, *Healing Power of the Breath*, 38.

310. Richard V. Palumbo et al., "Interpersonal Autonomic Physiology: A Systematic Review of the Literature," *Personality and Social Psychology Review* 21, no. 2 (2017): 99–141, https://doi.org/10.1177/1088868316628405.
311. Aaron Earls, "Public Trust in Pastors Continues Steep Decline," Lifeway Research, January 16, 2025, https://research.lifeway.com/2025/01/16/public-trust-in-pastors-continues-steep-decline/.
312. Patti Normille, "St. Francis of Assisi and His Canticle of the Sun," *Franciscan Media* (blog), January 27, 2023, https://www.franciscanmedia.org/franciscan-spirit-blog/st-francis-of-assisi-and-his-canticle-of-the-sun/.
313. Craig, *To Light Their Way*, 170–171.
314. Cowan, *Breathwork for Pregnancy*, 42.
315. Dana, *Anchored*, 21.
316. Dana, *Anchored*, 114.
317. Dana, *Anchored*, 112.
318. "Feeding America Harnesses Collective Action This Hunger Action Month," Feeding America, August 27, 2025, https://www.feedingamerica.org/about-us/press-room/hunger-action-month-2025.
319. "Global Food Crisis: 10 Countries Suffering the Most from Hunger," World Food Program USA, updated June 25, 2024, https://www.wfpusa.org/news/global-food-crisis-10-countries-suffering-the-most-from-hunger/.
320. "Isaiah 58:10," Bible Hub, accessed December 19, 2025, https://biblehub.com/isaiah/58-10.htm#study.
321. April Yamasaki, *Sacred Pauses: Spiritual Practices for Personal Renewal* (Herald Press, 2013), 160.
322. Yamasaki, *Sacred Pauses*, 160.
323. "Amos 5:24," Bible Hub, accessed December 19, 2025, https://biblehub.com/study/amos/5-24.htm.
324. Rolheiser, *Holy Longing*, 64.
325. Monica DiCristina, *Your Pain Has a Name: A Therapist's Invitation to Understanding Your Story and Sorting Out Who You Are from What Hurts* (Worthy Books, 2025), 173.
326. Peterson, *Long Obedience*, 96.
327. "Try Grounding Exercises," Mindscape, accessed December 18, 2025, https://www.health.harvard.edu/mindscape/for-young-people/what-creates-mental-wellness/try-grounding-exercises.
328. Darrell N. Kotton and Edward E. Morrisey, "Lung Regeneration: Mechanisms, Applications and Emerging Stem Cell Populations," *Nature Medicine* 20, no. 8 (2014): 822–832, https://pmc.ncbi.nlm.nih.gov/articles/PMC4229034/.
329. "What Defines a Kairos Moment?," Bible Hub.
330. Rohr, *Everything Belongs*, 142.
331. Wendell Berry, "The sky bright after summer-ending rain," in *The Peace of Wild Things and Other Poems* (Penguin, 2018), 116.
332. Saad, *Contemplative Life*, 177.
333. John D. Kelly IV, "Forgiveness: A Key Resiliency Builder," *Clinical Orthopaedics and Related Research* 476, no. 2 (2018): 203–204, https://pmc.ncbi.nlm.nih.gov/articles/PMC6259716/.
334. "Mark 12:30," Bible Hub, accessed December 18, 2025, https://biblehub.com/mark/12-30.htm#study.
335. James Bryan Smith, *A Spiritual Formation Workbook: Small Group Resources for Nurturing Christian Growth* (HarperSanFrancisco, 1993), 14–17; "Streams" were originally developed by Richard J. Foster, founder of Renovaré. There is now a sixth stream, "incarnational." You can learn more at "The Six Streams," Renovaré, accessed December 18, 2025, https://renovare.org/about/ideas/the-six-streams.
336. Smith, *Spiritual Formation Workbook*, 17.
337. Smith, *Spiritual Formation Workbook*, 17.
338. Frederick Buechner, *Alphabet of Grace* (HarperCollins, 1989), 38.
339. "Ecclesiastes 11:5," Bible Hub, accessed December 18, 2025, https://biblehub.com/ecclesiastes/11-5.htm#study; "Ruach," Bible Hub.
340. Matthew Solan, "Ease Anxiety and Stress: Take a (Belly) Breather," *Harvard Health Publishing* (blog), January 10, 2025, https://www.health.harvard.edu/blog/ease-anxiety-and-stress-take-a-belly-breather-201904261861.
341. Solan, "Ease Anxiety and Stress."
342. Dorothy Day, "On Pilgrimage," *Catholic Worker*, December 1965, 7, https://merton.bellarmine.edu/s/cw/item/41094.
343. Buechner, *Alphabet of Grace*, 40.
344. Pádraig Ó Tuama, *Daily Prayer with the Corrymeela Community* (Canterbury Press, 2017), xx.
345. Danielle Hitchen, "Allhallowtide," in *Sacred Seasons: A Family Guide to Center Your Year Around Jesus* (Harvest House, 2023).
346. Craig, *Every Season Sacred*, 65.
347. Yingst, *Everything Could Be a Prayer*, 2.
348. Adapted from "A Prayer for All Saints' Day," in Craig, *To Light Their Way*, 172.
349. Adapted from "A Prayer for All Saints' Day," in Craig, *To Light Their Way*, 172.
350. Buechner, *Wishful Thinking*, 58.
351. Saad, *Contemplative Life*, 70.
352. Adapted from Saad, *Contemplative Life*, chap. 5.
353. Trammel and Trent, *Counselor's Guide to Christian Mindfulness*, 9–10.
354. Laura Kelly Fanucci, *Living Easter: 50 Days to Practice Resurrection*, 145
355. Terri Yablonsky Stat, "Be Generous: It's a Simple Way to Stay Healthier," University of Michigan Department of Psychology, August 31, 2015, https://lsa.umich.edu/psych/news-events/all-news/archived-news/2015/08/be-generous--it-s-a-simple-way-to-stay-healthier.html.
356. "How Box Breathing Can Help You Destress," Cleveland Clinic, August 17, 2021, https://health.clevelandclinic.org/box-breathing-benefits.
357. Wuellner, *Prayer and Our Bodies*, 60.
358. Oakes, *Practice the Pause*, 111.
359. "Pneuma," Bible Hub; "Ruach," Bible Hub.
360. Trammel and Trent, *Counselor's Guide to Christian Mindfulness*, 23.
361. Buechner, *Wishful Thinking*, 39.
362. Nichols, *Peace Is a Practice*, 15.

363. "Ruach," Bible Hub.
364. Wuellner, *Prayer and Our Bodies*, 53.
365. Stephen, *Breath Taking*, 18.
366. Stephen, *Breath Taking*, 18.
367. Nichols, *Peace Is a Practice*, 87.
368. Ron Marshall, "How Many Ads Do You See in One Day?" Red Crow Marketing Inc., September 10, 2015, https://www.redcrowmarketing.com/blog/many-ads-see-one-day/.
369. "Luke 12:15," Bible Hub, accessed December 19, 2025, https://biblehub.com/luke/12-15.htm#study.
370. Thompson, *Anatomy of the Soul*, 169.
371. T. Äärimaa et al., "Interaction of Heart Rate and Respiration in Newborn Babies," *Pediatric Research* 24 (December 1988): 745–750, https://doi.org/10.1203/00006450-198812000-00019.
372. Thompson, *Anatomy of the Soul*, 80.
373. "Matthew 6:21," Bible Hub, accessed December 19, 2025, https://biblehub.com/matthew/6-21.htm#study.
374. Adapted from "A Prayer for a Grateful Spirit," in Craig, *To Light Their Way*, 115.
375. David Steindl-Rast, *A Listening Heart: The Art of Contemplative Living* (Crossroad, 1983), 12.
376. Emma Bowman, "Most Black Friday Shoppers Bagged Their Deals Online This Year, with Record Spending," NPR, December 1, 2024, https://www.npr.org/2024/12/01/g-s1-36310/black-friday-cyber-monday-record-spending.
377. Adapted from "A Prayer for Consumerism," in Craig, *To Light Their Way*, 120–121.
378. Adapted from "A Prayer for Consumerism," in Craig, *To Light Their Way*, 120–122.
379. "Breath Meditation: A Great Way to Relieve Stress," Harvard Health Publishing, April 15, 2014, https://www.health.harvard.edu/mind-and-mood/breath-meditation-a-great-way-to-relieve-stress.
380. Meister Eckhart, "Where God Enters," in *Watch for the Light*, 57.
381. L'Engle, "A Sky Full of Children," in *Watch for the Light*, 78.
382. Buechner, *Alphabet of Grace*, 39.
383. Adapted from Craig, *Every Season Sacred*, 117.
384. Adapted from "A Prayer for Advent," in Craig, *To Light Their Way*, 175–176.
385. Marcia Johnson, "The Gospel According to Caesar?," Bridges to the Bible, January 14, 2023, https://bridgestothebible.com/2023/01/the-gospel-according-to-caesar/.
386. Yingst, *Everything Could Be a Prayer*, 62.
387. Ned Bustard, *Saint Nicholas the Giftgiver: The History and Legends of the Real Santa Claus* (IVP Kids, 2021).
388. Adapted from "A Prayer for the Feast Day of St. Nicholas," in Craig, *To Light Their Way*, 177.
389. Adapted from "A Prayer for Advent," in Craig, *To Light Their Way*, 175.
390. Madeleine L'Engle, "After Annunciation," in *A Cry Like a Bell* (Harold Shaw Publishers, 1987), 58.
391. Adapted from "Bearing Witness," in Craig, *Every Season Sacred*, 100.
392. Susan L. Smalley and Diana Winston, *Fully Present: The Science, Art, and Practice of Mindfulness* (Da Capo Lifelong Books, 2010), 6.
393. Dietrich Bonhoeffer, "The Coming of Jesus in Our Midst," in *Watch for the Light*, 206–207.
394. Bonhoeffer, "Coming of Jesus in Our Midst," in *Watch for the Light*, 207.
395. Guy William Fincham et al., "Effect of Breathwork on Stress and Mental Health: A Meta-Analysis of Randomised-Controlled Trials," *Scientific Reports* 13 (January 2023): 432, https://doi.org/10.1038/s41598-022-27247-y.
396. "John 1:5," Bible Hub, accessed December 19, 2025, https://biblehub.com/john/1-5.htm#study.
397. "A Prayer for Winter," in Craig, *Every Season Sacred*, 88–89.
398. Adapted from "Vulnerable God," in Craig, *Every Season Sacred*, 122.
399. Greg Miller, "The Vital Crosstalk Between Breath and Brain," *Knowable Magazine*, October 6, 2022, https://knowablemagazine.org/content/article/mind/2022/vital-crosstalk-between-breath-brain.
400. Mariah Chuprinski, "Breathing May Measurably Modulate Neural Responses Across Brain, Study Finds," Pennsylvania State University, November 10, 2022, https://www.psu.edu/news/engineering/story/breathing-may-measurably-modulate-neural-responses-across-brain-study-finds.
401. Dent, "Breathing with God," 2.
402. Adapted from Dent, "Breathing with God," 3–4.
403. Adapted from "A Light Still Shines," in Craig, *Every Season Sacred*, 132.
404. Rolheiser, *Holy Longing*, 75.
405. Donald P. McNeill et al., *Compassion: A Reflection on the Christian Life* (Image Books, 1982), 15.
406. Adapted from "The Word," in Craig, *Every Season Sacred*, 94.
407. Timothy Keller, *The Prodigal God: Recovering the Heart of the Christian Faith* (Penguin Publishing Group, 2008), 24.
408. Brennan Manning, "Shipwrecked at the Stable," in *Watch for the Light*, 187.
409. "A Prayer for Advent," in Craig, *To Light Their Way*, 176.
410. "A Prayer for Christmas Morning," in Craig, *To Light Their Way*, 180.
411. Thurman, *Essential Writings*, 84.
412. Gustavo Gutiérrez, "Christ's History, and Ours," in *Watch for the Light*, 252.
413. This devotion is adapted from Craig, *Every Season Sacred*, 296–298.
414. This poem was inspired by a poetry prompt in Fasano, *Magic Words*, 105.
415. Adapted from "A Prayer for Winter," in Craig, *Every Season Sacred*, 90.

ABOUT THE AUTHOR

KAYLA CRAIG is a former journalist, bestselling author, and spiritual director whose work blends contemplative faith with fierce tenderness for the world God loves. She brings curiosity, compassion, and a love of connection to her writing, and her books include *To Light Their Way* and *Every Season Sacred*. Kayla's *Year of Breath* newsletter reaches readers in all fifty states and more than one hundred countries. Her nuanced, relatable reflections appear in an array of books and devotionals and have been featured by *Christianity Today* and Hallmark's DaySpring.

Kayla created the well-loved Liturgies for Parents Instagram account and speaks at retreats and conferences, helping peace feel possible and prayer feel doable in everyday life. She has trained in Christian spiritual direction and formation at Columbia Theological Seminary. Kayla lives in Iowa with her husband, four kids, and two dogs, where silence is . . . aspirational.

Find breathing room for your soul at kaylacraig.com.

Also by Kayla Craig

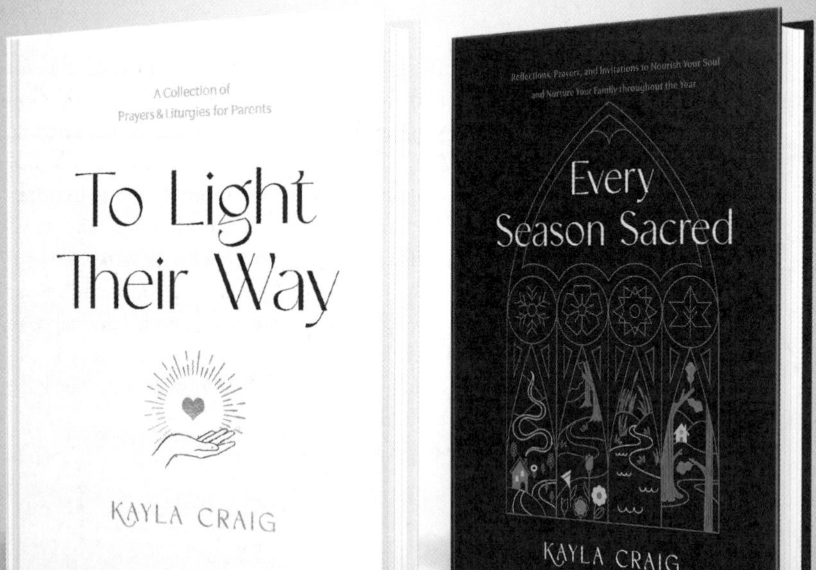

Available wherever books are sold.

CP1860